Student Plagiarism in an Online World:
Problems and Solutions

160101

Tim S. Roberts
Central Queensland University, Australia

INFORMATION SCIENCE REFERENCE

Hershey · New York

Acquisitions Editor:	Kristin Klinger
Development Editor:	Kristin M. Roth
Editorial Assistants:	Jessica Thompson and Ross Miller
Senior Managing Editor:	Jennifer Neidig
Managing Editor:	Sara Reed
Copy Editor:	Jennifer Young
Typesetter:	Lindasy Bergman
Cover Design:	Lisa Tosheff
Printed at:	Yurchak Printing Inc.

Published in the United States of America by
   Information Science Reference (an imprint of IGI Global)
   701 E. Chocolate Avenue, Suite 200
   Hershey PA 17033
   Tel: 717-533-8845
   Fax: 717-533-8661
   E-mail: cust@igi-global.com
   Web site: http://www.igi-global.com

and in the United Kingdom by
   Information Science Reference (an imprint of IGI Global)
   3 Henrietta Street
   Covent Garden
   London WC2E 8LU
   Tel: 44 20 7240 0856
   Fax: 44 20 7379 0609
   Web site: http://www.eurospanonline.com

Library of Congress Cataloging-in-Publication Data

Student plagiarism in an online world : problems and solutions / Tim Roberts, editor.
       p. cm.
  Summary: "This book describes the legal and ethical issues surrounding plagiarism, the tools and techniques available to combat the spreading of this problem, and real-life situational examples to further the understanding of the scholars, practitioners, educators, and instructional designers who will find this book an invaluable resource"--Provided by publisher.
  Includes bibliographical references and index.
  ISBN 978-1-59904-801-7 (hardcover) -- ISBN 978-1-59904-803-1 (ebook)
  1. Plagiarism--Prevention. 2. Cheating (Education)--Prevention. 3. Internet research--Moral and ethical aspects. I. Roberts, Tim S., 1955-
PN167.S78 2008
  371.5'8--dc22
                          2007023449

British Cataloguing in Publication Data
A Cataloguing in Publication record for this book is available from the British Library.

All work contributed to this book set is new, previously-unpublished material. The views expressed in this book are those of the authors, but not necessarily of the publisher.

This book is dedicated to my wife Jane, my daughter Rickie-Lee, and my son Mitchell. What did I do to deserve such good luck?

Table of Contents

Foreword / *Chris Park*.. xiv

Foreword / *Mark Brown* xvi

Preface.. xix

Section I:
Some Groundwork

Chapter I
Student Plagiarism in an Online World: An Introduction / *Tim S. Roberts* 1

Chapter II
Student Perspective of Plagiarism / *Craig Zimitat* 10

Chapter III
Controlling Plagiarism: A Study of Lecturer Attitudes / *Erik J. Eriksson
and Kirk P. H. Sullivan* 23

Section II:
Two Particular Case Studies

Chapter IV
Dealing with Plagiarism as an Ethical Issue / *Barbara Cogdell and Dorothy Aidulis* 38

Chapter V
Working Together to Educate Students / *Frankie Wilson and Kate Ippolito* 60

Section III:
EFL and International Students

Chapter VI
EFL Students: Factors Contributing to Online Plagiarism / *Teresa Chen
and Nai-Kuang Teresa Ku*.. 77

Chapter VII

International Students: A Conceptual Framework for Dealing with
Unintentional Plagiarism / *Ursula McGowan* 92

Chapter VIII

International Students and Plagiarism Detection Systems: Detecting Plagiarism,
Copying, or Learning? / *Lucas Introna and Niall Hayes* 108

Section IV:
Two Specific Issues

Chapter IX

Plagiarism and the Community College / *Teri Thomson Maddox* 124

Chapter X

The Phenomena of Contract Cheating / *Thomas Lancaster and Robert Clarke* 144

Section V:
Prevention is Better than Cure

Chapter XI

Prevention is Better than Cure: Addressing Cheating and Plagiarism Based on
the IT Student Perspective / *Martin Dick, Judithe Sheard, and Maurie Hasen* 160

Chapter XII

Plagiarism, Instruction, and Blogs / *Michael Hanrahan* 183

Chapter XIII

Minimizing Plagiarism by Redesigning the Learning Environment
and Assessment / *Madhumita Bhattacharya and Lone Jorgensen* 194

Chapter XIV

Expect Originality! Using Taxonomies to Structure Assignments
that Support Original Work / *Janet Salmons* 208

Section VI:
Two Looks to the Future

Chapter XV

Substantial, Verbatim, Unattributed, Misleading: Applying Criteria to
Assess Textual Plagiarism / *Wilfried Decoo* 228

Chapter XVI

Students and the Internet: The Dissolution of Boundaries / *Jon R. Ramsey* 244

Compilation of References 263

About the Contributors 287

Index 292

Detailed Table of Contents

Foreword / *Chris Park*... xiv

Foreword / *Mark Brown* xvi

Preface.. xix

Section I:
Some Groundwork

Chapter I

Student Plagiarism in an Online World: An Introduction / *Tim S. Roberts* 1

The purpose of this chapter is to provide an introduction to the problem of student plagiarism in an environment where use of the Internet is commonplace. What is plagiarism, and to what extent is it a problem? Why do students plagiarize, and what are typical attitudes towards such plagiarism? Why are academics, and institutions themselves, often reluctant to progress cases through official channels? What are some of the technologies used by students to plagiarise, and by academics to detect plagiarism? What solutions are possible, and what potential solutions might be just over the horizon? This chapter attempts to provide answers to all of these questions.

Chapter II

Student Perspective of Plagiarism / *Craig Zimitat* 10

This chapter reports on an Australian study of undergraduate students' engagement in plagiarism-related behaviours, their knowledge of plagiarism and their academic writing skills. Students were surveyed to: (i) estimate the incidence of plagiarism behaviours; (ii) examine students' self-reported academic writing skills; (iii) estimate their knowledge of plagiarism; and (iv) estimate their ability to identify plagiarised work. Across all three undergraduate years, approximately 90 percent of students believed that direct copying of text or ideas without acknowledgement constituted plagiarism, whilst around 5 percent were unsure if it constituted plagiarism. The majority of students (80 percent or more) claimed never to have plagiarized. About 80 percent of undergraduate students said they possessed the skills of note-taking, paraphrasing, citing and referencing, and so on, but barely half of students in each year group reported confidence with these skills. Students were able to distinguish between clear-cut cases of plagiarism and paraphrasing when presented with either different writing processes or different work samples, but they were less able to distinguish between "borderline cases." There are clear implications for classroom practice. First, students need the opportunity to practice and develop their academic writing skills, in the context of articulating their understandings of their own discipline. This requires teachers to recognise that academic writing is a developmental skill and to learn how to improve the writing skills of their students. Second, in this process, teachers need to ensure that students are inducted into the conventions of the academy that relate to the use, manipulation, and transformation of knowledge.

Chapter III
Controlling Plagiarism: A Study of Lecturer Attitudes / *Erik J. Eriksson and Kirk P. H. Sullivan* 23

Plagiarism is viewed as increasing problem in the academy. When plagiarism is discussed it is often in personal negative terms that refer to the "lazy" modern student. Previous studies have suggested that the largest cause of plagiarism is ignorance on the part of the student. This chapter examines lecturers' knowledge of, and attitude to, plagiarism, how they pass their knowledge on to students, and the lecturers' knowledge of disciplinary procedures. This examination teases out the lecturers' responsibility for continuing student plagiarism. It was found that academics are unsure of their definitions of plagiarism, have varied attitudes towards different types of plagiarism and do not effectively teach how to work with a text to avoid plagiarism. We suggest a wider discussion of plagiarism in the academy, extending beyond how to deter and catch plagiarists, and the writing of policy statements, to preventing plagiarism though education of both student and academic.

Section II:
Two Particular Case Studies

Chapter IV
Dealing with Plagiarism as an Ethical Issue / *Barbara Cogdell and Dorothy Aidulis* 38

This chapter outlines various strategies employed to reduce plagiarism both at a departmental and an institutional level. A detailed description and evaluation is given of two workshops that were designed specifically to educate students about the nature of plagiarism. The workshops also aim to provide students with alternatives to plagiarism by improving their writing skills. Most importantly we believe that students should learn about plagiarism in the context of professional ethics and an ethical attitude should be promoted throughout their study. By using both an ethical and educational approach to dealing with plagiarism, we hope that students will learn that they have nothing to gain from plagiarising and be confident in their own skills.

Chapter V
Working Together to Educate Students / *Frankie Wilson and Kate Ippolito* 60

This chapter presents a descriptive case study of how a UK University has addressed the problem of plagiarism through collaboration between academic staff, student support professionals, and the students' union. It outlines the developmental process undergone in devising, piloting, evaluating, and implementing the programme designed to educate students about plagiarism. Specific details of the tools and techniques used to achieve the intended pedagogical aims are included. The chapter identifies aspects of the institutional culture operating within our universities, such as discipline specific conceptions of knowledge and the diversity of students' and staff's previous educational experiences, which make tackling plagiarism problematic. Findings indicate that the approaches described are valued by students and staff but that barriers to achieving University-wide adoption persist. Suggestions for ways forward for any institution interested in tackling plagiarism are offered. It is anticipated that this chapter will stimulate discussion and inspire learning support professionals, including academics, by the success a collaborative approach can bring—not just a system of detecting and punishing plagiarism, but a method of educating students about what it is, why it is wrong, and how it can be avoided.

Section III:
EFL and International Students

Chapter VI
EFL Students: Factors Contributing to Online Plagiarism / *Teresa Chen and Nai-Kuang Teresa Ku*.. 77

This chapter reports on a survey study that investigates English-as-a-Foreign-Language (EFL) students' experiences with online plagiarism and the factors associated with these practices among the students. With reference to the important factors concerning plagiarism identified in previous studies, the survey focused on students' awareness of the definition of plagiarism, their perceptions of text borrowing, possible causes of their plagiarism, the role of print versus electronic media in plagiarism, and teachers' policies and enforcement of the policies. Based on the findings from the survey, the chapter presents the students' perspectives and provides suggestions on ways to prevent students from online plagiarism. It is hoped that the chapter will contribute to a series of dialogues regarding text borrowing by presenting students' experiences and points of view.

Chapter VII
International Students: A Conceptual Framework for Dealing with Unintentional Plagiarism / *Ursula McGowan*.. 92

This chapter addresses the incidence of unintentional plagiarism among international students whose native language is not English. Terminology widely used in plagiarism policies and in the literature indicates an overriding view of plagiarism as an offence. I have developed a conceptual framework to present an alternative position. The framework provides a matrix for tracing the progress of an international student's induction into the culture and language of academic research. Based on insights from this framework, undergraduate students would be regarded as apprentice researchers who require guidance in developing skills and language for scholarly writing. During the early phases of their apprenticeship, students would be shown the use of genre analysis for "harvesting" genre-specific language. Feedback on instances of inadvertent plagiarism would be non-judgmental, constructive, and formative. I suggest that this approach should be adopted in the core curriculum so that all students can benefit from an academic apprenticeship and so avoid unintentional plagiarism.

Chapter VIII

International Students and Plagiarism Detection Systems: Detecting Plagiarism,
Copying, or Learning? / *Niall Hayes and Lucas Introna*... 108

This chapter explores the question of plagiarism by international students (non-native speakers). It argues that the inappropriate use of electronic plagiarism detection systems (such as Turnitin) could lead to the unfair and unjust construction of international students as plagiarists. We argue that the use of detection systems should take into account the writing practices used by those who write as novices in a non-native language as well as the way "plagiarism" or plagiaristic forms of writing are valued in other cultures. It calls for a move away from a punitive legalistic approach to plagiarism that equates copying to plagiarism and move to a progressive and formative approach. If taken up, such an approach will have very important implications for the way universities in the west deal with plagiarism in their learning and teaching practice as well as their disciplinary procedures.

Section IV:
Two Specific Issues

Chapter IX

Plagiarism and the Community College / *Teri Thomson Maddox*.. 124

Although plagiarism is a problem in all educational institutions, the diversity of the community college student population and of the community college mission creates even more challenges. The purpose of this chapter is to discuss characteristics of community college students, define intentional and unintentional plagiarism, and provide methods that faculty can use to help students avoid both kinds of plagiarism.

Chapter X

The Phenomena of Contract Cheating / *Thomas Lancaster and Robert Clarke*................................. 144

This chapter discusses the issue of contract cheating. This is where students have work completed on their behalf which is then submitted for academic credit. A thorough background to this phenomenon is presented. A list of the main contract cheating Web sites is also given. These contract cheating sites are placed into four classifications: auctions sites, discussion forums, essay mills, and feed aggregators. Approaches are proposed for tutors to set assigned work that is less susceptible to contract cheating than standard assessments. The chapter concludes by arguing that urgent attention needs to be paid to contract cheating to avoid it becoming an educational problem of the same scale as plagiarism.

Section V:
Prevention is Better than Cure

Chapter XI

Prevention is Better than Cure: Addressing Cheating and Plagiarism Based on
the IT Student Perspective / *Martin Dick, Judithe Sheard, and Maurie Hasen*................................. 160

This chapter adopts a four-aspect model to address cheating and plagiarism in universities—education, prevention, detection, and consequence. The research focused on the two aspects of education and prevention as the authors feel that this area has not been considered in detail by the research. Building on past research, a series of eight focus groups (72 students) were conducted with students from information technology degrees at an Australian university. The students were asked to comment and discuss the phenomenon of cheating from their perspective. The chapter presents in detail the responses of the students as analysed by the researchers and then builds a set of guidelines for educators to use in the areas of education and prevention in relation to student cheating.

Chapter XII

Plagiarism, Instruction, and Blogs / *Michael Hanrahan* 183

This chapter takes as its point of departure the Colby, Bates, and Bowdoin Plagiarism Project (http://leeds. bates.edu/cbb), which sought to approach the problem of undergraduate plagiarism as a pedagogical challenge. By revisiting the decision to publish the project's content by means of a web log, the chapter considers the ways in which web logs provide a reflective tool and medium for engaging plagiarism. It considers web log practice and use and offers examples that attest to the instructional value of web logs, especially their ability to foster learning communities and to promote the appropriate use of information and intellectual property

Chapter XIII

Minimizing Plagiarism by Redesigning the Learning Environment
and Assessment / *Madhumita Bhattacharya and Lone Jorgensen* 194

In this chapter, we have raised a number of questions and made attempts to respond. These questions are: Can plagiarism be stopped? Should we stop students from using the information available on the Internet? Is it enough if the students just acknowledge the sources in their work? What action is required to minimize the harmful, and maximize the useful, aspects of internet use in the educational setting? We want our students to learn, and demonstrate their learning with honesty and integrity. In the institutions of higher education, student learning is judged through assessment tasks in the form of assignments, tests, and examinations. We have to ensure that high stakes assessments do not act as an inspiration to cheating in the form of plagiarism. We have provided arguments in support of the integration of process approach with deliverables at the end of the course for assessment of students learning.

Chapter XIV
Expect Originality! Using Taxonomies to Structure Assignments
that Support Original Work / *Janet Salmons* 208

The online world offers opportunities to appropriate others' work, while simultaneously offering opportunities for valuable research and creative exchange. The use of secondary research materials in academic writing can be represented as a continuum, with "plagiarism" on one end and "original work" on the other. Educators can take steps to prevent plagiarism by designing assignments that expect learners to respect others' ideas and strive toward creating their own original work. Educational taxonomies, including the cognitive and affective domains of bloom's taxonomy, and the author's taxonomy of collaborative e-learning, can serve as conceptual frameworks for designing assignments that expect learners to present original work; provide opportunities for learners to develop new ideas through meaningful online interaction; and value learners' ideas while respecting published authors' intellectual property.

**Section VI:
Two Looks to the Future**

Chapter XV
Substantial, Verbatim, Unattributed, Misleading: Applying Criteria to
Assess Textual Plagiarism / *Wilfried Decoo* 228

This chapter examines how to measure textual plagiarism more precisely, using as basis the four criteria of the American-based Office of Research Integrity's definition of plagiarism: to what extent is the reuse of someone else's text substantial, (nearly) verbatim, unattributed, and misleading? Each of these criteria is studied in its variables, leading to the proposal of a scale. Next the implications for the verdict are discussed. This criterion-based approach does not claim to offer an easily workable solution in all cases, but at least stresses the need to achieve greater consensus and impartiality in assessing alleged plagiarism. Indeed, such cases are often handled very differently in terms of disclosure, assessment, and decision-making. For the sake of fairness, an allegation as serious as plagiarism requires the establishment and acceptance of more solid criteria.

Chapter XVI
Students and the Internet: The Dissolution of Boundaries / *Jon R. Ramsey* 244

This chapter explores the information revolution represented by the Internet. It argues that a number of contemporary debates over the nature of authorship and the ownership of ideas and information present serious challenges to traditional concepts of plagiarism. Especially considered are students' many types of interactions with digital technologies and the effect of a "flat world" on their thinking and information-gathering practices. The author then offers suggestions for improving faculty and student understanding of the new information environment and for sustaining academic integrity in the midst of a knowledge revolution.

Compilation of References 263

About the Contributors 287

Index 292

Foreword

"There is nothing new under the sun," wrote the author of Ecclesiastes. Whilst he doubtless had other things in mind when he wrote it, the quote applies equally well to the re-use of other people's words, expressions or ideas. Even a decade ago plagiarism in higher education was very much a minority interest, and few of us paid much real attention to it. We trusted our students to play fair, and to attribute material properly, using established academic conventions and protocols. But there now is a growing evidence base that shows student plagiarism to be on the increase. It is matched by a growing body of research and published literature that deconstructs a phenomenon which at first glance seems simple—students cheat, deliberately, by copying words, phrases, or even large chunks of text from other (usually published) sources—but which in reality is complex, as the chapters in this book amply demonstrate.

Of course, students didn't invent plagiarism, nor are they the only group to engage in it. History is replete with examples of alleged plagiarism. Famous writers accused of borrowing or stealing words or ideas from others include William Shakespeare and Mark Twain. Other famous alleged plagiarists include song writers such as Celine Dion and Michael Jackson, film director Stephen Spielberg, scientists such as Pythagoras and Einstein, philosophers such as Descartes and Wittgenstein, and church men such as John Wesley and Martin Luther King. Students who plagiarise are in good company!

There must always have been students who decided to play Russian Roulette with their coursework, by copying chunks of text from published sources, either to save time (writing the essay the night before it's due in is an age-old practice) and/or effort (why bother to look at multiple sources if you have one conveniently sitting on the desk in front of you), or for other reasons. Such practices have always been regarded as cheating, but in the past the likelihood of catching students cheating in this way was small, certainly when compared with being caught cheating in exams. Motive (efficiency gain) and lack of deterrent (being caught) were often enough to incubate plagiarism behaviours, and institutions largely appealed (often implicitly) to students' consciences and sense of fair play to keep such behaviours in proportion.

Add means to motive, and you have a potent mix. In the past, although copying text from published sources was a much more efficient use of a student's time than spending multiple hours digging about in the library, it still took time. But even the drudgery of sitting and writing or typing out copies of other people's words is now a thing of the past, thanks to digital technologies which have brought us such things as word processors, the Internet, and digital archives. As various chapters in this collection illustrate, students now have access to an unrivalled wealth of material in digital format which can be readily downloaded, cut-and-pasted into essays, and passed off as their own work. And the Internet is accessible 24x7, from the student's own room, thus removing even the need to pop along to the library to find a printed source to copy from.

Yet this new digital technology is very much a double-edged sword, because whilst it does offer students a treasure trove of digital sources which are easy to access and use, it also provides the means by which plagiarism can be detected. At first sight, plagiarism detection software appears to offer a convenient and consistent means by which student's work can be checked for plagiarism, by comparing it with other textual material available on the Internet. The speed of this comparison and the breadth of material it is checked against are impressive. But such software does not offer the magic-bullet solution that some would like, because inevitably it has constraints (for example, it cannot compare against text that is not available online). There are operational issues to take into account too, such as agreeing thresholds (how much text, or how many words in sequence, would be needed to trigger a "plagiarism" case, for example?).

The broader literature and the chapters in this book indicate that we are entering a new phase in the understanding of student plagiarism. Hallmarks of this new phase include much better awareness of the multiple factors which give rise to plagiarism by students and the significant differences between deliberate and accidental plagiarism, and greater sensitivity to understanding how important it is to help students to develop appropriate study skills (particularly note-taking, essay-planning and writing skills) which minimise the risk of inadvertent plagiarism. Other hallmarks include much more informed understanding of the different practices, assumptions and skills of different groups of students (particularly international students) and the impact of such factors on apparent plagiarism behaviours, more grounded appreciation of the need to minimise the risk of plagiarism at source by setting appropriate assignments, and more sophisticated development of approaches to tackling student plagiarism within institutions.

Taken together, the chapters in this book bring the student plagiarism story up-to-date set it into context, and illustrate the more nuanced understanding of this complex phenomenon that is now emerging. As with most things, the more we learn about student plagiarism, the more we realise we don't know and the more clearly we see the need for further research and inquiry. But already there are clear implications emerging, about how we teach, how students study and learn, how we assess students' work, and even about what sort of work is most appropriate to expect from our students. Even if "there is nothing new under the sun", we owe it to our students—and indeed to the future credibility of the academy—to help them develop ways of writing and expressing themselves which are informed by the work of others, but avoid the risk of deliberate or accidental plagiarism.

Chris Park
Lancaster University, UK

Foreword

This book is timely, because in the age of the Internet, concern about patchwriting and cyber-plagiarism has become increasingly common. The term *patchwriting* refers to words and phrases by others, patched together in new sentences without acknowledgement, whereas *cyber-plagiarism* usually suggests large chucks or entire works downloaded from the Internet (Edmonds, 2006). Popular belief fuelled by the media is that ease of "copying and pasting" from the Web and the advent of online "paper mills" has led to a dramatic increase in plagiarism. Although the battle against plagiarism is nothing new, there is general acceptance that this problem has grown since widespread access to the Internet (McCabe & Stephens, 2006). However, evidence on the true extent of the problem remains inconclusive and empirical data does not necessarily support an epidemic of plagiarism (Scanlon, 2006).

Whether or not plagiarism is on the rise, a new kind of "game" exists, as there is little doubt that students and faculty are downloading unprecedented amounts of information in an electronic form. In attempting to redefine the rules of this new game by getting under the surface of plagiarism, the editor has compiled a diverse and impressive collection of works. Taken as a whole, the book illustrates that the problem of plagiarism is no longer as simple as students *copying someone else's work*—either accidentally or knowingly. Historically this distinction between intent has been central to the standard definition of plagiarism (Jenson & De Castell, 2004). In the digital age, however, plagiarism has become a complex and multi-faceted concept and this book shows why concerns about the growth of intellectual dishonesty and copyright violations should it be taken seriously.

While on the surface the text shows the issue of plagiarism can be controlled—if not solved—by a number of sophisticated software solutions, there is more for faculty and university policy-makers to consider than adopting systems that police the problem. Arguably, this kind of response to the threat of plagiarism merely scrapes the surface and is more about compliance than a genuine commitment to ethics and intellectual integrity. As Scanlon (2006) points out, attempting to stamp out plagiarism by employing plagiarism-checkers does little or nothing to address the real issue. The root cause of the problem itself must be put under the spotlight. We need to ask the fundamental question: why do students plagiarise?

The fact is that students plagiarise for the variety of reasons. According to the Canadian Library Association, students plagiarize because they may not know how to correctly cite published works; they may not understand the difference between quoting and paraphrasing; they may consider material on the Internet as public knowledge; or "they may turn to plagiarism when under stress from deadlines and failing marks" (Oliphant, 2002; cited in Edmonds, 2006, para. 40). In considering all of these reasons, the book invites the reader to rethink traditional conceptions of plagiarism. It offers a scholarly response to the concern about plagiarism by challenging the reader to critically reflect on three basic questions:

1. What is plagiarism?
2. How do you prevent plagiarism?
3. How do you educate people about plagiarism?

Each of these questions is multi-layered, as illustrated by the variety of contributions and international perspectives of plagiarism contained in the book. Indeed, a real strength of the book is the way the editor has brought together authors from around the world including Australia, New Zealand, Europe, the United States, and the United Kingdom. In an increasingly globalized world, the book shows that plagiarism is truly an international problem. At a technical level, it has become easier to detect plagiarism through online services such as *Turnitin,* but the true extent and definition of the problem remains a thorny issue.

In light of the argument that students learn and are frequently encouraged by parents to take advantage of subtle forms of cheating from a young age (Thompson, 2006), the focus rightly needs to be on educative rather than punitive measures. Such an approach is often described as the "3Ps" strategy towards plagiarism—that is, pedagogy, promotion, and policing (Dodd, 2006). While the "3Ps" have popular appeal, the emerging educative approach that Devlin (2006) and several contributors to this book advocate is centred on a comprehensive four-part strategy:

- A collaborative effort to recognize and counter plagiarism.
- Thoroughly educating students about the expected conventions of authorship.
- Designing approaches to assessment that minimize the possibility for plagiarism.
- Adopting highly visible procedures for monitoring and detecting plagiarism (p.47).

The last point acknowledges that plagiarism is more likely to flourish in institutional settings with few consequences (Thompson, 2006). It follows that educational institutions cannot afford to adopt a lassez faire approach to the new game. However, a culture of compliance, or as Devlin (2006, p.47) describes, a "catch-'n'-punish" approach, is unlikely to address the real sources of the problem and it may even drive the serial plagiarist further underground.

Instead, a more holistic and multi-layered "4P" approach is promoted incorporating policy, preparation, prevention, and processes (Devlin, 2006). That said, it is noteworthy that this approach goes beyond a pure ethics-based strategy as it acknowledges that plagiarism by students (and staff) is not always deliberate. This point recognises that the role of education is crucial in order to fulfill Lathrop and Foss' (2005) goal of guiding students from cheating and plagiarism to a culture of honesty and integrity. In my experience, students are far more likely to adopt academic conventions and practice ethical conduct when they respect and understand the reasons why this is important. However, education also needs to extend to academic staff as the book highlights the importance of setting original tasks that make plagiarism very difficult. The key point is that the responsibility for avoiding plagiarism must be shared by staff and students.

This book should appeal to a wide readership from a variety of higher education backgrounds. Having said that, this book is not the final word on patchwriting and cyber-plagiarism, and no doubt plagiarism will continue to be a thorny topic for many decades; for this reason the last word is left to Wilson Mizner (1876-1933), a playwright, raconteur, and entrepreneur: "If you steal from one author, it's plagiarism; if you steal from many, it's research" (Quotations Page).

REFERENCES

Devlin, M. (2006). Policy, preparation, and prevention: Proactive minimization of student plagiarism. *Journal of Higher Education Policy and Management, 28*(1), 45-58.

Dodd, T. (2006). Teaching, plagiarism, and the new and improved term paper mill. *Teachers College Record, October 17,* [online]. Retrieved October 22, 2006 from http://www.tcrecord.org

Edmonds, K. (2006). Off with their heads! Copyright infringement in the Canadian online higher educational environment. *Canadian Journal of Learning and Technology, 32*(2), [online]. Retrieved January 12, 2007 from http://www.cjlt.ca/content/vol32.2/edmonds.html

Jenson, J., & De Castrell, S. (2004). "Turn it in": Technological challenges to academic ethics. *Education, Communication & Information, 4*(2/3), 311-330.

Lathrop, A., & Foss, K. (2005). *Guiding students from cheating and plagiarism to honesty and integrity: Strategies for change.* Westport, Connecticut: Libraries Unlimited.

McCabe, D., & Stephens, J. (2006). "Epidemic" as opportunity: Internet plagiarism as a lever for cultural change. *Teachers College Record, November 30,* [online]. Retrieved December 2, 2006 from http://www.tcrecord.org

Quotations Page. Wilson Mizner [online]. Retrieved April 4, 2007 from http://www.quotationspage.com/quotes/Wilson_Mizner

Scanlon, P. (2006). Solving the problem of Internet plagiarism? The technological expediency of online plagiarism-checkers. *Teachers College Record, October 18,* [online]. Retrieved October 22, 2006 from http://www.tcrecord.org

Thompson, C. (2006). Unintended lessons: Plagiarism and the university. *Teachers College Record, 108*(12), 2439-2449.

Mark Brown
Massey University

Preface

Sometimes an editor just gets lucky. A collection of 16 articles by different authors, gathered together as chapters in one volume, can easily turn out to be a disappointment. Perhaps the quality of the articles is not up to scratch, or the articles do not gel together to form a coherent whole.

I am delighted to say that I am confident that neither of these faults is apparent in the current volume. Whilst some chapters have a distinctly different flavour to others, they all directly address the issue of online student plagiarism in a scholarly and professional manner, and the problems and solutions discussed within these pages range over a wide variety of possible contexts. Together, the authors contributing to this volume have managed to provide a comprehensive examination of all of the major issues of concern to researchers and practitioners in this increasingly important area.

Taken as a whole, the chapters that make up the body of the book display an interesting tension—between those authors who accept, almost as a basic tenet of faith, that existing values regarding plagiarism are vitally important, and between those who think there may be some value to be had in considering the current generation's attitude towards copyright issues—as, for example, in the widespread acceptance (especially amongst the young) of free downloading of music tracks and videos.

Within each group there are further tensions; for example between those who believe that emphasis should be placed on education and prevention and those who believe that greater benefit can be had by emphasising detection and punitive action. It is tempting to call the first group *idealists*, and the second group *realists*, but such categorisation is perhaps unduly simplistic, and many would classify themselves as somewhere in the middle. Equally, there is tension between those who believe that our current views on plagiarism should be relaxed a little (if the categorisation is to be continued, perhaps people with such views could be labelled *pragmatists?*), and those who believe that our outlook requires some more fundamental overhaul (*futurists?*).

I would not dream of attempting to apply, in any sort of rigorous fashion, such categories here to the authors of the different chapters in the book. As they say in all of the best texts, such categorisation will be left as an interesting exercise for the reader. However, the chapters have indeed been grouped, into six sections, to help in finding one's way around.

Section I consists of three chapters, laying the basic groundwork: an introduction, a study of student attitudes, and a study of lecturer attitudes about plagiarism. Section II examines two particular case studies of methods to deal with plagiarism, both from universities in the UK. All three chapters in Section III examine the politically sensitive issue of handling plagiarism amongst international students and those for whom English is a second language.

Section IV contains two chapters, both of which deal with a very specific topic; Chapter IX deals with plagiarism at community colleges, and Chapter X covers the hot issue of the use of cheat sites which provide essays, reports and papers for a fee. Section V, the largest in the book, consists of four chapters, all based around the theme that prevention is better than cure. Finally, Section VI contains perhaps the two most controversial chapters of all. The first is a clarion call for greater consensus and fairness. The second looks at a possible future where our underlying assumptions about plagiarism may be challenged.

To start at the beginning, with Section I: the first chapter, "Student Plagiarism in an Online World: An Introduction," serves as a basis for the rest of the book. It attempts, in a scholarly but informal and easy-to-read fashion, to describe the extent of the problem, detail some of the major issues, and list some of the Web sites used by students in their acts of plagiarism, and some used by academics to detect such acts.

The chapter then outlines some of the techniques currently being used to prevent or solve the problem and concludes, perhaps controversially, by suggesting two promising, but very different, solutions. The first involves using technology to detect plagiarism before it occurs; the second, handling plagiarism by returning more control back to academics.

The second chapter, "A Student Perspective on Plagiarism," by Craig Zimitat, of Griffith University in Australia, critically examines data from nearly 1,500 native English-speaking undergraduate students, mostly enrolled on a full-time basis in degree programs, at all year-levels, across four major academic groups.

There are some real gems in here, including the fact that some 36 percent of students admit to helping friends to write their assignments. Some 57 percent admit to giving their notes to friends to help them with their assignment tasks. The bulk of the article looks at the students' recognition of plagiarism and paraphrasing and at their abilities and confidence in academic writing.

Zimitat's conclusions, that teachers need to improve the writing skills of their students, and to ensure that their students are familiarised with the conventions of the institution that relate to the use, manipulation, and transformation of knowledge, set the groundwork for much of what follows.

What about lecturers' attitudes to plagiarism? Chapter III is by Erik Eriksson and Kirk Sullivan, of Umea University in Sweden. "Controlling Plagiarism: A Study of Lecturer Attitudes," examines lecturers' knowledge of, and attitude to, plagiarism, how they pass their knowledge onto students, and the lecturers' knowledge of the disciplinary procedures for suspected plagiarism in their university.

This examination teases out the lecturers' responsibility for student plagiarism and its apparent rise in the online world. They found that academics are not sure of their definitions of plagiarism, have varied attitudes towards different types of plagiarism, and do not effectively teach how to avoid plagiarism. They suggest a wider discussion of plagiarism in the academy that extends beyond how to deter and catch plagiarists, to preventing plagiarism though the appropriate education of both student and academic.

Next, there are two particular case studies. First in Section II, in their chapter appropriately titled "Dealing with Plagiarism as an Ethical Issue," Barbara Cogdell and Dorothy Aidulis of Glasgow University in Scotland describe the range of approaches that are being developed in biology at the University of Glasgow to try to minimise the incidence of plagiarism by developing the students' ethical skills.

They describe in detail a level 3 workshop designed to improve scientific writing skills and a postgraduate workshop focused on research ethics. Although mainly teaching using traditional methods, they are now making increasing use of the virtual learning environment (VLE) Moodle to supplement courses, especially in the area of ethical training.

In "Working Together to Educate Students," Frankie Wilson and Kate Ippolito describe how another British institution, Brunel University, dealt with plagiarism in 2004, when it instigated a "zero tolerance" approach.

To complement what many might regard as a tough—perhaps too tough?—line, a working party was established to share best practice in deterring plagiarism among academics, student support professionals, and the students' union. This group decided to create a programme to enable students to effectively learn about plagiarism and how to avoid it.

The bulk of the chapter details the development of this programme, including the principles that underpinned it and the teaching and learning materials that were developed. The chapter also reports the results of a pilot study of this programme and the methods so far used to roll it out across the University. The chapter concludes with some reflections on the Brunel approach and a look to the future.

Plagiarism often has been seen to be an especially serious problem amongst international students for whom English is a second language and who may have been brought up with different cultural traditions and ethical values. The next three chapters address this issue head on, beginning with Teresa Chen and Nai-Kuang Teresa Ku's chapter "EFL Students: Factors Contributing to Online Plagiarism."

Chen and Ku, from California State University, report on a survey study that investigates English-as-a-Foreign-Language (EFL) students' experiences with online plagiarism and the factors associated with these practices among the students. Two hundred and thirty-five English majors from four universities in Taiwan participated in this study. Based on the findings from the survey, the chapter presents the students' perspectives on plagiarism and, with reference to these students' input, provides suggestions on ways to prevent students from online plagiarism.

Ursula McGowan, from the University of Adelaide, points out in her chapter "International Students: A Conceptual Framework for Dealing with Unintentional Plagiarism" that students for whom English is an additional language are easily recognised for inappropriate use of extraneous sources.

Many tell-tale signs may alert the assessor to the possibility of inappropriate use of source material. If appropriate checks confirm the suspicion of plagiarism, the assessor faces a dilemma: was there an intention to deceive, or was the act of downloading done innocently, from lack of knowledge of the expectations, lack of skills in referencing, or lack of appropriate language?

This chapter teases out these concerns, and presents a possible solution by introducing a conceptual framework which places student learning at the centre of deliberations, and in which the inappropriate use of sources is understood to be part the process of induction into the culture and language of enquiry of the academic environment.

Lucas Introna and Niall Hayes from Lancaster University in the UK argue in Chapter VIII, "International Students and Plagiarism Detection Systems: Detecting Plagiarism, Copying or Learning?" that the inappropriate use of electronic plagiarism detection could lead to the unfair and unjust construction of international students as plagiarists. They argue that the use of detection systems should take into account the writing practices used by those who write as novices in a non-native language as well as the way "plagiarism" or plagiaristic forms of writing are valued in other cultures.

The chapter focuses on a technique seemingly frequently used by international students: copying from some online source, deleting a few words, and substituting others with synonyms. It then moves on to look at algorithms which are often used to detect such plagiarism, and looks at their commonalities and differences.

In conclusion, they call for a move away from a punitive legalistic approach to plagiarism that equates copying to plagiarism and move to a progressive and formative approach.

To open Section IV, a return to a more traditional audience: in "Plagiarism at the Community College," Teri Maddox, from Jackson State Community College, examines plagiarism by community college students and suggests that the diversity of ages, backgrounds, races, cultures, abilities, motivations, and personalities such students bring with them to the classroom present both problems and opportunities for teachers.

Are community college students that different from university students? Probably. Are the teaching and learning strategies that community college faculty should use to combat intentional and unintentional plagiarism different from those that university faculty should use? Probably not.

The area of contract cheating has not, as yet, received much examination in the literature. Self-reporting of contract cheating tends to be much lower than for other forms of plagiarism, typically ranging from 3 percent to 5 percent. But this low level is perhaps to be expected, given that it is commonly considered to be an even more serious crime than the "copy-and-paste" variety of plagiarism. In Chapter X, "The Phenomena Of Contract Cheating," Thomas Lancaster and Robert Clarke look in detail at the whole area of contract cheating.

In a particularly interesting table, they list no fewer than 42 sites which provide to the needs of contract cheaters, classifying them as either auction sites, discussion fora, essay mills, feed aggregators. Of course, by the time this book is in print, many will have disappeared, and many others will have taken their place.

Lancaster and Clarke, from UCE Birmingham in England, point out the difficulty of catching plagiarists using such sites and express their strongly-held belief that more thought needs to be directed to assignment design, and more tutors need to be aware that some original coursework submitted by their students may not be the results of the labour of those students.

The next four chapters, which make up Section V, all are guided by the oft-repeated cliché that prevention is better than cure, and concentrate on methods which might be used to prevent--or at least greatly reduce--the problem. In their chapter "Minimising Plagiarism by Education and Prevention," Martin Dick from RMIT and Judithe Sheard and Maurie Hasen, both from Monash University, provide an excellent reminder that time and effort expended to prevent plagiarism can repay itself many times over in terms of time and effort (and stress) saved in detection and policing.

While the chapter is based on a series of eight focus groups conducted with information technology students at an Australian university, the responses and lessons drawn would seem to have universal applicability.

In Chapter XII, "Plagiarism, Instruction, & Blogs," Michael Hanrahan describes the CBB Plagiarism Project, which promotes the responsible use, re-use, and re-purposing of its resources so instructors and librarians can address the problem of plagiarism at the level of local institutional practices, values, and concerns. CBB here stands for the Colby, Bates, and Bowdoin, the three colleges involved in the development of a Web site to act as a clearinghouse for information on plagiarism

Hanrahan, from Bates College, believes that the decision to publish content by means of a weblog has in retrospect leveraged a technology that has unexpectedly provided a reflective tool and medium for engaging plagiarism.

Some researchers and practitioners have put forward the idea that the most effective solutions lie primarily in a redesign of the methods of assessment, so as to make them less amenable to plagiarism. In their chapter "Minimising Plagiarism by Redesigning the Learning Environment and Assessment," Madhumita Bhattacharaya and Lone Jorgensen, both from Massey University in New Zealand, argue that teachers will need to change their approach to assessment.

They suggest that both processes and products will have to change in order to ensure the authenticity of students' work. Consequently, the authors propose a model for the design and development of assessment tasks, and the learning environment, to prevent plagiarism.

Along similar, but slightly different, lines, in Chapter XIV, "Expect Originality! Using Taxonomies to Structure Assignments that Support Original Work," Janet Salmons, from Vision2Lead Inc., argues that educators can take steps to prevent plagiarism by designing assignments that expect learners to respect others' ideas and strive toward creating their own original work.

xxiii

She argues that educational taxonomies, including the cognitive and affective domains of bloom's taxonomy, and her own taxonomy of collaborative e-learning, can serve as conceptual frameworks for designing assignments that 1) expect learners to present original work; 2) provide opportunities for learners to develop new ideas through meaningful online interaction; and 3) value learners' ideas while respecting published authors' intellectual property.

To finish, Section VI consists of two very different perspectives. In his chapter "Substantial, Verbatim, Unattributed, Misleading: Applying Criteria to Assess Textual Plagiarism," William Decoo, from the University of Antwerp, in Belgium, argues that both individuals and institutions handle cases of alleged plagiarism very differently in terms of disclosure, assessment, and decision-making.

The consequences therefore will vary greatly. A trivial instance, if highly publicized, may destroy a student's career, while a case of massive copying may be kept completely quiet and end in tacit exoneration. For the sake of justice, an allegation as serious as plagiarism requires the establishment and the wide acceptance of more solid criteria. Using the American-based Office of Research Integrity's definition of textual plagiarism, this chapter examines some of the variables to consider and suggests ways to achieve greater consensus and fairness in cases of alleged plagiarism.

Readers will undoubtedly have strong opinions about the final chapter, which concludes Section VI and provides a fitting end to the book. The chapter, "Students and the Internet: The Dissolution of Boundaries" by Jon Ramsey, is quite unlike any other, in both format and content.

Ramsey, of the University of California in Santa Barbara, looks bravely to the future: are we perhaps witnessing a possible dissolution of boundaries? As he himself says, "...(t)he traditional aspirations of academia need not be lost in translation if we look creatively for points of connection with the world in which the students operate daily--in particular, the myriad technological interconnections that increasingly inform students' understanding of information and ideas...".

Many will disagree with his outlook, but careful consideration of his thoughts as outlined in this chapter make for an interesting discussion. What better way in which to end?

Tim S. Roberts
Central Queensland University, Australia

Acknowledgment

Any book such as this is the result of the hard work of a large number of people. First and foremost, I would like to thank Chris Park and Mark Brown for their forewords for the book and all of the chapter authors—Dorothy Aidulis, Madhumita Bhattacharya, Teresa Chen, Robert Clarke, Barbara Cogdell, Wilfried Decoo, Martin Dick, Erik J Eriksson, Michael Hanrahan, Maurie Hasen, Niall Hayes, Lucas D. Introna, Lone Jorgensen, Nai-Kuang Teresa Ku, Thomas Lancaster, Teri Thomson Maddox, Ursula McGowan, Jon R. Ramsey, Janet Salmons, Judithe Sheard, Kate Ippolito, Kirk P H Sullivan, Frankie Wilson, and Craig Zimitat—all of whom have provided thought-provoking insights into the increasingly important problem of student plagiarism—a problem which seems to be almost systemic to the online world in which most of us live.

Many thanks also to all of those who served as reviewers, without whose critical but always constructive comments this book would never have seen the light of day. Special mention in this regard must go to Sharon Argov, Michael Barbour, Linda Bergmann, Haydn Blackey, Tim Bottorff, Ugur Demiray, Lisa Emerson, Robert Holley, Gulsun Kurubacak, Becky Mangin, Kathy Marlock, Tommy McDonnell, Joanne McInnerney, June Mogensen, Marion Smith, and Sue Thompson.

Editing this book would have been a much tougher task had it not been for the very helpful and professional staff at IGI Global. Extra special thanks must go to Lynley Lapp, Ross Miller, and Jessica Thompson, all of whom responded to my various requests with patience and good humour, especially when I was called for jury service at the last moment!

Last but very definitely not least: my thanks to you, the readers of this book. There is much more to be said about student plagiarism in an online world than can be contained in a single book, and I would welcome your thoughts and feedback. My e-mail address is t.roberts@cqu.edu.au.

Section I
Some Groundwork

Chapter I
Student Plagiarism in an Online World:
An Introduction

Tim S. Roberts
Central Queensland University, Australia

ABSTRACT

The purpose of this chapter is to provide an introduction to the problem of student plagiarism in an environment where use of the Internet is commonplace. What is plagiarism, and to what extent is it a problem? Why do students plagiarize, and what are typical attitudes towards such plagiarism? Why are academics, and institutions themselves, often reluctant to progress cases through official channels? What are some of the technologies used by students to plagiarise, and by academics to detect plagiarism? What solutions are possible, and what potential solutions might be just over the horizon? This chapter attempts to provide answers to all of these questions.

INTRODUCTION

The advent of the internet has made plagiarism by students not only easier, but also, easier to detect.

Statistics in this area tend to vary a little depending upon the methods used for their collection and calculation, but whether the percentage of students self-reporting plagiarism is 35 percent in one survey, or 45 percent in another, the conclusion is the same. Plagiarism no longer can be considered as a crime committed by a poor unfortunate few with questionable morals; rather, it is a crime (if it is indeed a crime) committed by a significant number of students, perhaps the majority, at one time or another.

WHAT IS PLAGIARISM?

Plagiarism...

*   ....is the act of representing as one's own original work the creative works of another, without appropriate acknowledgment of the author or source (University of Melbourne, 2007).
*   ....is the theft of someone else's ideas and work. Whether a student copies verbatim or simply rephrases the ideas of another without properly acknowledging the source, the theft is the same (Harvard University Extension School, 2007).
*   ....is the copying or paraphrasing of other people's work or ideas into your own work without full acknowledgement (University of Oxford, 2007).

What can we deduce from such definitions? First, that the plagiarist is using someone else's work, or ideas; second, that he or she does so without proper acknowledgement; and third, that mere paraphrasing or rephrasing of such work or ideas in no way mitigates the crime.

Plagiarism sometimes is delineated as to whether or not the student has set out intentionally to deceive; if so, the crime is perceived to be more serious than if the plagiarism has been unintentional. At the extremely serious end of the scale would generally be such acts as purchasing an essay or a term paper from a "cheat" site on the Internet; at the least serious end of the spectrum might be the employment of a phrase taken from a source which has been incorrectly referenced, or perhaps not referenced at all.

WHY DO STUDENTS PLAGIARIZE?

Lists of reasons as to why students engage in plagiarism can be found in many places. A typical list might look something like the following,

taken from the University of Alabama in Huntsville (2007):

*   Lack of research skills
*   Lack of writing skills
*   Problems evaluating Internet sources
*   Confusion about how to cite sources
*   Misconceptions about terminology
*   Pressure
*   Poor time management and organizational skills
*   Product-oriented writing assignments
*   Cultural factors

A list of reasons why students plagiarize compiled by someone with a more cynical turn of mind might come up with one more item: because they can. So long as the objective is to achieve a particular grade, rather than to learn, and there are reasonable prospects of avoiding detection, then students are optimizing their time and resources by plagiarizing. Potential solutions which fail to recognize this basic underlying fact are unlikely to be successful.

THE EXTENT OF THE PROBLEM

Statistics in this area must be necessarily treated with caution, for at least two reasons.

First, since the online environment is changing all the time, it is possible that students' attitudes to plagiarism are, too. Witness, for example, the changing attitudes to copyright issues in the music and video industries. So it is perhaps important to give more weight to evidence gathered in the last few years, rather than to that with origins in the last century.

Second, almost all such statistics are gathered through self-reporting. It should be fairly obvious, therefore, that such statistics might be quite unreliable; and perhaps more likely to underestimate the problem, rather than the reverse.

Those two concerns aside, the findings tend to be fairly consistent.

In 2002, a survey of some 700 undergraduate students revealed that some 25 percent of respondents had gone online to cut-and-paste without citation (Scanlon & Neumann, 2002).

In a survey of some 35,000 students conducted in the 2002/2003 academic year in the U.S and Canada, McCabe reported that around 36 percent of respondents voluntarily reported one or more instances of "cut-and-paste" plagiarism from Internet sources. Response rates were around 20 percent (McCabe, 2003). Presumably then, of around 7,000 respondents, almost 2,500 chose to "turn themselves in."

As noted above, with almost all such surveys, it is unlikely that students would self-report if they had not plagiarised; while the converse is not the case. It is quite conceivable that fear of the consequences could indeed cause many respondents to answer dishonestly. If this is accepted, statistics arising out of such surveys may perhaps best be regarded as minima.

In a 2006 Canadian survey, "more than half of the undergraduates and 35 percent of the graduate students surveyed admitted to some form of cheating on written course work, such as failing to footnote, turning in someone else's work, or falsifying a bibliography" (Birchard, 2006). Also in 2006, the Josephson Institute of Ethics reported that 33 percent of high-school students surveyed admitted to copying an Internet document for a classroom assignment within the past 12 months—18 percent did so two or more times (Josephson Institute, 2006).

LECTURER ATTITUDES AND A MEA CULPA

Let me relate an experience of my own, from a few years ago at another institution. In one of the computer science classes, it was quite a common occurrence to spot cases of plagiarism, some mi-nor, some major, amongst perhaps 25 percent of the students. I tended to deal with these personally, since the institution at which I was then employed was not to keen to spend much time investigating cases (quite rightly, in my opinion—a university should have as its core business teaching and leaning, not policing and punishment).

But then one particular term I decided to use an automated tool to check for plagiarism. This reported that the vast majority—I forget the exact statistic, but 70 percent would have been a rough figure—of the students had copied from each other or from available sources on the Web.

What was I supposed to do with this? Well, what I was supposed to do and what I actually did were two different things. The very first thing I did was to resolve not to use a plagiarism-detection tool ever again (at least, until I had a reasonable solution to the problem).

And what did I do in response to the cases I had detected? With regard to the less-serious cases, I made it clear that they had been found out, and gave a warning. With the more serious cases, I called them in, explained the evidence against them carefully, and either reduced their marks, or awarded them zero.

Why did I not follow official procedures? Well, self-justification is an imperfect science at best, so let me instead mention some of the reasons most often cited by other academics who have found themselves in similar situations:

- The time required is not worth it. More time on detection and follow-up procedures means less time devoted to teaching and learning.
- The stress involved is high and lasts for a long time, for all of the parties involved. Almost inevitably, official procedures result in an adversarial environment, where the academic is pitted against the student. Ideally, the academic's role should be to help the student, not punish him or her.

- The student is perhaps not entirely to blame. Maybe the student has not been taught what is appropriate and what is not? Maybe the culture from which the student comes is different, and the student is not fully aware of the seriousness of his or her actions?
- The launching of official procedures can bring attention to the academic and to the course. Why, some will want to know, are colleagues teaching other courses not reporting similar problems? Several possible reasons suggest themselves.
- Even after enduring the time, stress, and workload involved, it is quite likely that the students concerned will be given a warning, or a light punishment. So, ultimately, what is the point?

It is likely that most, if not all, of the above facts played a part in my decision not to pursue many cases through the official channels.

One extra point is perhaps worth noting: if my own experience is at all typical, then one can deduce that the number of reported cases recorded in official university documents represents the proverbial tip of the iceberg.

PAPER MILL SITES

There are a large and ever-growing number of "cheat" sites, where students can purchase term papers or essays to fit their assignment criteria. A selection of these can be found at Roberts (2007). A more comprehensive list is given by Stoerger (2006). A brief and not necessarily representative sample might include:

- Schoolsucks.com, a brilliantly titled site designed to appeal to the disaffected, which is "based on a free collection of term papers," and invites students to "download your workload." A recent search on "Abraham Lincoln" takes you to Termpapersmonthly. com, which claims to be "one of the largest collections of term papers, essays, book reports, and research papers," and produces 732 possible papers available for download. Membership is US$29.95 for 30 days, or US$89.95 for 180 days.
- Coursework.info invites students to search "133,021 pieces of coursework from the UK's largest coursework library." A recent search on "Abraham Lincoln" produced 210 essays. It is possible to purchase essays for free in return for supplying three of your own or paying £4.99.
- Cheathouse.com advertises a "library of essays, research and term papers, book reports, case studies" and invites you to "get inspired, use other's research and bibliographies" (!). Three days' access is US$9.90, or you can choose the 6-month option, for US$69.95. A search for "Abraham Lincoln" produced 410 possible essays.
- Essayschool.com has no membership fees, but charges US$9.95 per page "delivered 24 hours a day via your choice of e-mail, fax, or FedEx." But buyers beware: a paltry 160 possible essays resulted when searching for "Abraham Lincoln."

Figures of students self-reporting instances of buying papers from such sites are quite low (typically between 1 percent and 5 percent), perhaps because this is seen as a more serious crime than "mere" copying-and-pasting. Even if these figures are accurate, however, the total number of students involved in such activities is still vast.

PLAGIARISM DETECTION SITES

Plagiarism detection sites are, for the most part, still very basic. Mostly, they are text-matching systems, relying on existing databases of material, against which submitted assignments are matched. As such, they suffer from at least two major weaknesses.

First, some minor rephrasing of the material will most likely result in the assignment escaping detection. Thus, such sites tend to be successful in picking up work from students who, for whatever reason, have made little effort to amend the original text, but to miss those who have amended, or changed the order of, a sufficient number of words or phrases.

Second, because they rely on text matching with existing databases of material, it is self-evident that assignments using plagiarized materials not included in such databases will avoid detection. Such materials might be copied from other students, either past or present, or from printed books or magazine articles, or any number of other sources.

Having expressed such reservations, there is no doubt that some sites can provide a useful level of detection. Among the most popular are:

- Turnitin.com, a tool that "enables instructors to manage grades and assignments online and instantly identify papers containing unoriginal material. Probably the most widely-used of all anti-plagiarism sites" (Turnitin, 2007).
- MyDropbox Suite, which "integrates a renowned plagiarism prevention technology with a versatile digital learning environment that enables instructors to manage online assignments, organize electronic submissions and mark papers on the Web" (MyDropBox, 2007).
- DOC Cop, which "scans one million words, a thousand thousand-word documents or Homer's Odyssey against Joyce's Ulysses within 20 minutes" (DOC Cop, 2007).
- Easy Verification Engine (EVE2), "a very powerful tool that allows professors and teachers at all levels of the education system

to determine if students have plagiarized material from the World Wide Web" (EVE2, 2007).
- Glatt Plagiarism.com, "a highly sophisticated Screening Program to detect plagiarism. Typically used in academic institutions or in the legal profession for cases of copyright infringement"(Glatt Plagiarism Services Inc, 2007).
- MOSS, which is an acronym for a Measure of Software Similarity, which provides "an automatic system for determining the similarity of C, C++, Java, Pascal, Ada, ML, Lisp, or Scheme programs" (Moss, 2007).

More comprehensive lists can be found in Roberts (2007) and Stoerger (2006). The provision of plagiarism detection software is seen to be a burgeoning area, and it can be expected that more such sites will come to prominence in the near future.

EXISTING STRATEGIES TO COUNTER PLAGIARISM

A variety of different strategies are commonly used to counter plagiarism. A basic underpinning to all strategies, however, is the understanding that students should have been educated as to what plagiarism is, that intentional plagiarism is unacceptable in any academic environment, and that unintentional plagiarism can usually be avoided by the application of proper referencing standards. Students cannot be expected to play by the rules if they are not acquainted with them.

Assuming that such education has taken place, and that plagiarism is still occurring, there are several potential remedies commonly referred to in the literature. The following list should not be viewed as exhaustive, but rather as a guide to generic solutions that are likely to vary widely in practice from institution to institution.

- The use of honor codes (and/or integrity policies)
- The teaching of ethics and ethical behavior
- The implementation of more efficient policing and detection
- The imposition of harsher penalties
- The modification of assessment

All of these methods have their adherents, but all have substantial difficulties.

Honor Codes and the Teaching of Ethical Behavior

Many researchers and practitioners, who might perhaps be called idealists, adopt what might be perceived as moral solutions: that the problem can be cured—or at least, greatly reduced—by the implementation of honor codes, or the teaching of ethical behaviour, or both.

Honor codes are not new, and usually cover a range of attitudes and behaviors beyond just plagiarism. For example, Stanford University's Honor Code states:

A. The *Honor Code is an undertaking of the students, individually and collectively:*

1. *that they will not give or receive aid in examinations; that they will not give or receive unpermitted aid in class work, in the preparation of reports, or in any other work that is to be used by the instructor as the basis of grading;*

2. *that they will do their share and take an active part in seeing to it that others as well as themselves uphold the spirit and letter of the Honor Code.*

B. *The faculty on its part manifests its confidence in the honor of its students by refraining from proctoring examinations and from taking unusual and unreasonable precautions to prevent the forms of dishonesty mentioned above. The faculty will also avoid,*

as far as practicable, academic procedures that create temptations to violate the Honor Code.

C. *While the faculty alone has the right and obligation to set academic requirements, the students and faculty will work together to establish optimal conditions for honorable academic work* (Stanford University, 2007).

The Texas A&M University Honor Code would appear to be of a briefer nature:

An Aggie does not lie, cheat, or steal, or tolerate those who do (Texas A&M University, 2007).

Honor codes are usually implemented on an institution-wide basis, and considerable institutional involvement is almost always required if such approaches are to be successful.

The instilling of ethical behaviour might be attempted in a variety of ways, but is likely to include the introduction into the curriculum of one or more courses specifically devoted to ethics.

Unfortunately, results seem to be mixed, anecdotally at least. There have been several cases reported of students copying-and-pasting when asked to write essays on ethics, for example; and there would appear to be many instances of honor codes not being honored.

However, it is possible that honor codes may reduce the incidences of cheating. McCabe, for example, says that "serious test cheating on campuses with honor codes is typically 1/3 to 1/2 lower than the level on campuses that do not have honor codes. The level of serious cheating on written assignments is 1/4 to 1/3 lower" (Center for Academic Integrity, 2007).

More Efficient Policing and Detection, and Harsher Penalties

This group of strategies are less idealistic. They may perhaps be best categorized as punitive

6

solutions, and their proponents as realists; they are based on the assumption that most students unconsciously perform a cost-benefit analysis of sorts, and come to the conclusion that the benefits of plagiarism outweigh the costs. The solution, then, is to decrease the benefits, perhaps by downsizing the length or difficulty of the assessment items; and/or increase the costs, which can be achieved by rigorous policing, and implementation of harsh penalties.

This would seem to be a reasonable approach, but success is dependent on a number of factors; most notably, the use of automated detection systems; the willingness of administrators and academics to devote the necessary time and effort to plagiarism detection; and the willingness of all parties involved to follow through the inevitably bureaucratic processes, while acknowledging and accepting the amount of resources and stress that such courses of action typically involve.

It also is perhaps worth noting that even when such processes are followed through to a conclusion, institutions are often reluctant to impose the most severe penalties (such as exclusion from the course), for fear of litigation.

Modifying the Assessment

Another group of strategies, which might perhaps be termed pragmatic solutions, and their advocates perhaps pragmatists, are based on an acceptance that if students can cheat with a reasonable possibility of not being caught, they will. If assessment items are structured so as to be amenable to plagiarism, then the assessors have only themselves to blame. Perhaps more effort should be put in to redesigning the methods of assessment.

This solution clearly puts the emphasis—and, some would say, the blame—on the instructor, who has various possible options. Certainly, in some contexts it may be feasible to change the methods of assessment to those which are less amenable to plagiarism. But changing from an essay to, say, a multiple choice test is rarely an option. Altering essay requirements from "Describe X" to "Contrast X and Y" may help a little, but only a little.

Other options designed to ensure originality, such as getting students to submit drafts prior to the final product, or keeping reflective journals which detail the development of their assessment, can be onerous and time-consuming for both students and instructors.

At the extreme are solutions where final grades are determined exclusively by end-of-term examinations, and other assessment items count for nothing. Most educationalists would not be entirely happy with such solutions, however, and for good reason. Assessment items are very frequently used as integral components of the learning process itself, and without incentives in the form of potential higher grades, students may be reluctant to devote much effort to their completion.

POSSIBLE NEW DIRECTIONS

All of the current methods of dealing with the problem of plagiarism, including the moralistic, punitive, and pragmatic solutions referred to above, have obvious shortcomings. What might the future hold? Two possible solutions, student use of technology and return of control to the academic, are suggested here.

Student Use of Technology

One possibility is the use of technology to detect plagiarism before it occurs, and relies on the development of software which can detect plagiarism of all varieties with a high degree of reliability.

The key idea is that instead of the software being used by academics to detect plagiarism after the event, it is run by the students themselves prior to submission. Based on the results, students then have the opportunity to refine their potential submissions.

Such refinements could include the removal of offending passages, or the addition of appropriate references, and so on. They then can repeat the process as many times as are necessary. When the software gives them a clean sheet, they are able to submit their work. It is worth noting, however, that unless the software is of a very high standard, this may well result in mere re-wording, rather than anything more intellectually substantial.

Return of Control to the Academic

A second possibility is perhaps more promising, and is one that could be achieved now, since it does not rely upon possible future technological developments. Instead, however, it relies on something which may be altogether more difficult to achieve—a change in the mindset of how plagiarism is dealt with.

More often than not, procedures for dealing with cases of plagiarism are bureaucratic, time-consuming, and stressful to all concerned, not least the academics involved. Further, institutions recognise this, and encouragements to detect and report plagiarism therefore tend to be half-hearted, at best.

What if the emphasis were to be shifted 180 degrees from the academic having to detect and report plagiarism, to the student having to convince the assessor that they had learnt the material?

What is being suggested here is radical because this 180 degree shift takes any accusation of a crime having been committed out of the picture.

Let us take a particular case: suppose an essay on the life of Abraham Lincoln is submitted by a student. The instructor, through whatever means, determines that there are significant passages taken straight from Wikipedia, or some other source. Thus, the instructor determines that the student has not demonstrated much (or perhaps any) learning about the life of Abraham Lincoln. Therefore, the assessor awards a low, or zero mark.

The student has failed to convince the assessor that they have learnt anything about the life of Abraham Lincoln.

Or another example: suppose two (or more) students hand in close-to-identical essays. Therefore, none has individually provided evidence that they have mastered the material, so again, marks are reduced, or lost altogether. Of course, the assessor may decide to call the students concerned in for a chat, or seek further evidence of individual learning, but there is no necessity to treat it as a crime, or to proceed through the bureaucratic processes.

The objection may be raised that this places an onus on the assessor to act fairly. Well, indeed so. But isn't this a requirement of most professions? And, as in any case of perceived unfairness, students do not give up any of the rights they had in relation to being able to protest against unfair marking, which may occur in a variety of circumstances completely unconnected with plagiarism.

At opposite ends of the spectrum, the technological solution and the human solution, as they may be termed, are of course not opposites at all; they could be employed together, without problems. Both have obvious advantages, and may appeal to a greater or lesser extent depending upon the particular circumstances.

Hopefully their brief outlining here will inspire others to develop successful solutions to this increasingly important problem. The author would welcome hearing from any readers so inspired.

REFERENCES

Birchard, K. (2006). Cheating is rampant at Canadian colleges. *The Chronicle of Higher Education, 53*(8).

Center for Academic Integrity. (2007). *CAI Research*. Retrieved February 19, 2007, from http://www.academicintegrity.org/cai_research.asp

DOC Cop. (2007). *Bright Ideas.* Retrieved February 8, 2007, from http://www.doccop.com/

EVE2. (2007). *Eve Plagiarism Detection System.* Retrieved February 8, 2007, from http://www.canexus.com/

Glatt Plagiarism Services Inc. (2007). *Glatt Plagiarism Screening Program (GPSP).* Retrieved February 8, 2007, from http://www.plagiarism.com/

Harvard University Extension School. (2007). *Statement on Plagiarism.* Retrieved February 19, 2007, from http://cyber.law.harvard.edu/ptc/Statement_on_Plagiarism

Josephson Institute. (2006). *The ethics of American youth: 2006 Josephson Institute report card.* Retrieved February 19, 2007, from http://www.josephsoninstitute.org/pdf/2006reportcard/Q43.pdf

McCabe, D. L. (2003). Promoting academic integrity: A US/Canadian Perspective. In *Educational Integrity: Plagiarism and Other Perplexities, Proceedings of the First Australasian Integrity Conference.* University of South Australia, Adelaide.

Moss. (2007). *A system for detecting software plagiarism.* Retrieved February 8, 2007, from http://theory.stanford.edu/~aiken/moss/

MyDropBox. (2007). *MyDropBox Suite.* Retrieved February 8, 2007, from http://www.mydropbox.com/

Roberts, T. S. (2007). *Assessment in higher education: Plagiarism.* Retrieved February 19, 2007, from http://ahe.cqu.edu.au/plagiarism.html

Scanlon, P. M., & Neumann, D. R. (2002). Internet plagiarism among college students. *Journal of College Student Development, 43*(3), 374-385.

Stanford University. (2007). *Honor code.* Retrieved April 3, 2007, from http://www.stanford.edu/dept/vpsa/judicialaffairs/guiding/pdf/honorcode.pdf

Stoerger, S. (2006). *Plagiarism.* Retrieved February 19, 2007, from http://www.web-miner.com/plagiarism

Texas A&M University. (2007). *Aggie honor code.* Retrieved April 3, 2007, from http://www.tamu.edu/aggiehonor/know.html

Turnitin. (2007). *Plagiarism prevention.* Retrieved February 8, 2007, from http://turnitin.com/static/plagiarism.html

University of Alabama in Huntsville. (2007). *Preventing plagiarism.* Retrieved February 19, 2007, from http://www.uah.edu/library/turnitin/facultypreventplag.htm

University of Melbourne. (2007). *Academic honesty and plagiarism.* Retrieved February 19, 2007, from http://academichonesty.unimelb.edu.au/plagiarism.html

University of Oxford. (2007). *Plagiarism: Educational policy and standards.* Retrieved February 19, 2007, from http://www.admin.ox.ac.uk/epsc/plagiarism/

Chapter II
A Student Perspective of Plagiarism

Craig Zimitat
Griffith University, Australia

ABSTRACT

This chapter reports on an Australian study of native-English speaking, undergraduate students' engagement in plagiarism-related behaviours, their knowledge of plagiarism and their academic writing skills. Students were surveyed to: (1) estimate the incidence of plagiarism behaviours; (2) examine students' self-reported academic writing skills; (3) their knowledge of plagiarism; and (4) their ability to identify plagiarised work. Across all three undergraduate years, approximately 90 percent of students believed that direct copying of text or ideas without acknowledgement constituted plagiarism, whilst around 5 percent were unsure if it constituted plagiarism. The majority of students (80 percent or more) claimed never to have plagiarized. About 80 percent of undergraduate students said they possessed the skills of note-taking, paraphrasing, citing, referencing, and so on, but barely half of students in each year group reported confidence with these skills. Students were able to distinguish between clear-cut cases of plagiarism and paraphrasing when presented with either different writing processes or different work samples, but they were less able to distinguish between "borderline cases." There are clear implications for classroom practice. First, students need the opportunity to practice and develop their academic writing skills, in the context of articulating their understandings of their own discipline. This requires teachers to recognise that academic writing is a developmental skill and to learn how to improve the writing skills of their students. Second, in this process, teachers need to ensure that students are inducted into the conventions of the academy that relate to the use, manipulation and transformation of knowledge.

INTRODUCTION

Key studies in the U.S., UK and Australia confirm that academic plagiarism is increasing in higher education. In cross-institutional U.S. studies, the proportion of students admitting to academic misconduct, characterised by use of unacknowledged text in written assignments, has increased threefold since 1999 (Centre for Academic Integrity, 2005). From these studies, it appears that students who admit to plagiarism commonly admit to other academic misconduct. In another self-report study involving four Australia universities, Marsden (2005b) surprisingly found that acts of plagiarism were admitted to by 81 percent of undergraduate students. More objective technical analyses of nearly 2000 assignments submitted by students across six Australian universities (O'Connor, 2003) have demonstrated that 14 percent of papers contained more than 5 percent non-attributed text. It can be determined that plagiarism was committed by about 14 percent of students in that study. The extent of plagiarism in written assignments is not clear in the self-report studies, but less than 2 percent of analysed assignments in O'Connor's study contained 40 percent or more of unattributed text. Overall, it would be reasonable to expect that at least 10 percent of academic work (JISC, 2005) submitted by students might need close scrutiny because of plagiarism issues.

There appear to be multiple factors contributing to the increase in plagiarism. Across universities and disciplines, there exists a wide variation of definitions, policies, and practices that leaves considerable scope for confusion around the issue of plagiarism (ACODE, 2005; McCabe & Drinan, 1999; Pecorari, 2006). In the higher education sector generally, issues such as the increasing diversity of the student population and increasing class sizes makes the teaching of writing more challenging and the monitoring of assessment more difficult and decreases the potential chance of detection; increasing casualisation of the academic workforce hinders professional development programs focusing on learning and teaching issues, and increasing research pressures on academic staff may challenge their abilities to respond adequately to the increasing diversity of skills of the student population. More fundamental though is the finding that academic staff, like students, have diverse views on plagiarism. Staff members' working definitions of plagiarism are influenced by their personal views, as well as their disciplinary context (Flint, Clegg, & Macdonald, 2006; Macdonald & Freewood, 2002). The diversity of views on plagiarism is matched by the diversity of ability amongst staff to distinguish between paraphrasing and plagiarism Roig (2001). When asked to paraphrase text in Roig's study, some academic staff generated a product considered by peers that clearly represented plagiarism. Solving the "student plagiarism problem" is not possible without due consideration of the "teacher plagiarism problem."

New technologies play a key role in plagiarism both in terms of providing mechanisms for detecting plagiarism on the one hand and of fuelling access and opportunities for plagiarism on the other hand (Ashworth, Bannister, & Thorne, 1997; Larkham & Manns, 2002; Marshall & Garry, 2005a; Park, 2003; Scanlon & Neumann, 2002). Nearly 60 percent of students enrolling in Australian higher education are of the "Net Generation" and have grown up in a technologically rich environment copying, manipulating and "mashing" text, audio and video from the Internet in ways not previously imagined. Their social use of information derived from the Internet is at odds with the way in which the Academy views appropriate use of information (Prensky, 2001). Students certainly use new technologies, and as they progress through their degree programs they use learning technologies to a significantly greater extent (Zimitat, 2004). Students do not appear to be able to adapt their technological skills for the purposes of academic work (Katz, 2005; p. 7), and many teachers may not be able to adequately help them in this enterprise.

The widespread admissions of plagiarism implicate all students, though some groups of students are more likely to be involved in academic dishonesty than others. In a survey of 80,000 students in the USA, younger students, males, and less academically able students were found to be more likely to plagiarise than others (McCabe & Trevino, 1997). Marsden (2005a) also reported significant differences in rates of self-reported acts of plagiarism based on gender, age, and discipline of study, with young males under 25 years more likely to plagiarise than any other group of students. First year students may be more likely than third year students to plagiarise (McCabe, 2005), though others report the reverse (Marsden, Carroll, & Neill, 2005b). International students from non-English speaking backgrounds also have been singled out for attention because they are disproportionately represented in institutional misconduct statistics (ACODE, 2005; JISC, 2005). It is argued that these students are at greatest risk of plagiarism because of their inexpert grasp of English and lack of experience with Western writing traditions (Introna, Hayes, Blair, & Wood, 2003). Motivations for plagiarism maybe related to an orientation towards achieving good grades at any cost Marsden (2005a), or more simply because students weigh the chances of the low risk of detection (Reference) in favour of better grades.

Poor academic writing skills appear to be one fundamental cause of plagiarism related behaviour. Many students entering higher education today have poor writing skills in general. Academic writing, with its focus on argument and evidence, takes time to learn through experience and feedback, across the continuum of undergraduate study (Haggis, 2003). Skills such as the ability to analyse the topic for an assignment, note-taking, comprehending the key message in text, critically analysing, and summarising information can all impact upon students' writing, just as much as English proficiency (Howard, 1995; Pecorari, 2003). The ability to paraphrase and following

rules for referencing and citing evidence are also necessary for academic writing (Roig, 2001), and breaches of these appear most frequently in technical analyses of assignments (O'Connor, 2003). Students' development of these skills is complicated by varying degrees of acceptable practice of paraphrasing, citing, and referencing by teaching staff (Roig, 1997, 2001) and across disciplines (Pecorari, 2006). Whilst much has been made of international students' limited academic writing skills, very little attention has been focused on the academic writing skills of native-English speaking domestics students who, on the basis of numbers, are plagiarising more frequently than international students.

THIS STUDY

Our particular interest was to explore Australian students' engagement in plagiarism-related behaviours, their knowledge of plagiarism and their academic writing skills. The study was conducted at a multi-campus, metropolitan Australian university. All undergraduate students were sent an invitation to participate in an online survey mid-way through their first, second, or third year of their undergraduate degree program. They were asked a range of questions to examine (1) the incidence of plagiarism behaviours; (2) their self-reported academic writing skills; (3) their knowledge of plagiarism; and (4) their ability to identify plagiarised work. The confidential online survey was conducted in 2006 and all participants provided consent at login to the survey. Respondents were assured that data specifically about their behaviour would not be reported to the university. The overall response rate for the survey was 28 percent. Only cases with more than 95 percent of data points were retained for this particular study. Data was analysed in SPSS (v. 12, www.spss.com) using bivariate correlations and ANOVA, allowing effects by year and discipline to emerge. In this report, we examine data from

Table 1. Demographic information

Demographic Information	Year 1	Year 2	Year 3	All
Number of students	562	469	455	1486
Gender: Female	74%	75%	68%	73%
Enrolment: Full time	94%	92%	84%	91%
Discipline Group Arts, Law & Education	40%	40%	42%	41%
Business	22%	23%	26%	23%
Health Sciences	25%	25%	18%	22%
Science & Technology	13%	12%	14%	13%

* Discipline groups are based on Faculty structures at this university.

1,486 native English-speaking undergraduate students, mostly enrolled on a full-time basis in degree programs across the four major academic groups at the university (Table 1).

COPYING BEHAVIOURS IN PREPARATION OF ASSIGNMENTS

Students were asked directly about the frequency of various behaviours related to the preparation and submission of assessment tasks, and their perception of those behaviours as related to plagiarism. A list of inappropriate student behaviours was generated through discussions with academic staff, learning services staff, the chair of the academic misconduct committee, and with reference to the literature (Marsden et al., 2005b; Marshall & Garry, 2005b). Two broad types of behaviour were of interest: those broadly related to academic misconduct and plagiarism (e.g., copying from others' essays), and those relating specifically to plagiarism. Behaviours were reported on a scale of frequency ranging from never, once or twice, and occasionally, to often and very often. The pattern of responses to these questions was similar across all years of undergraduate programs, so data are presented here for all students. There were less than 1 percent of responses in the often and very often category, so for the purposes of reporting, the frequencies of behaviour have been grouped and described as never and occasionally.

We focused initially on behaviours related to unacknowledged assistance in completion of assessment tasks. Only 30% of students claimed never to have engaged in any of these behaviours. Looking at each behaviour specifically, the majority of students claimed never to have engaged in each of these behaviours (Table 2). Nearly 40 percent of all students admitted to occasionally giving their notes to friends to assist in the preparation of their written tasks for assessment, and about 30 percent of all students went further by occasionally helping friends to write their assessment tasks, whilst 20 percent borrowed friends' notes to use in preparation of their own assessment tasks (Table 2). Nearly one quarter of students reported that they worked with others to complete assessment tasks that were supposed to be undertaken individually. Overall, the majority of all students (about 80 percent) considered these collegial-type of activities not to warrant dishonesty or plagiarism.

We then turned to clear acts of plagiarism, primarily in the context of dealing with information from the Internet. Across all years, approximately 90 percent of students believed that direct copying of text or ideas without acknowledgement constituted plagiarism, whilst around 5 percent were unsure if it constituted plagiarism. The

Table 2. Students' self-reported behaviours related to plagiarism (% of 1486 students)

Behaviour	Never done	Have done occasionally
Helped friend to write their assignment	64	36
Given notes to friend to help them with assessment tasks	43	57
Borrowed friends' notes to complete assessment tasks	72	18
Copied information from a friend's assignment	90	10
Copied information directly from Web sites without acknowledgement	89	11
Copied information directly from texts without acknowledgement	89	11
Not used quotation marks to identify text taken directly from other sources	80	20

majority of students (80 percent or more) claimed never to have plagiarised (Table 2). About 11 percent of all students reported occasional direct copying of information from Web sites or books without acknowledgement, and more than one quarter reported using creative ideas arising from original sources in their assessment tasks without acknowledgement. Nearly one-fifth of all students reported that they did not identify quoted text taken from source documents. For those students that reported occasional acts of direct copying from Web sites, articles or books without acknowledgement, or occasional failure to identify quotations, 80 percent or more of them knew for certain that their actions constituted plagiarism.

ACKNOWLEDGMENT OF SOURCES

Does the source of the idea or original text need to be acknowledged? Students were first asked if an idea in a section of text in an article, book or Web site needed to be acknowledged in an essay for assessment, even if the original text was totally rewritten in their own words (i.e., properly paraphrased). The pattern of responses to these questions was similar across all years and all disciplines. Half of students (55 percent), across all years, believed that an acknowledgment of the original source was required, even if the original text had been totally rewritten and paraphrased.

Less than 20 percent of all students believed that the idea could be used without acknowledgement, even though the original text may have been well paraphrased. Approximately one quarter of students indicated that they were unsure if acknowledgement was necessary. In general, there was a broad understanding of the need for acknowledging the work of others was similar across years and across the four discipline areas.

Recognising Plagiarism and Paraphrasing

Can students identify the process of plagiarising and plagiarised text as appropriate or inappropriate? Two parallel tasks were set. Students were first asked to categorise a range of ways of using text in academic writing as appropriate and inappropriate usage. Secondly they were asked to correctly identify paraphrased and plagiarized versions of a paragraph of text.

Recognising Appropriate Ways to use of Original Source Text

In what ways can text be treated appropriately in academic writing? Students were presented with a list of six different ways in which they could use a short section of text in an essay or assignment. The six different ways of using text were modified from those described by Swales and Feak (1994), and ranged from inappropriate use of the text (i.e., plagiarism—represented by Treatments 1-4), to appropriate uses of the text (i.e., paraphrasing in Treatment 5, or quoting in Treatment 6) (Table 3). Students were asked to identify which uses of the text would result in paraphrasing or plagiarism, or indicate if they were unsure (Table 3). Overall, the majority of students were able to correctly identify Treatments 1 and 2 as plagiarism, and Treatments 5 (paraphrasing with acknowledgement) and 6 (quotation with acknowledgement) as appropriate ways in which the text could be used. In Treatment 3, a process of resequencing sentences of the original text, there was considerable confusion amongst students as to whether this was, or was not, an appropriate use of the original text. Just half of students in all years (44 to 50 percent) correctly believed the treatment represented plagiarism, while about

one quarter of students incorrectly believed the treatment represented paraphrasing. Treatment 4, essentially reusing phrases of the original text, was widely considered to be an appropriate use of the original text. Less than 20 percent of students correctly believed this treatment to represent plagiarism, whilst around two-thirds of students in each year (65 to 70 percent) incorrectly believed this treatment to represent paraphrasing. There appeared to be a view that appropriate use of the text related to some difference between the original and rewritten text, though the mechanisms to achieve this were not clear.

Values in parentheses represent % of students believing that action represented appropriate treatment of the text. Students could indicate if they were unsure, and this proportion can be calculated by subtraction.

Table 3. Student views regarding six approaches to treating text from a Web site, and whether each treatment would result in plagiarism. (% of 1486 students)

Treatments	Year 1 (N=562)	Year 2 (N=469)	Year 3 (N=455)	All (N=1486)
1. Cutting and pasting the paragraph word-for-word, there is no need to make any acknowledgement.	90	85	90	89
2. Copying the paragraph word-for-word, but change a few verbs, add some different words, change the punctuation and list the book in a bibliography.	57	52	62	57
3. Cutting and pasting the paragraph using whole sentences from the original source but omitting one or two words and/or putting one or two in different order; no quotation marks; with in-text acknowledgment and a bibliographical acknowledgment.	49 (25)	44 (32)	50 (27)	48 (28)
4. Composing a new paragraph by taking short phrases from the original source and putting them together with words of your own to make a coherent whole, with an in-text acknowledgment and a bibliographical acknowledgment.	16 (65)	15 (65)	16 (70)	16 (67)
5. Paraphrasing the paragraph by rewriting with major changes in language and organisation; the new version has changes in the amount of detail used and the examples used, in-text citation and source in bibliography.	10 (77)	9 (76)	8 (80)	9 (77)
6. Quoting the paragraph by placing it in block format with the source cited in text and in the bibliography.	10 (80)	10 (75)	8 (83)	9.5 (80)

Recognising Appropriately Used Original Source Text

In case students were not able to interpret the more abstract description of the writing processes associated with plagiarising and paraphrasing, modified samples of a short piece text representing paraphrasing and plagiarism were presented to students. The modified text samples related loosely to the various treatments of text illustrated in Table 3. The topic of the original text (and the modified text samples) about astrology were three sentences and less than 50 words in length and accessible to most students (Roig, 1998). Students were asked to assume that they wished to use the original paragraph of Web site text in an assignment. Their task was to compare the original text and the modified text and indicate if the rewritten text represented plagiarism, paraphrasing, or if they were unable to determine which it represented.

The ability of students to identify paraphrased and plagiarised text is illustrated in Table 4. The majority of students in all years were able to correctly identify the paraphrased text (illustrated in Samples 5 and 6) and the plagiarized text illustrated in Samples 1, 2 and 3 (Table 4). A minority of students, approximately 10 to 15 percent, were unable to determine if the modified text in these samples was plagiarized or paraphrased. Students had the greatest difficulty with Samples 3 and 4 which represent plagiarized text characterised by significant changes in internal sentence structure. The proportion of students that claimed they could not identify the modified text in Samples 3 and 4 as plagiarism or paraphrasing almost doubled. A change in the opening phrase(s) of the new text appeared to have a major influence on identifying the modified text as paraphrased. There were no significant differences based upon discipline, however there were significant differences between first and third year students in their ability to correctly identify Sample 4 as paraphrased or plagiarized text ($F = 11.27$, df $= 1418, p < .001$). Overall, students' apparent failure to understand the mechanics of paraphrasing is broadly consistent with their failure to identify paraphrased text.

Table 4. Six different treatments of text and student ratings of the text as paraphrased or plagiarised. (% of 1419 students)

Sample of modified text	Modified text is Paraphrased			Modified text is Plagiarised		
(Differences compared with original)	Yr 1	Yr 2	Yr 3	Yr 1	Yr 2	Yr 3
1. Plagiarised. Changes in sentence order only.	34	35	30	47	44	49
2. Plagiarised. Several word substitutions and change in order of several words.	26	24	24	53	57	65
3. Plagiarised. Several word substitutions, change in order of several words, insertion of additional words and internal re-ordering of some sentences. Original wording remains largely intact.	17	27	27	61	51	55
4. Plagiarised. New opening, some word substitutions, changes in tense, internal reorganization of original sentences and restructuring of phrases. Original wording remains largely intact.	76	52	58	6	27	24
5. Paraphrased. Significant changes to sentence structure and organisation, use of synonyms and alternate words.	77	82	85	3	4	3
6. Paraphrased. Significant changes to sentence structure and organisation, use of synonyms and alternate words.	49	67	70	21	9	10

ACADEMIC WRITING: ABILITY AND CONFIDENCE

Academic writing skills that may relate to plagiarising include the ability to analyse a question, take notes and summarise, plan for writing, develop a logical argument supported by evidence, and to use appropriate techniques for acknowledging the work of others. In this study, students were asked to report their ability regarding different academic writing skills (on a scale of not capable, some ability, capable), and their level of confidence with those skills (not confident, OK, confident) (Table 5).

How Well Do Students Rate Their Own Academic Writing Skills?

The majority of all students reported that they were capable of using a range of academic writing skills. Less than 1 percent of students, across all years and disciplines, indicated that they had not developed these skills and less than 10 percent indicated that they had "some ability" in these areas. There were no significant differences across years regarding these capabilities. Students in science and technology programs tended to report under-development of all these skills in comparison to those in business, health and arts, education, and law.

How Confident are Students with their Academic Writing?

Whilst a high proportion of students reported positively on their writing abilities, only about half of students reported high levels of confidence in those abilities. Two-fifths of students in all years reported confidence in their academic writing abilities (Table 5), with a roughly similar proportion of students in each year indicated that their abilities were "OK." The skills in which students

Table 5. Percentage of students in each year indicating their capability and confidence in difference aspects of academic writing. (N=1460)

Skill	Capability			Confidence			
	Yr 1	Yr 2	Yr 3	Yr 1	Yr 2	Yr 3	*r*
Analysing a question or task for assessment	82	84	87	40	43	44	.489
Taking notes and tracking sources of ideas and information	81	81	84	38	40	40	.515
Identifying key message in article, video, artistic work	75	77	84	33	36	39	.495
Making a brief summary of information in an article, video, artistic work	85	83	87	43	42	44	.443
Paraphrasing information from article, video or artistic work	82	84	88	39	39	44	.479
Planning an essay or assignment	82	85	87	38	40	40	.472
Establishing a point of view supported with evidence	83	81	87	41	37	41	.455
Using citations correctly	87	87	90	34	35	36	.450
Using quotations correctly	88	89	91	38	36	36	.410
Making reference list in appropriate format	87	89	92	38	36	31	.393

Correlation between capability and confidence was significant $p < .01$ for all pairs.

were least confident are those related to technical aspects (e.g., application of citation rules) of referencing. Students in science and technology reported significantly lower confidence (p<.001) in paraphrasing text in comparison to students enrolled in business, health and art, education, and law. Overall, science and technology students tended to report lower confidence across the range of academic writing skills compared with students in the other disciplines.

How Have Students Developed Their Academic Writing Skills?

Most students indicated that they had developed academic skills prior to entry to university. Nearly half of students in each year, and each discipline area, indicated that academic writing skills had been learned in their course of study at university, with a significant proportion of these students also undertaking workshops with academic learning support services. This represents the positive face about learning of writing skills. Despite a significant degree of confidence in academic writing, between 30 and 40 percent of students still recognised the need to continue to develop their academic writing skills over time.

Relationships between Academic Writing Skills and Knowledge

Relationships between self-reported skill and confidence in academic writing and demonstrated ability to distinguish between paraphrasing and plagiarism were examined. A score representing writing confidence was generated by summing self-reported confidence in each writing skill listed in Table 5 such that the score increases with confidence. Similarly, a score representing practical knowledge of plagiarism was generated by summing the number of correctly labelled writing processes in Table 3 (Swales score), by summing the number of correctly labelled rewritten paragraphs in Table 4 (Roig score) and summing

the Roig and Swales scores (practical knowledge score). There was a significant correlation between self-reported capability in each academic writing skill and confidence with that skill (r > 0.4 for all skills). There was a significant correlation ($r=0.524$, $p< .001$) between the Swales score and the Roig score that is, between the different ways of assessing practical knowledge. Finally, student's writing confidence score correlated significantly with their practical knowledge score ($r=0.302$, $p< .001$).

Discussion

There were two significant findings arising out of this study. First, knowledge of plagiarism and paraphrasing was high, though students were not always able to put that knowledge into practice. Second, there was a correlation between confidence in academic writing and practical knowledge of plagiarism.

INCIDENCE OF PLAGIARISM-RELATED BEHAVIOURS

In this study we asked students to self report behaviours that might lead to plagiarism, as well as those widely accepted as plagiarism. Overall, 30 percent of students claimed never to have engaged in any of these behaviours, similar to the 28 percent of New Zealand students that claimed never to have engaged in obvious acts plagiarism (Marshall & Garry, 2005a). Between 20 and 50 percent of students admitted to collegial activities such as sharing notes or helping friends to write assignments, whilst 10 to 20 percent admitted to unacknowledged use of source text in their assignments. As in USA and New Zealand studies, students considered collegial activities to be less serious than "direct copying" types of plagiarism (Marshall & Garry, 2005a; McCabe, 2003). The proportion of students admitting to unacknowledged collaboration in the preparation of written assessment tasks is similar to that reported in the cross-institutional USA study conducted by the Academic Integrity Centre (McCabe, 2005), where 24 percent of students admitted receiving help in a written assignment and 42 percent of students admitted collaborating on work that was to be done individually. On the other hand, the proportion of students admitting to acts of plagiarism lies well below the high 81 percent reported in another Australian study (Marsden et al., 2005b), and the 40 percent reported in the USA (McCabe, 2005). Some differences between studies could be attributed to variations in the methodology used. In addition, this study used a confidential (i.e., non-anonymous) survey approach, so it is possible that students may have been more willing to admit to less serious behaviours than to those they considered to be more serious.

Plagiarism Knowledge

Students were able to distinguish between clear-cut cases of plagiarism and paraphrasing when presented with either different writing processes or different work samples, but they were less able to distinguish between "borderline cases." In this study, a change to the opening phrase and/or internal structural changes to the paragraph appear to be acceptable practice to students. Confirming the work of Roig (1997) and Marshall & Garry (2005a), students were confused as to whether minor changes to the original text, changes to the order of phases in sentences, or swapping sentences within a paragraph are considered as legitimate paraphrasing. Students are not alone in their confusion, Roig (2001) has demonstrated clearly that many teaching staff have difficulties in determining what is acceptable paraphrasing and plagiarism. Further adding to the confusion, McCabe (2005) suggests that the boundaries of acceptable practice may be changing.

Students appear to be familiar with the concepts of referencing, paraphrasing and plagiarism, but have difficulty in distinguishing between these

inter-related issues. For example, "If I paraphrase, do I have to cite the source?" "Do I have to paraphrase a lot if I don't cite the original source?" "Should I always paraphrase?" The majority of students agreed that original sources of text and ideas should be acknowledged in written assignments, even if the original source was correctly paraphrased. Less than 10 percent of students disagreed with this fundamental principle, and nearly a quarter of them were unsure. This is an example of one grey area, where students appear to become confused between the need to acknowledge the work done by others and writing in their own words.

Academic Writing and Knowledge of Plagiarism

The greatest difficulty for most students appears to lie in the domain of academic writing. Whilst 80 percent of undergraduate students said they possessed the skills of note-taking, paraphrasing, citing, referencing, and so on, only half of students across all years reported confidence with these skills. There was a correlation between confidence in academic writing and their demonstrated ability to correctly identify processes leading to paraphrasing and plagiarism and distinguishing between them. The developmental nature of academic writing is recognised by students, of whom at least one third identified the need to continue improving their skills which will ultimately lead to less inadvertent plagiarism. Over the last two decades the demographics of participation in higher education have moved to include more students from alternative educational pathways, different social strata, and a wider range of cultural and language backgrounds. Unfortunately, many university teaching staff are unable to respond to this new diversity and appear to view academic writing as a deficit issue and a problem for secondary schools, not a skill that is developed throughout years of undergraduate and postgraduate study.

Poor academic writing and research skills can easily lead to unintentional plagiarism. One area for students to pay attention is note-taking. Failing to keep records of sources and not distinguishing between original source text and paraphrased text can lead to confusion in the writing process (Abasi, Akbari, & Graves, 2006). In addition, students should know, and be clear in their intentions to either paraphrase or summarise their original source information. In the latter, a writer captures the essence of the original text, perhaps by using a large number of words, or even phrases from the original text, whereas in the former the writer conveys the meaning of the original source information in the context of the topic question. However, these skills are not all that is required. Scholars new to a discipline area tend to have a limited vocabulary and rarely fully comprehend all that they read in preparation for an assignment. During the transition from novice to expert in the discipline area, they are likely to use a process of patchwriting (Howard, 1995) where some phrases of original source text are interwoven with their own writing. One of the keys to responding to plagiarism is to ensure that students have the opportunity to properly develop the skills necessary for academic success.

Implications for Teaching and Learning

Arising from this study are some broad inter-related implications for teaching and learning if higher education institutions are committed to minimizing plagiarism. In the first instance, teachers need to recognise that academic writing is a developmental skill. Not only do students need to know about academic writing and its related conventions, they need to practice writing. Students need the opportunity to practice and develop their academic writing skills, in the context of articulating their learning about their own discipline. This does not mean "teaching students to write," but encourages teachers to use writing, peer interaction, and feedback as tools to engage students with writing in class and online. To be effective, this process requires that teachers and tutors, collectively, discuss their own conceptions of academic writing and appropriate referencing processes and then communicate their expectations clearly to students so that they have a consistent point of reference. More broadly, institutions ought to acknowledge the developmental nature of academic writing in their academic misconduct policies. If patchwriting is indeed a transitionary phase, then institutions need to take care when implementing software driven plagiarism detections systems to ensure that they may have a dual purpose: targeting detection as well as providing formative information to assist the development of academic writing skills. The utility of the latter purpose needs further research. In conclusion, it is clear that addressing plagiarism at university requires both engagement of teaching staff and students, within a broader university context of dedication to quality in all aspects of the learning and teaching enterprise.

ACKNOWLEDGEMENT

Sincere thanks to the students that participated in this study. This study was conducted using http://www.surveymaker.com.au.

REFERENCES

Abasi, A. R., Akbari, N., & Graves, B. (2006). Discourse appropriation, construction of identities and the complex issue of plagiarism: ESL students writing in graduate school. *Journal of Second Language Writing, 15*, 102-117.

ACODE. (2005). Audit of academic integrity and plagiarism issues in Australia and New Zealand. Retrieved April 30, 2006, from http://www.tlc.murdoch.edu.au/project/acode/

Ashworth, P., Bannister, P., & Thorne, P. (1997). Guilty in whose eyes? University students' perceptions of cheating and plagiarism in academic work and assessment. *Studies in Higher Education, 22*, 187-203.

Centre for Academic Integrity. (2005). Levels of Cheating and plagiarism remain high. Honor codes and modified codes are shown to be effective in reducing academic misconduct. Retrieved October 15, 2006.

Haggis, T. (2003). Constructing images of ourselves? A critical investigation into "Approaches to Learning" research in higher education. *British Educational Research Journal, 29*(1), 89-104.

Howard, R. M. (1995). Plagiarisms, authorships and the academic death penalty. *College English, 57*, 788-805.

Introna, L. D., Hayes, N., Blair, L., & Wood, E. (2003). *Cultural attitudes towards plagiarism: Developing a better understanding of the needs of students from divers backgrounds relating to issues of plagiarism.* Lancaster, UK: Lancaster University.

JISC. (2005). Institutional issues in deterring, detecting and dealing with student plagiarism [Electronic Version]. Retrieved October 14, 2006 from http://www.jisc.ac.uk/uploaded_documents/plagFinal.pdf

Katz, R. (2005). In R. Kvavik & J. Caruso, *ECAR Study of students and information technology, 2005.* Retrieved from http://www.educause.edu

Larkham, P. J., & Manns, S. (2002). Plagiarism and its treatment in higher education. *Journal of Further and Higher Education, 26*, 339-349.

Marsden, H., Carroll, M., & Neill, J. T. (2005a). The contribution of demographic, situational and psychological factors to dishonest academic behaviours *Australian Journal of Psychology, 57*, 1-10.

Marsden, H., Carroll, M., & Neill, J. T. (2005b). Who cheats at university? A self-report study of dishonest academic behaviours in a sample of Australian university students. *Australian Journal of Psychology, 57*, 1-10.

Marshall, S., & Garry, M. (2005a, December 3-6). *How well do students really understand plagiarism?* Paper presented at the Annual *ascilite* conference., Brisbane, Australia.

Marshall, S., & Garry, M. (2005b, December 2-3). *NESB and ESB students' attitudes and percpetions of plagiarism.* Paper presented at the 2nd Asia-Pacific Educational Conference (Newcastle). Retrieved October 8, 2007, from htp://www.newcastle.edu/au/conference/apeic/papers_pdf/marshall_0519.edd.pdf

McCabe, D. L. (2003). Promoting academic integrity: A U.S./Canadian perspective in educational integrity: Plagiarism and other perplexities. In H. H. Marsden, M. (Ed.), *Educational integrity: Plagiarism and Other Perplexities, Refereed Proceedings of the Inaugural Educational Integrity Conference.* Adelaide, South Australia: University of South Australia.

McCabe, D. L. (2005). Cheating among college and university students: A North American perspective. *International Journal for Educational Integrity, 1*(1). Retrieved October 8, 2007, from http://www.ojs.unisa.edu.au/index.php/IJEI/article/viewFile/14/9

McCabe, D. L., & Drinan, P. (1999). Toward a culture of academic integrity. *Chronicle of Higher Education, 46*(8), B7.

McCabe, D. L., & Trevino, L. (1997). Individual and contextual influences on academic dishonesty: A multicampus investigation. *Research in Higher Education, 38*, 379-396.

O'Connor, S. (2003, May 6-9). *Cheating and electronic plagiarism—Scope consequences and detection.* In Proceedings of EDUCAUSE in Australia, Adelaide.

Park, C. (2003). In other (people's) words. Plagiarism by university students: Literature and lessons. *Assessment & Evaluation in Higher Education, 28,* 471-488.

Pecorari, D. (2003). Good and original: Plagiarism and patchwriting in academic second language writing. *Journal of Second Language Writing, 12,* 317-345.

Pecorari, D. (2006). Visible and occluded citation features in postgraduate second language writing. *English for specific purposes, 25,* 4-29.

Prensky, M. (2001). Digital natives, digital immigrants. Do they really think differently? *On the Horizen, 9*(6), 1-6.

Roig, M. (1997). Can undergraduate students determine whether text has been plagiarised. *The Psychological Record, 47,* 113-122.

Roig, M. (1998). *Undergraduates judgements of plagiarism and correct paraphrasing revisited.* Paper presented at the 69th Annual Meeting of the Eastern Pscyhological Association, Boston, MA.

Roig, M. (2001). Plagiarism and paraphrasing criteria of college and university professors. *Ethics & Behaviour, 11,* 307-323.

Scanlon, P. M., & Neumann, D. R. (2002). Internet plagiarism amongst college students. *Journal of College Student Development, 43,* 374-385.

Swales, J. M., & Feak, C. B. (1994). *Academic writing for graduate students: Essential tasks and skills.* Ann Arbor, MI: The University of Michigan.

Zimitat, C. (2004, December 5-8). *Changing student use and perceptions of learning technologies, 2002-2004.* Paper presented at the 21st Annual ASCILITE Conference, Perth, WA.

Chapter III
Controlling Plagiarism:
A Study of Lecturer Attitudes

Erik J. Eriksson
Umeå University, Sweden

Kirk P. H. Sullivan
Umeå University, Sweden

ABSTRACT

Plagiarism is viewed as an increasing problem in the academy. When plagiarism is discussed it is often in personal negative terms that refer to the "lazy" modern student. Previous studies have suggested that the largest cause of plagiarism is ignorance on the part of the student. This paper examines lecturers' knowledge of, and attitude to, plagiarism, how they pass their knowledge on to students, and the lecturers' knowledge of disciplinary procedures. This examination teases out the lecturers' responsibility for continuing student plagiarism. It was found that academics are unsure of their definitions of plagiarism, have varied attitudes towards different types of plagiarism and do not effectively teach how to work with a text to avoid plagiarism. We suggest a wider discussion of plagiarism in the academy, extending beyond how to deter and catch plagiarists, and the writing of policy statements, to preventing plagiarism though education of both student and academic.

INTRODUCTION

Cheating and plagiarism are behaviours that are regarded as malpractice in academic work. Suspicion can result in investigation and possible repercussions; for the academic this can result in loss of research reputation and employment, and for the student loss of course credits, suspension or expulsion. In spite of such possible repercussions, plagiarism occurs and according to the vice-chancellor of Umeå University, Sweden, Professor Göran Sandberg: "In today's Web-based world cheating in education is unfortunately common" (Sandberg, online, authors' translation).

A common view held by both students and academics is that many students plagiarize out of ignorance (Harris, 2001; Hult & Hult, 2003). Plagiarism exists outside of the academic community. Students may begin their university studies believing that plagiarism is appropriate behaviour in the academy in the way they have seen plagiarism elsewhere. However, if it is the case that ignorance of plagiarism continues beyond the initial weeks of a student's first semester of study, is this a result of lecturers being unclear as to how they wish students to view plagiarism and how to avoid it, or is it because the distance between the faculty definition of plagiarism and the students' perception of plagiarism is too great, or is it an interaction of these factors, or perhaps it is a result of faculty themselves being unclear as to what plagiarism is? This paper examines lecturers' knowledge of, and attitude to, plagiarism, how they pass their knowledge on to students and their knowledge of the disciplinary procedures for suspected plagiarism in their university. This examination aims to tease out the lecturers' responsibility for students continuing to plagiarise and its apparent rise in the online world (Nilsson, Eklöf & Ottosson, 2005), and suggest areas for improvement that can result in fewer instances of student plagiarism.

Although many (e.g., Harris, 2001) have argued that increased use of the Internet and computers in an online world has encouraged students to plagiarise, most of the reported increase was explained by an increased willingness of faculty members to report plagiarism.

THE CASE STUDY

To examine salaried academics knowledge of, and attitude to, plagiarism, how they pass this knowledge on to students, and their knowledge of disciplinary procedures for suspected plagiarism in their university as a route to teasing out the

lecturers' responsibility for student plagiarism and its apparent rise in the online world, an online questionnaire was devised and distributed. The questionnaire was piloted prior to the study and a couple of minor changes were made based on pilot feedback. The study is an extension of Eriksson (2005).

The Participants

The participants were 62 salaried academics from Umeå University, Northern Sweden, who answered the questionnaire. Umeå University is a 1960s university. Founded in 1965, it is the fifth largest university in Sweden. Three professors, four readers, 27 senior lecturers, 12 lecturers, 14 PhD students and two people who provided no job category, responded to the questionnaire. The largest group of participants came from the faculty of medicine (22), followed in descending order by the faculty of science and technology (15), the faculty of social sciences (14), the faculty of arts (7) and the teacher education faculty (7). The reported numbers of years of teaching experience reported by the participants were: 0-5 years (13), 6-10 (8), 11-15 (4), 16-20 (10), 20+ (12).

The Questionnaire

The questionnaire is presented in Appendix A and collected personal information about the participants before proceeding to collect information on the following four broad topics:

1. Defining plagiarism: the questions in this topic aimed at capturing the range of definitions within the academy as to what constitutes plagiarism and how different academics delimit plagiarism. These questions asked for free-text answers and did not prompt the respondents to consider anything in particular as plagiarism.

2. Informing students about plagiarism: the questions in this topic aimed at discovering how and when during a degree course academics informed, or taught, their students what plagiarism is and how to present work without plagiarizing.

3. Attitude to different types of plagiarism: the questions in this topic aimed to reveal the respondents attitudes to plagiarism as cheating, and to a range of different types of plagiarism, for example, copying someone's text, paraphrasing, and copying one's own text.

4. Reporting plagiarism; the questions in this topic aimed at discovering how academics link their personal definitions of plagiarism to those used in university policy documents and if the respondents were aware of how to report plagiarism or not.

Biographic data was automatically removed from the other responses to guarantee participant anonymity. To strengthen the participants' belief that they could not be individually identified, gender and age were not requested.

The Procedure

The Web address of the questionnaire, together with the password to access it, was e-mailed to academics teaching in higher education courses in each of the university's faculties. Departments were selected based on personal contact with a member of staff; we hoped this personal element would increase the number of completed questionnaires. All those who received the e-mail were encouraged to pass the details on to other colleagues. The e-mail informed potential participants that their responses be automatically disconnected from their personal details and that they would remain anonymous.

Participants logged into the Web page and answered the questions either by selecting a given option or by giving a free text answer. Once the respondent had answered a question and move on to the next it was impossible to go back and alter an earlier answer. This stopped questions towards the end feeding into the answers of questions at the beginning of the questionnaire. The questionnaire took around 20 minutes to answer.

THE RESPONSES

Responses are discussed by category.

Defining Plagiarism

Question 4 asked the participants to define, in their own words, the term plagiarism. Twenty participants provided no definition of plagiarism. The definitions provided were sorted into four categories: emphasizing illegal action, emphasizing the presentation of someone else's work as one's own, emphasizing the use of ill-formed references, and generally weak or ambiguous definitions.

Table 1 provides illustrative definitions for each category along with the number of definitions sorted into each category.

In the category, that emphasizes the illegal action of plagiarism (Category One), the definitions given by the participants indicate that the act of plagiarism is something that is, or should be, punishable. These definitions suggest that these participants strongly view plagiarism as malpractice. Definitions 1 and 2 include the modifying clause "without specifying source"; to avoid plagiarism the source needs to be given. The definitions state that the act, per se, is illegal, yet using or stealing information from a source and specifying this makes the theft permissible. The illegal act is not resolved by specifying source, according to these definitions. In fact, to avoid stealing, according to definitions 1 and 2, students would have to write their own material, with no information or text from other sources. With these definitions students could become confused, as

Table 1. Definitions of plagiarism: Illustrative definitions for each category along with the number of definitions sorted into each category

Category	No. of Definitions	Example Definitions
Emphasizing illegal action	3	(1) to steal information from someone else without specifying source (2) textual copying or theft of content without specifying source (3) that one copies someone else's work and uses it as one's own which is despicable and criminal
Emphasizing the presentation of someone else's work as one's own	14	(4) That someone takes a pre-existing text, piece of music etc., leaves out the source and puts their own name to make it out as one's own work (5) to present as one's own original text or original idea, a text or idea which is taken from another source
Emphasizing the use of ill-formed references	12	(6) to use others' words and reasoning without correct usage of quotation or presenting sources (7) undue usage of someone else's material, for example by not including quotations or references (8) to copy a piece of work without specifying source
Generally weak or ambiguous definitions	13	(9) using whole paragraphs or sentences directly taken from other sources without reformulation (10) the usage, in more than insignificant size, material that someone else has created in one's own name (11) Plagiarism=something that is copied from something else so that it is close to identical (12) copying of another's work and taking credit it for it, i.e., not providing a reference. Or if one references too much to another's work which it is not a review (13) It would probably take me a day or two to come up with an ok definition. Therefore I don't provide one

the application of morals relating to stealing from outside of the academy does not appear to apply when writing an academic piece of work. The idea of stealing something and admitting where you stole it from, and that this is ok, does not work as a defence in court when caught driving a stolen BMW.

The category emphasizing the presentation of someone else's work as one's own (Category Two), defines plagiarism as something to do with cheating. The act involves taking material from a source with the goal of presenting it as one's own. These definitions do not frame plagiarism in terms of illegal acts as the definition found in Category One, yet they do emphasize the taking of someone else's work. They are, thus, less strong than Category One definitions. The definitions in this category, such as definitions 4 and 5, do not

help students who which to know how to avoid plagiarism. They specify, albeit implicitly, that acknowledging the source is important, yet the definitions do not provide answers to how this should be done.

The category emphasizing the use of ill-formed references (Category Three) focuses on providing help to the student as to how to avoid plagiarism. The participants, through their definitions such definitions 6, 7, and 8, specify what plagiarism is and how to avoid it. Definition 8 was not grouped into category one (emphasizing illegal action) as the definition is not phrased in terms of thieving or stealing.

The category of weak and ambiguous definitions (Category Four), includes definitions that are either ambiguous, incomplete, or both. Definition 9 is incomplete and apart from suggesting the use of paraphrasing does not offer any help to the student who wants to learn how to avoid plagiarism. According to this definition, paraphrasing is not plagiarism, even if there is no reference to the source. This is, however, a definition that we, and many others, do not agree with. Paraphrasing is to show that the idea is someone else's, but the text is the writers (Harris, 2001); how can this be achieved without a reference to the source of the idea?

Definition 10 presents a different problem. It suggests there should be a lower limit below which, using unreferenced material, is not considered plagiarism. Thus, a series of words must be a specific length before its use constitutes plagiarism. This definition completely ignores paraphrasing or copying of ideas. Definition 11, on the other hand both identifies copying as plagiarism, and tries to handle paraphrasing as well, but the definition is ambiguous and hard to implement ("close to identical" is highly subjective). Definition 12 begins by defining plagiarism according to Definition

11, but then rather oddly suggests that plagiarism occurs if one references too much. Interestingly the participant who provided Definition 13 views plagiarism as complex and avoids providing a definition by saying it is too complex to define. This type of definition avoidance is not helpful to the student wishing to learn how to avoid being accused of plagiarism.

Informing Students About Plagiarism

The participants were asked how much information they provide to the students about plagiarism (Question 5). The responses were divided into five categories relating to the quantity of information made available to students, and two categories relating to the time, the point in a degree course, the information is provided. Forty-two participants responded to this question. Responses were independently categorized for "Quantity" and "Timing." Hence, some responses were categorized twice, once based on "Quantity" and once based

Table 2. The amount of information given to students about plagiarism and when it is given during the student's studies

Response Category	Number of responses	Example Responses	
No information	5	(14)	Most students I teach have no written work, so I have no need to discuss it up with the students. As PhD supervisor, there is of course no need to use the word plagiarism as one always goes to the source
Little information	21	(15)	We only inform about the risks associated with the law framework surrounding cheating
Some information	5	(16)	I am clear that I do not accept it and that, in their work, it shall be clear who has said what.
Lots of information	4	(17)	Lots!
Vague response	6	(18)	The teacher group was informed of this through examples.
Early in the course	3	(19)	Information about the rules and regulations to the students at course start; Reminder in connection with take-home assignments of essay type
Late in the course	12	(20)	It is mentioned to different extent in C and D level courses.

on "Timing." Table Two lists these categories, the number of participants whose answers fell into each category and an example response.

What is apparent from this data is that students are poorly informed about plagiarism and any information that is provided is most often given a late stage in their courses/programmes. There were no responses indicating that information is given progressively or repeatedly, or that departments had developed a teaching programme for plagiarism.

Question 6 asked how students are informed about plagiarism and how to avoid it. From Table 3, that presents an overview of the responses, it can be seen that the majority of the participants, 25, rely on oral information alone to inform students what constitutes plagiarism and how to avoid it. These academics rely on students understanding what they say and taking good lecture notes. The responses to this question also revealed that none of the participants simply handed out written information relating to plagiarism without discussing them with the students.

When collating responses to Questions 5 and 6 about when and how much information about plagiarism is provided to students, it is surprising there are not more cases of plagiarism detected in the online world. The data suggests that most students are not fully informed about plagiarism, nor given examples or exercises to reinforce the little they are told. Yet in spite of this, the majority of students do not plagiarize. Further, many of those who do may well continue to do so, as has been suggested, out of ignorance. This continuation of this ignorance beyond the first weeks of a student entering the academy may be the result of teaching by academics who are not sure as to what constitutes plagiarism and are thus ill prepared to teach students the techniques needed to be able to ground written work in the literature and not plagiarize. The continuation of some types of student plagiarism could also be due the attitudes lecturers hold about these different types.

Attitudes to Different Types of Plagiarism

The responses to these questions are presented in Table 4.

The summary of the responses presented in Table 4 supports the idea that some occurrences of plagiarism could be due to differing attitudes among academic staff about some forms of plagiarism. For example, self-plagiarism (Question 20) reveals a high level of insecurity within the academy as to whether this is plagiarism or not, as does undertaking work in pairs but not referring to this in submitted reports (Question 19). This parallels the ethics of research team publications, publication based on student work and the passing off of the work of others as one's own in a journal paper.

Table 3. How information about plagiarism is given to students

Form of information	Number of responses
Written handouts only	0
Oral presentation only	25
Oral presentation combined with written handouts	10
Oral presentation combined with personal Web site	2
Oral presentation combined with departmental Web site	6
Oral presentation combined with University policy Web site	3

Table 4. The questions and responses for the questions relating to attitudes towards plagiarism and it various forms

Question No.	Question Text	Answer: YES	Answer: NO	Answer: Unsure
13	Is plagiarism cheating?	33	1	5
15	Do you believe plagiarism and cheating could be reduced by making students more responsible for their own learning?	27	4	10
16	Are there occasions when plagiarism is justifiable?	3	34	4
17	Is it plagiarism to word-by-word copy a text, include a reference, but leave out quotation marks?	24	9	7
18	Is it plagiarism to translate a text to Swedish without quotation or references?	37		3
19	A task is undertaken in pairs. The ability to work together is important but each student is to submit individually. Is it plagiarism if two students submit highly similar reports, yet do not reference each other?	15	12	13
20	Is it plagiarism to use one's own work without referencing?	16	7	17

In the responses to Questions 13 and 15 - 20, we again see academics being unsure about what is covered by the concept of plagiarism. Their attitudes to these different scenarios vary. Yet, to the direct question is plagiarism cheating (Question 13) there is a near universal view that it is. Though, oddly, marginally more participants believe there are occasions when plagiarism is justified (Question 16). From our personal knowledge of discussions at pedagogical seminars, we offer a weak interpretation of these responses as indicating that a student cannot be disciplined for plagiarism if the student has never been informed of what plagiarism is and taught how to avoid it.

Although academics are unsure in their definitions of plagiarism and how it is delimited, academics are supposed to work from policy statements when judging, reporting, and punishing plagiarism.

Institutional Definitions, Reporting Plagiarism and Punishment

Question 9 asked if the participant's department, faculty or university had guidelines for how plagia-

rism is classified and how it should be reported. A total of 42 responses were received; 19 answered that such guidelines do exist, four that they did not and 19 were uncertain. Question 10 asked the participants the level at which they believed guidelines should be set: five thought university level, four, faculty level, three, department level and one, national level as defined in the Higher Educational Ordinance.

The participant referring to the Higher Educational Ordinance demonstrated a lack of knowledge of this legal document. Chapter 10, Paragraph 1 of this ordinance states: "Disciplinary action can be taken against a student who has: By the use of unauthorized aids or in some other way has tried to cheat during an examination or when a student presentation is to be judged." This paragraph is the nearest the ordinance comes to mentioning plagiarism.

The confusion relating to the Higher Educational Ordinance recurs in responses to Question 12, which asks if their department, faculty or university's clear definition concurred with their personal definition. Among the 12 responses to this question one person wrote "We can only follow the definition in the higher educational ordinance." The participants answering this question had answered yes to Question 11: "Does your department, faculty or university have a clear definition of plagiarism?" Fifteen participants answered yes to this question, four no, and 23 responded that they were unsure.

Confusion over the definition of plagiarism among those who responded yes to Question 11, is demonstrated not only by the participant referring, incorrectly, to the Higher Educational Ordinance, but also by such responses as: "We have an Urkund programme [A Swedish plagiarism control programme] that I have never used," "I assume that there is a definition," and "Yes and No. Definitions are bad as they exclude things that may be cheating but that are not explicitly mentioned."

Responses to questions 9 - 12 should have reflected that only two faculties of Umeå University's five faculties have policy documents that cover plagiarism. The Faculty of Arts defines plagiarism as: "To, in a piece of work use others' ideas or formulations with the purpose of making the reader believe that they are one's own" (Umeå University, Faculty of Arts, online, author's translation).The Faculty of medicine defines plagiarism in a similar way: "To, in a piece of work, use others' formulations, data, illustrations, summaries or published ideas with the intent to make the reader believe that they are one's own" (Umeå Univeristy, Faculty of Medicine, online, author's translation).

A few departments at Umeå University have their own definitions and policy documents. Some of these documents highlight the importance of references, for instance "Plagiarism is text collected, for example, from the Internet, a book, a journal, etc. and used in an assignment, etc. without referencing" (Umeå University, Department of Applied physics and Electronics, online, author's translation).

Surprisingly, the majority of respondents were unaware of these guidelines, and many believed that a central university definition existed. Here we see a belief in guidelines that participants assume exist, yet that it is clear most have not read them, and in some cases they do not exist.

This lack of knowledge of university policy is reflected in the answers to Question 8, "to whom should cases of plagiarism be reported?" The given responses were: The vice-chancellor (3), the university lawyer (1), the university disciplinary committee (9), the head of department (12), the departmental director of studies (20), course/programme director (5) my nearest boss (2), a person in my department (1), and "no idea, but I can find out in five minutes the day I need to know" (1). The route for reporting suspected cases of plagiarism is clearly not universally understood by this group of salaried academics who teach higher educational courses. This is even more alarming when one considers that 21 of the participants reported they had discovered plagiarism (Question 7) and eight participants were uncertain as to whether they had discovered cases of plagiarism of not. Thirteen respondents had not discovered any cases of plagiarism.

Question 14 asked participants what they considered to be an appropriate disciplinary measure for cases of plagiarism. Twenty-four thought suspension, thirteen said it depended on specific circumstances, seven thought the student should fail the module, three that the student should be given a warning, two did not know, two said it was not their decision and two thought a permanent comment should be included in the student's transcript. This question revealed a lack of recognition of plagiarism as an educational problem. Only 13 thought that it depended upon the circumstances. Most were in favour of the most severe punishment a Swedish university can give: suspension.

GENERAL DISCUSSION AND CONCLUSION

Although the study presented in this chapter was conducted in Sweden, we believe that similar results are likely to be found elsewhere. Previous studies have shown that explanations of why students plagiarise in Sweden are similar to those of students in other countries. Hult and Hult (2003) asked Swedish faculty members and students why students plagiarize. The top response given was to be able to hand in an assignment on time. Other reasons given included: the Internet makes it easy, increased anonymity with increased student group sizes, teaching and examination forms, greater cooperation and collaboration among students, "everybody else is doing it," the risk of being caught is low, and personal morals. These explanations are mirrored in non-Swedish studies such as Harris (2001) and Bowman (2004). Similarly, the definitions of plagiarism found in Umeå University's documents are comparable to those found outside Sweden. These definitions are similar to definitions found abroad; for instance at the University of Wales, plagiarism is defined as:

Plagiarism is the act of claiming the work of others as your own work. 'Others' in this context can include fellow students and the authors of books, journals, and Internet material. (University of Wales, Validation Handbook of Quality Assessment: p. 91, online)

At Stanford University, plagiarism is defined as:

The use, without giving reasonable and appropriate credit to or acknowledging the author or source, of another person's original work, whether such work is made up of code, formulas, ideas, language, research, strategies, writing, or other form(s). (Standford University, online)

Looking at the definitions provided for plagiarism, the attitudes toward specific kinds of plagiarism, the way students are informed of plagiarism, and the desire to punish the offending student that were evident from this study, it is clear that the problem needs to be addressed. It will not be solved by increased use of plagiarism control programmes or more disciplinary action against students (and academics?), but by education of both student and academic.

Academics have a tendency to forget that they learnt things as students and rarely question if their knowledge of general academic matters such as plagiarism is better than the students' or not. This case study suggests that their knowledge is not better when it comes to plagiarism and their opinions are particularly divergent with regard to issues such as self-plagiarism. The following three quotes from three different papers (the differences are indicated in bold) would be viewed as unproblematic by some, but as severe cases of plagiarism by others [see Giles (2005) for a discussion of self-plagiarism].

*The case of Sweden is also an interesting one. Sweden has long been a multiethnic society, despite the presumption in the 1960s of "one language, one race and no religion" (Andrae-Tein & Elgqvist-Salzmen, 1987, p. 4). Often forgotten in today's discussions are the number of Swedish-born minorities—Sami (Laplanders), Finnish Swedes, Roma, and Jews—each of which has made significant contributions to Swedish society and culture over the centuries (Proposition 1998/99, p. 143). Today, of Sweden's nine million inhabitants, approximately 10 percent (over 900,000) were born abroad. Of these, 40 percent have lived in Sweden for 20 years or more. An additional 700,000 have at least one parent from abroad (Proposition 1997/98). **It is estimated that, by the end of 2010, every third child born in Sweden will have at least one parent with a foreign background.** (Gaine, Hällgren, Domínguez, Noguera and Weiner, 2003: 321-322)*

Sweden has long been a multiethnic society, despite the presumption in the 1960s of "one language, one race and no religion" (Andrae-Tein & Elgqvist-Salzmen, 1987, p. 4). Often forgotten in today's discussions are the number of Swedish-born minorities—Sami (Laplanders), Finnish Swedes, Roma, and Jews—each of which has made significant contributions to Swedish society and culture over the centuries (Regeringens Proposition 1998/99). Today, of Sweden's nine million inhabitants, approximately 10 percent (over 900,000) were born abroad. Of these, 40 percent have lived in Sweden for 20 years or more. An additional 700,000 have at least one parent from abroad (Regeringens Proposition 1997/98). **At present, a quarter of all children in Sweden have such a background—excluding national minorities** *(SCB, 2000) (Hällgren and Weiner, 2003: 321).*

As pointed out in a paper, 'Why here, why now' (Hällgren & Weiner, 2003), *Sweden has long been a multiethnic society, despite the presumption in the 1960s of "one language, one race and no religion" (Andrae-Tein & Elgqvist-Salzmen, 1987, p. 4). Swedish-born minorities—Sami,* **Swedish Finns, Tornedalers,** *Roma, and Jews (Regeringens Proposition, 1999, p. 143), each of which has made significant contributions to Swedish society and culture over the centuries.* **Currently (2004),** *of Sweden's nine million inhabitants, approximately 10 percent (over 900,000) were born abroad. Of these, 40 percent have lived in Sweden for 20 years or more. An additional 800,000 who were born in Sweden have at least one parent from abroad. Altogether this means that nearly two million people living in Sweden have a foreign background (Regeringens Proposition, 1997; Kulturdepartementet, 2000, p. 43)* **At present, a quarter of all children in Sweden have such a background—excluding national minorities** *(SCB, 2000). (Hällgren, 2005: 219-220).*

An issue that is aligned to plagiarism, and one of particular importance in the online era, is that of copyright permission. Diagrams, photos, and other figures can readily be copied into documents. In student work, sometimes the source is referenced and sometimes it is not; sometimes plagiarized and sometimes not. In books and paper published by major publishers obtaining of copyright permission is demanded and along with this, the source must be clearly stated in the text. In books and working papers published by universities, this is not always the case.

Based on the responses to this study, it is apparent that academics view plagiarism as wrong and that they believe students should be punished for it. However, it is also apparent many academics are ignorant of what plagiarism covers and how and where it is defined, and do not teach students how to avoid plagiarising. The attitude is clear, but the praxis is not. It is the praxis that needs to be focused on to prevent plagiarism occurring due to ignorance. Only when academic and teaching praxis has been improved, can academics legitimately assume that a student (or academic) caught plagiarizing, or using figures without copyright permission, has done so with intent. Ignorance is no defence, but a realistic chance to have learnt both what plagiarism is and how to avoid it, is needed for disciplinary actions to have validity with student and academic bodies.

In our view, the skill of how to avoid plagiarism needs to be taught, and that like most skills, this skill will take time to learn. The complexities of teaching and deterring plagiarism are clear from Carroll (2002). As it takes time to learn about plagiarism, when the act of plagiarism occurs in a student's university career and how much the student has been taught (and warned) about plagiarism ought to impact upon the disciplinary measures taken. It is also important to remember that this group of academics defined plagiarism in many different ways, and were poor at teaching/informing students about it and how to avoid it. There is a degree of double morality in the academic construction of plagiarism, what it is, and why it occurs in student work.

We suggest that plagiarism should not simply be taught once and the student given a Web site to check the details. We propose that plagiarism should be gradually taught over the course of a degree programme, so that when the student writes his or her final year project paper dissertation, he or she is familiar with and can recognise the core aspects of plagiarism, and is aware of the issues surrounding those aspects of writing that not all view as plagiarism and copyright. Further, plagiarism should be taught, not as something that is criminal, but as a guide to operating within academic writing confines and why this rule/framework surrounding the use of others ideas, texts, and figures in one's own work exists. To achieve this, the academic body needs to discuss plagiarism and stop assuming we all know what it is, that all can write correctly, and all know how to avoid it. Many universities now demand that new lecturers attend higher education teaching and learning courses. These courses could be designed to include local definitions and policy on plagiarism and how best to teach plagiarism avoidance. Part of training of such lecturer training should also consider when and how to teach different aspects of plagiarism avoidance. This would, for example, permit the lecturer who is teaching during, for example semester three, to know what plagiarism avoidance skills the students have and which they have yet to learn. It is unrealistic to assume a first semester student knows how to write, quote and cite in an academic manner when even academics at times fail to do these things correctly.

REFERENCES

Bowman, V. (2004). Teaching intellectual honesty in a tragically hip world: A pop-culture perspective. In V. Bowman (Ed), *The Plagiarism Plague* (pp. 3-9). New York: Neal-Schuman Publishers, Inc.

Carroll, J. (2002). *A handbook for deterring plagiarism in higher education.* Oxford: Oxford Centre for Staff and Learning Development, Oxford Brookes University.

Eriksson, E. J. (2005). *Plagiarism control: Lectures' attitudes.* Unpublished PhD course paper, Department of Philosophy and Linguistics, Umeå University, Sweden.

Gaine, C., Hällgren, C., Domínguez, S. P., Noguera, J. S., & Weiner, G. (2003). "Eurokid": An innovative pedagogical approach to developing intercultural and anti-racist education on the Web. *Intercultural Education, 14*(3), 317-329.

Giles, J. (2005). Taking on the cheats. *Nature, 435,* 258–259.

Hällgren C. (2005). "Working harder to be the same:" Everyday racism among young men and women in Sweden. *Race, Ethnicity and Education, 8*(3), 319-341.

Hällgren, C., & Wiener, G. (2003). The Web, antiracism, education and the state in Sweden: Why here? Why now? In N. M. Bloch, K. Holmlund, I. Moqvist, & T. S. Popkewitz (Eds), *Restructuring the governing patterns of the child, education and the welfare state* (pp. 313–333*).* New York: Palgrave Publishing Co.

Harris, R. A. (2001). *The plagiarism handbook.* Los Angeles: Pyrczak Publishing.

Hult, Å., & Hult, H. (2003). Att fuska och plagiera – Ett sätt att leva eller ett sätt att överleva? *Report Centrum för undervisning och lärande, No 6.* Linköping, Sweden: Linköping University.

Högskoleförordningen (online) Retrieved December 19, 2005 from http://web2.hsv.se/sok_publika-tion/search/readmore.jsp?-folder=/appl/docs/publikationer/lagar_regler&filename=hogskolelagen. shtml

Högskoleverket (HSV) (2005). Disciplinärenden 2004 vid högskolor och univeristet med statligt huvudmannaskap. *Högskoleverkets rapportserie: 2005:28 R*, Stockholm, Sweden: Högskoleverket. Retrieved December 19, 2005 from http://web2. hsv.se/publikationer/rapporter/2005/0528R.pdf

Nilsson, L. -E., Eklöf, A., & Ottosson, T. (2005). Copy-and-paste plagiarism: Technology as a blind alley or a road to better learning? *Proceedings of the 33rd congress of the Nordic Educational Research Association (NERA)*. Oslo, Norway. March 10 – 12, 2005.

Sandberg, G. (online). Blog. Retrieved December 19, 2005 from http://www.vk.se/Article.jsp?articl e=36545&leftmenu =132

Stanford University (online) *What is plagiarism?* Retrieved December 19, 2005 from http://www. stanford.edu/dept/vpsa/judicialaffairs/students/ plagiarism.sources.htm

Umeå University, Department of Applied Physics and Electronics (online). *Studenthandbok*. Retrieved December 19, 2005 from http://www. tfe.umu.se/studieinformation/Studentguide.htm

Umeå University, Faculty of Arts (online). *Plagiatpolicy för den humanistiska fakulteten*. Retrieved December 19, 2005 from http://www.umu. se/humfak/internt/images/plagiatpolicy.pdf

Umeå University, Faculty of Medicine (online) *Plagiatpolicy för den medicinska fakulteten*, Retrieved December 19, 2005 from http://www. odont.umu.se/utbildning/Plagiatpolicy.pdf

University of Wales, *Validation Handbook of Quality Assurance – Policies and procedures* (online) Retrieved on December 19, 2005 from http://www.wales.ac.uk/newpages/external/e612. asp?E,VALQAA

APPENDIX A: THE QUESTIONNAIRE

1.   What position do you have?

    Lecturer   PhD student

    Professor   Reader

    Associate Professor   Other

2.   How many years of tertiary teaching experience do you have?

3.   In which faculty do you teach the most?

    Medical   Science and Technology

    Social sciences   Teacher Education

    Arts

4.   What is your definition of plagiarism?

5.   How much information do you provide your students about your view on plagiarism?

6.   By what means do you supply your students your view on plagiarism?

7.   Have you ever discovered cases of plagiarism?

    Yes   No

    Unsure

8.   To whom should cases of plagiarism be reported?

9.   Are there at your department, faculty, or institution clear guidelines for classifying plagiarism / cheating and how to report such cases?

    Yes   No

    Unsure

10. If yes, please provide details (links, or other information)

11. Are there at your department, faculty, or institution clear definitions what constitutes plagiarism?

    Yes   No

    Unsure

12. If yes, please provide them and do they concur with your personal views?

    Yes   No

    Unsure

13. Is plagiarism cheating?

    Yes   No

    Unsure

14. What is a reasonable punishment for plagiarism?

15. Do you believe plagiarism and cheating could be reduced by making students more responsible for their own learning?

    Yes   No

    Unsure

16. Are there occasions when plagiarism is justifiable?

    Yes   No

    Unsure

17. Is it plagiarism to word-by-word copy a text, include a reference, but leave out quotation marks?

    Yes   No

    Unsure

18. Is it plagiarism to translate a text to Swedish without quotation or references?

    Yes   No

    Unsure

19. A task is undertaken in pairs. The ability to work together is important but each student is to submit individually. Is it plagiarism if two students submit highly similar reports, yet do not reference each other?

    Yes   No

    Unsure

20. Is it plagiarism to use one's own work without referencing?

    Yes   No

    Unsure

Section II
Two Particular Case Studies

Chapter IV
Dealing with Plagiarism as an Ethical Issue

Barbara Cogdell
University of Glasgow, UK

Dorothy Aidulis
University of Glasgow, UK

ABSTRACT

This chapter outlines various strategies employed to reduce plagiarism both at a departmental and an institutional level. A detailed description and evaluation is given of two workshops that were designed specifically to educate students about the nature of plagiarism. The workshops also aim to provide students with alternatives to plagiarism by improving their writing skills. Most importantly, we believe that students should learn about plagiarism in the context of professional ethics and an ethical attitude should be promoted throughout their study. By using both an ethical and educational approach to dealing with plagiarism, we hope that students will learn that they have nothing to gain from plagiarising and be confident in their own skills.

INTRODUCTION

Plagiarism is unprofessional, unethical, devalues degrees, and is an issue that has to be taken seriously if the integrity of university qualifications is to be maintained (Ashworth, 2003; Carroll, 2002; Carroll & Appleton, 2001). It can lead to a loss of writing and thinking skills in students.

Moreover, they can spend a lot of "misplaced" effort and ingenuity in plagiarising and not studying (Netskills, 2004).

Plagiarism has always existed, but the growth of the Internet in an online world has made it much easier to do and, therefore, more of a temptation to students (BBC news, 2006a, 2006b). At the same time, other changes in the nature of university education in Britain have also inadvertently encouraged the practice of plagiarism (Ashworth, Bannister & Thorne, 1997; Franklyn-Stokes & Newstead, 1995). Student numbers have greatly increased, there are lower staff-student ratios, and continuous assessment of course work has increasingly replaced traditional exams.

Our experience is in teaching and assessing students in the Institute of Biomedical and Life Sciences (IBLS) at the University of Glasgow. By UK standards, we have one of the largest bioscience classes in the UK with 500-700 students in each of four years. Cases of plagiarism are found in each year.

The reasons why students plagiarise are many and varied (Carroll, 2002; Howard, 2001), and although a detailed analysis of these is beyond the scope of this chapter, they have been taken into account in designing our strategies.

This chapter describes the range of approaches that we are developing in biology at the University of Glasgow to try to minimise the incidence of plagiarism by developing the ethical skills of our students. Although we mainly teach using traditional methods we are now making increasing use of the virtual learning environment (VLE) Moodle (2006) to supplement our courses especially in this area of ethical training.

BACKGROUND

IBLS is a department within the University of Glasgow, one of the oldest universities in the UK (over 550 years old), located in the west of Scotland. The University has 15,486 undergraduate students and 4,061 postgraduates (University of Glasgow, 2006a). IBLS offers courses in a large number of biological subjects ranging from the study of molecules up to whole organisms, including medical biochemistry, genetics, marine and aquatic bioscience, and anatomy. These courses contribute to both three- and four-year undergraduate degree programmes that lead to either a designated BSc (three years) or a BSc with Honours (four years). IBLS has a wide range of postgraduate degree programmes leading to MSc (both taught and by research), MRes and PhD. IBLS staff also provide important contributions to the teaching of professional courses such as medicine, dentistry, and nursing.

The standard four-year degree programme is divided into four levels. Normally, Level 1 is completed in the first year that a student attends and so on. There is, however, the possibility that some students may enter directly into the University at Levels 2 or 3 depending on their previous qualifications. Most students come directly from British high schools at age 17 or 18, but there are many students with a wide variety of other backgrounds, ages, and nationalities.

At Level 1, all IBLS students study a common biology course, one third of their first year requirements. There typically are between 650 and 720 Level 1 students each year, making it one of the largest biology courses in the UK. Some of these students go on to study subjects outside biology, so at Level 2 there are about 550 students who study a variety of optional courses. Each of the Level 2 biology courses is designed to occupy 1/12 of the timetable and an IBLS student will typically choose between six and 12 biology courses in the year. In the final two years of their study, Levels 3 and 4, the students take courses specific to their final degree choice. An advantage of this system is its flexibility, as students do not have to decide on their final degree subject until the end of Level 2.

IBLS requires all its postgraduate students (just under 300) to complete a number of specific courses designed to improve their generic skills. This includes a course on research ethics, and later in this chapter we describe in detail the contents of a new workshop that forms part of this course.

PERSONAL EXPERIENCES AND MOTIVATION

One of us (BC) first became interested in the subject of academic honesty on discovering in 1999 that three groups of students (seven students) had submitted identical answers to problems in a "take-home" test. As a result, BC undertook a study (Cogdell, Matthew, & Gray, 2003) of attitudes of medical students to cheating using a modified form of a questionnaire devised by Franklyn-Stokes and Newstead (1995) and a semi-structured group interview. Results from the questionnaire confirmed the findings of Franklyn-Stokes and Newstead, that students did not consider plagiarism a serious offence.

Ashworth et al. (1997) found that there was a strong moral basis to the students' views, and the study by Cogdell et al. (2003) agreed with this. Students were firm about what they did or did not consider cheating. Interestingly though, using essay banks was viewed as very serious, but omitting sources was not, implying they found this practice relatively acceptable. This highlights that the issues surrounding plagiarism are confusing and require clarification. In addition, students clearly have a sense of ethics, but do not necessarily view different forms of plagiarism as cheating. Our intention is to build on the beginnings of this ethical thinking, to "bridge the gap," and help students see that plagiarism is cheating. This requires first and foremost that students (and staff) have a clearer idea of what constitutes plagiarism; it then can be viewed as part of a wider ethical issue. Our strategy entails educating the students on what plagiarism is, particularly the less obvious "grey areas," and to include this into the wider context of ethical considerations. This will involve short-term and longer-term aspects, and we believe this holistic approach will lead to the longer-term objective of strengthening students' moral attitudes so that they clearly see plagiarism as wrong.

DA became involved in the plagiarism issue around 2003-2004 on discovering a few instances of plagiarism in Level 3 laboratory reports. The extent of this was not great, and resulted in a few marks being lost, but more importantly it highlighted a need to address students' misconceptions of acceptable writing practice. Around this time there were also some cases reported in the media, in particular one of a final year student at an English university who was being disciplined for plagiarism, but who attempted to sue the university (Baty, 2004; Consilio, 2004). His defence was that he had not been properly educated in what plagiarism was, and that the university in question had been negligent in this regard. As a result of this, DA realised that we needed to provide much more detailed information for our students on these issues. Furthermore, she found plagiarism in an honours thesis, involving multiple cut and pastes from journal articles. The subsequent disciplinary procedure required full documentation of the incident, with every instance marked and original sources detailed. This was extremely labour intensive. Bearing in mind the situation described above, intervention and prevention is paramount before events progress this far. This made us determined to deliver our courses so as to persuade students, especially by the end of their degrees, that plagiarism is unacceptable, and indeed avoidable.

EXTENT OF PLAGIARISM IN THE INSTITUTE OF BIOMEDICAL AND LIFE SCIENCES

While there is no evidence that plagiarism is any more or less prevalent at Glasgow University compared to elsewhere, it is an issue we take very seriously. The number of students in the whole university penalised officially for offences classified as plagiarism by the Senate Assessors for Discipline over the past four years is very small. However, the university policy is that at Levels 1, 2, and 3, "first offenders" are dealt with within their departments, while only final year cases or repeat offenders are sent to the Senate Assessors and it is these cases that are included in the official figures. In the session 2001-2002, 42 students were officially penalised and the numbers for the following three years were 16, 16, and 24 respectively (University of Glasgow, 2006b). These numbers are especially small considering that there are over 19,000 students in the University, and the total number of pieces of course work submitted is enormous. It is entirely possible that the actual number of cases is greater than the number detected. We therefore consider plagiarism an issue for action, not least because it is the potentially lifelong skills of students that are at stake. In addition, students should be treated consistently and fairly, and those who do not plagiarise have the right to expect that their work is awarded fair grades and that they are not ranked behind students who have plagiarised. In other words plagiarism cheats a range of people for different reasons: firstly the plagiarists themselves who are failing to learn good practice; secondly the honest students who may be getting poorer grades than the undetected cheats; and lastly the institution who may suffer a reputation loss by giving degrees under false pretences.

Although the Internet has undoubtedly contributed to the volume of plagiarism worldwide, electronic means are also instrumental in its detection, and several forms of plagiarism detection software are now available (Bull, Collins, Coughlin & Sharp, 2001; Netskills, 2004). We have chosen not to go down this route however. It would require all students to submit all pieces of work electronically and we believe this process would have a detrimental effect on staff-student relationships as it automatically sets up a climate of distrust. All potential instances of plagiarism detected by such software must also be checked manually anyway, as legitimate quotes, for example, can lead to false positives. The use of these

programs therefore has consequences for staff time and resources. Furthermore, they cannot detect every case, for example translations from foreign languages, use of obscure books which are not online, and other students' work. These arguments against electronic detection are firmly in accordance with those set out by Howard (2001), who also points out that student texts scanned in this way are automatically added to the detection software database, a consequence which in itself has questionable ethics. More importantly, we believe that it is not the prime role of the staff to act as policemen or judges, again agreeing with Howard (2001). Even though staff need to be vigilant, and act on any cases discovered, it is better if we can educate the students not to plagiarise in the first place. The aims of our strategy are, therefore, to reduce the incidence of plagiarism and thereby reduce the burden of detection and subsequent disciplinary procedures.

AIMS OF OUR APPROACH TO COMBATING PLAGIARISM

It is not sufficient simply to tell students not to plagiarise, especially since the concept of plagiarism is quite difficult to explain (Carroll, 2002; Freewood, Macdonald, & Ashworth, 2003). Some examples lie in a grey area and even experienced academics do not always agree what is or is not acceptable. Furthermore, students do not always rank plagiarism as a serious offence (Cogdell et al., 2003, Franklyn-Stokes & Newstead, 1995). We therefore propose that a multifaceted approach should be taken.

Our long term objective is to change the attitude of students and to create a climate where plagiarism is ethically unacceptable. This requires a four-pronged attack:

- A consistent institutional approach towards plagiarism

41

- Removing, as far as possible, opportunities for plagiarism
- Educating the students to understand what plagiarism is and how it can be avoided
- Perhaps most importantly, promoting ethical behaviour in their academic work

We believe that students should learn about plagiarism in the context of professional ethics and that this message needs to be repeated as in the method of the spiral curriculum proposed by Bruner (1960). Bioethics courses provide the ideal place to get over the principles of professional ethics including attitudes to plagiarism. Bioethics is a topic that has recently been included in the Quality Assurance Agency benchmarks (2002) for biosciences teaching at British universities. Plagiarism also has been recognised as an ethical issue in scientific publications in general (Benos, Fabres, Farmer, Gutierrez, Hennessy, Kosek, et al., 2005). Learning about these issues in the context of professional ethics will develop a mature approach in students towards their own academic studies and their future behaviour and also help them to realise why plagiarism is unacceptable and indeed self-defeating.

STRATEGY TO ACHIEVE OUR AIMS

Dealing effectively with plagiarism requires a clear strategy that involves action both locally at departmental level and across the university as a whole. Below are listed some of the different ways that our comprehensive strategy deals with each of the four lines of attack outlined above. Many of these approaches can be employed whether a course is online or traditional.

Institutional Approach

- Clear policies with appropriate discipline, available on university Web site

- Policies written in course information documents, available on departmental and course Web sites
- Sessions including information about policies at the beginning of each academic session
- Students signing anti-plagiarism statements before handing in course work

Avoiding Opportunities for Plagiarism

- Course work done under examination conditions
- Assessments designed to make plagiarism difficult

Education

- Exercises to help the understanding of plagiarism
- Practice in referencing
- Improvement of writing skills so that students are more confident in their own abilities and therefore less likely to feel the need to plagiarise

Promotion of Ethical Behaviour

- Incorporation into bioethics and research ethics courses

Until recently, IBLS did not have a consistent coherent strategy to deal with plagiarism. Groups of staff had developed numerous ad hoc ways of dealing with the various aspects of this problem. However, as we learnt more about the nature of plagiarism and students perceptions of it, it became clear that there was a need to develop a well-thought-out, integrated approach to tackle the issue. In this chapter we describe the present status of implementing this approach.

We were helped in developing this strategy when one of us (DA) went to a workshop on

"Detecting and deterring plagiarism. The Web: hindrance or help?"organised by Netskills (2004), which was attended by academics from other British Higher Education establishments. This proved a valuable experience and made us realise that we also needed to train staff to deal with the plagiarism problem. On returning from the workshop DA disseminated what she had learnt to other staff. The workshop also provided the stimulus to set up the Level 3 "Scientific Writing Skills" workshop that will be described later in this chapter.

INSTITUTIONAL APPROACH

The University of Glasgow has an official policy on plagiarism (University of Glasgow, 2005). It is important that students are aware of this policy and can access it. Staff also needs to know about this and the procedures to follow if they detect a case of plagiarism, so that they respond in a consistent, fair and prompt manner.

Dissemination of Policy

Based on the university policy, IBLS includes a detailed statement about plagiarism in every course information document (CID) that it publishes. CIDs are documents that are issued to the students at the beginning of each academic session containing course outlines, aims, and objectives as well as university rules and regulations. They also are available online. CIDs are provided for all courses both at undergraduate and at postgraduate level. The students need to be fully aware of these regulations and so all students are strongly encouraged to read their CIDs.

Plagiarism also is highlighted in the introductory lectures at the beginning of each year from Level 1 to Level 4. These lectures have different formats and contents for each year and subject area, but cover common themes. A typical example is the situation for the Level 3 Physiology and Sports Science class. On their induction day, students receive a 20 minute talk which defines plagiarism, gives some examples, says why they should not do it and describes what will happen to them if they are caught.

Guidance for Staff

It is essential that all staff members within our department are clear and consistent when dealing with plagiarism. Guidance notes currently are being developed which will outline precisely the procedures to be followed on detection of plagiarism, including what information is required for records (see below), and where it should be sent. In order to facilitate the commitment of staff to a coherent approach towards plagiarism and other ethical issues, an IBLS Ethics Teaching Group has been established. Staff are further supported by the activities of the Higher Education Academy's Biosciences Ethics Working Party (HEA, 2005). This provides a valuable forum for discussion and exchange of ideas.

Signed Statements

For all Level 2 courses, the students are required to sign a non-plagiarism statement each time they submit a piece of course work. This currently is being extended to other courses.

Record Keeping

Record keeping is essential for tracking numbers of plagiarism cases, trends, and identification of repeat offenders, as well as providing information on the effectiveness of strategies to combat plagiarism. We keep records of cases of plagiarism locally in our department. These local records are more informative than university-wide figures in terms of being able to evaluate the success or otherwise of our anti-plagiarism measures. Instructions on their collection are incorporated into staff guidelines.

AVOIDING OPPORTUNITIES FOR PLAGIARISM

The second line of attack is to try to avoid continuous assessment tasks that can be easily plagiarised. One way to do this is to require all written exercises to be completed under exam conditions. Indeed, the Education Authority for England has just announced an extensive reduction in the amount of unsupervised course work included in secondary school exams (BBC, 2006c; Mulholland, 2006). Our Level 1 students now write their one hour essays in laboratories with invigilators. They are given the topic beforehand to prepare material in advance, and then write their essays without notes under supervision.

Another way to minimise plagiarism in course work includes designing questions whose answers are inherently more difficult to copy from other sources. Sometimes this requires considerable imagination, but answering these sorts of questions require deeper thought and understanding, so as well as avoiding plagiarism there is an educational benefit. Essays titles can be set which do not just ask for descriptions. A variety of similar solutions have been suggested by Jude Carroll (2002).

At Levels 3 and 4 it is important that students learn how to write longer pieces of work, research topics in depth, write literary reviews and project dissertations, and are able to be trusted to do this without plagiarising. Project supervisors need to discuss with their students how to quote from the literature and how to cite the references in the text. It also is helpful if supervisors are encouraged to look out for any instances of plagiarism when they are reading draft copies of the students' write-ups. At this point, discussions with the student should lead to them being able to adopt

better writing techniques before they hand in their final versions.

EDUCATION AND PROMOTION OF ETHICAL BEHAVIOUR

Initially it might seem that the two approaches outlined above would be enough to prevent plagiarism. Though the official policies and the introductory lectures raise awareness and stress the seriousness of committing plagiarism, they do not necessarily help the students to understand what plagiarism really entails and why they should not do it. In addition, knowing that punishment/sanctions exist is not necessarily an effective deterrent, but more importantly gives no information on the correct way to go about writing. Likewise, designing all course work so that the tasks make plagiarism impossible does not help students cope with writing tasks when they eventually have to write reports on their own. It would clearly be better if the students fully appreciate why they should not plagiarise and develop the necessary skills to avoid it. These points lead to our final two prongs of attack against plagiarism, education, and promotion of ethical behaviour.

These two lines of attack complement each other and both should be embedded within the curriculum. Learning how to avoid plagiarism in these ways should be considered a study skill that needs to be developed in students. Wingate (2006) proposed that the learning of such skills is better when they are integrated in the core subject teaching. We agree with this philosophy, and believe our approach will foster deeper levels of learning, and lead to longer-term benefits for the students throughout their university careers and beyond.

The avoidance of plagiarism is a topic that needs to be revisited at all levels of a student's career. However, it must be done in a way that the students do not just think "Oh no, not plagiarism again." This can be achieved by dealing with the topic in different ways and we will describe some examples of our approach towards educating the students not to plagiarise and promoting ethical behaviour. When plagiarism is very blatant, it is obvious. However at the margins, what is or is not plagiarism can be very confusing. It is clear from published work that students do not always appreciate exactly, or indeed agree on, what plagiarism is (Carroll, 2002; Freewood et al., 2003). Similarly, plagiarism as an ethical issue requires a conceptual shift, (Meyer & Land, 2003, 2005), and it is only when students engage with this on a deeper level that they will actively seek ways to avoid it.

Below are some brief examples from each level showing how the issue of plagiarism is incorporated into our curricula.

Level 1: Various measures including a non-plagiarism declaration which must be signed on enrolment; a keynote lecture on ethics which includes plagiarism; and the completion of a plagiarism exercise based on that devised by Willmott and Harrison (2003). A complete description of all the measures used in the Level 1 Biology class is given by Tierney, Brown, and Neil (2006).

Level 2: Science Communication course. This course deals with plagiarism as an ethical issue and the topic is introduced in a lecture on "scientific misconduct." It is also included in group discussion sessions on scientific ethics.

Level 3: Scientific Writing Skills workshops given to students in the human biology group of degrees. This workshop was designed for Level 3 students, to gauge their general understanding of what is meant by plagiarism, to address the confusing and grey areas encountered, and to provide guidelines on referencing sources correctly.

Level 4: Bioethics course. This is an optional course open to all students in Level 4 IBLS. It is a five-week course with two three-hour sessions per week. A variety of ethical issues based in the biosciences are dealt with including research ethics.

Postgraduate: Research Ethics course. This includes a workshop where ethical issues such as plagiarism are discussed by small groups of students.

The rest of the chapter will describe in detail two examples of our strategy. The first takes the education approach and is the Level 3 workshop on "Scientific Writing Skills." Although this workshop deals mainly with promoting good writing practices it does emphasise the ethical reasons for not plagiarising. The second example describes a workshop from the postgraduate Research Ethics course, which puts the discussion of plagiarism wholly in an ethical context.

LEVEL 3 "SCIENTIFIC WRITING SKILLS" WORKSHOP

Description

The workshop has been run for the past three years. It is taken by most of the students studying for degrees in human biology, that is, anatomy, physiology, pharmacology and neuroscience. Each year this is typically 120 students, and so the workshop runs in four repeat sessions. There is a general feeling that if workshops are optional, attendance will be patchy, therefore the workshops have been incorporated into the regular laboratory timetable. Furthermore, the workshop is run in conjunction with the University of Glasgow's Student Learning Service, who support Wingate's (2006) concept that skills should be taught within courses, and emphasises our approach that plagiarism is not a stand-alone issue.

Level 3 is an appropriate place to have such a workshop as this is the first stage where students are expected on all courses to read original journal articles and to be able to cite references correctly. The workshop was initially named "Plagiarism Workshop", but we have renamed it as "Scientific Writing Skills" as it was felt this would create a more positive climate.

Figure 1. Flow chart showing structure of the Level 3 writing-skills workshop; the duration of each activity is shown on the left.

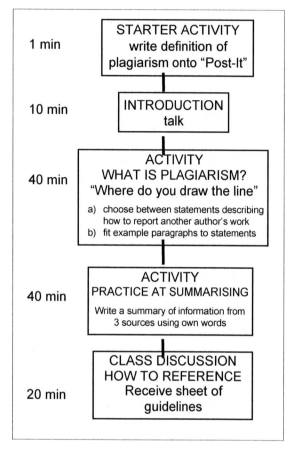

The workshop is split into three main sections, (1) "Where do you draw the line?" (2) Summarising from sources; and (3) Referencing, as outlined in Figure 1. The first section is designed to clarify what plagiarism is, the second provides practice in summarising, and the third contains guidance in referencing sources correctly.

To gauge students' general understanding of plagiarism, before looking at any material in the workshop, they are asked to write on a "Post-it" note what they think plagiarism means. Their "Post-its" are then stuck round a board at the front of the class, referred to during the workshop, and kept for analysis later. In addition, a copy of the University Plagiarism Statement (University of Glasgow, 2005) is given to every student who attends the workshop. It is also available online on the Moodle pages for all the courses taking the workshop, as it is crucial that (a) students know there is an official policy, (b) it will be acted on, and (c) they can easily access it.

The first activity "Where do you draw the line?" is based on an exercise by John Swales and Christine Feak (1994), as described by Jude Carroll (2002). Students are given a series of six descriptions of how an article can be written, beginning with copying word-for-word (clearly plagiarism) and ending with quoting a paragraph in the correct way (in quotes, set apart from the main text, and referenced; clearly not plagiarism). The descriptions in between gradually get "better" and the students must discuss and decide "where to draw the line," so that the statements above the line are clearly plagiarism, and those below the line are not.

The students are seated in groups to do this exercise, and demonstrators are on hand to facilitate discussion. Then a whole-class discussion takes place where each group is asked to report where they "drew the line." Group answers are noted on the blackboard, so everyone has a visual picture of where the discrepancies lie. The class teacher then facilitates a discussion on why each group chose their particular place, as not all groups agree. This discussion is crucial as it pinpoints where the main points of controversy are, and helps to clear up misunderstandings surrounding definitions and examples of plagiarism. Group work was chosen as the main teaching methodology as it is an excellent way of enabling students to engage with tasks (Tiberius, 1999). Managed effectively, small-group teaching can be very empowering for students as each can have their say when they may otherwise be inhibited to contribute (Tiberius, 1999). Discussions also can continue online, encouraging further participation and hence deeper engagement. This online aspect using the Moodle VLE will be described further under "Future Trends."

The next stage of the activity is to look at examples of writing in their own subject area. The material was prepared again using Jude Carroll's book for guidance. A paragraph from a journal article was taken ("original article"), then six versions of this were prepared according to the descriptions in the "Where do you draw the line?" exercise. As an illustration, for version 1 (copying verbatim), the paragraph was preceded by "It has recently been shown that," the rest of the paragraph following word-for-word, and ending with "more studies need to be done." In groups, students look at each version, compare them to the descriptions in "Where do you draw the line?" and match each version to the correct description. In this way, by looking at actual examples rather than abstract statements, students gain more understanding of what each description actually means. A whole-class discussion then follows to clarify which version was which (straight copy, properly quoted paragraph, and all versions in between). Again, those versions falling in the "grey areas" provide interesting discussion and help to clear up some misconceptions. The class also is given highlighter pens, and asked to highlight on each version parts that are identical to the original. They are asked to hold up any which fall into a grey area, and very quickly a visual assessment of highlighted areas helps in the decision. This also helps to illustrate the idea that changing a few words here and there does not make an original article. Indeed, one student had asked "how much do you have to change something before it isn't plagiarism?" but literally seeing the highlighted words jump out of the page helped him very quickly to see that this was entirely the wrong question to ask.

The second activity to give the students practice in summarising, but keeping in mind the concepts highlighted above. Each group of students is given three articles on one general scientific topic, using different types of sources (for example Internet, journal, and news articles), asked to discuss these together and make notes, then summarise, on their own, particular aspects of the information (for example, benefits and risks). Guidance is given on how to avoid simply writing down the same words as the original article, placing emphasis on discussion, highlighting relevant information, listing important points, drawing diagrams and so on. Using all these different methods involves much more processing by the brain than a single step of "read articles, write summary," and group discussion helps to clear up questions and aid understanding. The increased understanding and processing allows actual synthesising of the information to take place and arguments to be constructed. One student pointed out that once you have read something, it is difficult to say it in a different way, but was then convinced that following the above methods means you are much less likely to have a sentence straight from the page in your head. Furthermore, as the learning is more active and on a deeper level than simple memory and reproduction, the writing will be of a better quality, and the learning at a higher level (Bloom, 1956), leading to longer term benefits.

Summarising exercises are common practice in skills-based activities such as those provided by the Student Learning Service. The advantage of doing this in the workshop is that the students do the summarising immediately following on from the exercise on what constitutes plagiarism. Links to ethical (or unethical) practice are mentioned throughout this process.

The final section of the workshop provides guidelines on referencing sources properly. Such information is freely available on the Internet and there are many good sites, however, the text can be very wordy and sometimes daunting, and it is not enough simply to refer students to a Web page. A two-sided sheet was prepared specifically to cover referencing from journals, books, book chapters, and Internet sources, tailored to the needs of the relevant degree subjects. The details on these sheets were agreed in advance with course organisers for each of the four subjects involved, to ensure classes were given consistent guidelines that adhere to departmental conventions, styles, and course requirements. Students were also given copies of journals to begin to familiarise themselves with referencing conventions. The main points on the information sheet were elucidated by a question and answer session. However, it is only by practice that many of the questions can be answered, for example "when do I put an in-text reference?" "if I don't use the same words do I need to reference it?" and so on. An electronic copy of the referencing guidelines sheet is posted on the Moodle pages for each course, and further resources will be added in future.

Evaluation

The starter activity where the students write on the "Post-it" notes gives them some "ownership" of the lesson. An analysis of what they have written reveals what they know before the workshop.

The students evaluated the workshop using a feedback form. The findings presented below are those obtained from the second year that the workshop was run. The results from the other two years are similar.

In 2005, 110 students in total completed the workshop and feedback form. Data showing how helpful the session was overall are shown in Figure 2a. Eighty percent of the students rated the session overall as 4 or 5 on the five point rating scale, where 5 is "very helpful" and 1 "waste of time." Only one student rated the session as a waste of time. Figures 2b, 2c and 2d illustrate the breakdown for each of the three exercises. "Where do you draw the line?" (Figure 2b) and "Referencing" (Figure 2d) were both rated by 75 percent or more of the students as 4 or 5 on the five-point scale. The exercise on Summarising was the least favourably received (Figure 2c), but the majority (57 percent) still chose either 4 or 5 on the rating scale and 32 percent chose the middle point of the scale. Several students who ranked this exercise worse than the other two exercises said

Figure 2. Graphs showing the students' responses to the evaluation questionnaire on the Level 3 writing skills workshop; (a) shows how helpful they found the workshop overall. (b), (c) and (d) show how helpful they found each of the three activities: (b) Where do you draw the line? (c) summarising from sources and (d) referencing

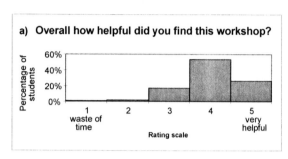

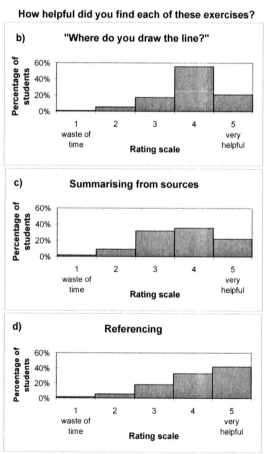

they would have liked more time; however some said this part of the workshop was too long.

The feedback form also asked students to give two examples of each of the following:

a. Something you didn't know about which has been clarified by this workshop.
b. Something this workshop has covered which you knew already.
c. Something you've changed your opinion about as a result of this workshop.

The students' responses revealed that, although they often indicated that they knew something already, for example, about referencing, their pre-existing understanding was limited and that they needed to revisit the whole area.

Some students chose only to complete the "tick-box" five-point rating, and did not add comments. In total, there were 20 "blanks" for (a), 51 for (b), and 52 for (c). However, some students gave more than one answer for each question. On analysis, there appeared to be four main categories of responses, and these have been grouped as "summarising," "referencing," "plagiarism," and

"other." Many of the responses were just simply "references" or "summarising," while others were more explicit. Examples of what was included in each category are shown in Table 1. The category "other" included all those items that did not fit into the other three categories.

Figure 3a shows the data summarising "Examples of something you didn't know about which has been clarified by this workshop." The great majority of students thought that they had not known about some aspects of referencing before and that these have been clarified by the workshop. A number of students (34) said that they had not known about plagiarism before. Hopefully these

Figure 3. Graphs showing the students reactions to the Level 3 writing skills workshop

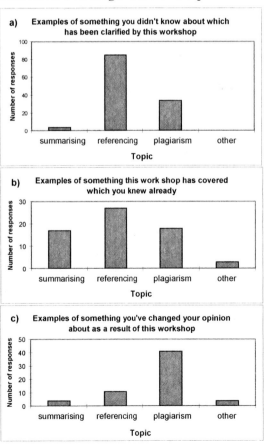

Table 1. The table shows examples of the students' responses placed within each of four categories

Summarising	Referencing	Plagiarism	Other
try to paraphrase	how to list references	exactly what constitutes plagiarism	how to approach work to hand in
	quoting from a source	limits of plagiarism	web-dubious articles
	journal referencing	ideas for avoiding	all the workshop
	citing in text	drawing the line	nothing
	anon means anonymous	plagiarism by mistake	
	Harvard system	not to copy	

students will be more likely to avoid plagiarism than they would otherwise have been, and this finding provides a good indication that the workshop has been effective at least for them.

Figure 3b might at first sight seem to contradict Figure 3a as the students again give referencing as the most popular answer, but this time for "Examples of something this workshop has covered which you knew already." However, the category of referencing can be further broken down into different aspects of referencing. For example, of the 85 responses categorised as referencing in Figure 3a, 31 of these responses were about citing in text and 11 were on how to reference Web sites. Only two of the responses to Figure 3b mentioned citing in the text and none referred to referencing Web sites. In fact, none of the responses in Figure 3a and Figure 3b from a single individual student were actually identical.

Figure 3b ("Examples of something this workshop has covered which you knew already") shows approximately equal numbers of choices for plagiarism and summarising. It is not surprising that students have at least heard of these issues before, but it is not possible to distinguish having heard of something, and having a good understanding of it, from this question.

Figure 3c shows the responses to something that the students have changed their opinion about as a result of this workshop. Here, the majority of students chose plagiarism. This is an excellent result as it demonstrates that the students were altering their perceptions of plagiarism as a result of attending the workshop.

These responses, as indicated above, also give support to the idea of plagiarism being a threshold concept (Meyer & Land, 2003, 2005). As such, it is something that needs special attention when designing a course, and this is what we have done in this workshop (Land, Cousin, Meyer & Davies, 2005). Interestingly, five students said "plagiarism" in answer to both (b) and (c), indicating that plagiarism was something that they already knew about, as well as being something

that they have changed their opinion about as a result of the workshop. This is to be expected if plagiarism is a threshold concept that requires a transformation of understanding before the student can progress.

Overall, the responses to these questions give strong support for the usefulness of the workshop. The students clearly learnt new information about techniques to avoid plagiarism (referencing and summarising), and they also now have a much clearer idea of what plagiarism is. This academic year (2006-2007) is only the third time that the workshop has run. It is, therefore, not yet possible to carry out an in-depth analysis of changes in students' behaviour in response to the workshop. However, preliminary indications are promising. No student completing the workshop has been referred for plagiarism in laboratory reports that DA has marked, which was one of the driving forces for setting up the workshop in the first place. Furthermore, another Level 3 subject group, which did not attend the workshop, has this year reported 18 students for plagiarism in laboratory reports. It will be interesting to analyse this more systematically over the coming years to find out whether this positive trend continues and can indeed be attributable to the measures, including this workshop, that we have put in place.

POSTGRADUATE WORKSHOP ON RESEARCH ETHICS

Description

This workshop was run for the first time earlier this year (2006) and will shortly be repeated with a larger number of students. Forty-five students attended. The students were at the beginning of their postgraduate courses and were studying the full range of bioscience subjects. They came from a variety of backgrounds. A few had completed their first degrees at the University of Glasgow, but the majority were from elsewhere. Many were from abroad and there were at least 10 different nationalities. This meant that many did not have English as their first language. Some had previously encountered ethics, while others had no experience at all. The workshop was designed to raise the level of ethical thinking in all these students.

The workshop lasts for four hours. The structure of the workshop is outlined in Figure 4. It begins with a one hour lecture on "Research

Figure 4. Flow chart showing the structure of the postgraduate research ethics workshop; the duration of each activity is shown on the left

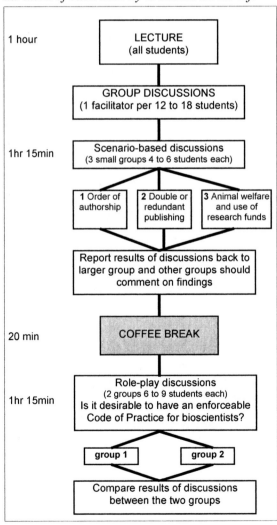

Ethics in the Biosciences" which all the students attend together. The content of the lecture includes ethical decision making with a brief introduction to some of the philosophical theories behind this; ethics and science; professional ethics with the key issues of fabrication, falsification, and plagiarism; issues of good practice which have an ethical dimension; and finally why the students are offered this short course in research ethics. The background for the topic sets the scene for the rest of the workshop, with particular emphasis in the lecture being that it is essential to discuss ethical issues with others in order to sort out what decisions to make.

The second part of the workshop involves group discussions of hypothetical scenarios (see Tiberius [1999] for more information on setting up group work). The students are initially divided into groups of 12 to 18 students. These groups are each then sent to a separate room with a facilitator. The facilitator's role is to promote the discussions, rather than to give answers or "teach" the students. Each group then is further divided into three small groups of four to six students, with a workplace scenario to discuss. After 30 to 40 minutes discussion in their small group, the students come together again in the larger group and present their findings to the rest of the students. All of the students are thus given the chance to learn about each of the three topics and express their views on any of them.

The three topics of the workplace scenarios were:

Order of authorship. This scenario was about the order in which names of authors of journal articles are listed. The position of an author's name can have serious consequences for their future job opportunities, promotion, and status (Nature, 1997).

Double or redundant publishing, see Box 1.

Animal welfare and use of research funds. This scenario concerned a scientist using external grant funding, awarded to maintain his experi-

Box 1. This is an example of a scenario used for the postgraduates' small group discussions

---

Scenario 2: Double or Redundant Publishing

Sarah has just completed the first year of her Ph.D. and she has obtained some very interesting results. Her supervisor Dr West says the data are good enough to publish and that it would complete a study that he is in the process of writing up. He gives the draft of his paper to Sarah and suggests that she adds her data to a section of the results. Sarah feels very proud that her results will be included but when she reads through the draft paper she realises that some of the paper is identical to an article previously published by her supervisor.

What should she do?

Activity

- What are the ethical issues involved?
- List all the parties involved.
- Do you need any further information?
- What are all the possible courses of action that might be taken?
- What might be the outcome of each course of action?

After discussing the issues raised, prepare a short presentation on the problem and your conclusions to feed back to the whole class.

---

mental animals, for other purposes. Consequently, the animals' welfare was suffering.

The scenario topics were deliberately chosen to be about issues that the students might encounter or worry about in their workplace during their research training. The text of the second scenario is given in full in Box 1. Although there is no explicit mention of plagiarism in the text, the students need to discuss plagiarism and what it means in the context of reporting science in order to fully explore the various issues raised in the scenario. A good place to find ideas for writing similar scenarios is from the Web site of the Committee of Publications Ethics (COPE, 2006). They give a wide range of real and made-up cases of ethical malpractice occurring in the publication of scientific journals, together with descriptions of how the cases were dealt with by the editors of the journals.

The final part of the workshop was a role-play scenario based on the desirability of introducing an enforceable code of practice in the biosciences, similar to those in the engineering and medical professions here in the UK. An example of such a code for the biosciences has been proposed by Jones (2005). The students were asked to consider the proposal from the viewpoints of a wide range of people, such as a senior executive in a biotechnology company, a member of parliament, a researcher for a wildlife conservation charity, and high ranking officials of religious groups. The task involved dividing the group into smaller discussion groups as before, although this time into two where both groups discussed the same topic. Again after about 30 minutes the groups reported back to each other and compared their findings.

As with the workplace based scenarios, the code of practice scenario deals with plagiarism in an ethical context not just in isolation. This code of practice scenario requires thought about how to define scientific misconduct and then how to turn this into explicit rules that can be applied. The definition of scientific misconduct typically refers to fabrication, falsification and plagiarism, but it is not always as straight forward as it seems, as was pointed out by Goodstein (2002).

Evaluation

At the end of the workshop the students were asked to complete an anonymous course evaluation questionnaire. The results were very encouraging and a summary of the findings that are relevant to this chapter is shown in the graphs in Figures 5 and 6. Figure 5a gives the evaluation of the short scenarios on ethical problems in the workplace. The vast majority (85 percent) of the students reported that the scenarios were thought provoking, relevant, and helpful. Some of the students chose more than one option. Indeed, one student commented that the scenarios seemed at first sight very simple, but then after the discussion he realised that

Figure 5. Evaluation of the scenario-based group discussions in the postgraduate research ethics workshop

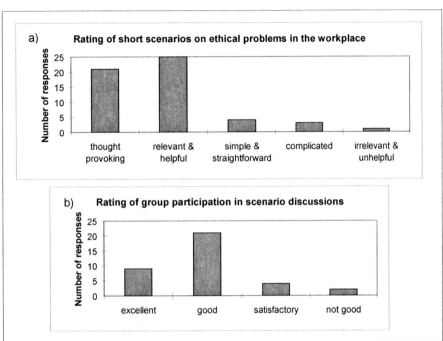

the issues were in fact quite complicated. These are exactly the sort of outcomes for which we were aiming. Likewise, Figure 5b shows a favourable rating for how the students perceived the group participation in the scenario discussions. Over 80 percent thought that the participation was good or excellent. As a facilitator of one of the sessions, BC can confirm that students were animated and had plenty to say particularly on the workplace scenarios. Indeed, she found it very difficult to stop the discussions and get the students to move on to the next activity. These findings provide strong support for the appropriateness of this teaching method (facilitated discussions).

Figure 6 shows the students' reactions to four statements about the workshop as a whole. Again, the responses are positive. Only 20 percent agreed with the statement: "I found the course largely a waste of time because I have already thought about the issues covered." Although we would

have liked this figure to be lower it does indicate that nearly 80 percent learnt something useful. The 23 percent of students who agreed with the statement: "The course was generally irrelevant to me because the issues covered were too far removed from the work I do" are a bit more worrying. The next time we run the course we shall place more emphasis on its relevance to research scientists. However, the course took place at the very beginning of some of the students' post-graduate courses and maybe they have not really encountered such issues before. The responses to the third question with over 70 percent agreeing or being neutral to the statement: "Compared to other 'generic' courses delivered in the first year of my PhD, this was interesting and enjoyable" is a very positive response. Finally the last statement: "I like the way the course gave us all a chance to discuss our views" supports the findings from the previous question reported in Figure 5b. However,

Figure 6. Students' overall impressions of the postgraduate research ethics workshop

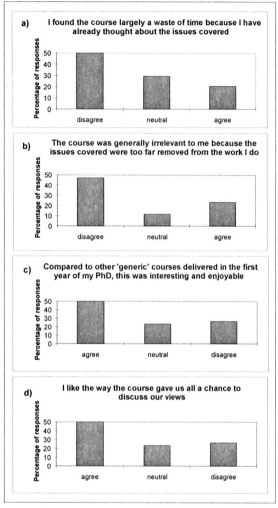

before the workshop so that the students can be better prepared.

It is important to note that even though several aspects of dealing with trying to prevent plagiarism can be delivered online, we have found that face to face discussions are very important to both really engage the students and to make them appreciate the complete picture. As noted below however, it is clear that online discussions via the Moodle VLE can be instrumental in helping the students formulate and share opinions, and is an area for future development.

FUTURE TRENDS

In this section, we will discuss how virtual learning environments, and conceptual changes in thinking, are two relatively new and emerging fields that serve to inform our current stance on plagiarism and that provide scope for developing our approach in the future.

Moodle

There now are several Virtual Learning Environments available, including WebCT, Blackboard, and Moodle (Carliner, 2005). These have greatly enhanced communication and discussion on both traditional and online courses (Carliner, 2005). In our institution it was the remit of GUIDE (Glasgow University Initiative in Distance Education) (University of Glasgow, 2006c) over the last few years to evaluate different VLEs. As a result of their findings, Moodle (Modular Object-Oriented Dynamic Learning Environment) was adopted by University of Glasgow for a number of reasons. It is technically easy to use and requires no specialist knowledge, so courses using it have more control over its content and applications. It is suitable for on- and off-campus learning and teaching, and students and tutors "build" the course pages together. Its design was educationally driven, and the intention of its creator Martin

the responses to this statement reveal more about how they felt as individuals within the group discussion than in the case of the earlier question. The 26 percent who disagreed with this statement might not be as negative as they seem. There were a number of students whose first language was not English and some of them commented that they could not contribute as much as they would have liked. We need to consider carefully how to improve the course for this last group of students and plan to make the scenarios available online

Dougiamas is to encourage socially constructivist learning (Dougiamas, 2006a, b).

We believe that the Moodle VLE is therefore ideally suited for our purposes, where course material, how it is presented, and how participants can interact with it is under complete control of the staff and students on the course. DA trialled a Moodle site first within her tutor group then within the Level 3 Pharmacology class during the 2005-2006 academic year. One of the most dynamic features is the Discussion Forum, where participants can start and respond to discussion topics. Networks of discussion (rather than a more linear model) can be built up, particularly if students are asked to both respond to a question or statement (for example, a particular view of plagiarism), and reply to a classmate's posting. Real active dialogue then results, where everyone contributes to and can access the picture being built up, and issues can be "thrashed out" in depth. This is conducive to developing a deeper understanding of hard-to-grasp concepts such as the "greyer" areas of plagiarism, and other areas of ethics. The skill of the tutor lies in knowing when it is appropriate to intervene and when to stay out of discussions, in order to maximise student input and understanding.

When managed well, small group teaching is an excellent and appropriate technique for promoting discussion and active learning, and we have adopted this pedagogy for the workshops described in this chapter. However, there can be several problems in small group teaching such as group dynamics and dealing with silence (Tiberius, 1999), and Moodle discussion forums remove many of the barriers associated with this. They are particularly good for quieter students, who may not otherwise get their views across, as discussions are not face-to-face and they can take time to formulate their thoughts. Moodle forums are therefore an ideal way to supplement and support our face-to-face teaching. Courses which combine traditional or face-to-face teaching methods with online and other electronic initia-

tives, have been described as "hybrid" by Taradi, Taradi, Radic, and Pokrajac (2005; p. 35). Such courses have been shown to significantly enhance student performance (Taradi & Taradi, 2004; Taradi et al., 2005). The biology courses within IBLS at Glasgow University can be described in a similar manner, with the introduction of Moodle in addition to other more established online communication systems such as e-mail.

We therefore intend to utilise and fully develop Moodle's applications in this regard to supplement and enhance our current ethics and scientific writing workshops. We also will continue to integrate these workshops with the actual science courses. One of the problem areas we have identified is students' confidence in dealing with primary research sources of scientific literature. Tierney et al. (2006) also document students' difficulties with referencing these sources. Gillen, Vaughan, and Lye (2004) describe an online tutorial designed to help non-science specialists make sense of scientific research literature and we are interested in exploring this area further. Wingate (2006) makes the case that embedding these sorts of skills within course teaching rather than providing them separately is the way forward. This is in accordance with our philosophy, presented in this chapter. Plagiarism, writing skills, and ethics involve complex issues, and we strongly feel that our approach is appropriate, indeed necessary, for longer-term, higher-level learning (Bloom, 1956) to take place.

Most of the exercises described in this chapter can be easily adapted to being mounted online on Moodle. In fact, versions of the "Where do you draw the line?" and the paragraph matching exercise already exist on the Internet. The paragraph matching exercise exists as part of the University of Essex Web pages on plagiarism (Brewis, n.d.). Webeducate (2006) is a small commercial company that provides e-learning tools including "pollster," which creates anonymous Web polls. They include the "Where do you draw the line?" exercise as an example of their polls and the results of this poll can be found by using the submit button following their poll on plagiarism.

A further advantage of using Moodle, rather than just a simple Web-based version of the exercises, is that Moodle creates comprehensive logs. This allows us to monitor how students are using the site and provides data on its usefulness. For example, we can see whether some resources are accessed more than others, and this can provide important data from which to evaluate the effectiveness of these exercises.

We are just beginning to use Moodle in the context of ethical training and anti-plagiarism strategies. An exciting area to be developed lies in the potential to engage in the issues on a global basis by the use of links to relevant articles describing "real-life" instances of plagiarism, and the resulting debates, available on the Internet. An example of such a debate is an interview by Amy Goodman (2003) for Democracy Now and a link to this has been posted on the Moodle pages. Being aware of the issues in a wider context should help students to develop their own ethical philosophy in making decisions about their own writing. Links also can be made to the many referencing and anti-plagiarism resources available on the Internet. It is important that these are screened by tutors to avoid confusion with possibly conflicting information and to select or adapt those most appropriate for their students' particular needs. As well as the global dimension, Moodle is an excellent medium for outlining and clarifying institutional policy, by posting these as fixed, readily-accessible documents.

Although it is feasible to do most of the activities we have described above online, we do not envisage using this as our sole approach to teaching about plagiarism. The evaluations of our workshops indicate that group discussions provide a good way of learning about plagiarism in an ethical context. It is likely that this can be powerfully enhanced by posting easily accessible resources, and engaging in discussions, via Moodle. Moodle is potentially of great benefit in helping students make the concept shifts necessary to develop their thinking.

Concept Shifts

Conceptual shifts in thinking have been likened to a "portal" which must be stepped through, before existing ways of thinking, and therefore writing, can be transformed (Meyer & Land, 2003, 2005). This involves deconstruction of previously held views, which are then re-synthesised in a new way. The problem (plagiarism) then can be viewed from a perspective different to that of the typical student, where plagiarism is sometimes acceptable to get things done, knowledge is static, and there is no other way to write about it. In fact more than one conceptual shift is required, for example plagiarism is an ethical issue; knowledge is not static; and writing skills are part of a lifelong skill-base. These conceptual shifts are part of an emerging school of thought (Meyer & Land, 2003, 2005), and the ways in which plagiarism are being tackled in IBLS at the University of Glasgow are likely to draw on this more and more. Implementation is dependent upon an effective management and dedicated, motivated staff. We are fortunate at Glasgow University that key staff at both teaching and management level are sufficiently skilled and motivated in this regard. However we recognise that this may be transient, therefore great effort has gone into implementing procedures at departmental and university level wherever possible.

CONCLUSION

It is generally acknowledged that plagiarism among students is on the increase, and it seems likely that the "age of information" and growth of the Internet has been a contributing factor. Conversely, technology also can be instrumental in its detection using search engines such as Google and plagiarism detection software packages. It is clear however that plagiarism is a multifactorial problem, and as such requires a number of measures to tackle it.

This chapter has described several strategies designed to combat plagiarism at the University of Glasgow. These include development of a consistent Institutional approach, removing opportunities for plagiarism, and educating students on the nature of plagiarism and its place in a wider ethical context (Benos et al., 2005).

At Glasgow University, we have therefore chosen to tackle plagiarism from a number of angles, using both institutional and educational measures. Our particular stance is that plagiarism can be viewed as part of a wider ethical debate, and increasing student (and staff) awareness of this is one of our main objectives. This however requires a conceptual shift in thinking, which can be facilitated by online resources such as Moodle. We believe this holistic approach is the key to "tackling student plagiarism in an online world."

ACKNOWLEDGMENT

The authors would like to thank Professor Roger Downie and Ms. Chris Growney for their help with preparation of this manuscript.

REFERENCES

Ashworth, P. D. (2003). Symposium on academic malpractice among students. In *Improving student learning theory and practice—10 years on*. Oxford: Oxford Centre for Staff and Learning Development, 363-398.

Ashworth, P. D., Bannister, P., & Thorne, P. (1997). Guilty in whose eyes? University students' perceptions of cheating and plagiarism in academic work and assessment. *Studies in Higher Education, 22*, 187-203.

Baty, P. (2004, May 28). Plagiarist student to sue university. *The Times Higher Education Supplement.* Retrieved October 15, 2006, from http://www.timesonline.co.uk/article/0,,3561-1126250,00.html

BBC news. (2006a). *Net students 'think copying OK.'* Retrieved June 19, 2006, from http://news.bbc.co.uk/go/pr/fr/-/hi/education/5093286.stm

BBC news. (2006b). *Students 'admit copying essays.'* Retrieved June 19, 2006, from http://news.bbc.co.uk/go/pr/fr/-/hi/education/4810522.stm

BBC news. (2006c). *Maths GCSE coursework is dropped.* Retrieved October 11, 2006, from http://news.bbc.co.uk/1/hi/education/5385556.stm

Benos, D. J., Fabres, J., Farmer, J., Gutierrez, J. P., Hennessy, K., Kosek, D., Lee, J. H., Olteanu, D., Russell, T., Shaikh, F., & Wang, K. (2005). Ethics and scientific publication. *Advances in Physiology Education, 29*, 59-74.

Bloom, B. S. (Ed.) (1956). *Taxonomy of educational objectives: The classification of education goals: Handbook I, cognitive domain.* New York, Toronto: Longmans, Green.

Brewis, J. (n.d.). *Test your understanding of plagiarism.* Retrieved October 2, 2006, from http://www.essex.ac.uk/plagiarism/test.htm

Bruner, J. (1960). *The process of education.* Cambridge, Massachusetts: Harvard University Press.

Bull, J., Collins, C., Coughlin, E., & Sharp, D. (2001). *Technical review of plagiarism detection software report.* Luton, UK: University of Luton and Computer Assisted Assessment Centre. Retrieved October 13, 2006, from http://www.jisc.ac.uk/uploaded_documents/luton.pdf

Carliner, S. (2005). Course management systems versus learning management systems. *Learning Circuits: American Society for Training &*

Development. Retrieved October 13, 2006, from http://www.learningcircuits.org/2005/nov2005/carliner.htm

Carroll, J. (2002). *A handbook for deterring plagiarism in higher education.* Oxford: Oxford Centre for Staff and Learning Development.

Carroll, J. (2003). Deterring student plagiarism: Where best to start. *Improving student learning theory and practice—10 years on* (pp. 365-373). Oxford: Oxford Centre for Staff and Learning Development.

Carroll, J., & Appleton, J. (2001). *Plagiarism: A good practice guide.* Retrieved October 14, 2006, from http://www.jisc.ac.uk/uploaded_documents/brookes.pdf

Cogdell, B., Matthew, B., & Gray, C. (2003). Academic cheating: An investigation of medical students' views of cheating on a problem based learning course. *Improving student learning theory and practice—10 years on* (pp. 384-398). Oxford: Oxford Centre for Staff and Learning Development.

Consilio. (2004, October18). Student may sue university for failing to spot plagiarism. *Consilio: The daily online magazine for law students.* London: Semple Piggot Rochez. Retrieved October 15, 2006, from http://www.spr-consilio.com/arteduc1.htm

COPE. (2006). *Cases.* Retrieved October 11, 2006 from http://www.publicationethics.org.uk/cases

Dougiamas, M. (2006a). *About Moodle – philosophy.* Retrieved October 13, 2006, from http://docs.moodle.org/en/Philosophy

Dougiamas, M. (2006b). *About Moodle—background.* Retrieved October 13, 2006, from http://docs.moodle.org/en/Background

Franklyn-Stokes, A., & Newstead, S. E. (1995). Undergraduate cheating: who does what and why? *Studies in Higher Education, 20,* 159-172.

Freewood, M., Macdonald, R., & Ashworth, P. D. (2003). Why simply policing plagiarism is not enough. *Improving student learning theory and practice—10 years on* (pp. 374-383). Oxford: Oxford Centre for Staff and Learning Development.

Gillen, C. M., Vaughan, J., & Lye, B. R. (2004). An online tutorial for helping nonscience majors read primary research literature in biology. *Advances in Physiology Education, 28,* 95-99

Goodman, A. (2003, September 24). Scholar Norman Finkelstein calls Professor Alan Dershowitz's new book on Israel a "hoax." *Democracy Now* [News program]. Retrieved February 21, 2007, from http://www.democracynow.org/static/dershowitzFin.shtml

Goodstein, D. (2002). Scientific misconduct. *Academe: Bulletin of the American Association of University Professors.* Retrieved October 11, 2006, from http://www.aaup.org/publications/2002/02JF/02jfgoo.htm

HEA. (2005). Special interest group: Teaching ethics to bioscience students. *The Higher Education Academy: Centre for Bioscience.* Retrieved February 21, 2007, from http://www.bioscience.heacademy.ac.uk/network/sigs/ethics/index.htm

Howard, R. M. (2001, November 16). Forget about policing plagiarism. Just teach. *The Chronicle of Higher Education.* Retrieved February 21, 2007, from http://leeds.bates.edu/cbb/events/docs/Howard_ForgeT.pdf

Jones, N. L. (2005). A code of ethics for bioscience. In J. Bryant, L. Baggott la Velle, & J. Searle, *Introduction to bioethics.* Chichester: John Wiley & Sons (pp. 217-223).

Land, R., Cousin, G., Meyer, J. H. F., & Davies, P. (2005). Threshold concepts and troublesome knowledge (3): Implications for course design and evaluation. *Improving student learning - equality and diversity.* Oxford: Oxford Centre for Staff and Learning Development, 53-64.

Meyer, J. H. F., & Land, R. (2003). Threshold concepts and troublesome knowledge: Linkages to ways of thinking and practising within the disciplines. *Improving student learning theory and practice—10 years on* (pp. 412-424). Oxford: Oxford Centre for Staff and Learning Development.

Meyer, J. H. F., & Land, R. (2005). Threshold concepts and troublesome knowledge (2): Epistemological considerations and a conceptual framework for teaching and learning. *Higher Education, 49*, 373-388.

Moodle. (2006). *Moodle homepage.* Retrieved October 15, 2006, from http://moodle.org

Mulholland, H. (2006, September 27). Johnson to scrap GCSE maths coursework. *The Guardian.* Retrieved October 11, 2006, from http://education.guardian.co.uk/policy/story/0,,1882294,00.html

Nature. (1997). Games people play with authors' names. Editorial. *Nature, 387*, 831.

Netskills. (2004, April 7). *Detecting and deterring plagiarism. The Web: hindrance or help?* Workshop held at Leeds Metropolitan University. Netskills, University of Newcastle. Retrieved October 14, 2006, from http://www.netskills.ac.uk/content/about/

QAA. (2002). *Biosciences: Subject benchmark statements.* Gloucester, UK: Quality Assurance Agency for Higher Education.

Swales, J. M., & Feak, C. B. (1994). *Academic writing for graduate students: Essential tasks and skills. A course for nonnative speakers of English.* Ann Arbor: University of Michigan.

Taradi, S. K., & Taradi, M. (2004). Expanding the traditional physiology class with asynchronous online discussions and collaborative projects. *Advances in Physiology Education, 28*, 73-78.

Taradi, S. K., Taradi, M., Radic, K., & Pokrajac, N. (2005). Blending problem-based learning with Web technology positively impacts student learning outcomes in acid-base physiology. *Advances in Physiology Education, 29*, 35-39.

Tiberius, R. G. (1999). *Small group teaching: a trouble-shooting guide.* London: Kogan Page.

Tierney, A. M., Brown, A., & Neil, D. (2006). Tackling plagiarism in the Level One Biology class—A work in progress. *Practice and Evidence of Scholarship of Teaching and Learning in Higher Education, 1*(1), 13-21. Retrieved October 11, 2006, from http://www.pestlhe.org.uk

University of Glasgow. (2005). University of Glasgow plagiarism statement. *Senate office.* Retrieved October 2, 2006, from http://senate.gla.ac.uk/discipline/plagiarism/plagstate.html

University of Glasgow. (2006a). Student numbers. *Facts and Figures.* Retrieved October 2, 2006, from http://senate.gla.ac.uk/publications/factsandfigures/studentnumbers.html

University of Glasgow. (2006b). Student discipline. *Senate office.* Retrieved October 2, 2006, from http://senate.gla.ac.uk/discipline/stats.html

University of Glasgow. (2006c). Moodle adoption. *Learning and Teaching Centre.* Retrieved October 15, 2006, from http://www.gla.ac.uk/services/learn/elearn/moodhis.html

Webeducate. (2006). *Pollster.* Retrieved October 11, 2006 from http://www.webducate.net/pollster.php

Willmott, C. J. R., & Harrison, T. (2003). An exercise to teach bioscience students about plagiarism. *Journal of Biological Education, 37*(3), 139-140.

Wingate, U. (2006). Doing away with "study skills." *Teaching in Higher Education, 11*(4), 457-469.

Chapter V
Working Together to Educate Students

Frankie Wilson
Brunel University, UK

Kate Ippolito
Brunel University, UK

ABSTRACT

This chapter presents a descriptive case study of how a UK university has addressed the problem of plagiarism through collaboration between academic staff, student support professionals, and the students' union. It outlines the developmental process undergone in devising, piloting, evaluating, and implementing the programme designed to educate students about plagiarism. Specific details of the tools and techniques used to achieve the intended pedagogical aims are included. The chapter identifies aspects of the institutional culture operating within our universities, such as discipline-specific conceptions of knowledge and the diversity of students' and staff's previous educational experiences, which make tackling plagiarism problematic. Findings indicate that the approaches described are valued by students and staff but that barriers to achieving university-wide adoption persist. Suggestions for ways forward for any institution interested in tackling plagiarism are offered. It is anticipated that this chapter will stimulate discussion and inspire learning support professionals, including academics, by the success a collaborative approach can bring—not just a system of detecting and punishing plagiarism, but a method of educating students about what it is, why it is wrong, and how it can be avoided.

INTRODUCTION

Brunel University is located in west London. It was founded in 1966, and a long succession of developments and mergers has brought it from modest beginnings to the institution it is today. Brunel University's traditional strengths were engineering, science, and technology, and it was a pioneer in sandwich courses (courses containing a work placement element). Today the subjects offered extend far beyond these fields, but all programmes endeavour to meet the needs of the real world and contribute in a practical way to progress in all walks of life. Brunel University currently caters for 14,000 students, including 3,000 postgraduates and 1,600 international students drawn from 110 countries.

The chapter starts with a description of how this institution dealt with plagiarism in 2004, when it enforced a "zero tolerance" approach. To complement this tough approach, a working party was established to share best practice in deterring student plagiarism among academics, student support professionals, and the students' union. This group decided to create a programme to enable students to learn effectively about plagiarism and how to avoid it. The bulk of the chapter details the development of this programme, including the principles that underpinned it, and the teaching and learning materials that were developed. The chapter also reports the results of a pilot study of this programme, and the methods so far used to roll it out across the university. The chapter concludes with some reflections on the Brunel approach, and a look to the future.

THE UNIVERSITY'S STARTING POSITION

Plagiarism has been viewed as an increasingly important issue in UK higher education since the early 1990s. From the turn of the millennium the issue had caused widespread outcry—featuring heavily in both the popular press and specialist publications such as Times Higher.

Against this background, Brunel University became explicit about treating plagiarism as a serious issue affecting academic standards. In 2004, the university Senate supported a proposal to change the penalties for plagiarism in line with the existing definition, which explicitly aligned plagiarism with cheating in examinations:

Cheating involves taking unauthorised material into an examination, actual, intended, or attempted deception and/or dishonest action on the part of a student in relation to any academic work of the University, and includes aiding, or attempting to aid, another candidate in deception or dishonest action, or any attempt at such action, with intent to gain advantage. Plagiarism is the knowing or reckless presentation of another person's thoughts, writings, inventions as one's own. It includes the incorporation of another person's work from published or unpublished sources, without indicating that the material is derived from those sources. It includes the use of material obtained from the Internet. (Senate Regulation 6.44)

Severe penalties (Figure 1) were sanctioned for anyone found to have committed plagiarism, with the aim of creating a culture of "zero tolerance."

Up until this point, plagiarism had been dealt with by departments, often by the course tutor

Figure 1. Penalties for committing plagiarism at Brunel University

Level 1 undergraduate students	A fine of £100 and a severe warning
Level 1 undergraduate students (repeat offence)	Expulsion without credits. Barred from re-admission to the University
Level 2 and 3 undergraduate students	Expulsion without credits. Barred from re-admission to the University
Postgraduate students	Expulsion without credits. Barred from re-admission to the University
Students at undergraduate Level 2 and 3, and postgraduate students, committing offences without clear premeditation	Expulsion but permitted to retain credits and/or award to which the credits lead. Barred from re-admission to the University

Figure 2. Number of plagiarism cases and expulsions a Brunel University

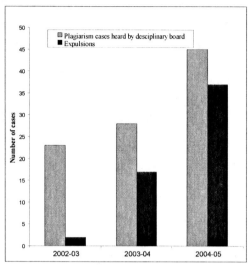

or senior tutor, with only the most serious cases being advanced to the disciplinary board. With the instigation of the "zero tolerance" approach, departmental practices adhered more closely to the procedures, and all suspected cases of plagiarism had to be passed on to the head of department (HoD), and then, if the HoD decided there was a case to answer, to the disciplinary board. This resulted in more students undertaking university disciplinary procedures accused of plagiarism, and more expulsions, as can be seen in Figure 2.

To complement this tough approach, the university recognised that it had a duty of care to its students. It convened a working group to bring together those who were currently working on the detection and deterrence of plagiarism in order to share best practice. The group was chaired by the head of registry (who has responsibility for the regulation of student disciplinary procedures) and invited a membership of: senior tutors; other interested academic staff; representatives from the students' union; the library; the Learning & Teaching Development Unit (LTDU); the graduate school; and Brunel International.

At that time, standard practice was to provide information to students about plagiarism in an introductory lecture when the students first arrived. Best practice included: providing details of the punishments for plagiarism in student handbooks or via lectures; running a compulsory lecture for all students in a subject area on plagiarism; providing details of how to reference correctly in student handbooks or on Web pages; and using electronic plagiarism detection software.

Based on the statistics (Figure 2), the working group felt that the zero tolerance approach combined with the minimal guidance outlined above was not working in deterring plagiarism. In addition, the working group felt that the university had a moral obligation to ensure that students really understood what plagiarism was and how to avoid it. The group was concerned that existing methods of presenting such information to students were lecturer-led and encouraged passive approaches to learning, and therefore were not sufficient to ensure that all students really *learnt* about plagiarism.

At the first meeting of the working group, the first author reported on the workshop session she had recently attended. This workshop titled "Detecting and Deterring Plagiarism" was run by Netskills[1]. Ostensibly a workshop about the use of Joint Information Systems Committee (JISC) plagiarism detection software[2], Netskills took the issue of plagiarism in its entirety, including how to educate students to avoid it. The working group was impressed by this approach and was inspired to create a programme to enable students to learn about plagiarism and how to avoid it.

THE DEVELOPMENT OF THE PROGRAMME

Four members of the plagiarism working party were asked to develop a programme for teaching students how to avoid plagiarising. They were the authors and:

- Sarah Batt (Union of Brunel Students): vice president with responsibility for education and welfare issues, 2004-2006, who made plagiarism her main campaign issue for her years in office;
- Mark Lycett (senior lecturer): then module leader for "Professional Development and Research," a module taken by all masters students in Information Systems and Computing, who was willing to pilot the programme with these students.

The team members were chosen because of their passion for the need to educate students about plagiarism. They also had day-to-day contact with students on plagiarism issues, and so had the requisite skills and knowledge in this area.

The team drew on a variety of sources to create the underlying principles of the programme. The first decision was on the format the programme should take. Brunel University operates on a devolved model where responsibility for teaching students falls entirely within the remit of their academic school. The only exception to this is information skills training, which is taught by the subject liaison librarian responsible for that school. It was not feasible for central service departments (library and LTDU) to undertake this programme with all students. In previous, similar instances, the LTDU had successfully used a "train the trainers" approach to teach the lecturers, who then taught the students.

In addition, more than one method of referencing is used at Brunel (specific styles by different subject areas), so a "one-size-fits-all" approach was not appropriate. Therefore the first principle was that the programme should comprise the "building blocks" of a session that could easily be taken by any lecturer and adapted for their own purposes. Materials would include briefing information about plagiarism, referencing, and the purpose of the seminar; facilitator lesson plan; student worksheet; handouts; PowerPoint presentation; and instructions for putting the session together. These materials would be provided as a "toolkit" for lecturers to use and adapt.

One of the main drivers for the programme was the need to ensure students actually learned how to avoid committing plagiarism, rather than just learnt a definition. The literature on pedagogic theory, especially Kolb's (1976) experiential learning theory, suggests that people learn by inputting information from concrete experience, or from abstract conceptual sources such as books or lectures. Information is then processed reflectively, or through active experimentation. Kolb argued that efficient learners use all four aspects of learning. However, most people develop a preferred learning style, which consists of a combination of a preferred style of inputting information and a preferred mode of information processing. The second principle was therefore that the session should be a student-focussed seminar that used a variety of pedagogical approaches to accommodate all students' learning styles.

Three of the four learning styles described by Kolb (1984) require an active learning experience for successful learning to occur. The third principle was therefore to ensure students had the opportunity to actively participate in the seminar in order to test their understanding and receive formative feedback.

The team's experience as teachers demonstrated that students tend to become fixated on the "grammar" of referencing ("Where do the commas go? Should this be a full stop?") and pay little attention to the underlying reason for referencing correctly. However, the team's individual experiences as learners suggested that students do appreciate specific "recipes" detailing exactly what should go where when referencing specific items in a particular style. Therefore, the fourth principle was to focus during the seminar on why referencing is necessary, as the academically acceptable method of avoiding committing plagiarism, and spend little time on the exact details of how to reference. These details would be provided for students as a handout to take away, so they would be able to refer to it when completing their assignments.

When determining the content of the seminar, the team drew on the information provided at the Netskills workshop (q.v.), in particular the exercise "Where do you draw the line," which was based on an exercise in Swales and Freak (1994) and also featured in Carroll (2002). The team also took into account that students would have different levels of awareness and understanding of what plagiarism was, based on their previous experience, including experiences at other universities or in other learning cultures.

Based on these principles and content, the seminar was designed to focus on:

1. Sharing of students' ideas and previous experiences
2. Presentation and discussion of theoretical constructs

3. "The rules"—Brunel University's interpretation of plagiarism
4. Peer learning by undertaking the "Where do you draw the line" exercise in small groups
5. Reflection on what is plagiarism and what is not plagiarism—applying theory in practice
6. Active experimentation in applying referencing techniques

THE SEMINAR

The seminar was split into four sections. The information in Box 1 is an elaborated version of the facilitator lesson plan. This is supported by a student worksheet and PowerPoint slides. Exemplars of all materials provided are available from http://people.brunel.ac.uk/~lbsrfcw/.

Box 1. Lesson plan for seminar

---

1. Purpose and Objectives

You should provide a short presentation on the purpose of the seminar, setting the concept of plagiarism into an appropriate academic (and subject) context. You may wish to use the PowerPoint presentation provided in the toolkit.

2. What Constitutes Plagiarism?   15 minutes

The objective of this section of the seminar is to review and discuss what plagiarism is. This involves students sharing their ideas and previous experiences; the presentation and discussion of the theoretical constructs of plagiarism; and the presentation of Brunel University's interpretation of plagiarism. The methods of transmitting information are active – involving small group discussion; plenary feedback; and slide presentation by you, as the facilitator.

➤ Ask students to form small groups and discuss the question 'What do you think plagiarism is?' **5 minutes discussion time**.

➤ If necessary, facilitate group discussions.

➤ Elicit feedback of three points relating to plagiarism from each group (plenary style).

➤ Following / during elaborating on feedback from the groups, ensure that the following points are raised (use the slide presentation as necessary):

o Whatever your view of what constitutes plagiarism, what is important is to understand what Brunel University views as plagiarism – it is the Brunel rules that must be followed.

o Plagiarism can be defined as "To take and use as one's own the thoughts, writings or inventions of another" (Oxford English Dictionary). Plagiarism therefore has two elements:

   • taking another's work; and
   • using the work as your own.

   If you take another's work but do not use it as your own – because you cite and reference it correctly – it is not plagiarism.

o Plagiarism can be:

   • copying – submission of someone else's entire work as your own. The original work could be from the internet, a classmate, or a student in a previous year;

(continued on next page)

Box 1. continued

- copying parts from a number of different books, journals, or internet sites, and linking the parts together with your own words;
- failing to indicate a direct quote (quotation marks should be used) in the text;
- paraphrasing or synthesising material from a book, journal article or internet site without acknowledging the source in the text;
- composing a paragraph by joining together sentences from a number of sources and not acknowledging them in the text.
   - Some reasons why people plagiarise (poor time management; failure to engage with the learning process; crisis at home; laziness). Emphasise that it doesn't matter what the reason is; there is no excuse for committing plagiarism.

3. Knowing Where to 'Draw the Line'   20 minutes
The objective of this section of the seminar is for students to apply theory about 'What constitutes plagiarism' to a concrete situation. Discussion following the exercise aims to highlight the discrepancy between what students and the University consider to be plagiarism, so students can adjust their mental constructs accordingly.

- ➢ In small groups, set the exercise 'Knowing where to draw the line'. Encourage discussion among participants about their reasoning. **10 minutes discussion time**.
- ➢ If necessary, facilitate group discussions.
- ➢ Elicit feedback of where each group would draw the line (plenary style).
- ➢ Feedback to students that **Brunel University** would draw the line between 4 and 5 (i.e. 4 is plagiarism; 5 is not). Research (Carroll, 2002) has shown that students generally tend to draw the line between 2 and 3 – they do not recognise 3 or 4 as plagiarism.
- ➢ Answer questions and facilitate whole group discussion.

4. Avoiding Plagiarism   15 minutes
The objective of this section of the seminar is for students to identify the stages involved in academic writing, to understand how plagiarism avoidance techniques can be built into this process, and to practise different types of citing and referencing techniques using concrete examples.

- ➢ Raise idea that avoiding plagiarism is something that needs to be built into all stages of academic work:
   - Reading and Note-taking
      - Where exactly did the information come from?
      - Can I express its meaning in my own words?
   - Drafting
      - Have I embedded references in the text as I write?
      - Have I got an up-to-date list of references?
   - Writing
      - Am I drawing together information from a variety of sources and creating an expression of my own understanding?
   - Proof-reading
      - Have I referenced everything that wasn't my own idea?
      - Have I checked that all my quotes are accurate?
      - Have I checked that the citations in my text cross-reference with the reference list?
- ➢ Introduce the principles of citing references in the body of the text. Detail the three main types of citing (citation, quotation, secondary citation).
- ➢ Ask students to discuss what the crucial elements are in these citations, and why. **5 minutes discussion time**
- ➢ Provide feedback on the reason for the essential elements:
   - Citation – Authors, date of work (shows not your work);
   - Direct Quote – Authors, date of work (shows not your work) PLUS quotation marks (shows not your words); page number (helps people find it);
   - Secondary source – Author and date of original source (shows who did the work) AND author and date of the source you read (shows you have taken their interpretation of the original work), and page number (helps people find it).
- ➢ Distribute one of the following to each group – monograph, edited or collected work (with 1 chapter indicated), journal (with one article indicated), print out of a webpage (if no internet access in the room).
- ➢ Ask students to read the information in their worksheet about the style of referencing. Ask students to discuss where they would find the information. You need to write a bibliographic entry for each of their items. **5 minutes discussion time**
- ➢ Answer questions.

5. Summary
A brief summary of the session, emphasising the sources of help available to students.

APPLICATION OF THE SEMINAR

The purpose of the seminar was to change the way Brunel students conceived of plagiarism and to enable them to use techniques to avoid committing plagiarism in their work. In order to determine whether the seminar had the desired impact, the team piloted the session with several groups:

- 120 masters (taught postgraduate) students in Information Systems and Computing, as part of the module "Professional Development and Research" (students in the UK and in Norway take this module).
- 170 international students, as part of their orientation programme.
- 45 undergraduate and postgraduate students in three mixed sessions as part of the Effective Learning Week programme of study skills workshops.

Students' feedback on the effectiveness of the seminar was collected via questionnaires (65 responses) and interviews (seven participants).

As can be seen in Figure 3, most students felt confident that they understood what plagiarism was and how to avoid it before taking part in the seminar.

However, as can be seen in Figure 4 most students felt that the seminar helped them to understand how to better avoid committing plagiarism.

Importantly, all of the student who responded "No" or "Not sure" when asked if they felt confident before the seminar reported that the seminar had helped them understand how better to avoid committing plagiarism. All the 12 percent of students who were "Not sure" if the seminar has helped them understand how to avoid committing plagiarism did respond that the seminar had helped their understanding of what plagiarism was.

The four aspects of the seminar that students found most useful were (1) the examples of how to cite/reference; (2) the "Where to draw the line" exercise; (3) the explanation of what plagiarism is and "discussing what plagiarism is and isn't"; and (4) guidance on how Brunel interprets plagiarism (Figure 5).

The findings that students still learnt from the seminar, even though they thought they understood what plagiarism was and how to avoid committing it, is powerful support for our

Figure 3. Proportion of students who felt confident they understood about plagiarism before the seminar

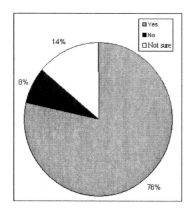

Figure 4. Proportion of students who felt the seminar helped them to better understand how to avoid committing plagiarism

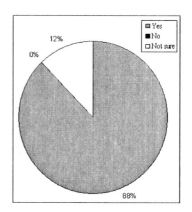

Figure 5. Aspects of the seminar that students found most useful

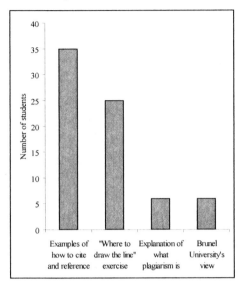

assertion that existing methods were not helping students learn. One student even said: "I thought I knew what plagiarism was." There are a number of reasons why this might be the case. Referencing and avoiding plagiarism are "often taken for granted" (Burke & Hermerschmidt, 2005, p. 353) academic practices which lecturers, and students themselves, assume students understand. After all, a learner cannot know what they do not know and will be guided by the assumptions that their lecturers make implicitly or explicitly. The seminar was successful in helping students realise the limitations of their existing knowledge and strategies around plagiarism. This meant they were more motivated to learn successful strategies for avoiding committing plagiarism.

However, despite this positive feedback, the responses also indicated that there were students who were not confident and neither equipped, nor thought they had sufficient resources to support them in avoiding plagiarism when producing their assignments.

Students also commented on aspects of the session that could have been altered or improved. Sixteen students commented that they would have liked more examples of how to reference and six said that they needed more time—a longer session or an additional session with time in between.

Interestingly, the feedback showed that it is not just university staff who feels that plagiarism is a serious issue. One student, in reference to how penalties against plagiarism are enforced, expressed his frustration:

I think plagiarism has been talked a lot about. It is good that you mention it but it doesn't work in practice as I've heard... (laughs) because people have plagiarised, they have been caught for it, but they haven't been ditched out of the course...or Brunel. I don't like that. Maybe I'm too harsh, maybe I'm just fair, but when it comes to that I have nothing left over for people who plagiarise. (International student).

This illustrates that, for many students, committing plagiarism is not just about ignoring an externally imposed rule. Plagiarism constitutes an act of disrespect towards the academic community of which they are part. It undermines the academic practice in which they are engaged and potentially devalues their degree.

In addition to student feedback, the seminar was tested with a number of different facilitators to ensure that it could be delivered by individual academic staff using centrally provided resources. Feedback was collected by the programme design team through participant observation, and a debriefing session with the facilitators. It was felt that the seminar was a valuable addition to the academic programme, both for educating students about plagiarism but also for providing academic staff with a greater insight into students' understandings than the previous lecture-based format offered. As one academic commented "doing the plagiarism exercise...I think it very firmly indicated to us that the grey area that we thought would be a grey area *was* in fact a grey area and that they struggled with that...The engagement side of things was really important to me."

The masters module leader observed a tangible outcome of the seminar in a reduction in the number of cases of plagiarism within the group compared with the previous year. However, he admitted that, if detection procedures were stepped up, more cases might be discovered.

The feedback from the pilot study, detailed above, enabled the team to refine the seminar. In particular, the amount of time spent defining plagiarism was reduced because students were already familiar with this from existing methods. In addition, it clarified the two most important parts of the session: the emphasis on the "Brunel University way," and the discussion that followed the "Where do you draw the line" exercise. The former offered the opportunity to address any cross-cultural barriers, while the latter enabled students to test their own understanding of plagiarism, and construct a subject- and context-specific set of rules to follow.

CROSS CULTURAL FACTORS

At a university with a diverse student population there is a tendency to assume that plagiarism is exclusively the problem of international student groups. It is widely conceived that lack of proficiency in English language is a primary reason for second language speakers committing plagiarism, because, when writing in a second language, it is less easy to distinguish between your own words and someone else's (Swain, 2004). However, it is also increasingly acknowledged that cultural differences in academic practices are equally significant, that plagiarism is not a universal concept, and its rules for application are not universal (Swain, 2004).

Feedback on the pilot session with postgraduate students indicated that home students found the session equally as beneficial as international students. Interestingly, 18 of the students who responded to the questionnaire were studying for a Brunel degree at a distance in Norway, and their responses followed the same pattern as the UK-based cohort. One emerging pattern was the discrepancy in education around, and enforcement of, plagiarism regulations across UK universities and therefore the importance of communicating the expectations at Brunel. For example, when asked if he valued the session, one interviewee responded:

Yes, I did, when I did my undergraduate [degree] the rules on papers were virtually non-existent. I think they basically said...don't do it, it's naughty. That was about it and I never heard of anybody even getting their wrist slapped for quite blatant plagiarism. So, I think, if that's not the case at Brunel, and obviously it's not, then I think it was vital to communicate that, in quite strong terms, to the students. And I think that was done quite well, and you know the session had [books and journals to work with] and so, as I say, not having really worked with papers before its something that was useful, useful for me. (Home student)

When asked what the main differences between university study at home and in the UK, one international student volunteered:

It's a lot different... I think there's a lot of transparency, because the thing about plagiarism is non-existent in Pakistan, we used to rip stuff off the Internet and just make assignments up... assessments are... not the difficult to do back in Pakistan you can ask your friends to do it for you. (International student)

Another student commented: "There are so many different ways of doing this, including different teachers saying different things" (Norway-based student).

The three quotes above were indicative of students' perspectives. They reinforce the proposition that academic practices such as avoidance of committing plagiarism, and correct referencing, are part of our specific Brunel University culture. It is clear that students from *all* cultural backgrounds need help in understanding academic cultural conventions, not just international students. It is the university's responsibility to ensure that all Brunel students understand the ideology underpinning plagiarism and how to avoid committing it at Brunel. This was strong support for our proposal that the seminar session should be delivered to *all* students by their academic tutors.

ROLL OUT OF THE PROGRAMME ACROSS THE UNIVERSITY

The first underlying principle of the programme was that lecturers should deliver the seminar to their own students. This principle was built on practical factors—central support services do not have the capacity to deliver small group training to all students. However, two further issues strengthen this principle.

Firstly, piloting of the session showed that students ask subject-specific questions that are best answered by academic staff. This was particularly the case with issues of what constitutes "common knowledge." Secondly, evidence from other information skills training sessions has shown that attendance is greater for sessions embedded within the curriculum, rather than offered as an extra-curricular option.

Furthermore, feedback from the pilot sessions demonstrated the need for avoidance of plagiarism to be embedded in the conceptualisation of knowledge in a discipline, and integrated into every stage of the discipline-based academic writing process. Without this, there is a danger of the mechanical procedure of referencing being viewed as all that students need to know in order to avoid committing plagiarism.

The development of the programme from pilot to roll out across the university over the last 12 months has so far involved:

1. Construction of a virtual learning package, containing all the materials and information needed to deliver the seminar
2. Strategic targeting of those responsible for teaching and learning within each subject area
3. Training the trainers
4. Supporting "early adopters"

Construction of a Virtual Learning Package

In order for academic staff to deliver the seminar themselves, a toolkit comprising the "building blocks" of the session had to be available centrally. Brunel University uses a Virtual Learning Environment (VLE) to support modules. Most staff members are familiar with this system, so it was decided that this was an appropriate forum to use. The staff-only VLE module was constructed to provide all the "building blocks:" the rationale for the seminar; briefing information about plagiarism, referencing, and the purpose of the seminar; facilitator lesson plan; student worksheet; handouts; PowerPoint presentation; and instructions for putting the session together.

An important addition to these materials is a discussion board, where staff can exchange ideas, information, and good practice. This includes examples where teaching staff have tailored the materials for use with their own students in the context of their teaching. It is hoped that this repository of good practice will become self-sustaining in the future.

Strategic Targeting of Those Responsible For Teaching and Learning

In order to ensure top-level support at subject level for rolling the programme out across the university, the authors devised a workshop titled 'Helping Students to Avoid Plagiarism.' Staff responsible for teaching and learning within each subject area (Deputy Heads for Teaching and Learning, undergraduate tutors and/or undergraduate and postgraduate programme leaders, or a colleague of their choosing with specific responsibility for academic quality issues) were strategically targeted and invited to attend the workshop. It was hoped that, following the workshop, they would feel it appropriate to incorporate the seminar into their curricula, for both undergraduate and postgraduate students. The workshop involved modelling the seminar, after which participants were invited to discuss aspects of the session that they felt they could usefully adopt, and to explore how they might effectively integrate this into the curriculum. They were also encouraged to share issues and challenges that they had experienced when trying to support students in avoiding plagiarism and in detecting cases of plagiarism. Thanks to persistent and targeted awareness-raising about the sessions, the number of participants was high (19 participants) and all subject areas were represented.

The feedback received from participants confirmed the need for such a programme to be rolled out across the university. Feedback included the following issues.

- Where possible, compulsory (not seen as additional to the curriculum) seminars for first years should be scheduled after induction but before they begin writing their first academic assignment.
- Similar sessions already exist in some modules but tend to be in a lecture format. These should be combined with the seminar and used as a model for other modules.
- Staff should run a refresher session for final year undergraduate students, when more is expected of them in terms of academic writing. Plagiarism seminars could be combined with expectation setting/information giving sessions for dissertation students.
- "One-way" presentations on plagiarism may be making students unnecessarily anxious. A small-group, interactive workshop might provide an environment/opportunity to calm anxiety.
- There was a positive response to interactive exercises that encourage students to consider how to avoid plagiarism at all stages of the academic writing process. The practical study tips were particularly liked, such a using different coloured pens for author's words, author's ideas, and students' own analysis/ideas.
- Participants felt the "Where do you draw the line" activity should be made available online for students to access at any point, and that they should possibly be *required* to complete the online exercise.
- Participants would like more information on which to base case studies, for example, the percentage of students found to have committed plagiarism. They would like access to some details of actual (anonymised) Disciplinary Board hearings from the Union of Brunel Students to give the students a first hand point of view.
- Understanding plagiarism is part of some secondary school curricula, so this may impact on some students, but the university can't make assumptions that students understand what the Brunel rules and penalties are.
- The university should not make assumptions that postgraduate students understand what plagiarism is and how to avoid it from their previous university experiences.

- There was concern over the implications for future professional behaviour of plagiarism that is undetected/"unpunished" by universities.
- Participants were concerned about detecting possible plagiarism, and providing the necessary evidence for cases of plagiarism. It was agreed that further information on plagiarism detection software would be useful.

This positive feedback supports our assertion of the need for the seminar, and also validates the contents and design of the seminar. Attendees pledged to work towards embedding the seminar into the curricula for their students.

Training the Trainers

Following the successful workshop for strategic staff, it was clear that a number of specific lecturers had been asked to incorporate the seminar into their modules, but that the contents of the authors' workshop had not been cascaded down to them.

Therefore, the authors identified and set up two "train the trainer" opportunities in order to engage with lecturing staff regarding the issue of plagiarism, and to guide them in embedding the materials and approaches into their teaching practice.

The first of these was a staff development workshop modelling the seminar and discussing issues around plagiarism for academic staff interested in running seminars with own students. Eight members of lecturing staff attended this workshop.

In addition, a shortened version of the staff development session has been incorporated into the Postgraduate Certificate in Teaching and Learning in Higher Education and Brunel Associate Practitioner Pathway programmes. This will ensure that all newly appointed lecturers and graduate teaching assistants undertaking these respective

programmes are aware of the issues, the resources, and potential solutions in this area.

Supporting the "Early Adopters"

In addition to the author-led interactions listed above, three lecturers pro-actively expressed interest in running the seminar with their own students. On the assumption that roll out across the university operates on a snowball principle (not just top down), the authors offered additional support to these "early adopters;" support that it would not be possible to offer to all interested staff.

A senior lecturer in the School of Engineering and Design was planning a session on plagiarism for postgraduate students "based on my experience over the years with the problem." He had heard about the work that the plagiarism working party had been engaged in and contacted the authors for comment on his approach. The authors offered feedback and suggested that he might like to use the materials that the team had developed, which he did. In the spirit of collaboration, he allowed his slide presentation to be mounted on the VLE so other lecturers could benefit from his experiences.

Secondly, two Biology lecturers approached the authors with the desire to run the seminar with their second year undergraduate students. They were provided with training in the use of the seminar, and helped to use the VLE module to create their own materials. They also allowed their slides to be added to the VLE.

This reciprocity is another example of Brunel University staff working together across subject/department boundaries in order to tackle the problem of plagiarism.

However, despite such examples of collaborative practice, the roll out of the programme has not been as fast or as comprehensive as was hoped for. In particular, despite pledging to embed the seminar into the curriculum for all students, this has only occurred for Business & Management undergraduates, Biology undergraduates, Information Systems & Computing postgraduates, and Engineering postgraduates (around 10 percent of the student population).

REFLECTIONS ON THE DEVELOPMENT OF THE PROGRAMME

The authors believe that the main reason for the successful development of the programme was the strong, multi-faceted approach taken by the working group, involving representatives of academic staff, student support services, and the students' union in the development team. Such a collaborative approach ensured that plagiarism was not seen as being solely the responsibility of one section of the university, but an issue on which all those working to support students had something to offer. By working together something was produced which was truly greater than anything that could have produced individually.

The authors believe that the actual programme has been successful so far, and is likely to be successful in the future, for two equally important reasons. Firstly, the impetus for developing the programme came from the highest level in the university. This is essential in ensuring that a uniform approach is taken in all subject areas. Secondly, the programme development team were all enthusiastic, passionate individuals, committed to educating students in how to avoid plagiarising. They were willing and able to invest a significant amount of time in developing the programme, and advocating its use. This was essential to "sell" the seminar and its benefits to academic staff. Finally, the data gathered from the pilot project meant that there was evidence to support the arguments of the necessity of teaching students about plagiarism in this way. The seminar design was strongly underpinned by pedagogical

theory, but it was the quotes from students and evidence about the reduction in the instances of plagiarism for the pilot students that convinced many academic staff.

However, despite all this promise and goodwill, the roll out of the seminar has been disappointingly poor. There are a number of possible reasons for this, three of which will be explored here. Firstly, there was a change in the senior management team of the university, including the vice-chancellor and the head of registry. This has resulted in the loss of the strong top-down impetus behind the working party and therefore the roll out.

The other two reasons will be familiar to anyone who works in the higher education sector. Feedback from the student interviews highlighted that committing plagiarism is less about applying the mechanical procedure of correct referencing and more about understanding fundamental aspects of academic writing, such as drawing on literature to support your arguments. Interview conversations indicated that some students had difficulty grasping the need for, and purpose of, referencing. Not all students understood the "orchestration of voices" metaphor (Lillis & Ramsey, 1997) to make sense of their role in argument building and the construction of knowledge. One student expressed that they were "still not sure of the concept of literature review" and, when writing reflectively about their own learning experience, puzzled "why should I need those papers to know?" If these underlying issues are left uncontested, it will make it impossible to tackle plagiarism in the way proposed. If educating students about how to avoid plagiarising is to be truly successful, significant work needs to be done with students to help them understand the purpose, principles, and process of academic writing.

Finally, despite the very positive response and unanimous support for the seminar from academic staff, translating such a response into a change in the curriculum meets resistance due to the great pressures in the timetable. Lecturing staff reported that they feel unable to include such a staff-intensive seminar in the often already over-loaded curriculum. Accepting that a small group seminar produces better results is one thing; changing from a one-hour lecture for 400 students to 13 two-hour seminars is another.

The authors have, as yet, no solutions to these three barriers to roll out. However, the following section describes some first steps towards overcoming them.

NEXT STEPS

Despite the success of the development of the programme, there is still a great deal to be done, specifically in integrating the seminar into the curriculum. As the university enters this next phase of the programme development, we are taking a number of approaches to work towards the goal of every student at Brunel University learning how they can avoid committing plagiarism.

The authors continue to promote the seminar and advertise the VLE module to academic staff, both to individuals, and through the academic management structure. Part of this promotion involves running regular staff development workshops to "train the trainers" by modelling the seminar and facilitating discussion around the subject of plagiarism. The authors have also provided extra support to lecturers who are interested in moving towards the seminar delivery. This approach is showing some signs of helping to overcome the "over-loaded curriculum" barrier. For example, the authors adapted the seminar for delivery to 200 Business & Management undergraduates in a lecture theatre. The key underlying principles of emphasising the "Brunel University way," the small group "Where do you draw the line" exercise, and the plenary question and answer session were preserved, though all other elements of the seminar were removed. While this was arguably less successful that the small group seminar, the

student feedback indicated that is was more successful at helping them understand how to avoid committing plagiarism than the lecture had been. The lecturer, along with the management of the academic school, is now looking at moving to a small group seminar format for delivering this module as a whole.

The university has also been able to extend the level of support for the process of academic writing available to students at the point of need. There is now an Effective Learning Advice Service that provides support for students with all aspects of academic skills, and can work one-to-one with a student to help them avoid plagiarism in a particular assignment.

At our "train the trainers" workshops, we received feedback that staff would like a VLE to enable students to access additional resources and to practise their techniques outside the classroom and when they felt was timely. This was supported by students' requests to have access to more examples of "correct referencing" and more time to practise. However, we were concerned that such provision would lead to teaching staff referring their students to the VLE for a self-led approach rather than embedding the face-to-face seminar in the curriculum. The evidence from the pilot study showed that the most useful parts of the seminar for helping students to understand were those involving facilitator-supported discussion, so we decided not to develop such a resource. However, online guidance on the technicalities of plagiarism and correct referencing is available to students via the Library and Effective Learning Advice Service Web sites.

Subsequently, two members of academic staff and the first author are developing an e-learning package, which uses a range of interactive online activities to teach students how to reference correctly and avoid committing plagiarism. These activities are underpinned by strong pedagogical theory. This year-long project was funded by the Brunel's Curriculum Innovation Fund and includes an evaluation of the success of such methods of learning. It is not anticipated that this package will replace the face-to-face seminar. Rather, it will offer an additional tier of support for students at the point of need.

In addition, the second author is a partner in the Higher Education Funding Council of England (HEFCE) funded "Centre of Excellence in Teaching and Learning" (CETL) project – *Learn-Higher*. This project is exploring learner development across 16 UK universities. Each partner is working to develop resources and approaches on one aspect of student academic skills. This is complemented by research into the effectiveness of these resources and approaches. The aim is that the whole suite of resources will be available to all UK higher education institutions. As a result, Brunel University will have access to additional peer reviewed and student-approved materials to help teach students how to avoid committing plagiarism.

Finally, the university is in the process of updating its learning and teaching strategy, and the aim is to incorporate the issue of educating students to avoid plagiarism within this. It is hoped that this will re-energise the impetus for roll out.

There are no targets for roll out of the programme across the university, and no mechanism to make the programme a compulsory part of the curriculum. Instead it is hope the "softly, softly" approaches detailed above will support academic staff in moving from viewing the seminar as "a good thing" to implementing it in practice.

CONCLUSION

A recent newspaper article (Davies, 2006) reported the extent of the UK problem of plagiarism in an online world. Coventry University had implemented the use of the JISC plagiarism detection software (q.v) and discovered 237 cases where students had committed plagiarism. Brunel University has yet to implement the use of this software universally, but we hope that the efforts described in this case study will mean that, when we do, we will catch fewer students out than Coventry did.

The authors are not proposing that the programme described here is a panacea to solve the problem of plagiarism. Instead, it is hoped that the process used to develop this programme may inspire others. The authors consider the key elements of the Brunel University approach to be as follows:

- There was very strong top-level support for addressing the issue of plagiarism through a combination of deterrent, detection, and education.
- There was a close working relationship with the student union. Sarah Batt (the vice-president for education and welfare) stayed in office for two years, and made plagiarism the main campaign issue of her term. Both the university and student union benefited from knowledge of the variety of support options available to students facing this issue.
- There has been pro-active collaboration between central services and different academic subject areas to ensure top-level support is translated into support at lecturer level.
- There is a single point of reference in the university about the correct method of referencing (taking into account the use of different referencing conventions).
- This standardised information is used in student handbooks detailing what plagiarism is; the penalties; and how to avoid it through correct referencing.
- Students have the opportunity to learn what plagiarism means for them, and how they can avoid it, through small group learning via the seminar.
- The seminar designers worked to understand how academic staff interact with students, and so ensure it is as easy as possible for

staff to provide the seminar for their own students.

- New academic staff members are taught what Brunel University considers to be plagiarism, how to teach their students to avoid it, how to detect it, and what the procedures are for reporting it.

REFERENCES

Burke, P. J., & Hermerschmidt, M. (2005). Deconstructing academic practices through self-reflexive pedagogies. In B. V. Street (Ed.), *Literacies across educational contexts: Mediating learning and teaching.* Philadephia: Caslon Publishing.

Carroll, J. (2002) *A handbook for deterring plagiarism in higher education.* Oxford: Oxford Centre for Staff and Learning Development.

Davies, R. (2006). University catches 237 cheats who trawl the Internet. *The Observer,* September 10, 2006.

Kolb, D. A. (1976). *Learning Styles Inventory: Technical manual.* Boston: McBer and Company.

Kolb, D. A. (1984). *Experiential learning: Experience as the source of learning and development.* New Jersey: Prentice-Hall.

Lillis, T. M., & Ramsey, M. (1997). Student status and the question of choice in academic writing. *Research and Practice in Adult Learning Bulletin,* Spring, 15-22.

Swain, H. (2004). I could not have put it better so I won't. *Times Higher Education Supplement,* June 25, 2004, p.23.

Swales, J., & Freak, C. (1994). *Academic writing for graduate students,* Ann Arbor: University of Michigan.

ENDNOTES

[1] Information available from: http://www.netskills.ac.uk/content/products/workshops/range/plag.html

[2] Information available from: http://www.jiscpas.ac.uk/

Section III
EFL and International Students

Chapter VI
EFL Students:
Factors Contributing to Online Plagiarism

Teresa Chen
California State University, USA

Nai-Kuang Teresa Ku
California State University, USA

ABSTRACT

This chapter reports on a survey study that investigates English-as-a-Foreign-Language (EFL) students' experiences with online plagiarism and the factors associated with these practices among the students. With reference to the important factors concerning plagiarism identified in previous studies, the survey focused on students' awareness of the definition of plagiarism, their perceptions of text borrowing, possible causes of their plagiarism, the role of print versus electronic media in plagiarism, and teachers' policies and enforcement of these policies. Based on the findings from the survey, the chapter presents the students' perspectives and provides suggestions on ways to prevent students from online plagiarism. It is hoped that the chapter will contribute to a series of dialogues regarding text borrowing by presenting students' experiences and points of view.

INTRODUCTION

This chapter reports on a survey study that investigates English-as-a-Foreign-Language (EFL) students' experiences with online plagiarism and the factors associated with these practices among the students. In the literature on second/foreign language writing, there has been a series of debates on the authorship of texts as well as to what degree students should be expected to comply with the dominant writing norm. While there has been little scholarly agreement upon the notion of plagiarism (see Chandrasoma, Thompson, & Pennycook, 2004; Deckert, 1993; Pennycook, 1994; Sapp, 2002), in the midst of the debates the study takes a more practical approach, by examining students' perspectives in a context in which English language learners are required to accommodate the mainstream writing conventions, including the relatively dominant view on plagiarism. It is expected that without waiting for the debates to settle, the study can offer suggestions conducive to learning and instruction after investigating students' points of view on current practices in the real world. It also is expected that the study concerning Chinese-heritage students in Taiwan will provide a base for understanding similar challenges faced by English language learners in the other regions of the world.

Building upon previous research, this study is significant in three ways. First, the study presents an up-to-date picture of the problem in a non-western context. Many studies on plagiarism have been conducted in North America (Park, 2003), but relatively speaking, little research has examined the extent of plagiarism in non-western universities. This study fills the void and brings to light an urgent problem that all educators need to address. The findings from this study will also help both traditional and online educators to better understand the behaviors of their students, who are more diverse than ever before. Second, the study examines students' experiences with plagiarism in both their first and foreign languages. Previous studies (e.g., Sowden, 2005) indicate that unfamiliarity with a new writing convention (in this case the convention rooted in Anglo-Saxon heritage) may account for students' plagiarism offenses. The study seeks to reveal the role that dissonance between traditional and new conventions plays in the incidents of students' plagiarism. Third, the study provides another perspective in examining personal factors by including self-efficacy. Although little research has explored the relationship between self-efficacy and plagiarism, self-efficacy has been regarded as a critical element in understanding students' learning and achievements. Bandura's (1986) sociocognitive perspective regards learners as proactive and self-regulated, equipped with self-beliefs that control

their thoughts, feelings, and actions. According to this line of thought, those who can adequately evaluate their own capabilities can better acquire knowledge and skills than those who are unable to do so. This study attempts to use self-efficacy as a predictor for students' online plagiarism offenses.

BACKGROUND

Some educators and researchers find it challenging to squarely define plagiarism, but a review of the definitions of plagiarism in sources easily accessible to college students, reveals some common themes. The *Webster's New World Dictionary* for college students considers plagiarism as "the act of plagiarizing" and defines plagiarize as "to take (ideas, writing, etc.) from (another) and pass them off as one's own" (Neufeldt & Guralnik, 1988, p. 1031). Hacker's (1996) *Rules for Writers* states, "to borrow another writer's language or ideas without proper acknowledgement is a form of dishonesty known as plagiarism" (p. 353). *The Publication Manual of the American Psychological Association* includes plagiarism as one of the ethical standards for the dissemination of scientific information and states that "Psychologists do not present substantial portions or elements of another's work or data as their own, even if the other work or data source is cited occasionally" (p. 395). Furthermore, a Web search for a definition generates numerous results, which seem to be in agreement with the printed sources mentioned above when indicating that plagiarism is to present others' language or ideas as one's own without giving credits to the original source. Several definitions on the Web include phrases such as "a form of cheating," "the theft of ideas," "academic malpractice," and "intellectual property violation." These definitions present the modern view of plagiarism in the English speaking world, even though the root of this word can not be traced in the *Old English Dictionary*, which includes lexis of an earlier form of English used between the mid-fifth and the mid-twelfth century. The word plagiarism is said to have been derived from the Latin word *plagiarus*, meaning "literary theft" (Park, 2003).

In the modern English writing convention, plagiarism is equated with "cheating" and "dishonesty," and sometimes it even has the connotation of a "crime." Nonetheless, writing conventions vary from culture to culture, and also from time to time within a culture. Not only is plagiarism a "Western" idea, but also it was not prevalent and had not become institutionalized until capitalism became widespread in modern society (Prochaska, 2001). As McLeod (1992) pointed out, authorship is a concept very foreign to people from cultures in which no one can claim ownership of any words or ideas. In these cultures, language is perceived as common and accordingly, some notions concerning plagiarism, such as "stealing someone else's words" and "taking another person's idea as one's own" do not exist at all. McLeod (1992) also mentioned that in ancient times, in which originality and individualism were not valued, "writers borrowed freely from one another" (p. 12). She suggested that the notion of plagiarism had germinated alongside the rise of individualism and the idea of private property. Nowadays, in the English-speaking world at least, language has become something that can be owned. Writers are encouraged to reveal their original ideas and are required to acknowledge their sources when using others' words or ideas.

Such cultural values also are reflected in research and instruction in academia, especially in academic practices within the cultures where "originality" and "change" are regarded as synonymous with "progress." Researchers follow the scientific methods, build on previous research findings, engage in problem-solving processes, and strive for innovative discovery. While they stand on their predecessors' shoulders in order to look for new insights, it is customary and oftentimes considered ethical for them to acknowledge these predecessors' contributions. It widely is acceptable in these cultures, for example, the modern western culture, that granting ownership to original ideas or attribution encourages innovation, which is the cornerstone of social progress. Following this line of thought, instruction explicitly or implicitly delivers the values, sets the standards of scholarship, and molds students to meet the standards. Value-laden standards prevail in academic policies and instruction, particularly in those on how to avoid plagiarism (see Yamada, 2003).

In the meantime, educators also conduct research on student plagiarism with the purposes of understanding the phenomenon and to deter students from such practice, which widely is considered as an academic problem. Especially in recent years, perhaps due to the widespread use of the Internet, plagiarism is on the rise (Auer & Krupar, 2001; Duggan, 2006; McKeever, 2006). Previous studies (e.g., McCabe, 2001) on plagiarism document this rising trend and look into possible factors that may account for this growing problem. Studies (e.g., Szabo & Underwood, 2004) that investigate native English-speaking students pay attention to personal and situational/contextual factors, whereas research (e.g., LoCastro & Masuko, 2002) involving non-native speakers also takes cultural factors into consideration.

Personal factors include students' personal circumstances and personal traits (Bennett, 2005). Students' insufficient personal investment in education, habits of procrastination, study skills, self-esteem, and desire for good grades are among the many personal factors associated with plagiarism. In addition, students' Internet experience and use as well as gender are considered important factors in previous research investigating academic offenses (Underwood & Szabo, 2003). Underwood and Szabo (2003) found that students who use the Internet frequently for their coursework tend to plagiarize more often than those who use it less frequently. Males seem to be associated with higher frequencies of academic misconduct, including plagiarism

(Roberts, Anderson, & Yanish, 1997; Szabo & Underwood, 2004). Nevertheless, Underwood and Szabo (2003) cautioned against painting a "female-good and male-bad" (p. 475) picture regarding academic offenses. Their data indicated that both gender groups might commit the offenses, though the incentives that triggered the offenses were different.

Self-efficacy is often used as a reliable predictor for factors contributing to students' academic performance, though it is far less often adopted in research on plagiarism. Self-efficacy refers to the perception of one's ability to perform a given task (Bandura, 1986, 1997). According to Bandura's hypothesis, self-efficacy plays a vital role in influencing an individual's choice of activities, the effort applied toward the activities, and the individual's persistence. The self-efficacy theory holds that people evaluate their capability to perform tasks based on their mastery accomplishments, observation of the other people's experiences, feedback from others, and physiological indexes.

Research based on Bandura's theory has demonstrated that students who believe that they can self-regulate or control their own learning tend to set higher academic goals and attain higher levels of performance than students who do not think they can manage their own learning (Schunk, 1991; Zimmerman, 1990). The latest research made efforts to examine the relationships between plagiarism and other psychological factors such as self-esteem and self-efficacy (Marsden, Carroll, & Neill, 2005). Self-esteem emphasizes the component of "affection" in one's self-belief while self-efficacy is defined as the judgment of one's competency (Pajares & Schunk, 2001). In referring to academically dishonest behaviors, Marsden et al. (2005) found self-efficacy had a strong relationship to plagiarism, cheating, and falsification. In this study, we also examined how students perceive their capabilities and how those perceptions are related to plagiarism.

Situational factors include easy access to on-line materials and lack of academic policies and enforcement to deter students from plagiarism (Bennett, 2005). In a study on plagiarism among graduate students, Love (1998) identified five sets of contributing factors: negative personal attitudes, lack of awareness, lack of competency, pressure, and leniency of professors. The study shows that situational factors are stronger than personal factors (respectively labeled external and internal factors in the study), with pressure (in terms of grades, time, or task) the strongest. McCabe (2001) also revealed that contextual factors had the strongest influence on students' cheating behaviors.

Cultural factors include differences in writing conventions, perceptions of text borrowing across cultures, and different approaches to learning. Researchers (e.g., Brennan & Durovic, 2005; Sowden, 2005) have pointed out that such cultural differences have generated claims of plagiarism against inexperienced student writers who are not familiar with Anglo-Saxon writing conventions. While the student writers acquire the new academic discourse and obtain concepts and skills important for them to become members of the mainstream scholarly community, they inevitably draw on their cultural resources and rely on their own writing conventions and learning approaches, which may not meet their new scholastic demands. Pennycook (1994) suggested that educators approach students' plagiarism in consideration of the context, including the students' concept of authorship, cultural and educational backgrounds, prior knowledge, and language competency. He also cautioned against viewing the western tradition as superior to other cultural practices and taking for granted that there is only one acceptable academic practice in the world.

The students' original approaches to learning and their assumptions concerning education play a vital role in their language learning process.

To understand these backgrounds, scholars have examined the cultures that students bring with them to language classes, though the cultures referred to in the research usually correspond to homogeneous ethnic traditions. For example, Jin and Cortazzi (1998) claimed that students' approaches and assumptions concerning learning had cultural roots, which shaped the students' perceptions of language learning. They used the term "culture of learning" to include culturally-based ideas about proper class behaviors and learning processes. Culture of learning is rooted in the cultural tradition of a society and is influenced by the social-economic conditions in the context. Several studies (e.g., Brenna & Durovic, 2005; Sapp, 2002) on plagiarism by Confucius-heritage students suggest that their culture of learning is in several ways at odds with the western approaches to learning. For instance, when copying text which is believed to belong to all, including the teachers, students do not deem it necessary to cite the source, which is, by default, known to all (see Bowden, 1996). Moreover, imitation and memorization are considered pedagogically valuable, on which base students obtain their understanding and share their work for others to imitate. Comparative studies (e.g., Jin & Cortazzi, 1998; Li, 2003) on cultures of learning provide a reference point to interpret student actions with regard to plagiarism. However, such research should be approached with caution because it easily can run the risk of oversimplification and ethnocentrism.

The limitations of the comparisons do not invalidate the studies, but they do restrict the kinds of findings that can be generated (LeTendre, 1999), and thus may unfortunately lead to stereotypes or prejudice. Based on the differences, cultural dichotomies, for example, individualism-holism and egocentric-sociocentric, have been constructed to contrast the West versus the rest (Hermans & Kempen, 1998). In particular, individualism-collectivism and its related constructs have been researched actively in American versus Asian contexts (Vandello & Cohen, 1999). Although the studies yield an understanding of second/foreign language learners' academic practices, they are problematic in that, while attributing students' behaviors simply to ethnic/cultural backgrounds, the studies obscure the intricate nature of the difficulties faced by the students. Because factors contributing to plagiarism are complex and multi-faceted, the study attempts to understand it holistically by incorporating the three sets of factors (personal, situational, and cultural) discussed previously.

ISSUES AND PROBLEMS

The issues associated with plagiarism not only frustrate teachers but also confuse students, especially English language learners. After teaching at a university in Beijing, China, Sapp (2002) reflected on his experience in confronting plagiarism and lamented his transformation from an engaging teacher to "a single-minded guardian of academic honor" (p. 72). Meanwhile, his students, who believed that cheating is a skill that they should master in order to compete in the global economy, challenged the "unfair" demand for academic honesty amid corporate scandals, government misconduct, and social injustice. The conflict in values creates dissonance, which can only be diminished through ongoing dialogues and mutual understanding among the concerned parties. This study set out to contribute to the series of dialogues by presenting students' experiences and perspectives. The elemental questions that guided this study are the following:

1. Is there any association between frequencies of plagiarism and possible contributing factors, such as gender, accessibility to computers, computer proficiency, English proficiency, self-efficacy, teachers' reinforcement, and students' understandings of plagiarism?

2. What are the students' perceptions of text borrowing and plagiarism?

Method

This study took place in four urban universities located in northern, central, and southern regions in Taiwan. The participants were a total of 235 junior undergraduate students (51 males and 184 females) who were English majors enrolled in second-year English composition classes. The students ranged in age from 20 to 25 years, with a mean age of 21.5 years. Survey participation occurred during class time two weeks before the final exams and was voluntary and anonymous.

The study used the following two instruments for data collection: (a) Bandura's Scale of Self-efficacy for Self-regulated Learning (Bandura, 2001) and (b) a self-report survey on students' perceptions and experiences with plagiarism. The two measures, like many other self-report instruments, certainly have their limitations, of which most noticeably is that the results completely rely on the participants' truthfulness in responding to the measures. It is true that performance-based measures may better meet the criterion of trustworthiness, but considering the practicality of data collection, the study had to adopt self-reported instruments in order to answer the research questions.

The construct of self-efficacy was the specific variable that was hypothesized to be associated with students' self-efficacy perceptions, gender, and frequencies of L1 and L2 plagiarism. Participating students were asked to rate their perceived capability in using various self-regulated learning strategies, such as concentrating on tasks, memorizing tasks or important concepts, organizing projects, planning ahead, seeking assistance or resources, and participating in class discussions. The students rated their self-regulated learning efficacy on 11 items using a 7-point Likert-type response scale (1= "not very well at all" to 7 = "very well").

All participants also were asked to voluntarily self-report their perceptions on and experiences with plagiarism. With reference to the important factors concerning plagiarism identified in previous studies, the survey on plagiarism solicited information on students' awareness of the definition of plagiarism, their perceptions of text borrowing, possible causes of their plagiarism, the role of print versus electronic media in plagiarism, teachers' policies and enforcement of the policies, and the trends for online plagiarism. In addition, the survey collected demographic data, such as gender, students' self-rated computer competency, numbers of years using computers, accessibility to computers, and degree of English proficiency.

Findings and Discussion

The findings indicated the prevalence of plagiarism among the participating students, with 73.6 percent of the respondents admitting to having plagiarism in English (L2) and 62.1 percent in Chinese (L1). Given the fact that many of the respondents' perceptions of plagiarism were to some degree different from the western notion of plagiarism, the practice of plagiarism to which the students admitted could have been less pronounced than it would have been when the western notion had been applied. For instance, the majority of the students (82.4 percent) did not consider "copying verbatim from the text *with the addition of one's own ideas*" plagiarism. It is not likely that these students would have admitted to plagiarism when they had inserted their ideas into a piece of text that they had copied verbatim. As long as the piece of text included their ideas or words, they simply did not consider such practice of text borrowing plagiarism. The findings revealed the students' confusion about the notion of plagiarism, which in turn suggested that the practice of plagiarism could have been even more widespread than that which was reported by the participating students.

The data analysis did not suggest a statistically significant correlation between frequencies of plagiarism and the possible contributing factors identified in the study. However, the descriptive and correlation analyses of the factors provide a reference point for the exploration of the reasons behind students' plagiarism in both L1 and L2. The discussion below first provides an overview of the participating students' experiences with and attitudes towards plagiarism, and then summarizes the findings obtained from the analyses of the contributing factors.

Experiences with and Attitudes Towards Plagiarism

As discussed previously, the majority of the participants plagiarized both in L1 and L2. The findings also revealed a parallel pattern regarding the frequencies of the students' plagiarism in both languages. Most of the students (34.5 percent in L1 and 44.7 percent in L2) reported that they had committed the offenses in 20 percent of their assignments; few (5.5 percent in L1 and 4.3 percent in L2) had plagiarized for every single assignment. Figures 1 and 2 show the frequencies of the students' plagiarism offenses when they worked on their assignments in L1 and L2, respectively.

Not only were the extent and frequency patterns of plagiarism similar in L1 and L2, but also were the sources that the students used for their plagiarism. The respondents identified the Internet (81 percent for L1 and 86.5 percent for L2) and print media (19 percent for L1 and 13 percent for L2) as the two major sources (see Figure 3). For those who plagiarized via the Internet, they started with search engines, among which the Google

Figure 1. Frequency of plagiarizing assignments in L1

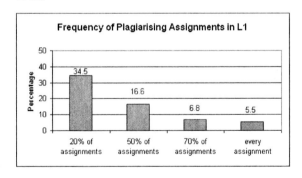

Figure 2. Frequency of plagiarizing assignments in L2

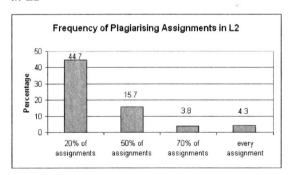

Figure 3. Sources of plagiarism for Chinese (L1) and English (L2) assignments

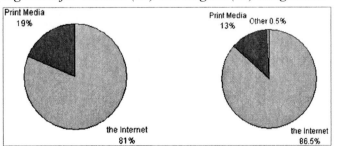

Figure 4. Attitudes toward plagiarism

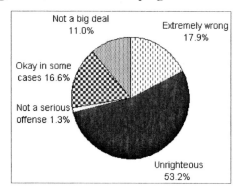

site was the one that was mentioned most often by the students.

With regard to the students' attitudes toward plagiarism (see Figure 4), the majority of them understood that it was not acceptable, with 53.2 percent of them considering it an "unrighteous" behavior, and 17.9 percent viewed plagiarism as "extremely wrong." Nevertheless, it is noteworthy that almost 30 percent of the respondents had lax attitudes, with 16.6 percent of them indicating that "it depends, it is okay to plagiarize in some cases," and 11 percent thought that "plagiarism is not a big deal."

The findings on students' experiences with and attitudes towards plagiarism showed that the majority of the students were willing to take risks in committing the offenses even though most of them realized that plagiarizing was not a proper behavior. Among the students who plagiarized, the minority of them had plagiarized for more than 50 percent of their assignments. The findings suggested the need to understand the incentives or stimuli that led to the offenses. Why did so many students plagiarize? Why did they plagiarize for one assignment but not for another? Moreover, as indicated by the students, the Internet was the major source of plagiarism. What were the students' perceptions of text borrowing from the Internet? The following discussion aims to answer these questions by providing information

about the factors that contributed to the students' plagiarism.

Personal Factors

The personal factors explored in this study included history and proficiency of computer use, English proficiency, and self-efficacy. In general, the majority of the students reported easy access to the Internet. The demographic survey pointed out that 91.9 percent of the students owned personal computers. About 80 percent of them had used the computer for more than four years. (Over 42.1 percent of the students reported that they had used computers for seven to 10 years; 37.9 percent of them for four to six years.) As shown in Figure 5, most students were skilled computer users; 63.4 percent of them reported an intermediate level of computer competency (i.e., being able to use a variety of productivity tools) and 15.3 percent reported an advanced level (i.e., being able to use multimedia editing software). Almost 60 percent of the respondents reported that they had spent more than 10 hours every week on the computer (see Figure 6).

The students' computer-using profiles provide a backdrop for the understanding of their plagiarism. Different from Underwood and Szabo's (2003) study, which showed that frequent Internet users (for coursework) had plagiarized more often, the present study did not find a correlation between the frequencies of students' plagiarism and their computer accessibility and competency. The findings from the present study suggest that with adequate access to the Internet and operative knowledge of the computer, students could engage in Internet plagiarism with ease if they chose to. Those who plagiarized most often were not necessarily frequent or advanced computer users.

With regard to English proficiency, 28.9 percent of the participants identified themselves as having an advanced level of proficiency, 63.4 percent with an intermediate level, and 6 percent with a basic level. The independent t-test revealed that there

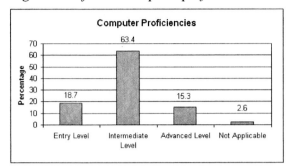

Figure 6. Self-rated computer proficiencies

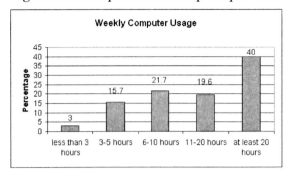

Figure 5. Hours spent on the computer per week

was no significant difference among the self-report scores on the measurement of English proficiency for the sample of male and female students. The data also did not suggest a statistically significant relationship between the frequencies of students' plagiarism and their self-rated English proficiency, in spite of the fact that 44.4 percent of those who had admitted to plagiarism in English attributed such practices to their difficulties expressing themselves in English and 30.6 percent to their inadequate English writing ability. The finding showed that the students' English proficiency was one of the key factors that triggered plagiarism offenses. Nevertheless, the finding did not imply that the lower the students' English proficiency was, the more frequently they had plagiarized in English.

On the self-efficacy measure, the mean obtained for the male group was 4.34 (SD = 0.87) and 4.64 (SD = 0.75) for the female group. An independent t-test revealed that there was a statistically significant (F [1, 322]=6.06, P< .05) difference among scores on the self-efficacy measure for the male and female groups. The findings indicated that the female group had a higher level of self-efficacy than did the male group. That is, the female participants perceived that they were able to manage their study (e.g., by applying learning strategies or resisting distractions), whereas their male counterparts rated themselves

as less able. However, there were no significant differences indicated on the self-reported scores of L2 plagiarism frequencies (F [1, 232]= .32, P>.05), L1 plagiarism frequencies (F [1, 232]= 1.77, P>.05) and self-efficacy. The degrees of the students' self-efficacy were found to not be correlated with their frequencies of plagiarism. The limited items in describing specific domains (such as subject and course contents) in which the students plagiarized might have accounted for the finding. Instead of adopting items general to all domains, future studies should direct students to specifically evaluate their capabilities in English writing. Further studies using more objective measures, such as GPA or teachers' ratings, are also needed in order to validate students' self-reports of self-efficacy and plagiarism in the specific domain.

Situational Factors

The study examined the following two situational factors: (a) policies on, and enforcement of, disciplinary measures for cheating and plagiarism and (b) the availability of the Internet. The items that addressed the policies and enforcement asked the respondents to identify the "success rate" of their plagiarism, teachers' policies, and the consequences of their offenses when caught. It is astonishing to note the high success rate shown in the self-report data. Given the prevalence of plagiarism among the respondents, 65 percent of them reported that they had never been caught in L2 plagiarism, and 74 percent had never been caught in L1 plagiarism. Although there were policies on plagiarism and they were made known to the students in the English composition classes at the beginning of the semester, it looked as if the policies had not always been effectively enforced. About 50 percent of the participants reported that their instructors did not impose any specific penalty on students' L1 plagiarism. As for the policies against L2 plagiarism, one third of them indicated that their instructors did not enforce the policies. Some students reported that the instructors usually gave an oral warning; some others mentioned that the instructors deducted a few points, asked students to rewrite their papers, or gave an incomplete grade. Evidently, from the students' points of view, the instructors were not very serious about the policy on plagiarism. The lax enforcement in turn might have served to nurture the seeds for plagiarism, as it became a practice associated with "low risk" and "high reward."

In addition to the lax enforcement that might have encouraged plagiarism, the students were also tempted by the availability of the Internet, which as a global repertoire of educational materials offers abundant opportunities for text borrowing. Fifty-six percent of the students perceived that the widespread use of the Internet had allured them and their peers to plagiarize. So far as the Internet is concerned, we believe that instructors should play a more important role in helping students resist the temptations of online plagiarism. As a matter of fact, there have been a variety of software programs that can effectively detect plagiarism from the Internet. Either as a policing or as an educational tool, the software can certainly help to minimize the offenses or to deter students' attempts to plagiarize. Unfortunately, from the students' self-report, it looked as if few instructors of these participating students had

taken advantage of such software programs. Because this study focused on students' perspectives, it did not obtain any data from instructors. Future studies on teachers' perspectives are needed in order to corroborate the students' account of teachers' enforcement and any assistance that they had provided to help students avoid plagiarism.

Cultural Factors and Students' Perceptions of Text Borrowing

In order to obtain data on students' perceptions of text borrowing, the survey included an open-ended question asking respondents to give a brief definition of plagiarism. The survey also presented 12 scenarios and had the students indicate whether each of the scenario consisted of plagiarism offenses or not. Their definitions, in general, resembled the western notion of plagiarism discussed previously, though one student included a note saying, "plagiarism is not necessarily bad." The majority of the students agreed that copying verbatim their peer's or other's work constitutes plagiarism (86.3 percent and 88.2 percent). However, a closer look at their responses to the other scenarios showed that the students' perceptions of text borrowing, to some degree, deviate from the definitions that they provided. Apparently, many of them considered copying word for word to be plagiarism but it is acceptable to paraphrase or use a few words or ideas without attribution. For instance, only 39.2 percent of the students equated "synthesizing online sources without citation" with plagiarism. Moreover, even though 74.5 percent considered copying verbatim from the textbook plagiarism, when it came to copying verbatim from the text *with the addition of one's own ideas*, only 17.7 percent associated the behavior with plagiarism. The venues for which the work is written also made a difference in their identifications of the offenses. On the one hand, 74.5 percent of them found it not acceptable to submit for publication work that includes about two lines of text copied from an encyclopedia, without giving credits. On the other hand, only 49 percent of them considered it plagiarism when the same work was submitted as a homework assignment to their teachers. The data not only suggested the convergence of the traditional and western notions of text borrowing but also demonstrated students' confusion about plagiarism.

The focus in Chinese-heritage education on "sharing excellence" (including good ideas and articles) with peers seemed to be in conflict with the western notions of plagiarism that the students were told to follow in the English composition classes. In an educational system that places much more emphasis on collaboration and harmony than on individualism and authorship, students had been taught to model and incorporate other individuals' masterpieces and points of view in order to strengthen their own writing, oftentimes without the need of attribution. As a matter of fact, the participating students had not been taught how to effectively synthesize reading materials nor to accurately cite and quote references until they had entered a university as English majors. Lacking western notions of plagiarism and practices, the students were not equipped with a clear definition of plagiarism and specific working knowledge about preventing it. In turn, many students did not

consider it a serious violation of academic honesty nor did they take its consequences seriously.

In addition to the similar patterns found regarding the frequencies and sources of students' plagiarism in L1 and L2, the factors contributing to their plagiarism in both languages were alike, except that students made note of their difficulties with English writing. Apparently, all the factors explored in the study play a role, though there were no correlations found between the frequencies of plagiarism and these factors. Table 1 below provides a summary of the prominent factors discussed previously. The overall findings from the study demonstrate the complexity in the attempt to explain EFL students' plagiarism.

SOLUTIONS AND RECOMMENDATIONS

Past research has provided a variety of recommendations for educators to use to combat both intentional and unintentional plagiarism. In the following, we summarize the recommendations that we consider important for teachers of EFL students in five dimensions and subsequently offer our suggestions based on the findings of our study. The five-prong approach is adopting plagiarism

Table 1. Factors contributing to EFL students' plagiarism

Factor	Findings
Perceptions of Plagiarism	Over half of the subjects perceived plagiarizing others' work as not right; yet, 27% perceive plagiarism as acceptable.
Definitions of Plagiarism	Copying word for word was considered plagiarism; paraphrasing or using a few words/ideas without attribution was thought to be allowable.
English Proficiency	Over 44% of the subjects responded as having difficulties with communication and expression in English.
Access to Computers/the Internet	Over 91% of the subjects owned personal computers; over 80% of the subjects reported the primary source of plagiarism in L1 and L2 was the Internet.
Lax Academic Policies/ Enforcement	74% of the subjects reported their instructors had not developed academic policies on students' L1 plagiarism; 65% of them reported their instructors did not fully enforce academic policies on L2 plagiarism.

detection tools, restructuring assessments, developing and reinforcing transparent academic policies (Conradson & Hernández-Ramos, 2004), providing tutorials or instructions, and taking students' cultural backgrounds into account. McKeever (2006) reviewed online detection services and suggested they be used in conjunction with human discretion. Walden and Peacock (2006) introduced another technical solution, but unlike the detection tools that aim at policing, the tool (known as i-Map) that they described integrates assessment into students' learning and facilitates their data-gathering and inquiry process. With regard to educational policies, Devlin (2006) questioned the punitive approach, such as outlining the penalties for offenses and advocates for the inclusion of an education-focused approach. As for the instruction that English language learners need, strategies on text-borrowing and paraphrasing, as well as inferential thinking (Yamada, 2003) are considered essential. In addition to educating students about plagiarism, it is suggested that while socializing their students into the English-speaking community, teachers should accept cultural diversity and recognize the difficulties faced by their students (Leask, 2006).

While this five-prong approach is helpful in deterring plagiarism, we believe that the following suggestions can further strengthen this approach: (a) having students examine different cultures of learning, (b) training students to become self-regulated learners, and (c) empowering teachers with training. The data in the study demonstrated that students' approaches to writing are based on their understanding of the Chinese writing conventions, which have a long history of development in their cultural and educational upbringing. In addition, before the students came into contact with English, they had acquired certain academic skills, learning strategies, and values that are not compatible with the standards for scholarship in the English-speaking world. A contrastive analysis of that incompatibility can foster a deeper understanding of the differences between their traditional and the new target language writing conventions. Whereas most instructions on plagiarism deal with the "whats" and "hows," such analysis can reveal the "whys" and "why nots" at an ideological level and give students a sense of purpose by providing rationale for the need to avoid plagiarism in their English writing.

In terms of instruction, it is also important for students to become aware of accurate citation methods, utilize more precise organizational skills to compose their writing, to identify original ideas, to evaluate and synthesize sources, and to monitor their own writing process. Furthermore, it is equally important for students to discover from the writing process, how to become independent learners who can regulate their own cognitive constructions. By eliciting students' self-knowledge on preventing plagiarism, teachers should be able to help students to use effective learning strategies, better budget their time for assignments, and become more accountable learners.

Students in this study reported that most of their plagiarism attempts had been successful. Their "success" may be attributed to the laxity of penalties imposed by the instructors and there are two possible reasons for the instructors' leniency. First, the instructors may not be fully aware of the mechanisms available to them for combating plagiarism. Second, the instructors, who speak English as a foreign language themselves, may not consider plagiarism a serious threat, nor worth waging a "war" against. As indicated in previous studies, social factors such as teachers' leniency are the strongest contributors to students' plagiarism, so it is important to empower teachers with knowledge and skills in order for them to deter plagiarism, at least in English writing. They may not agree with western writing conventions, but as instructors who prepare students for academic studies and professional careers in the interconnected world in which English is a universal language, they have the responsibility of ensuring that their students follow the target language writing conventions.

FUTURE TRENDS

With reference to our review of existing literature and to the findings of our study, we predict the future directions concerning plagiarism will be in the following three areas: assessment practices, cultural values, and computer technology.

First, it is likely that the incidences of plagiarism will continue to rise if the current assessment practices remain unchanged. Performance assessments, such as the process-approach to writing, have gradually emerged as valid measures to determine students' levels of knowledge and skills. Different from traditional instruments that only evaluate learning outcomes in test settings, performance assessments capture individuals' learning performances and provide evidence of their learning for analysis and improvement. Many writing classes have adopted performance assessments from which teachers are aware of their students' idea development and writing processes. However, in large classes where teachers have little opportunity to review students' multiple drafts, the process-approach is less common.

Second, the question as to what extent students should conform to the target language writing conventions remains an issue. It is true that language reflects cultural values (Harklau, 1999) and all language learning implies acculturation. Along with the spread of English around the globe, the values and ideologies associated with the language also penetrate its learners. Similar to the resistance to globalization around the world, there has been critique and resistance to the "hegemony of academic discourse" (Atkinson, 1999, p. 648). Resistance and acculturation are not mutually exclusive; they are likely to continue at the same time. It is also worth noting that when the Chinese-heritage students accommodate to the notions of plagiarism and intellectual property rights, they may apply those notions to their writing in Chinese.

Lastly, the advancement of computer technologies will certainly continue to attempt to find solutions concerning plagiarism. Even though the data in the study did not support the hypothesis that students who have easier access to computers and those who have higher computer proficiency are more likely to plagiarize, the majority of the participating students indicated that the widespread use of the Internet encouraged them and their peers to plagiarize online. As the new medium exacerbates the problem, it also offers possible means for tackling the problem. As mentioned previously, there have been several tools for detection and facilitating students' learning. We believe that like the approach to academic policies, a more instruction-focused, rather than punishment-focused, approach to software development will be more effective in dissuading students from plagiarism.

REFERENCES

American Psychological Association (2001). *Publication manual of the American Psychological Association* (5th ed.). Washington, DC: Author.

Atkinson, D. (1999). TESOL and culture. *TESOL Quarterly, 33*(4), 625-654.

Auer, N. J., & Krupar, E. M. (2001). Mouse click plagiarism: The role of technology in plagiarism and the librarian's role in combating it. *Library Trends, 49*(3), 415-432.

Bandura, A. (1986). *Social foundations of thought and action: A social cognitive theory.* Englewood Cliff, NJ: Prentice-Hall.

Bandura, A. (1990). *Multidimentional scales of perceived self-efficacy.* Stanford, CA: Stanford University.

Bennett, R. (2005). Factors associated with student plagiarism in a post-1992 university. *Assessment & Evaluation of Higher Education, 30*(2), 137-162.

Bowden, D. (1996, April). Coming to terms. *English Journal*, 82-83.

Brenna, L., & Durovic, J. (2005, December). *"Plagiarism" and the Confucian Heritage Culture (CHC) students: Broadening the concept before blaming the student.* Paper presented at the Australia and New Zealand Marketing Academy Conference, Fremantle, Australia. Retrieved July 3, 2006, from http://anzmac2005.conf.uwa.edu.au/Program&Papers/pdfs/8-Mktg-Edn/8-Brennan.pdf

Chandrasoma, R., Thompson, C., & Pennycook, A. (2004). Beyond plagiarism: Transgressive and nontransgressive intertextuality. *Journal of Language, Identity, and Education, 3*(3), 171-193.

Conradson, S., & Hernández-Ramos, P. (2004). Computers, the Internet, and cheating among secondary school students: Some implications for educators. *Practical assessment, research & evaluation, 9*(9). Retrieved October 6, 2006 from http://PAREonline.net/getvn.asp?v=9&n=9

Deckert, G. (1993). Perspectives on plagiarism from ESL students in Hong Kong. *Journal of Second Language Writing*, 2, 131-148.

Devlin, M. (2006). Policy, preparation, and prevention: Proactive minimization of student plagiarism. *Assessment & Evaluation in Higher Education, 28*(1), 45-58.

Duggan, F. (2006). Plagiarism: Prevention, practice and policy. *Assessment & Evaluation in Higher Education, 31*(2), 151-154.

Hacker, D. (1996). *Rules for writer* (3rd ed.). Boston: Bedford/St. Martin's.

Harklau, L. (1999). Representing culture in the ESL writing classroom. In E. Hinkel (Ed.), *Culture in second language teaching and learning* (pp. 109-130). Cambridge: Cambridge University Press.

Hermans, H. J. M., & Kempen, H. J. G. (1998). Moving cultures: The perilous problems of cultural dichotomies in a globalizing society. *American Psychologist, 53*(10), 1111-1120.

Jin, L., & Cortazzi, M. (1998). The culture the learner brings: A bridge or a barrier? In M. Byram & M. Fleming. (Eds.), *Language learning in intercultural perspective: Approaches through drama and ethnology* (pp. 98-118). Cambridge: Cambridge University Press.

Leask, B. (2006). Plagiarism, cultural diversity and metaphor – Implications for academic staff development. *Assessment & Evaluation in Higher Education, 31*(2), 183-199.

LeTendre, G. K. (1999). The problem of Japan: Qualitative studies and international educational comparisons. *Educational Researcher, 28*(2), 38-45.

Li, J. (2003). U.S. and Chinese cultural beliefs about learning. *Journal of Educational Psychology, 95*(2), 258-267.

LoCastro, V., & Masuko, M. (2002). Plagiarism and academic writing of learners of English. *Hermes, Journal of Linguistics, 28*, 11-38.

Love, P. G. (1998). Factor influencing cheating and plagiarism among graduate students in a college of education. *College Student Journal, 32*(4), 539-550.

Marsden H., Carroll M., & Neill, J. (2005). Who cheats at university? A self-report study of dishonest academic behaviors in a sample of Australian university students. *Australian Journal of Psychology, 57*, 1-10.

McCabe, D. L. (2001). Cheating in academic institutions: A decade of research. *Ethics & Behavior, 11*(3), 219.

Mckeever, L. (2006). Online plagiarism detection service – Saviour or scourge? *Assessment & Evaluation in Higher Education, 31*(2), 155-165.

McLeod, S. H. (1992). Responding to plagiarism: The role of the WPA. *Writing Program Administration, 15*(3), 7-16.

Neufeldt, V., & Guralnik, D. B. (Eds.). (1988). *Webster's new world dictionary of American English* (3rd ed.). New York: Simon & Schuster.

Pajares, F., & Schunk, D. H. (2001). Self-beliefs and school success: Self-efficacy, self-concept, and school achievement. In R. Riding & S. Rayner (Eds.), *Perception* (pp. 239-266). London: Ablex Publishing.

Park, C. (2003). In other (people's) words: Plagiarism by university students – Literature and lessons. *Assessment & Evaluation of Higher Education, 28*(5), 471-488.

Pennycook, A. (1994). The complex contexts of plagiarism: A reply to Deckert. *Journal of Second Language Writing, 3*(3), 277-284.

Prochaska, E. (2001). Western rhetoric and plagiarism: Gatekeeping for an English-only international academia. *Writing on the Edge, 12*(2). 65-79.

Roberts, P., Anderson, J., & Yanish, P. (1997, October). *Academic misconduct: Where do we start?* Paper presented at the Annual Conference of the Northern Rocky Mountain Educational Research Association. Jackson, Wyoming.

Sapp, D. A. (2002). Towards an international and intercultural understanding of plagiarism and academic dishonesty in composition: Reflections from the People's Republic of China. *Issues in Writing, 13*(1), 58-79.

Shih, H. P. (2006). Assessing the effects of self-efficacy and competence on individual satisfaction with computer use: An IT student perspective. *Computer in Human Behavior, 22*(6), 1012-1026.

Szabo, A., & Underwood, J. (2004). Cybercheats: Is information and communication technology fuelling academic dishonesty?. *Learning in Higher Education, 5*(2), 180-199.

Schunk, D. H. (1991). Self-efficacy and academic motivation. *Educational Psychologist, 26*(3&4), 207-231.

Sowden, C. (2005). Plagiarism and the culture of multilingual students in higher education abroad. *ESL Journal, 59*(3), 226-233.

Underwood, J., & Szabo, A. (2003). Academic offences and e-learning: Individual propensities in cheating. *British Journal of Educational Technology, 34*(4), 467-477.

Vandello, J. A., & Cohen, D. (1999). Patterns of individualism and collectivism across the United States. *Journal of Personality and Social Psychology, 77*(2), 279-292.

Walden, K., & Peacock, A. (2006). The i-Map: A process-centered response to plagiarism. *Assessment & Evaluation in Higher Education, 31*(2), 201-214.

Yamada, K. (2003). What prevents ESL/EFL writers from avoiding plagiarism?: Analyses of 10 North-American college websites. *System, 31*, 247-258.

Zimmerman, B. J. (1990). Self-regulating academic learning and achievement: The emergence of a social cognitive perspective. *Educational Psychology Review, 2*, 173-201.

Chapter VII
International Students:
A Conceptual Framework for Dealing with Unintentional Plagiarism

Ursula McGowan
The University of Adelaide, Australia

ABSTRACT

This chapter addresses the incidence of unintentional plagiarism among international students whose native language is not English. Terminology widely used in plagiarism policies and in the literature indicates an overriding view of plagiarism as an offence. I have developed a conceptual framework to present an alternative position. The framework provides a matrix for tracing the progress of an international student's induction into the culture and language of academic research. Based on insights from this framework, undergraduate students would be regarded as apprentice researchers who require guidance in developing skills and language for scholarly writing. During the early phases of their apprenticeship, students would be shown the use of genre analysis for "harvesting" genre-specific language. Feedback on instances of inadvertent plagiarism would be non-judgmental, constructive, and formative. I suggest that this approach should be adopted in the core curriculum so that all students can benefit from an academic apprenticeship and so avoid unintentional plagiarism.

INTRODUCTION

In the online environment of today, downloading information from Internet sources and re-using it in an undigested way has become commonplace among students. The evident increase in plagiarism associated with this practice in universities located in Australasia as well as North America and the United Kingdom is generally deplored in educational literature (McCabe, 2005; Park, 2003). The attention that has in recent times been given by the media to some extreme examples of plagiarism incidents, in particular those involving international students, has caused some Australian universities to review their plagiarism policies and procedures for sanctioning unacceptable conduct (Devlin, 2006). They do so in the hope of reducing the occurrence of deceptive student behaviour and avoiding media scandals. However, there are question marks over the effectiveness of policies and procedures in reducing the incidence of plagiarism or cheating.

At the heart of a perceived rise in plagiarism is the dual reality of higher education in the 21st century: the ubiquitous availability of online resources on the one hand and a phenomenal increase in international student numbers on the other.

Ubiquitous Availability of Online Resources

The first reality is that online resources have become a permanent fact of life. Successive intakes of today's "net-generation" students who cannot remember a world without the Internet have embraced the ever-increasing variety of online tools, from search engines to learning management systems, from e-mails and discussion boards to webinars, wickis, podcasts, streaming, and more (Oblinger & Oblinger, 2005). However, the runaway pace of online advances that have made copy-and-paste technology a matter of course has also resulted in the inappropriate use of this facility within the academic context. As the incidence of plagiarism cases detected continues to rise, tertiary institutions and individual academics are challenged in their traditional role of guarding and promoting intellectual integrity and upholding academic standards.

International Student Numbers

The second reality that now must be faced in many countries is that, in this era of the internationalisation of education, growing numbers of students are studying in a foreign country and in a language that is not their own native tongue.

Higher education institutions in North America, the United Kingdom, and Australasia are particularly sought after as destinations where students seek to gain both educational qualifications and improved proficiency in English. In Australia, the number of international students has been growing over the past decade, to the extent that they now form a sizeable proportion of the student population (Australian Government, 2004). In my own university, an internal report stated that in 2006 upward of 20 percent of students enrolled were international students, with some classes containing as many as 75 percent to 99 percent, and that by far the majority of these students originated from China and other Asian countries (Bain, 2007). For these students, still adjusting to their new cultural environments, and uncertain of their competence to meet unfamiliar learning demands, the Internet is a ready resource to be utilised, not only for content but also language that is more sophisticated than that of the English classrooms of their past. In the absence of skills for producing academic English to express their own views, and without the necessary knowledge of academic conventions, these students fall all too easily into the "trap" of plagiarism.

Concern and Purpose of this Chapter

Concern arises from the fact that assignments written by students for whom English is an additional language (EAL)[1] are easily identified if extraneous sources are used inappropriately. An EAL student's sudden burst of flawless, sophisticated prose within an otherwise basic, perhaps somewhat laboured or grammatically flawed text will alert an assessor to the likelihood of plagiarism. A quick Google check may confirm this suspicion, and the assessor then faces a dilemma, as it may be unclear whether there was an intention to deceive or whether the unacknowledged material was used innocently. A decision then has to be made: should the student be given another chance or is it an incident that must be reported?

There is a further dilemma that has serious consequences for student morale and the academic integrity of the entire university. While easily recognised occurrences of plagiarism are detected and the students subjected to procedures laid down by policy, there may be others whose downloaded material has been more successfully integrated with their own style and who cheat without being detected. The negative effect of blatant dishonesty by their peers ripples through the student community in several ways. If the action of students who cheat remains undetected, it will confirm them in their dishonest behaviour; some students who do not cheat and observe others "getting away with it" may be outraged but may also decide to follow their example; and students whose plagiarism was unintentional will feel the injustice of being punished for an offence they don't understand, as well as loss of face at the shame of being subjected to the university's investigative procedures.

The purpose of this chapter is to address these concerns by means of a conceptual framework which I have developed and applied in academic staff development (McGowan, 2006). The initial focus is on EAL students, particularly international students from China and other Asian cultures, who are studying in the academic context of Australian universities. However, I suggest that the insights gained from the use of this framework, if incorporated into the core curriculum, will potentially assist not only international students, but all students, native and non-native English speakers alike, who are in transition to tertiary studies.

Structure of the Chapter

I begin by presenting and examining terminology that refers to plagiarism in the recent educational literature and in plagiarism policies of Australasian universities. The effectiveness of the use of punitive terminology for avoiding or deterring plagiarism is questioned in the light of learning issues experienced by international students whose first language is not English. The conceptual framework is then introduced and I propose a pre-emptive curriculum-based solution to unintentional plagiarism that should also have the effect of freeing up resources for dealing more effectively with behaviour that is intentionally deceptive.

BACKGROUND

Plagiarism Terminology

To set the scene, the terminology currently in use in relation to plagiarism and academic integrity was extracted from a relatively small sample of recent literature selected from the vast array of publications in which the topic has been addressed. The sample of publications was taken from the discipline of education found on the Educational Resource Information Center (ERIC) database. The search was restricted to a small window of three years from 2004 to 2006 and to items whose titles or abstracts contained the terms "plagiarism" or "academic integrity." Terminology that either defined or described the issues was extracted from the titles, abstracts, and key words in the first 35 titles that appeared. The limitations set were somewhat arbitrary; however, the aim was simply to gain an overview of the range of terminology used in relation to plagiarism. For this reason, too, repetitions were in general elided. The results of this search are displayed in Tables 1 and 2 and grouped under the broad headings of student conduct and values (Table 1) and student skills and education (Table 2). A third table was drawn up from a list of terminology extracted from a 2005 "snapshot" of the plagiarism policies of Australian and New Zealand universities (ACODE, 2005). The purpose of Table 3 is to

Table 1. Plagiarism terminology: Student conduct / values

PLAGIARISM AS OFFENCE / LACK OF INTEGRITY	
CRIME / MISCONDUCT	**INTEGRITY / PROFESSIONALISM**
Admitting to cut-and-paste plagiarism	Academic / educational integrity
Cheating	Academic standards
Collusion	Attitude
Commit an offence	Core pillars
Consequences of cheating	Educational integrity
Consistent application of sanctions	Educational values are compromised
Copyright infringement	Ethical responsibility to inform…
Crime against the academic community	Ethicality of the practice
Cyber-plagiarism	Ethics
Cyber-pseudepigaphy (false authorship)	Ethos of integrity
Detection (software)	Range of values & attitudes
Deterrence	Responsibility
Digital fingerprints	Shared responsibility between student, staff, and
Drop below the radar	institution
Enforcement strategies	Standards
Fear of penalties…fear of failing	Transparency
Increased scrutiny	Trust
Infringement	Unfair
Investigate	Values
Lab reports routinely copied	Culturally loaded
Malpractice	
Metaphors of war and battle	
Misconduct	
Offence	
Ownership	
Perpetrators	
Protect against cheating	
Punishing with appropriate fairness/consistency	
Safeguards	
Sanctions	
Serial plagiarism	
Stealing	
Submit as their own	
Student behaviour	
Vigilant	
Violations	

Plagiarism Terminology in Educational Literature. Source: Keywords and abstracts in ERIC educational literature search 2004-2006. Retrieved October 3, 2006, from http://www.eric.ed.gov

provide an overview of the terminology that is conveyed to students and staff in Australasian tertiary institutions.

Plagiarism as Crime, Misconduct, Lack of Integrity

In Table 1 (student conduct and values) the first column lists terminology for student conduct in legalistic terms of (1) crime (commit, offence, malpractice, perpetrators, serial plagiarism, stealing) (2) misconduct (cheating, collusion, copied, infringement, violations) (3) detection (digital fingerprints, drop below the radar, fear, investigate, scrutiny) and (4) punishment (consequences, deterrence, enforcement, punishing, sanctions). As these lists are taken from only a small sample of recent literature, no doubt more expressions

Table 2. Plagiarism terminology: Student skills / education

PLAGIARISM AS PART OF THE LEARNING PROCESS		
INFORMATION / SKILLS	**INSTITUTION / CURRICULUM**	**ACADEMIC CULTURE / RESEARCH**
Adequate guidance Anti-plagiarism resources / sessions Avoid P. Clear warnings Consequences Educate users…what constitutes academic integrity Educative approach Explaining the precise nature of P. How to properly work with sources Information literacy May not know Mismatch between staff and student expectations Training & educational initiatives Unambiguous definition Understanding	Address causes of P. Assessment Assessment-led solutions Complex, culturally loaded concept—P. as intercultural encounter Culturally constructed concept Cultural influences Debate about pedagogical issues associated with P. Deter P by encouraging…engagement with cultural diversity Environment for holistic revision of institutional practice Faculty responsibility Lack of understanding of P. Low-stakes formative assessment (cf high stakes summative) Negligence rampant Professors neglect their casual responsibility Student diversity Western academic practice	Academic culture Acknowledge that ideas and language are necessarily derivative Document the enquiry process Focus on … issues of writing, identity, power, knowledge Disciplinary dynamics and discourse that underlie intertextuality (Chandrasoma 2004) Help to understand academic culture Improving language control Online detection…a positive teaching aid…diagnostic tool Poor scholarship Value of originality

Plagiarism Terminology in Educational Literature. Source: Keywords and abstracts in ERIC search 2004-2006. Retrieved October 3, 2006, from http://www.eric.ed.gov

can be found. Words such as "case," "theft," or more dramatically, "academic death penalty" are some that come to mind. Items listed in the second column, (integrity and professionalism), appeal to a sense of honour, responsibility, and fairness in terms such as ethics, standards, values, and honor codes.

Plagiarism as Part of a Learning Process

Table 2 (student skills and education) lists terms relating to plagiarism prevention as part of the learning process. These range from "information and skills" to "institutional responsibilities" and include references to "academic culture" and "scholarship." The educative strategies suggested include mandatory staff development requirements, provision of information and learning resources, as well as learning centre support

for students, appropriate assignment setting and assessment approaches, and—of particular interest for this chapter—"documenting the enquiry process."

Plagiarism Policies

Table 3 shows terminology extracted from Australian and New Zealand plagiarism policies. The general tenor of plagiarism policies is to combine disciplinary with educative approaches. Warnings to students include detection of misconduct such as "academic dishonesty" and "cheating;" prescriptive directives to give "scrupulous acknowledgment" performed "in the precise manner specified;" the categorisation of "levels of offences;" the requirement of a signed statement by students declaring that they "understand what plagiarism is and that the work is their own;" the existence of a "flowchart for dealing with plagiarism;" "conduct

Table 3. Terminology in plagiarism policies, guidelines and staff education (2005)

DEFINING / DESCRIBING PLAGIARISM		DEALING WITH / FORESTALLING PLAGIARISM	
PLAGIARISM	**ACADEMIC HONESTY / INTEGRITY**	**BY WARNINGS / DISCIPLINARY ACTIONS**	**BY INFORMATION / LEARNING / TEACHING / RESEARCH**
Plagiarism has no place in a university Plagiarism is a form of cheating... A person's words, work, or thoughts Another person's ideas, designs, words or works... Material that is not the student's own work Copying or paraphrasing another's work... ...take and use... ...pass them off... ...presenting it as one's own... ...borrowed material... Must be acknowledged clearly in the manner specified... Reproduction without acknowledgment... Unless the source...is clearly acknowledged Scrupulous acknowledgement	Academic honesty is a core value of the university...observe the highest ethical standards... University is committed to high standards of professional conduct... Academic integrity means honesty and responsibility in scholarship through respecting the work of others University upholds the values of academic integrity as fundamental to scholarship... The belief that honesty is at the core of exemplary scholarship codes of practice Accepted ethical practice...	Will be subjected to disciplinary action Serious P. may lead to exclusion from the University..... Penalising academic dishonesty and all forms of cheating...students...complete a cover sheet...which indicates that they have completed the work, that they understand what plagiarism is and that the work is their own... Detection software Discipline: procedure for dealing with breaches Student Academic Conduct Officer Offences (levels 1, 2, 3) Serious acts of plagiarism Natural justice, transparency, confidentiality, equity, representation / support, balance of probabilities Flowchart (for dealing with plagiarism) Plagiarism Register	Awarding due credit for honestly conducted scholarly work Responsibility of the academic staff to...teaching their students ethical learning and research practices ...responsibility of the students to acquire a clear understanding of how to avoid unethical practices.... University...to provide a secure, yet challenging environment for teaching and learning assessment policy and procedures Setting assignments that predispose students to go out and 'do' rather than to plagiarise / do not invite copy / paste methods of internet copying Mandatory staff development...includes a session on academic integrity Resources for staff...fact sheets...advice to staff Workshops on citation are available to students... Mandatory for first year students.... (address cultural differences) by printing handouts in languages other than English (e.g., Chinese characters...) Student have access to...learning centre Self-paced online modules for students... "Avoiding Plagiarism" website Unit outline contain a statement about academic integrity referencing guide Code of Ethical Conduct...the University and its students: responsibilities and expectations
Plagiarism Terminology in Educational Literature. Source: ACODE, 2005			

officers;" a "plagiarism register;" and "penalties," including the possibility of "serious plagiarism" leading to "exclusion from the university." These are high stakes indeed.

Most of this terminology will no doubt have a familiar ring to anyone in the area of tertiary education. However, the intention in drawing them together in such concentration has been to conceptualise the message they convey to the members—staff and students—of the university.

Analysis of Plagiarism Terminology

It comes as no surprise that the range of expressions from the perspective of "student conduct and values" (Table 1) is found to be considerably broader and more creative than that referring to the issue of "student skills and education" (Table 2). After all, the word plagiarism itself derives from the Greek word for "kidnapping," which aptly applies to cases of deliberate cheating, false authorship, and other forms of fraud.

A major thrust that emerges from the terminology is to represent plagiarism from the perspective of the institution, rather than the learner. The vocabulary of plagiarism as "crime" or "lack of integrity" projects an image of tertiary institutions as embattled fortresses, threatened, and requiring "safeguards" and "protection" of their values against the ill intent of students. It is an image that basically views plagiarism as synonymous with cheating. From this perspective the default position is "misdemeanour" which may, in certain circumstances, be treated with leniency or understanding. This theme is continued in the less legalistic but similarly high-minded appeal to moral values, with exhortations to students to commit to "fundamental" values of "honesty, trust, respect, fairness, responsibility" (Center for Academic Integrity, 1999).

The need for promoting these values in the face of widespread cheating has been amply demonstrated by large-scale research projects undertaken by McCabe (2005), and recurs in many smaller studies. A particularly challenging development is the growth of false authorship, or "cyber-pseudepigraphy," through so-called "paper mills" that sell personalised assignments on the Internet (Page, 2004). The point is well made by Carroll and others that when cheating goes undetected, it appears to be condoned. Seeing their peers get away with deceptive practices produces a sense of injustice, undermines student morale, and is therefore rightly categorised in these terms (Carroll, 2002; Carroll & Appleton, 2005).

However, the important task of engendering and fostering in students the "fundamental values of academic integrity" as part of their tertiary education has not been well served by the automatic inclusion of plagiarism in the list of unacceptable, deceitful behaviours. The blurred lines between willful actions, designed to deceive the assessor in order to gain unfair advantage over fellow students, and mistakes made due to a lack of understanding or a lack of skills, deserve to be re-examined, with a view to re-casting plagiarism into a framework that addresses this reality.

PROBLEMS

A negative consequence of simply equating plagiarism with cheating is that it can create a block to learning and teaching, as mistakes made by students can be interpreted by assessors as offences rather than as opportunities for learning (Briggs, 2003). Furthermore, there is little provision in most plagiarism policies or much of the literature for a systematic approach to teaching new students the basics of scholarly writing. A reliance on providing students with "clear" definitions and information on plagiarism policies, or offering remedial support in developing skills for appropriate acknowledgment of sources, can only be seen as a small gesture in the direction of student learning, that leaves to the student the responsibility for finding their way into the meaning and practices of academic culture.

An approach that highlights student education appears to be offered by Dodd (2006):

While Internet technologies may provide easy opportunity for students to corrupt research processes, educators also possess tools to teach honest scholarship. The "3 Ps" strategy—pedagogy, promotion, and a little policing—assists students in developing the necessary academic and ethical skill sets to resist the temptation to violate academic integrity norms. (Abstract)

But although he suggests pedagogy as a strategy, the primary purpose of this strategy is still cast in terms of plagiarism as an offence, rather than a process of learning the "new rules" of a "new game" (Leask, 2006). Dodd's approach does not seem to concede the complexity of plagiarism issues (Carroll, 2002; O'Regan, 2006) and in particular, that new students may have no means of knowing that their assignments are intended to be pieces of research and scholarly writing.

Induction into the Culture of Enquiry

There is, generally speaking, no reason to assume that students in transition to the university would have an understanding of what it is that characterises research writing. There is very little in the day-to-day environment outside university to suggest the need for "acknowledging sources." Within the university culture, notions such as "stating a point of view" or presenting an "argument" take on specialised meanings, different from the "common sense meanings" outside the academy (Chanock, 2004, p.3). Outside the academic research environment, examples of how opinions, arguments, or factual information may be stated are commonly found in entertainment literature, news reports, opinion columns, commentaries, or TV documentaries, but there is no requirement for these to demonstrate the constraints of acknowledgment, let alone of citing and referencing, that are requirements in higher education. Academic staff may lose sight of the fact that university represents a new culture, a culture that is characterised by research, in which knowledge is based on evidence, and in which opinions are explicitly grounded in the documented ideas and prior research of others (James et al., 2002).

But this is not at all self-evident to beginners. There is no reason why it should be, as they have not been exposed to examples of source acknowledgment in their day-to-day environment. Students in transition to academia need to learn that:

... in undertaking tertiary study they place themselves into a research tradition. This means that they need to learn to acknowledge that at least some aspects of what they are writing about have been dealt with before, and that the opinions they express need to be backed up by evidence. They must become familiar with a new culture: the "culture of enquiry" (McGowan, 2005a, p.292).

Individual programs aimed at enculturation into academic ways do exist. A pilot project on developing, trialling and evaluating a Research Skill Development Framework by Willison and O'Regan (2007) is a practical example of taking a mainstream approach to an active student induction into the culture of enquiry. However, there is as yet little evidence of a systematic academic induction for undergraduates in the Australian tertiary system.

EAL Language Development

The effectiveness of mechanisms for avoiding or deterring plagiarism must be questioned in the light of learning issues experienced by international students whose first language is not English. Although there are currently no precise statistics available on the overall incidence of plagiarism in Australasia (Devlin, 2006), anecdotal evidence from academics suggests that EAL students form a significant part of the problem. For example, in

2005 the University of Waikato, New Zealand, found that "there is a disproportionate number of students who are facing disciplinary proceedings for plagiarism," and that "Asian students comprise … 75 percent of plagiarism complaints and 79 percent of misconduct findings of plagiarism" (cited in ACODE, 2005).

A disproportionate statistic of this order makes it highly unlikely that the intention to cheat would have been the motivation for students' plagiarism in all these cases (McGowan, 2005b). Certainly the shortcuts offered by the availability of cut-and-paste online resources would be at lest as tempting to EAL students as it is to native speakers of English.

However, a further consideration is the acquisition and development of the appropriate language for scholarly writing. As Pennycook (1996) noted, there is an "obvious problem" for EAL learners:

… who, while constantly being told to be original and critical, and to write things in their "own words," are nevertheless only too aware that they are at the same time required to acquire a fixed canon of knowledge and a fixed canon of terminology to go with it. (p. 213)

In Australian universities, international EAL students are currently admitted to undergraduate study at English language levels of 6, 6.5 or 7 (out of a possible 9 levels) on the International English Language Testing System (IELTS) scale, the precise requirement varying across universities and for individual faculties. The band scores are described in the IELTS Handbook (2005) as follows:

BAND 6: Competent user. Has generally effective command of the language despite some inaccuracies, inappropriacies and misunderstandings.

Can use and understand fairly complex language, particularly in familiar situations.

BAND 7. Good user. Has operational command of the language, though with occasional inaccuracies, inappropriacies and misunderstandings in some situations. Generally handles complex language well and understands detailed reasoning.

These levels represent base starting points from which the more specific academic language of a student's discipline needs to develop. This is not always understood by university teachers or administrators. Because the students are deemed to have "generally effective command of the English language," it is assumed that they will be self-directed in further developing their language, not only to overcome their "inaccuracies" but also the "inappropriacies and misunderstandings" that are evident at their entry level.

There are no models of appropriate academic writing for the student in the day-today experience outside academic study. More disturbingly, however, even within university work there generally does not exist a culture of providing models for EAL students to draw on in order to develop their written language to an appropriately academic level. Much of the English to which they are exposed within the university is in an informal, spoken mode, during lectures, tutorials and peer discussion. Even textbooks often take on a didactic "spoken" tone that does not necessarily serve as an appropriate model for use in an assignment (McGowan, 2005b). On the other hand, the polished and concentrated style of published academic articles on their reading lists is often too difficult for new EAL students to unpack, with the result that students may, in desperation, resort to copying and pasting material into a patchwork that is identified as plagiarism.

A PROPOSED SOLUTION AND RECOMMENDATION

Curriculum: Issues of Learning, Teaching and Assessment

The fact of Internet plagiarism and the growth of international student numbers may be a blessing in disguise (Hunt, 2002) because these two factors have drawn attention to flaws in the reasoning which posits morality as the starting point for dealing with plagiarism. If a new focus leads to an acceptance of the reality of international students as a feature of the Australasian Higher Education system, a resolution to address plagiarism in the first instance as an educational issue, rather than a moral one, may provide the welcome additional benefit of an overall rise in students' academic and professional standards. It could become an

aim for universities that learning, teaching, and assessment are consciously relocated within the new realities: that students are seen as apprentice researchers (as recommended by the Boyer Commission, 1998) and are inducted into the values, language, and scholarly approaches of the university cultures; that online strategies are employed in creative and educationally sound ways; that students' use of Internet resources is not only accepted, but that students are taught to subject online information to the same processes of critique and analysis as have always been expected; and above all that scholarly approaches are explicitly described and rewarded in assessment criteria and associated rubrics (Willison & O'Regan, 2007).

For the ideal to become a reality, there needs to be an institutional shift from framing student plagiarism as an attack on academic integrity to

Figure 1. Unintentional plagiarism: language and cultural factors (adapted from McGowan, 2006)

PLAGIARISM FRAMEWORK: STUDENT AS APPRENTICE RESEARCHER				
INTERNATIONAL STUDENT EXPERIENCE				
	1. PRE- / EXTRA-UNIVERSITY	**2. EARLY APPRENTICE RESEARCHER**	**3. EMERGING RESEARCHER**	**4. COMPETENT RESEARCHER**
A. Culture	Diversity: Home country vs Australian cultures	Need for induction into academic culture of enquiry, learning as research, scholarly writing	Recognition of culture of enquiry, reasons for referencing conventions (i.e. transparency of research steps)	Academic values, integrity, autonomy, scrupulousness with data, attribution
B. Informal English language INPUT	English class text-book and lessons, websites, Spoken: Australian colloquial, TV drama etc.	Language of lectures and tutorials, peers, one-to-one advice, websites, LMS, course guides	Language of lectures and tutorials, peers, one-to-one advice, websites, LMS, course guides	Language of lectures and tutorials, peers, one-to-one advice, websites, LMS, course guides
C. Formal English Language INPUT	Newspapers, radio, websites, TV news, commentary, documentaries etc.	Course text-books, academic articles, websites (mainly for content)	Course text-books, academic articles, websites (for content, some language)	Variety of academic genres, articles, books seminar papers, research reports (for content and language)
D. Written English language OUTPUT	Personal: letters, application forms etc.	Mixture of informal language and quotations, uncertainty of conventions Awareness of own language inadequacies Inadvertent plagiarism	Recognition of writing as part of research Reader provided with information to sources Some uncertainty of conventions Occasional instances of plagiarism	Use of readings to shape writing Use of academic conventions Recognition of common Knowledge and language 'Harvesting' of discipline-specific language

putting it into a learning framework which positions the student as "apprentice researcher." Such a conceptual framework is presented in Figure 1.

Conceptual Framework

As a step towards a solution to the plagiarism problem, I have devised a conceptual framework which I have used to good effect in academic staff development. This framework provides the basis for a systematic, educative approach that accepts the dual reality that the largest and steadily growing minority of students in many higher education institutions consists of non-native speakers of English, and that online cut-and-paste plagiarism is widespread. The framework is designed to open up a fresh perspective for academic staff and assist them in providing students with an entry into their discipline-specific language and culture. It reverses the trend of viewing plagiarism primarily from the perspective of the institution's need to defend its integrity. Instead, it presents the issue as a student's journey from a non-academic environment into an increasing awareness of and competence in the culture of enquiry of the research environment encountered in an Australian, North American, or British university.

The journey takes the students through four learning phases, from the non-academic pre- or extra-university environment (phase 1), to the experience of being an early apprentice researcher (phase 2), an emerging researcher (phase 3), and finally a competent researcher (phase 4). It needs to be said at the outset that this is not a strictly linear progression. In particular, the starting point, the experience of the non-academic world of phase 1 is never left behind but is a continuing experience concurrent with a student's progress through the stages of a research apprenticeship. The experience of the cultural environments, together with the examples of the informal and formal English language that students encounter during each of the four phases (their language "input"), constitutes the resources they can draw on to produce their own written work (or "output"). Clearly, the quality of their output will be limited by the range and quality of the input experiences available to them.

In phase 1, the cultural experiences of international students may vary greatly from those of local students. There are many differences in expectations between home and host countries in everyday living that require adjustment and adaptation. In addition, the experience of informal and formal English input available to students outside their university environment is restricted to non-academic examples that provide no clues to their cultural and linguistic development needs during phase 2, the beginning of their apprenticeship into the research environment of tertiary study.

In phase 2 there is provision for an induction into the academic culture of enquiry of the university, in line with recommendations by the Boyer Commission (1998). I envisage that this induction should take place over an extended period of time covering phases 2 and 3, and that it is treated as a learning phase embedded into the overall learning.

During phases 2 and 3 the plagiarism produced by these students can be understood as a natural step in their effort, by trial and error, to transform their casual, spoken language to the more formal, written style used in research genres. If it were treated as errors rather than offences, plagiarism by students who are "emerging researchers" could then be dealt with as being unintentional, in a similar manner to the treatment of grammatical errors in the development of communication skills. Above all, the occurrence of plagiarism during these two phases should flag the need for universities to accept responsibility for explicitly apprenticing students into the university's culture of research and assisting them in the complicated process of acquiring the necessary skills in the language and conventions of that culture.

The induction of students into an understanding of the principles of research and the norms of scholarly writing within the curriculum is a necessary first step in this process. But my concern is that for EAL students this needs to be accompanied by a comparable induction into the means for acquiring the language that is required for a range of written genres which they have to master for their assignments. This may be achieved by helping students to learn the skills of genre analysis, a process for using their reading as models to improve their writing.

Genre Analysis

Potentially the most useful language models for EAL students in a research context would be annotated examples of assignment answers or academic articles written in the desired style (Ingleton & Wake, 1996). Comments in the margins and arrows to relevant items could be used to label stages in the structure of the text. In addition, commonly used words, phrases, and sentence patterns would be highlighted as "reusable language." The process is described in McGowan (2005b) and is based in genre pedagogy for which there is a large body of literature (Cope & Kalantzis, 1993; Halliday & Hasan, 1985; Halliday & Martin, 1993; The New London Group, 2000; Swales, 1990, 2004). Genre pedagogy is based on the understanding that different genres of communication have developed their specific structures and their own "canon" of words that are "re-used" and that characterise that particular type of writing. By analysing a number of examples of the required genres, such as essays, short answers or research reports, students can learn to identify the "content-free" word sequences that bind the text and communicate the content. These can be noted and used again in a different context to communicate a student's own ideas.

The metaphor of "harvesting" language is a useful one in this context. The richness and variation in language that students can find in the readings within their disciplines is a constantly renewing resource from which to harvest language that is not only "correct" but also "appropriate" for the purpose of scholarly writing and so fast-track their apprenticeship into the academic culture.

An approach based on genre pedagogy as outlined here is currently being applied to good effect in a specialised program with off-shore EAL academics aiming to publish their research in English language journals (Cargill, 2004; Cargill & O'Connor, 2006). In the context of Australian universities, the process of assisting students in accordance with my framework will require cooperation from content lecturers who, in turn, need reassurance that the effort involved is likely to pay dividends in the long run. Their time spent in providing models and guiding students into the skills of genre analysis should save much of the time that is currently wasted in pursing those EAL students whose plagiarism is no more than their failed attempts at acquiring what Pennycook called the "fixed canon of terminology" of academic genres.

FUTURE TRENDS

If the concepts of the framework were accepted in designing university policies, the prevailing view of plagiarism as an offence could be transformed into one that recognises its occurrence as part of a developmental process. Instead of relying on systems of warnings, and referrals to extra-curricular remediation as a solution to plagiarism, institutions could find space for the induction of all students into the culture of evidence-based writing within the core curriculum. Saltmarsh (2005) describes the "Western rationalities of superiority and worth" in terms of racism and argues for a position:

...in which the focus is shifted from pejoratively constituted "Others" toward a renewed emphasis on both developing pedagogic processes which

effectively meet language, learning and equity needs across the full range of student cohorts. (Conclusion—no pagination given)

The framework presented here is designed to provide that emphasis by treating students as apprentice researchers. Academics can help them not only to gain insights into the requirements of a scholarly approach but also to develop skills in genre analysis as a simple tool for fast-tracking the development of their academic writing, by "harvesting" academic language from the growing range of genres for communicating research results (McGowan, 2005c). It will require staff development to achieve the necessary shift of focus (McGowan, 2005d). It also will need recognition and support at the institutional level to gain acceptance among academics that language learning is integral to content learning, that new genres and new language must be learnt by students during their research apprenticeships, and that in this context feedback on incidences of inadvertent plagiarism should be non-judgmental, constructive, and formative. If this shift in focus could be achieved, the learning of scholarly practice would become recognised as an integral part of the purpose of tertiary study as envisaged by the Boyer Commission (1998), and support the development not only of international EAL students but also local students who are native speakers of English.

CONCLUSION

The conceptual framework presented here provides for a student focus on plagiarism issues that are traditionally seen more from an institutional perspective. By modelling the stages of the culture and language successively experienced by EAL students, the framework provides some insights into issues affecting their academic writing development. If new students are regarded as apprentice researchers and inducted into the culture of enquiry they receive a firm grounding for understanding and mastering the academic conventions required of them. In addition, by assisting students in developing the skills of genre analysis as a tool for life long language learning—I call it "the 4 Ls"—it is possible to provide more effective means for avoiding some of the commonly found traps of inadvertent plagiarism. My suggestion has been that this approach be adopted in the design of the core curriculum to assist all undergraduate students, both EAL and native speakers of English. It is to be hoped that by treating students as apprentice researchers, academics would be taking a first step towards reducing the overall incidence of unintentional plagiarism and so allow the full force of disciplinary resources to be devoted to detecting and dealing with those students who are genuinely engaged in deception, cheating, or academic fraud (McGowan, 2005c; JISC, 2005).

Perhaps, with reference to Hunt's (2002) article "Four reasons to be happy about Internet plagiarism," it has been "a good thing" that EAL issues and the Internet have combined to bring some of the problems around plagiarism to a head and cause scholars to re-examine what is really involved. In meeting the challenge posed by a particular group and a new technology, the academy may move towards a renewal of educational practices to embrace a more broadly based approach to learning and teaching in order to benefit all students in transition to tertiary study, and as Hunt puts it, to "help our students learn… the most important thing they can learn at university: just how intellectual enterprise and scholarship really works."

ACKNOWLEDGMENT

I gratefully acknowledge the valuable advice and support I received from John McGowan and Kerry O'Regan in finalising this chapter.

REFERENCES

Australasian Council on Open, Distance and E-learning (ACODE) (2005). *Academic Integrity Project: Audit of Academic Integrity and Plagiarism Issues in Australia and New Zealand.* Prepared by the Teaching and Learning Centre, Murdoch University. Retrieved September 6, 2006, from http://www.tlc.murdoch.edu.au/project/acode/

Australian Government (2004). *International higher education students: How do they differ from other education students?* (Research Note No. 2). Department of Education, Science and Training. Retrieved January 15, 2007, from http://www.dest.gov.au/sectors/international_education/publications_resources/profiles/international_higher_education_students.htm

Bain, A. (2007). *Distribution of International Students.* Paper for the Working Party on Interactions between International and Local Students. South Australia. Adelaide: The University of Adelaide.

Boyer Commission (1998). *Reinventing undergraduate education: A blueprint for America's research universities.* Stony Brook, NY: Carnegie foundation for University Teaching. Retrieved August 15, 2006, from http://naples.cc.sunysb.edu/Pres/boyer.nsf/

Briggs, R. (2003). Shameless! *Australian Universities Review, 46*(1), 19-23.

Carroll, J. (2002). *A Handbook for deterring plagiarism in higher education.* Oxford: Oxford Centre for Learning and Staff Development: Oxford Brookes University.

Carroll, J., & Appleton, J. (2005). Towards consistent penalty decisions for breaches of academic regulations in one UK university. *International Journal for Educational Integrity, 1*(1), No pagination. Retrieved March 23, 2006, from http://www.ojs.unisa.edu.au/index.php/IJEI/issue/view/3

Cargill, M. (2004).Transferable skills within research degrees: A collaborative genre-based approach to developing publication skills and its implications for research education. *Teaching in Higher Education, 9*(1), 83–98.

Cargill, M., & O'Connor, P. (2006). Developing Chinese scientists' skills for publishing in English: Evaluating collaborating-colleague workshops based on genre analysis. *Journal of English for Academic Purposes, 5*(3), 207-221.

Center for Academic Integrity (1999). *The Fundamental Values of Academic Integrity.* Retrieved September 3, 2006, from http://www.academicintegrity.org/

Chanock, K. (2004). *Introducing student to the culture of enquiry in an arts degree.* HERDSA Guide. Milparra New South Wales: Higher Education Research and Development Society of Australasia.

Cope, B., & Kalantzis, M. (1993). How a genre approach to literacy can transform the way literacy is taught. In B. Cope & M. Kalantzis (Eds.), *The powers of literacy: A genre approach to the teaching of writing* (pp. 1-21). London: Falmer Press.

Devlin, M. (2006). Policy, preparation and prevention: Proactive minimization of student plagiarism. *Journal of Higher Education Policy and Management, 28*(1), 45-58.

Dodd, T. (2006). Teaching, plagiarism, and the new and improved term paper mill. *Teachers College Record.* Date Published: October 17, 2006. Retrieved February 24, 2007, from http://www.tcrecord.org, ID Number: 12794.

Halliday, M.A.K., & Hasan, R. (1985). *Language context and text: Aspects of language in a social semiotic perspective.* Geelong: Deakin University Press.

Halliday, M.A.K., & Martin, J. R. (1993). *Writing science. Literacy and discursive power.* London: Falmer Press.

Hunt, R. (2002). Four reasons to be happy about Internet plagiarism. *Teaching Perspectives.* St. Thomas University, Canada. Retrieved May 25, 2005, from http://www.stu.ca/~hunt/4reasons.htm

Ingleton, C. & Wake, B. (1996). *Literacy Matters.* Adelaide, South Australia: Advisory Centre for University Education, University of Adelaide.

International English Language Testing System (IELTS) (2005). *International English Language Test Score Handbook.* Retrieved September 30, 2005, from http://www.ielts.org/_lib/pdf/1649_IELTShbk_2005.pdf

Joint Information Systems Committee (JISC) (2005). *Deterring, detecting, and dealing with plagiarism.* Joint Information Systems Committee. Retrieved June 20, 2005, from http://www.jisc.ac.uk/

James, R., & Baldwin, G. (2002). *Nine principles guiding teaching and learning in the University of Melbourne.* Centre for the Study of Higher Education. Retrieved June 21, 2005, from http://www.cshe.unimelb.edu.au/pdfs/9principles.pdf

Leask, B., (2006). Plagiarism, cultural diversity, and metaphor – Implications for academic staff development. *Assessment and Evaluation in Higher Education, 31*(2), 183-199.

McCabe, D. (2005). Cheating among college students. A North American perspective. *International Journal for Educational Integrity, 1*(1), No pagination. Retrieved March 23, 2006, from http://www.ojs.unisa.edu.au/index.php/IJEI/issue/view/3

McGowan, U. (2005a). Plagiarism detection and prevention. Are we putting the cart before the horse? In A. Brew & C. Asmar (Eds.), *Higher education in a changing world. Proceedings of the HERDSA Conference* (pp. 287-293). Sydney. Retrieved August 15, 2005, from http://www.itl.

usyd.edu.au/herdsa2005/pdf/refereed/paper_412.pdf

McGowan, U. (2005b). Does educational integrity mean teaching students NOT to "use their own words?" *International Journal for Educational Integrity, 1*(1), no pagination. Retrieved March 23, 2006, from http://www.ojs.unisa.edu.au/index.php/IJEI/issue/view/3

McGowan, U. (2005c). Educational integrity: A strategic approach to anti-plagiarism. Paper presented at the 2nd Asia Pacific Educational Integrity Conference (pp. 1-10). Newcastle, Australia, December 1-3. Retrieved January 15, 2007, from http://www.newcastle.edu.au/conference/apeic/papers.html

McGowan, U. (2005d). Academic integrity: An awareness and development issue for students and staff. *Journal of University Teaching and learning Practice, 2*(3a), 48-57. Retrieved January 20, 2007, from http://jutlp.uow.edu.au

McGowan, U. (2006). Plagiarism framework: Student as apprentice researcher. The University of Adelaide Web site: Resources for Staff. Retrieved December 15, 2006, from http://www.adelaide.edu.au/clpd/plagiarism/staff/

The New London Group (2000). A pedagogy of multiliteracies. In B. Cope & M. Kalantzis (Eds.), *Muliliteracies. Literacy learning and the design for social futures.* Melbourne: Macmillan Publishers Australia.

Oblinger, D. G. & Oblinger, J. L. (2005). Is it age or IT: First steps toward understanding the Net generation. In D. G. Oblinger & J. L. Oblinger (Eds.), *Educating the Net Generation.* An Educause e-book. Retrieved October 10, 2006, from http://www.educause.edu/EducatingtheNetGeneration/5989

O'Regan, K. (2006). Policing—or, at least, policying—plagiarism at one Australian university.

Journal of University Teaching and learning Practice, 3(2), 114-123. Retrieved January 20, 2007, from http://jutlp.uow.edu.au

Page, J. S. (2004). Cyber-pseudepigraphy: A new challenge for higher education policy and management. *Journal for Higher Education Policy and Management, 26*(3), 429-433.

Park, C. (2003). In other (people's) words: Plagiarism by university students—Literature and lessons. *Assessment & Evaluation in Higher Education, 28*(5), 471-488.

Pennycook, A. (1996). Borrowing others' words: Text, ownership memory, and plagiarism. *TESOL Quarterly, 30*(2), 201-230.

Saltmarsh, S. (2005). "White pages" in the academy: Plagiarism, consumption, and racist rationalities. *International Journal for Educational Integrity, 1*(1), no pagination. Retrieved March 23, 2006, from http://www.ojs.unisa.edu.au/index. php/IJEI/issue/view/3

Swales, J. (1990). *Genre analysis. English in academic research settings.* New York: Cambridge University Press.

Swales, J. (2004). *Research genres. Exploration and applications.* New York: Cambridge University Press.

Willison, J. & O'Regan, K. (2007) Commonly known, commonly not known, totally unknown: A framework for students becoming researchers. *Higher Education Research and Development, 26*(4), 393-409.

ENDNOTE

[1] EAL (English as an additional language) is the descriptor that is gaining favour over ESL (English as a second language) as a recognition of, and a mark of respect to, the students who are at home in not just two but multiple languages and cultures.

Chapter VIII
International Students and Plagiarism Detection Systems:
Detecting Plagiarism, Copying, or Learning?

Lucas D. Introna
Lancaster University Management School, UK

Niall Hayes
Lancaster University Management School, UK

ABSTRACT

This chapter explores the question of plagiarism by international students (non-native speakers). It argues that the inappropriate use of electronic plagiarism detection systems (such as Turnitin) could lead to the unfair and unjust construction of international students as plagiarists. We argue that the use of detection systems should take into account the writing practices used by those who write as novices in a non-native language as well as the way "plagiarism" or plagiaristic forms of writing are valued in other cultures. It calls for a move away from a punitive legalistic approach to plagiarism that equates copying to plagiarism and move to a progressive and formative approach. If taken up, such an approach will have very important implications for the way universities in the west deal with plagiarism in their learning and teaching practice as well as their disciplinary procedures.

INTRODUCTION

The issue of academic integrity within higher education has received considerable attention in the literature over recent years (Carroll & Appleton, 2001; Deckert, 1993; Dryden, 1999; Harris, 2001; Howard, 1995, 1993; Kolich, 1983; Lathrop, 2000; Myers, 1998; Pennycook, 1996; Scollon, 1995; Sherman, 1992). Much of this literature, coupled with the considerable anecdotal evidence amongst colleagues within our own and other universities, suggests that plagiarism is on the increase. O'Connor (2003) describes one recent Australian study that spanned 20 subjects and six universities. This saw 1,925 essays being submitted into Turnitin, an electronic detection service that compares electronic work submitted with the 2.6 billion publicly available pages on the Internet, and to all the essays previously submitted to Turnitin for checking. This study found that 14 percent of essays "contained unacceptable levels of unattributed materials." Further, unacceptable levels of plagiarism were found to be present in all six universities and in over 70 percent of the subjects. The report also highlighted that what was detected electronically is just the tip of the iceberg, as Turnitin did not cover most books, journals, paper mills, and so on (O'Connor, 2003).

In relation to the literature that has considered why students plagiarise, Carroll (2002) has suggested that most students are unsure what plagiarism is. She argues that this lack of understanding of what is and what is not plagiarism contributes to students plagiarising unintentionally. Furthermore, Angelil-Carter (2000) claims that there is also a lack of clarity across a university about what constitutes plagiarism and a discrepancy in the way plagiarism is detected and enforced (Biggs, 1994; Ryan, 2000; Scollon, 1995). Others have highlighted the growing staff student ratio as being implicated in the rise in the number of cases of plagiarism. They suggest this results in staff having less time to deal with students as individuals and hence less opportunity to talk through issues regarding writing practices (Angelova & Riazantseva, 1999; O'Donoghue, 1996). Carroll (2002) also argues that the move from examination to coursework and project based assessment has resulted in not just over assessment, but students experiencing continual pressure to attain high marks (Carroll, 2000). Others suggest that poor time management by students, or the institutions setting simultaneous deadlines is a major contributing factor (Errey, 2002).

The purpose of this chapter is not to revisit these arguments about the increase (or not) of plagiarism or why students find themselves plagiarising. It is our view that many of these papers and arguments deal with a rather oversimplified view of plagiarism, especially with regard to international students[1] (i.e., non-native English speakers). The purpose of this chapter is rather to explore the complex interaction between cultural values, writing practices and electronic plagiarism detection systems as depicted in Figure 1.

The central argument of this chapter is that the inappropriate use of electronic plagiarism detection systems (such as Turnitin) could lead to the unfair and unjust construction of international students as plagiarists, with obvious devastating consequences. This "inappropriate" use that we refer to flows from three sets of interrelated assumptions or misunderstandings:

a. A misunderstanding of the writing practices used by those who write as novices in a non-native language.

b. Inappropriate assumptions about the way "plagiarism" or plagiaristic forms of writing (such as copying) are valued in other cultures.

c. A dualistic view of plagiarism that does not take into account the practices and values referred to in (a) and (b) above.

We would argue that plagiarism is not a simple phenomenon. It is not a simple choice between

Figure 1. Conditions that mediate the construction of international students as plagiarists

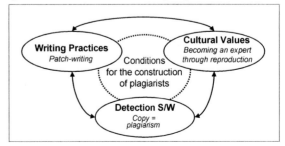

cheating and not cheating. There are a number of complex conditions that are shaping the actual writing practices of students (and international students in particular). It is not realistic or fair for us to take a reductionistic approach in dealing with plagiarism by international students. Further, researching the conditions that mediate the construction of international students as plagiarists requires us to attend to literatures in many different fields of study, such as literature in cultural analysis, academic writing, and higher education policy. We acknowledge that full consideration of all these literatures is not necessarily possible within the scope of a book chapter. The following sections will consider these literatures in more detail.

Becoming an Academic "Speaker" (With the Help of Patches)

Non-native speakers and novices in a discourse often "speak" or write by means of a practice Howard (1993) calls "patch-writing." Howard (1993) defines patch-writing as "copying from a source text and then deleting some words, altering grammatical structures, or plugging in one-for-one synonym-substitutes" (p. 213). She argues that writers often turn to patch-writing when they are unsure of their understanding of the material or lack confidence in the use of a particular language (such as academic language and phraseology). Patch-writing can be seen as a form of mimicking behaviour. Students normally understand how important it is to "speak" like the teachers and the people whose material they read to become accepted into the community. Howard argues, following Hull and Rose (1989) that patch-writing is a legitimate attempt to "interact with the text, relate it to your own experiences, derive your own meaning from it" (p. 150). This interaction directly with the text in order to derive one's own meaning from it is something most novice readers/writers do in unfamiliar contexts. This type of engagement often is characterised

by copying (mimicking) with ever increasing adoption as confidence grows. Defending patch-writing seems reasonable when we consider that we all learn new skills by mimicking or copying others considered exemplary. Let us consider the example of learning a new language, which seems appropriate in this case. One even could argue that native English speakers also need to learn a new language when they are expected to express their ideas in academic writing. In the case of non-native speakers there is a double hurdle to cross.

Most language courses do not teach you the vocabulary and the grammar separately and then expect you to independently construct meaningful sentences; they tend to follow a very different approach. They normally start by teaching you meaningful phrases in situated contexts, such as how to ask for a glass of water in a restaurant. Only once you have mastered a sufficiently large set of situated phrases and understand when and how to use them appropriately can you begin the next step. In the next step you are expected to selectively and carefully change parts of the phrases in appropriate ways. The way you would converse as a beginner then would be to use these phrases as "building blocks" changing them ever so slightly in various situations in order to express meaningfully in that particular situation. Only once you have become competent at this level of expression can you begin to build phrases independently in order to convey your intentions more precisely. This account of becoming an expert, moving from the "standard patterns" to specific situated instances, was used by Hubert Dreyfus (1992) to provide a devastating critique of artificial intelligence research.

If we use this basic model for learning a language to understand the steps that international students might be going through when learning to do academic writing then it is easy to understand how they tend to use patch-writing as a way to deal with their lack of skills. When international students go to study in the UK, USA, and Australia[2], they are given the vocabulary (theoretical ideas) and the grammar (academic style of writing, rules of structure, rules of argumentation, conventions for referencing, etc.) and then are expected to be expert users of the academic language and to be able to converse (write an essay) by directly creating independent phrases. However, these ideas, rules, and conventions (even if they are individually understood) do not provide non-native students with the necessary skill to speak the academic language, as it does not with speaking any other language. What is in fact happening is that, as beginners, they are using exemplary sentences and paragraphs as situated phrases (or patches in Howard's terminology) to develop competency in "speaking" academically. This strategy is evident in this comment by a Greek student in an earlier study (Hayes & Introna, 2005): "taking a bit here and there helps with getting meaning across. Paraphrasing if you are not a native speaker is difficult." Even the more competent "speakers" will tend to use meaningfully modified phrases as a way to sustain a conversation (essay)—as is clear from this comment by an English speaking student during the same piece of research: "If you take all the sentences/paragraphs from other authors—then you have to do the work to put it together—you have learned and need a certain understanding of the topic, it is not just blatant copying" (Hayes & Introna, 2005).

Furthermore, it is possible to show that students can use patches from an original document to say something quite different from that which the original author has said. Consider the example below in Table 1. In this example, the original text is making the argument that computers in writing can lead to a better quality outcome. The patch-written text uses the original base text as a patch, both in terms of providing meaningful formulations of certain ideas as well as providing an overall narrative structure. Nevertheless, the patch-writer—using the majority of the original text—expresses an *independent* argument to sug-

gest that the research surveyed is only relevant for particular situations and that one cannot make general conclusions from these about the value of computers in writing. Clearly, the patch-written text below normally would be considered in Western universities as being plagiaristic.[3] Nevertheless, we would argue it also indicates independent thought based on informed and sound logical argumentation. In this case, the patch-writing is not very sophisticated. More sophisticated forms of patch-writing may use patches from a variety of documents patched together around an independently formulated argument.

This view of an engagement with texts through patch-writing seems to be acceptable practice in many Asian universities as confirmed by a Japanese professor Dryden (1999): "students are supposed to show how well they can understand several books and digest them in a report or a paper. They aren't asked for original ideas or opinions. They are simply asked to show a beautiful patchwork…as long as you mention all the books in your bibliography, you can present the ideas from the books as if they were yours, especially if your patchwork is beautiful" (p. 80). The notion of a "beautiful patchwork" may seem strange to academics in western universities, but it clearly seems to be quite unproblematic to international students and the institutions they come from.

To conclude: we would claim that patch-writing can and should be seen as a step towards independence in academic writing. Furthermore, we would argue that students can express their own independent arguments through patch-writing that demonstrates *an active and informed engagement with a text*—as indicated by our example above and suggested by Howard (1993) and Pennycook (1996)—rather than mere "mindless" copying. Thus, we would argue that it is important to move away from a simplistic "copy = plagiarism" interpretation of patch-writing if effective strategies to deal with plagiarism are to be developed.

Table 1. Example of a patch-written text

The original text	The patch-written text (<u>added text</u>)
In general, the research on word processors and student writing conducted during the 1980's and early 1990's suggests many ways in which writing on computers may help students produce better work. Although much of this research was performed before large numbers of computers were present in schools, formal studies report that when students write on computer they tend to produce more text and make more revisions (Dauite, 1986; Vacc, 1987). Studies that compare student work produced on computer with work produced on paper find that for some groups of students, writing on computer also had a positive effect on the quality of student writing (Hannafin & Dalton, 1987; Owston, 1991;). This positive effect is strongest for students with learning disabilities, early elementary-aged students and college-aged students (Hass & Hayes, 1986; Phoenix & Hannan, 1984; Sitko & Crealock, 1986). Additionally, when applied to meet curricular goals, education technology provides alternative approaches to sustaining student interest, developing student knowledge and skill, and provides supplementary materials that teachers can use to extend student learning. Although earlier research syntheses reveal just modest trends, individual studies of that era have shown that writing with a computer can increase the amount of writing students perform, the extent to which students edit their writing (Dauite, 1986; Etchinson, 1989; Vacc, 1987), which, in turn, leads to higher quality writing (Hannafin & Dalton, 1987; Kerchner & Kistinger, 1984; Williamson & Pence, 1989). **Text from:** Goldberg, A., Russell, M., & Cook, A. (2003). The effect of computers on student writing: A metaanalysis of studies from 1992 to 2002. *Journal of Technology, Learning, and Assessment, 2*(1). Available from http://www.jtla.org.	In general, the research on word processors and student writing conducted during the 1980's and early 1990's suggests <u>that there might be</u> many ways in which writing on computers may <u>not always be</u> help<u>ful for</u> students <u>to</u> produce better work, <u>except in very particular cases or task situations.</u> Although much of this research was performed before large numbers of computers were present in schools, formal studies report that when students write on computer they tend to produce more text and make more revisions (Dauite, 1986; Vacc, 1987). <u>More text and more revisions could lead to better work but not always. One could also argue that it might lead to less disciplined thought processes. Moreover, if students become depended on the possibility of multiple revisions what would that mean for their general writing ability?</u> There are <u>some</u> studies that compare student work produced on computer with work produced on paper find that for <u>only</u> some groups of students, writing on computer also had a positive effect on the quality of student writing (Hannafin & Dalton, 1987; Owston, 1991;). <u>It is however necessary to point out that the notion of 'quality' used in these studies is not uncontroversial. Nevertheless,</u> this positive effect is strongest for students with learning disabilities, <u>early</u> elementary <u>school</u> students and <u>older university level</u> students (Hass & Hayes, 1986; Phoenix & Hannan, 1984; Sitko & Crealock, 1986). <u>This would suggest that the use of computer in writing is not a simple quick fix for all. Nevertheless,</u> when applied to meet curricular <u>boarder educational</u> goals, education technology provides alternative approaches to sustaining student interest, developing student knowledge and skill, and provides supplementary materials that teachers can use to extend student learning. <u>However it should be emphasised that the</u> syntheses of earlier research reveal <u>only</u> modest trends. <u>Thus,</u> although individual studies of that era have shown that writing with a computer <u>may</u> increase the amount of writing students perform, the extent to which students edit their writing (Dauite, 1986; Etchinson, 1989; Vacc, 1987), which, in turn, <u>may</u> lead to higher quality writing (Hannafin & Dalton, 1987; Kerchner & Kistinger, 1984; Williamson & Pence, 1989), <u>there are still significant doubts as to the degree these conclusions can be taken as significant for the larger population.</u>

Becoming an Expert Through Reproduction

"If you want to write a poem you must first copy three hundred good poems"
A Chinese proverb according to a Chinese teacher

Patch-writing makes even more sense in other cultures with a different philosophy of language and learning and whose cultural values that do not value individualism, creativity, and autonomy. In many Asian cultures, copying, especially through large amounts of repetition, is seen as the true route to learning. Young learners are encouraged to copy good expression and exemplars that they appreciate or are told to be exemplary. This has as much to do with their pedagogical approach as it has to do with their view of language. For example, Pennycook (1996) has argued that the Chinese view of language is quite different to ours:

In this [view of language] primacy is accorded to language and not to the 'real' world, notions such as metaphor, which suggests that some word 'stands for' something else, become quite different because reality is in the language and not in the world. (p. 221)

The sinologist Hans-Georg Moeller (2003, p. 75) also expresses this view clearly:

Chinese theory of 'forms and names' granted an equal ontological status to both the matter and *the designation of the things. To use a more formal expression, not only the signified but also the signifier was considered to be inherent in the things.* The signifier was not conceived of as an arbitrary 'label' or as being only attached to things a posteriori. Its name belonged to the thing just as much as its form. *The ancient Taoist text Zhuangzi (see Zhuangzi 1947: 72/25/76) says: 'It has a name and it has a shape: this is what establishes a thing.'* (Emphasis added)

Obviously, there is an issue with regard to the degree that this ancient view of language is still evident in contemporary everyday practice. Nevertheless, to the degree that it still is, it would suggest that for Chinese students altering the exact expression of something might plausibly be seen as altering the reality of the world itself. Where would the authority to do this come from for a student? Furthermore, capturing the exact expression—through meticulous memorisation—would be seen as capturing the reality as such. Thus, students would be encouraged to express reality by using the words, the exact expression of the expert since the exact expression contain in them the meaning and expertise that they want access to. Several Chinese students mentioned that precise memorising of texts has been the focus of their learning experience throughout all levels of education. Turner (2000) confirms this mode of teaching and learning in her telling account of the Chinese educational context:

In the classroom, the teacher speaks and the students listen. Asking questions in class is actively discouraged—the teacher/lecturer may ask one or two favoured students questions but may not ask questions at all ... The questions are likely to be factual—it is not normal practice to ask students to venture an opinion. Should a student provide an incorrect answer, they tend to receive some kind of rebuke or punishment from the lecturer ... [T]he teacher will provide the students with structured notes—usually on the blackboard which the students will copy—and students are not encouraged to take notes independently. ... Owing to the competition for places in Chinese higher education ... [w]ork is entirely individual—and almost completely examination-based. ... [W]riting, in the form of how to style, structure and present a piece of writing is not taught in China ... Students, therefore, are unlikely to have encountered essay-writing to any extent ... Nor will they have any experience of using references or multiple sources of information to inform their written work or their thinking ... The teaching method emphasises the correct memorisation and reproduction of teacher's notes or text book information—referencing is not used, since almost the entire essay [in the exam] may be in the form of *memorised sections of text.* Information is viewed in a unitary way: the teaching of facts. Critical examination of different perspectives on a subject, and the development of an argument is absent within Chinese education. (Emphasis added)

We are not making a judgement about the validity or appropriateness of this pedagogical approach as such. There is some research to suggest that this approach to learning may indeed be effective (Biggs, 1994, 1996). Nevertheless, we are claiming that this approach—which is common in Asia (Marsh & Morris, 1991; Morris & Sweeting, 1995)—would tend to create the conditions under which the exact reproduction of the expert's expression and formulations (as contained in the prescribed textbook) might be seen as necessary to succeed. As one Indian student indicated in our earlier study, the exam questions "will ask us to repeat definitions word for word from the textbook" (Hayes & Introna, 2005).

There could not be a starker contrast to what is expected from international students when they enter the learning and teaching environments in western universities. Instead of relying on the authority of the lecturer and the textbook, international students—especially at postgraduate level—are expected to gain their understanding of a topic from a multitude of sources (journals, books, Internet papers, case studies, etc.) expressed in the reading list. They are required to be able to read the material and distil from it the important points, arguments and issues, that is, be able to evaluate the material with regard to authority, content, relevance, and appropriateness. International students are expected to be able to give a critical account of the literature and to be able to formulate their own position, pertaining to the material suggested, which they must be able to justify. International students may be expected to present and justify these views openly through discussion and questioning in a group or lecture context. The good students are expected them to move beyond the reading list, which most non-native students will already consider to be extensive. Further, they are required to find their own sources, evaluate them critically and incorporate them in an appropriate manner into their arguments. It is clear that completely different sets of skills are called for in these two approaches. In this situation, the typical non-native student will often find himself or herself in a situation where they have a huge skills deficit. In such a situation they will tend to fall back on what has worked in the past, memorisation and the reproduction of "canonical" phrases as expressions of expertise.

Once western views of language and values in learning are set aside it becomes possible to start appreciating the behaviour of some of the international students in Australian, U.S., and UK universities. In particular, the importance that memorisation and the use of exact expressions play in their way of understanding and knowing the world.

Becoming Seen as a Plagiarist

Main Entry: **pla·gia·rize**
Pronunciation: 'plA-j&-"rIz also -jE-&-
Etymology: plagiary (to kidnap) transitive senses : to steal and pass off (the ideas or words of another) as one's own : use (another's production) without crediting the source intransitive senses : to commit literary theft : present as new and original an idea or product derived from an existing source (from Merriam-Webster Online Dictionary)

How does patch-writing and the copying (mimicking) of the expert manifest itself in the texts of international students? Clearly it is not simply a matter of "lazy" students "cutting and pasting" the work of others and presenting this "as their own" as the definition above suggests. Obviously this does sometimes happen and ought to be taken very seriously. However, it seems rather that there is a complex process of learning and valuing at play in the construction of texts by international students. It is most certainly the intentional use of another's words—as indicated in part of definition above. However, it seems that it is mostly *not* an attempt to present it as original (i.e., as if their own work)—as indicated in the other part of definition above. Thus, the intention is not to deceive but rather to conform to perceived expectations of what it means to learn.

The debate about cases of plagiarism is often characterised by a *dualistic* perspective. Teachers in countries such as the USA and UK often argue that if a text contained "copied" material then it was either intentionally copied (which would be cheating) or it was unintentionally incorporated (which would be sloppy or bad writing practice). With an increased use of plagiarism detection systems they will refer to the reports such systems generate to reinforce such views.[4] This dualistic view of plagiarism does not allow for the account we gave above where a student intentionally uses parts of texts as "patches" as well as a means to retain the expressions of the expert, yet does not present it, or mean to present it, as their own independent work. Indeed the question of whether it is there own work or not does not come up as relevant at all—as novices it was never expected to be in the first place. In other words, we want to argue that there are significant pedagogical and cultural reasons for using part copies of texts (as patches) that are not simply plagiaristic behaviour.

It is this form of "plagiarism," which we will call "grey" plagiarism, that is our concern. This is not an ideal term as "plagiarism" essentially refers to the intention to deceive, which is mostly not the case. However, we do want to retain it as an acknowledgement that grey plagiarism should only function as *a step towards* independent work and not as an end in itself. Thus, we are proposing a progressive and formative view of plagiarism that sees patch-writing as a step towards independent and critical thought. This is in contrast to the dualistic and punitive view often held in Australian, UK, and U.S. higher education institutions.

It is our claim that the implementation of plagiarism detection software (such as Tutnitin) implicitly operates with, or is used with a dualistic punitive approach to plagiarism—that is, copy = plagiarism = requires discipline. Thus, many international students that engage in patch writing or use parts of texts to retain the expressions of the expert could, and is being, identified as "plagiarists" by our electronic detection systems. This is both with regard to the design of algorithms as such and the way in which it is implemented. We now will turn to this "technical" issue.

ALGORITHMS AND THE DETECTION OF PLAGIARISM

Plagiarism detection software detects *copies*, not plagiarism. How does it detect copies? A simple approach that could have been adopted by the developers would be to compare a document character by character. However, this approach has a number of problems: (a) it is very time-consuming and resource intensive; (b) it is not sensitive to white spaces, formatting, and ordering changes; (c) it cannot detect partial copies from multiple sources. To deal with these problems, a number of algorithms have been developed. Unfortunately, many of these (such ad Turnitin and EVE) now are proprietary software and therefore not available for analysis. However, there is one that we can consider as a basis to understand how these algorithms work; it is an algorithm called "winnowing" (Schleimer, Wilkerson, & Aiken, 2003)[5].

Winnowing, like many other algorithms, makes a digital fingerprint of a document which it then uses to compare documents against each other. The fingerprint is a small and compact representation of the content of the document that can serve as a basis for determining correspondence between two documents (or parts of it). A fingerprint is created in a number of steps indicated in the Table 2.

It is in step 4 where most algorithms differ. There are a variety of techniques for determining which hashes to keep as the document fingerprint (see also Brin, Davis, and Garcia-Molina, 1995). The ratio between the total population of hashes and the sample selected for the fingerprint is called the *density* of the fingerprint. Obviously there is a trade-off to consider here. If the fingerprint were not dense enough then it would not be unique and would lead to many false positives

Table 2. Steps of a typical plagiarism detection algorithm (based on Schleimer et al., 2003)

Sample text submitted to algorithm:
 	
"How to make a cup of tea
    1.   Get a cup
    2.   Place a teabag in the cup
    3.   Fill the kettle and boil
    4.   Pour boiling water into cup with teabag
    5.   Wait one minute to brew
    6. Add milk and sugar to taste"*		

Step in the fingerprinting algorithm	**Example execution using sample text**	**Comments**
1. Remove irrelevant information from text	howtomakeacupoftea1getacup2 placeateabaginthecup3fillthekett leandboil4pourboilingwaterintoc upwithteabag5waitoneminutetob rew6addmilkandsugartotaste	Remove all white space and punctuation to create a continuous (145) character string
2. Create k-grams of the Step 1 text where k is a parameter (here chosen as 5)	howto, owtom, wtoma, tomak, omake, makea, akeac, keacu, eacup, acupo, cupof, upoft, pofte, oftea, fteag, teage, eaget, ageta, getac, etacu, tacup, …	The 5-grams are created as follows: take the first 5 characters together; move one character right; take the next 5 characters together; and continue until the whole document is done. Here we have only done the first 21 characters. There will normally be almost as many k-grams as there are characters in the document (145 in our case)
3. Convert all k-grams into hashes using a hash function	[**77**, 74, 42, 17], [**98**, 50, 17, 98],[**8**, 88, 67, 39],[**77**, 74, 42, 17],[**99**, 29, 80, 52],[**75**, … (these are hypothetical examples)	A hash function[6] is a program that converts a character string into an integer (in the example 'howto' becomes '77'). Note that the conversion does not always produce a unique result.
4. Take a sample of consecutive hashes from the string of all the hashes (at least one from each window) and store this as the digital fingerprint of the document	77, 98, 8, 77, 99, 75	The technique for selecting the sample from the population of hashes (created in step 3) is crucial. If the gap between successive hashed is too big then the 'identity' of chunks of the document can be lost. If it is too small then a large amount of information will be stored as the fingerprint, which will be inefficient (and costly in terms of resources). Winnowing requires at least one hash from a window of hashes indicated by the [] in step 3 above.
5. Store fingerprint for detection purpose		

(incorrect identification of text as "copies"). On the other hand if it is too dense then it will be inefficient, as it would require a huge amount of computing resources to process the fingerprints when a comparison is made. What does this mean in practice?

In experiments done by the authors of winnowing using 500,000 Web pages (in HTML format), it was found that these consisted of 7,182,692,852 bytes of text (approximately 14,300 bytes per page). After step 1, these were reduced to 1,940,576,448 bytes of data. This represents an enormous 73 percent reduction. This means that 73 percent of the documents consisted of white spaces and formatting data and only 27 percent was actual content. This is the redundancy required to make our documents easy to read (spaces between words, lines between paragraphs, headings, formatting, etc.). The results of the first step were hashed in step 3 to create 1,940,576,399 hashes. From these hashes 38,530,846 fingerprints were selected as the fingerprint of the 500,000 Web pages (approximately 78 bytes of fingerprint per page text). This is a reduction gives a fingerprint density of 1.9855 percent. This means that the size of the fingerprint (selected hashes) is only 0.536 percent of the original document size. This implies that we can uniquely identify a document with a fingerprint that is only 0.536 percent of the size of the original document. Stated differently, it is the same as saying a typical research paper of 8,000 words can be uniquely identified by a "fingerprint" that is the equivalent of a sequence of 43 words selected from the document—obviously the algorithm is more complex than such a comparison would suggest.

With such a reduction, will it not be possible that there will be many documents that end up having the same fingerprint? In their experiments with winnowing, Schleimer et al. (2003) have found that: "82 percent of the fingerprints selected by winnowing were chosen [occurred] only once; 14 percent were selected twice; and only 2 percent occurred three times." Thus, they are fairly confident that they will be able to detect the source document if given a sufficiently large "chunk" from it. In the case of winnowing, it has to be greater than the window (or chunk) size, which is a user parameter that was set as approximately 100 characters in the reported experiments. This is because the algorithm ensures that it takes at least one unique hash from each window for the fingerprint.[7] Most sentences in this chapter vary between 50 and 300 characters. The vast majority is over 100. Thus, any partial copy of a document—greater than 100 characters—will map onto a part of the fingerprint, making it possible to identify the part as belonging to the document identified by the fingerprint. Furthermore, the use of k-grams (k successive sequence of characters) means that the algorithm will be robust against "noise," that is, it will not simply match common phrases with copies of those phrases in other documents.

From this discussion, it is clear that plagiarism detection algorithms are reasonably robust at linking copies or part copies back to its source document. Let us now consider some of the implications of the implementation of the algorithms for detecting plagiarism.

We need to start by reminding ourselves that plagiarism detection systems (contrary to their name) *do not detect plagiarism*. They only detect copies (or part copies) of documents. This is an important point. Not all copies are plagiarised and not all plagiarism comes in the form of exact text copies. Thus, there is not a one-to-one relationship between copies and plagiarism.

To Copy is Not Always to Plagiarise

There may be a variety of reasons why a copy does not represent plagiarism. It may be a legitimately referenced quote. It also may be a phrase that coincidently corresponds to a phrase in another document. However, most important for us, it may be a patch in a patch-written text. As argued above, it is very likely that international students, who are novices in academic writing, may present their work through patch-writing. This issue becomes more acute when student essays are batch submitted for checking and a threshold as a percentage of a document copied is set quite low (as one can do in these systems) for cases to be further investigated. One might argue that the international student's patch-writing and use of familiar sources to expressions of the expert will exaggerate the difference between them and the native students even if it is legitimately referenced, thereby "pushing" the native-speaker down below the line of detection. It is also likely that native speakers will be more able to use patches in such a way that they may be identified as paraphrases rather than direct copies. This easily can be done by the careful use of synonyms and slight changes in the structure of sentences. However, such more subtle changes require a more sophisticated linguistic ability that may be beyond the level of a non-native speaker.

To Plagiarise is Not Always to Copy

Plagiarism detection systems are based on the principle of character sequence detection, as seen above. This means that it can only identify plagiarism where there is an exact copy made of a string of characters (irrespective of location on the page). This sort of detection will obviously tend to show up those students who tend do retain exact copies of phrases or sentences. It therefore will not detect those that copy structure, arguments, or ideas but express these in "their own words." Thus, plagiarism detection systems operate with the assumption that to plagiarise one needs to use the exact words of another. This is a very "legalistic" view of plagiarism. It is similar to the legal view of copyright—adopted in most western countries—which suggests that one can only copyright expression and not ideas. Clearly this is a very narrow definition of plagiarism; an assumption that favours the native speaker and disproportionately penalises the non-native speaker. The native speaker has the linguistic skills to eloquently re-express the work of others and remain undetected by the detection algorithm. It is evident that if the task of plagiarism detection is "delegated" to algorithms, then there is a strong possibility that this might create the conditions for constructing international students as plagiarists while also allowing for native speaking plagiarists to remain undetected.

ON THE (UN)CONSTRUCTION OF PLAGIARISTS

There is no doubt that plagiarism is a problem for most universities in Australia, the UK, and the USA and that this is a complex problem that defies simplistic solutions—as most authors in the field will agree. It is our argument that a reactive punitive response to plagiarism based on an algorithmic detection approach is unfair for the following reasons:

a. It makes inappropriate assumptions about plagiarism, for example, copy = plagiarism.

b. International students are predisposed to the use of exact copies in their writing practice (in patch-writing and keeping the master's voice) and are therefore inappropriately identified as plagiarists. This often leads to further more detailed and meticulous scrutiny, something other students are not subjected to.

c. Thus, international students tend to be disproportionately identified as plagiarists to the benefit of native speakers who may plagiarise through the unattributed copying of ideas and arguments of others and yet remain undetected.

d. Plagiarism algorithms, or more specifically the assumptions embedded in them, are developed within a western cultural context which makes particular assumptions about the nature of teaching and learning. As such they may unfairly discriminate against those from non-western backgrounds.

Obviously, this argument still is somewhat tentative and needs further evidence for it to become sufficiently robust. Nevertheless, it seems at least plausible. As such we would suggest that there are a number of things that staff in Australian, British, and North American institutions could and need to do to address the issues raised by this chapter. Let us briefly state them.

a. The issue of plagiarism detection cannot be delegated to an electronic detection system or service. As the quality guru

Edwards Deming (1986) said: "you cannot inspect quality into the product." Quality is a systemic outcome of the whole system. Likewise, plagiarism cannot be "detected" out of the learning process. The elimination of plagiarism requires a systemic approach which involves the whole system.

b. An appreciation and understanding of the learning and teaching environment from which our international students come is required in order to create the mechanisms and resources that will make their transition to western systems as easy as possible.

c. Western universities ought to take a formative attitude to plagiarism in which they accept that patch-writing may be a legitimate interim step to the development of independent writing skills. In this regard, plagiarism detection systems can act as a mechanism to help students and lecturers to become aware and monitor this transition to independence. This will have important implications for how institutional rules and frameworks for dealing with plagiarism will be formulated and implemented.

d. There is a need to develop a much better understanding of how plagiarism detection systems work. What are the assumptions the make? How do the different parameters interact? How do these favour some forms of plagiarism and not others? This may be difficult as most systems are based on proprietary systems where the algorithms and code is not available for inspection.

CONCLUSION

Our chapter seeks to provide further insights into why some students may be identified as plagiarists. We accept that students may plagiarise as a consequence of poor time management, a marks orientation, and so on. We also accept that due to being disaffected from their studies, students may deliberately plagiarise. Indeed, when there is no or little interest in a subject, plagiarism could be an attractive option. But what about those students who are interested and committed to a subject who are identified as plagiarists? In relation to non-native students, we suggest that there may be an alternate series of explanations for why many non-native students are incorrectly identified as plagiarists. We do acknowledge that some international students have an awareness of the need to reference (Dryden, 1999), but we argue that it is one thing to be aware of referencing and another to know how to undertake the practices required of them within specific cultural contexts; namely, due to their lack of familiarity with the education context in the west, their limited ability to develop an independent argument, and importantly, them learning to undertake academic writing in a second or third language. Our chapter has pointed to the strong possibility that international students are more likely to be detected as having significant strings of unattributed characters that are copied from another source. This may be due to writing in patches or to native students being much better at remaining undetected, and as a consequence, non-native writers may be rendered more visible. We suggest that utilising detection systems too early may take away the opportunities for learning that are required by such students in order to become embedded in a different education context and to develop all the practices that are required to succeed. Detecting such possibilities to learn while also upholding academic integrity is thus an important challenge when thinking through the use of plagiarism detection systems among overseas students in western universities.

In relation to further research in better understanding the plagiarism detection systems and the conditions that mediate the construction of international students as plagiarists, we suggest first that this requires rigorous analysis of the leading plagiarism detection vendors' proprietary algorithms and the ways they are appropriated in universities. We acknowledge that this will no doubt be challenging but will indicate how such systems differ to our findings with regard to winnowing's algorithm. Second, we have highlighted that in order to better understand the ways in which plagiarism detection systems may configure international students as plagiarists, future research needs to draw on literature that are diverse and span many different fields of study. We hope that this chapter can act as a springboard for ourselves and others to pursue these themes in subsequent research.

ACKNOWLEDGMENT

A previous version of this chapter, Introna and Hayes (2004) "Plagiarism, detection, and intentionality: On the construction of plagiarists," was presented and included in the proceedings of *Plagiarism: Prevention, Practice & Policy Conference*. St James Park, Newcastle upon Tyne 28-30 June. Newcastle: Northumbria University Press.

REFERENCES

Angelil-Carter, S. (2000). *Stolen language? Plagiarism in writing*. UK: Pearson Education Limited.

Angelova, M., & Riazantseva, A. (1999). "If you don't tell me, how can I know?": A case study of four international students learning to write the U.S. way." *Written Communication,16*(4), 491-525.

Bao, J. P., Shen, J. Y., Liu, X. D., & Liu, H. Y. (2006). A fast document copy detection model. *Soft Computing, 10*(1), 41-46.

Biggs, J. (1994). Asian learners through Western eyes: An astigmatic paradox. *Australian and New Zealand Journal of Vocational Educational Research, 2*(2), 40-63.

Biggs, J., & Watkins, D. (1996). *The Chinese learner*. Hong Kong: Comparative Education Research Centre.

Brin, S., Davis, J., and Garcia-Molina, H. (1995) Copy detection mechanisms for digital documents. In the *proceedings of the ACM SIGMOD Conference*, pp.398-409.

Carroll, J. (2002). Suggestions for teaching international students more effectively. Learning and Teaching Briefing Papers Series, Oxford Brookes University, www.brookesac.uk/services/ocsd

Carroll, J., & Appleton, J. (2001). *Plagiarism: A good practice guide*. Oxford: JISC, Oxford Brookes University.

Deckert, G. (1993). Perspectives on plagiarism from ESL students in Hong Kong. *Journal of Second Language Writing,2*(2), 131-148.

Deming, W. E. (1986). *Out of the crisis*. Cambridge, MA: Massachusetts Institute of Technology Press.

Dreyfus, H. L. (1992). *What computers still can't do*. Cambridge, MA: Massachusetts Institute of Technology Press.

Dryden, L. (1999). A distant mirror or through the looking glass? Plagiarism and intellectual property in Japanese education. In L. Buranen & A. Roy (Eds.), *Perspectives on plagiarism and intellectual property in a postmodern world* (pp. 75-85). Albany, NY: State University of New York Press.

Errey, L. (2002). *Plagiarism: Something fishy? ...Or just a fish out of water?* OCSLD

Harris, R. A. (2001). *The plagiarism handbook: Strategies for preventing, detecting, and dealing with plagiarism*. Los Angeles: Pyrczak Publishing.

Hayes, N. & Introna. L. (2005). Cultural values, plagiarism, and fairness: When plagiarism gets in the way of learning, *Ethics and Behavior, 15*(3), 213-231.

Heintze, N. (1996). Scalable document fingerprinting. In *Proceedings of the Second USENIX Electronic Commerce Workshop*, pp. 191-200.

Howard, R. (1993). A plagiarism pentimento. *Journal of Teaching Writing, 11*(2), 233-245.

Howard, R. (1995) Plagiarism, authorship, and the academic death penalty. *College English, 57*(1), 788-805.

Hull, G. & Rose, M. (1989). Rethinking remediation: Toward a social-cognitive understanding of problematic reading and writing. *Written Communication, 6*(2), 139-154.

Kolich, A. M. (1983). Plagiarism: The worm of reason. *College English,* 4, 141-148.

Lathrop, A. (2000). *Student cheating and plagiarism in the Internet era: A wake-up call.* Englewood, CO: Libraries Unlimited.

Marsh, C. & Morris, P. (eds.) (1991). *Curriculum development in East Asia.* London: Falmer Press.

Morris, P. & Sweeting, A.(eds.) (1995). *Education and development in East Asia.* New York and London: Garland Publishing Inc.

Moeller, H. (2003). Before and after representation. *Semiotica, 143*(1/4), 69–77.

Myers, S. (1998). Questioning author(ity): ESL/EFL, science, and teaching about plagiarism. *Teaching English as a Second or Foreign Language, 3*(2). http://www-writing.berkeley.edu/TESL-EJ/ej10/a2.html

O'Connor, S. (2003, May 6-9). Cheating and electronic plagiarism—Scope, consequences, and detection. In *Proceedings EDUCAUSE in Australasia,* Adelaide, (CD-ROM).

O'Donoghue, T. (1996). Malaysian Chinese student's perceptions of what is necessary for their academic success in Australia: A case study at one university. *Journal of Further and Higher Education, 20*(2), 67-80.

Pennycook, A. (1996). Borrowing others' words: Text, ownership, memory, and plagiarism. *TESOL Quarterly, 30*(2), 210-230.

Ryan, J. (2000). *A guide to teaching international students.* Oxford: Oxford Centre for Staff Development, Oxford Brookes University.

Schleimer, S., Wilkerson, D.,& Aiken, A. (2003, June). Winnowing: Local algorithms for document fingerprinting. In *Proceedings of the ACM SIGMOD International Conference on Management of Data,* 76-85.

Scollon, R. (1995). Plagiarism and ideology: Identity in intercultural discourse. *Language in Society, 24*(1), 1-28.

Sherman, J. (1992). Your own thoughts in your own words. *ELT Journal, 46*(2), 190-198.

Turner, Y. (2000). Chinese students: Teaching, learning, and equality in UK higher education. *Higher Education Equal Opportunities Network, National Network Newsletter for Equal Opportunities Practitioners,* Spring, Issue 13, http://www.worc.ac.uk/services/equalopps/HEEON/newsonline.htm#Yvonne%27s

ENDNOTES

[1]   We use the term "international student" to refer to those students that come from a culture in which copying is valued differently—as compared to the UK—and who are non-native English speakers, that is,

have English as a second or third language. Currently these students represent 26 percent of the UK postgraduate populations (UKCOSA).

[2] Australia, the UK and the USA are the three most popular destinations for international students. However, our analysis is also equally relevant to countries whose educations systems resemble these three.

[3] We use the term Western to refer to universities in Australia, UK and North America. However, it also refers to all countries whose universities are based on the argumentative style that typifies the institutions in the three countries listed above.

[4] Such reports indicate the percentage of copied text for the documents as a whole, they list them in rank by module, and then the individual reports highlight the sources that text that is identified as being copied derives from.

[5] Also refer to Heintze (1996) and Bao, Shen, Liu, and Liu (2006) for alternative methods.

[6] A more technical definition of hash function is "A **hash function** is a function that converts an input from a (typically) large domain [input values] into an output in a (typically) smaller range (the *hash value*, often a subset of the integers). (from http://en.wikipedia.org/wiki/Hash_function)

[7] Unless consecutive hashes are the same, then it is omitted, which is why there are less hashes than there are sentences in a document.

Section IV
Two Specific Issues

Chapter IX
Plagiarism and the Community College

Teri Thomson Maddox
Jackson State Community College, USA

ABSTRACT

Although plagiarism is a problem in all educational institutions, the diversity of the community college student population and of the community college mission creates even more challenges. The purpose of this chapter is to discuss characteristics of community college students, define intentional and unintentional plagiarism, and provide methods that faculty can use to help students avoid both kinds of plagiarism.

INTRODUCTION

Most sources agree that plagiarism is a major problem for educational institutions (Breen & Maassen, 2005; Ercegovac & Richardson, 2004; Furedi, 2004; Martin, 1994; Ryan, 2004; Standler, 2000). In their literature review of academic dishonesty and plagiarism, Ercegovac and Richardson (2004) quote a Bronfenbrenner et al. report, *The State of Americans,* "Virtually every high school student in 1989 (97 percent) admits having let another student copy from his or her work" (p. 311). More recently, the Internet has helped make copy and paste plagiarism fast and easy; furthermore, Internet paper mills are relatively

inexpensive and offer papers that are harder for teachers to detect (Bloomfield, 2004; Bombak, 2005; Edlund, 2000; Ercegovac & Richardson, 2004; Harris, 2004; Howard, 2001; Leland, 2002; McKenzie, 1998; Murray, 2002; Plagiarism.org, 2005; Rocklin, 1998; Ryan, 2004; Scanlon, 2003; Standler, 2000; Sterngold, 2004). Amazon.com has a "Search Inside the Book" feature that allows users to search for ideas and content within specific texts (Sterngold, 2004), certainly a valuable research tool but also a plagiarist's golden opportunity. The Council of Writing Program Administrators (WPA) states that the ease of Internet plagiarism "has begun to affect teachers at all levels, at times diverting them from the work of developing students' writing, reading, and critical thinking abilities."

If technology has amplified the problem of plagiarism for all educational institutions, the problem seems especially pronounced in the community college setting because of the diversity of the student population and because of the emphasis that community colleges put on meeting their students' changing needs. This chapter will define plagiarism, describe the growth of the community college and characteristics of community college students, and provide instructional approaches faculty can use to help students avoid both intentional and unintentional plagiarism.

PLAGIARISM CONFUSION

Students and faculty have difficulties with plagiarism on college campuses because the concept of plagiarism is misunderstood (Breen & Maassen, 2005; Ercegovac & Richardson, 2004; Scanlon, 2003). Even though almost every institution's Web site contains definitions of academic dishonesty and plagiarism, Breen and Maassen (2005) state that it is clear that "the existence of a policy was not sufficient in and of itself to eliminate plagiarism." Scanlon (2003) says that the "amount of misconception on this topic appears to have grown exponentially in the past few years, as access to the Internet becomes nearly universal." He cites several studies that suggest that students are not sure what plagiarism is and that they do not think it is as serious an issue as faculty does.

Faculty also may be unclear about plagiarism definitions, types, and consequences (Breen & Maassen, 2005; Ercegovac & Richardson, 2004; Scanlon, 2003). In their literature review of academic dishonesty, Ercegovac and Richardson (2004) cite a study by Burke of faculty at a two-year college: "The fact that 86 percent of the studied faculty suspected academic dishonesty in their classroom but did not perceive it to be a major problem should be investigated further" (p. 310).

They cite other studies that find that although faculty members complain about cheating and plagiarism, "many do little or nothing about it … It seems there is a lack of alignment between offences and punishment and a lack of communication among administrators, faculty, parents, and students" (p. 311).

The WPA Council Web site, "Defining and Avoiding Plagiarism," states that students may be confused because "academicians and scholars may define plagiarism differently or more stringently than have instructors or administrators in students' earlier education or in other writing situations." For Murray (2002), these definitions vary widely even "across and within departments, allowing students wiggle room and making it tempting for faculty to ignore potential problems."

DEFINITIONS OF PLAGIARISM

McLemee (2004) cites the Oxford English Dictionary's definition of *plagiarism*: it is derived from the Latin *plagiarius*, meaning "one who abducts the child or slave of another," and "the word plagiarism was first used in its current sense by the Roman poet Martial, in the first century AD, as a sarcastic put-down of another writer who had cribbed some of Martial's verse" (p. A9). Today, most educational institutions consider plagiarism a threat to ethical standards; The Purdue Online Writing Lab (OWL) says that "There are few intellectual offenses more serious than plagiarism in academic and professional contexts," (Stolley, 2006), and Bolkan (2006) calls it "the unoriginal sin" (p. 13).

The Council of Writing Program Administrators (WPA) seems to take a moderate approach to the issue, defining plagiarism in the following way: "In an instructional setting, plagiarism occurs when a writer deliberately uses someone else's language, ideas, or other original (not common knowledge) material without acknowledging its source." The key term here seems to be *deliber-*

ately. The WPA Council distinguishes between plagiarism and misuse of sources:

students are not guilty of plagiarism when they try in good faith to acknowledge others' work but fail to do so accurately or fully. These failures are largely the result of failures in prior teaching and learning: students lack the knowledge of and ability to use the conventions of authorial attribution.

Like the word *deliberate*, the words *in good faith* take into account student *intentions*, not just the results. Several sources agree that many plagiarism cases are probably inadvert (Breen & Maassen, 2005; Martin, 1994). Martin (1994) says, "Students are apprentices, and some of them learn the scholarly trade slowly" (p. 37).

On the other hand, other sources do not try to judge whether the use was deliberate or not and make no distinction between plagiarism and misuse of sources. In fact, for Standler (2000), "the intent of a plagiarist is *ir*relevant. The act of quoting material without including the indicia of a quotation is sufficient to convict someone of plagiarism. It is *no defense* for the plagiarist to say 'I forgot.' or 'It is only a rough draft.' or 'I did not know it was plagiarism.'"

Like Standler, several university Web sites do not take into account the writer's intention. Stolley, on the Purdue OWL Web site, "Avoiding Plagiarism," warns students that even "inadvertent mistakes can lead to charges of plagiarism … A charge of plagiarism can have severe consequences, including expulsion from a university or loss of a job, not to mention a writer's loss of credibility and professional standing." These are very strong words, perhaps intending to scare students into taking the issue seriously. The Georgetown University "What Is Plagiarism?" Web site informs students that "even using one of [a source's] small,

characteristic phrases without quotation marks is considered plagiarism." Similarly, McLemee (2004) defines plagiarism in this way: "A writer who fails to give appropriate acknowledgment when repeating another's wording or particularly apt term, paraphrasing another's argument, or presenting another's line of thinking is guilty of plagiarism." These definitions make no distinction between deliberate plagiarism and inadvertent plagiarism or misuse of sources.

These examples seem to illustrate that there are major differences that hinge on whether institutions make allowance for intention or deliberateness. However, McCullen (2003) acknowledges that "it is not so easy to draw a hard and fast line between what is a deliberate case of plagiarism and an unintentional error in citation" (p. 40).

Because community colleges attract diverse students with diverse educational goals, faculty members need to acknowledge the problems their students face when given a writing or research project and help them avoid both intentional and unintentional plagiarism. Intentional plagiarism, which takes place when a student buys a paper from a paper mill, uses another student's paper as if it were his or her own, or fabricates sources or citations, can be addressed by restructuring assignments, helping students develop better time management skills, and using learner-centered teaching methods. Unintentional plagiarism, which occurs when the student uses a phrase from a source and cites it but does not put it in quotation marks, when the student copies and pastes to such an extent that he or she loses control of the paper, or when the student inaccurately records source material, can be addressed using student/teacher conferences, portfolios, and peer evaluations.

In order to understand why plagiarism is a problem in community colleges, a discussion of the characteristics of community college students is provided.

GROWTH OF COMMUNITY COLLEGES

Since the beginnings of the community college system in 1901 when Mt. Juliet Community College in Illinois was begun as an outgrowth of high school, community colleges have altered the American postsecondary educational system, making college more accessible and more affordable. Kasper (2002-2003), an economist for the Office of Occupational Statistics, states, "No other segment of postsecondary education has been more responsive to its community's workforce needs. At community colleges, students can learn at any point in their lives while taking advantage of low tuition, convenient campus locations, open admissions, and comprehensive course offerings" (p. 14). Enrollments in community colleges have grown faster than four-year institutions. According to Kasper, "enrollment at public four-year colleges and universities roughly doubled from 1965 to 1999, while enrollment at public community colleges increased about fivefold" (p. 14). Kasper states that although 26 percent of all students attending public degree-granting institutions in 1965 attended community colleges, that percentage had almost doubled in 1992 to 48 percent (p. 14). More than 11.5 million students attend nearly 1200 community colleges (Lamkin, 2004).

Community colleges might have begun as a low cost alternative for students seeking a four-year degree who were denied access to universities, but the mission of community colleges has expanded to include career certificate training, workplace training, continuing education opportunities, associate degrees, and associate of applied science degrees. Many students attend a community college to transfer to a four-year institution, but others want to fulfill short-term goals. This diversity of mission is one way that community colleges differ from four-year institutions. Carnevale (2001) highlights the advantages of a community college education:

Unlike company-training programs, which usually omit academic preparation, and four-year colleges, which provide academic challenges but rarely link them to occupational constructs, community colleges are able to provide students with the tools they need to sustain career in the modern economy by developing a curricula that incorporates both academic knowledge and occupational skill training.

This goal of bridging academia and the work place can be accomplished by focusing on student needs, but this task is made difficult because of the diverse student population in the community college.

THE COMMUNITY COLLEGE STUDENT

Besides the differences in their educational mission, community colleges and four-year institutions also differ in student diversity. According to Lamkin (2004), the image of a typical college student as "a recent high school graduate, a young, white, middle-or upper-income person pursuing a four-year degree on a residential campus" (p. 12) has changed. Perhaps this image may describe students at many four-year institutions, but not community colleges, which now account for about half of the U.S. postsecondary student population (Sampson, 2004). Lamkin (2004) states, "attracting particularly high proportions of underserved students, including low-income students, first-generation college-goers, and students of color, community colleges enroll 46 percent of all African American, 55 percent of all Hispanic, and 55 percent of all Native American students" (p. 12). Asians and Hispanics are the fastest growing minorities (American Association of Community Colleges, 2000). "As with other groups before them, upwardly mobile ethnic and racial groups will rely on community colleges as their on-ramp to the higher education highway" (Carnevale, 2001).

Lamkin (2004) reports that community college students are often at-risk; more than half of them have at least two of the seven characteristics that have been shown to influence drop out rates: delayed enrollment after high school graduation, lack of a high school diploma, part-time enrollment, full-time work (at least 30 hours a week), financial independence from parents, dependants other than a spouse, or single parenthood. "Low income and students of color are especially likely to exhibit these characteristics" (p. 12).

Teaching students how to avoid plagiarism may make sense in the white majority American culture with its emphasis on the importance of the individual, copyright law, and the legality of ownership of individual ideas. However, other cultures may not value this kind of individual ownership, so plagiarism of words and ideas may not be something community college students from non-white cultures see any reason to avoid. English as a second language (ESL) students may have particular problems understanding plagiarism issues since they have a language as well as a culture difference from mainstream America (Breen & Maassen, 2005; Ercegovac & Richardson, 2004).

UNDERPREPARED STUDENTS

The open door policy of most community colleges allows students who would never have been able to attend a university to begin a college education, even with poor high school GPAs, low placement tests, and limited financial resources. Shemo (2006) describes hundreds of thousands of students arriving at community college doors, "eager but unready." Many of these students are the first in their families or neighborhood to attend college, so they have no mentors in their families or peer group. Most underprepared students lack academic writing and research skills. They may

not be able to comprehend a syllabus description on how to avoid plagiarism or understand Web site examples of plagiarism.

On its Web site, The University of Alberta lists the following reasons why students plagiarize, all of which may be exacerbated by underprepared students' lack of academic experience:

- Lack of research skills
- Problems evaluating Internet sources
- Confusion between plagiarism and paraphrasing
- Careless note taking
- Confusion about how to properly cite sources
- Misconception of plagiarism
- Misconception of intellectual property, copyright, and public domain
- Misconception of common knowledge
- Perception of online information as public knowledge
- Poor time management and organizational skills
- The commodification of knowledge and education

Although most campuses have some kind of tutoring centers that provide free support for students who are delving into writing or research projects, the irony is that underprepared students often are the very ones who do not take advantage of the opportunity. They know they have academic limitations, but they are afraid to take the very public step into an academic assistance center for fear of announcing their weaknesses to the world. Faculty can help students overcome their embarrassment by sharing information and statistics from the centers that show that many A and B students take advantage of tutors and academic support. Another suggestion is to have the staff from the center visit the classroom, or even better to take the entire class over to visit the center so that students will be familiar with the people and environment. Often a class visit is all it takes to give underprepared students the confidence to ask for help.

Since their scholastic experience is limited, underprepared students are often confused by the idea of common knowledge. A definition is given by Stolley on the Purdue OWL Web site: "Generally speaking, you can regard something as common knowledge if you find the same information undocumented in at least five credible sources. Additionally, it might be common knowledge if you think the information you're presenting is something your readers will already know, or something that a person could easily find in general reference sources." However, underprepared students might have problems understanding the meaning of "undocumented," "credible sources," and "general reference sources."

Paraphrasing is also difficult for underprepared students. Lacking formal academic language, they often cannot state in their own words what a source is saying. In order to avoid plagiarism, they instead quote whole sections of source material rather than summarizing or paraphrasing. Until underprepared students have the expanded vocabulary that comes with educational experience, paraphrasing will remain a difficult task for them. Faculty who receive an overly quoted paper should realize that the student is trying to follow the academic rules of citing sources and needs to be guided to gain control over those sources in small steps. Requiring students to print out and attach source material to their research paper rather than allowing students to rely on copying and pasting is one way teachers can help students begin the critical thinking process it takes to paraphrase and summarize.

A research paper or project is "one of the most challenging projects students undertake in college because it requires strong research, writing, and critical thinking skills to carry out successfully" (Sterngold, 2004), and the lessons learned from such a project are crucial to students' educational experience. Unfortunately, because of the bad experiences community college faculty have had

when they get poorly documented papers, riddled with organizational and grammar errors, many stop requiring a research paper.

To help support underprepared students, many colleges offer developmental courses. Nordstrom (1997) states that according to the National Center for Education Statistics (NCES), 78 percent of all postsecondary institutions offered at least one developmental reading, writing, or mathematics course in 1995. Virtually all public two-year institutions and 81 percent of public four-year institutions offered developmental courses, while 63 percent of private two- and four-year institutions offered them. Developmental classes help older students review academic skills they may have forgotten and help recent high school graduates develop college-level skills they may have never been taught. Students who graduate from high school on a technical track, for example, may not have taken a foreign language, history, algebra, or academic writing class, so if they decide to attend college, they are deficient in many college-level areas.

FIRST GENERATION STUDENTS

Community colleges are often the choice for first generation students, but being the first person in the family to attend college is intimidating. Bureaucratic red tape, which is frustrating for most all students, is almost insurmountable for students who have no family or peer mentors. Technology has made it possible to put many of the traditional print-based institutional documents online, including class schedules, the catalog, and the student handbook. In addition, the admissions process, financial aid process, class selection process, and registration process at many institutions are also online, so students may feel like they have no face-to-face help to advise them either at school or at home. In addition, first generation students are often unprepared for college demands; Pascarella et al. (1996) suggest that first generation students enter college academically at risk and are not likely to experience conditions positively related to persistence, performance, and learning. They have weaker reading and creative thinking skills, lower degree aspirations, study less, take fewer humanities and fine arts courses, work more, complete fewer hours, less frequently attend racial or cultural awareness activities, and receive less encouragement from friends to continue enrollment.

MINORITY STUDENTS

Even though community colleges attract a high percentage of minority students, the degree attainment rates for minority students are dismal. Laden (2004) reports that in 2000, over 230,000 students earned community college degrees, with three-fourths of those degrees going to white students. "Despite the growing presence of nonwhite students, only 9.6 percent of associate degrees were awarded to African Americans, 10.1 percent to Hispanics, 5.3 percent to Asian American and Pacific Islanders, and 1.0 percent to American Indians and Alaska Natives" (p. 9). Many factors play a role in why many minority students fail to complete a degree, so institutions should continue to focus on the social, financial, and academic problems facing students and provide prompt assistance when warning signs appear.

SOCIOECONOMIC FACTORS

Community students often have financial issues. Tuition and fees have increased at community colleges, but not as fast as four-year institutions. Kasper (2002-2003) states that in-state tuition for community colleges for the academic year 1976-77 was an average of $283 and by 2001-2001 had increased to $1,359, an increase of 380 percent, while four-year public institutions' tuition rose

from an average $617 to $3,506, an increase of 468 percent.

Two out of five students enrolled in developmental courses receive some form of financial aid (Boylan, 1999) and Knopp (1996) found that nearly one quarter (22 percent) of those taking developmental courses reported an annual family income of less than $20,000, while only 14 percent of those not enrolled in these courses reported the same income level. Many of these students do not have computers at home, so they may be as unsure of the rules of the Internet as they are the methods of online research, factors that might lead to unintentional plagiarism.

ADULT LEARNERS

In "Facilitating Responsibility for Learning in Adult Community College Students," Howell (2001) states that more than 2.5 million adult students (age 25 and older) attend community colleges, and Phillippe (2000) uses statistics from the National Center for Educational Statistics to show that in 1997, 32 percent of community college students were 30 years of age or older and 46 percent were 25 or older. Nordstrom (1997) found a 50 percent increase in the number of college students in the U.S. who are 25 years old or older, and the total number of adult students increased from 32 percent of the population in 1991 to 40 percent in 1995.

Many adult students need remediation, according to Roueche and Roueche (1999), who state that high school graduates who do not enroll in college immediately after leaving high school are more likely to need remediation in more than one subject area than graduates who enroll immediately. Therefore, as the adult population in college swells, so does the number of underprepared students.

Even though adult students may need developmental courses or extra support services to brush up on academic skills they may have forgotten, most studies including one by Whisnant, Sullivan, and Slayton (1992) find that older, nontraditional students perform at a higher academic level than younger, traditional students. Most college faculty are happy to have nontraditional students in their classes because they bring experience, life-lessons, maturity, and what Whisnant et al. call "an educationally focused personality" with them, attributes which motivate them to have a serious academic bent. Many are paying for their classes themselves since they are no longer dependent on parental support, so they intend to get their money's worth.

Focusing on adult learners as a separate area of study from younger learners was first championed by Knowles (1984) who proposed a new label for adult learning, *andragogy,* to distinguish adult learning theory from *pedagogy.* Knowles' model lists the following characteristics of adult learners:

1. Adults both desire and enact a tendency to be self directed;
2. Adults' experiences are a rich resource for learning;
3. Adults are aware of specific learning needs generated by real life tasks or problems;
4. Adults are competency-based learners: they want to apply newly acquired skills or knowledge to their immediate circumstances; and
5. They are problem-centered rather than subject centered.

Although there is a debate about whether andragogy can be defined as a distinct learning theory (see Merriam & Caffarella, 1999, pp. 272-278), it offers educators a new way of looking at their students, allowing them more opportunity to choose, plan, and evaluate their educational experiences. Because adults want to apply their learning to their immediate circumstances, they may become frustrated with writing a research paper for its own sake, especially if the topic seems irrelevant or the task seems overly burdensome. Adult learners want to be able to connect material to their own experiences; learning needs to be relevant and practical, so adults may feel that typical writing or research assignments are busy work. Bloomfield (2004) states, "If students believe an assignment is 'busy work,' some will be busy cheating." Pearson (2004) states that "given the pressures students feel to produce a number of papers and to get good grades, they may feel it is not worth their time to write an original paper for a class not in their major."

Adult learners bring a certain set of characteristics with them according to Horne and Carroll (1996): they are more likely to attend part-time, to enroll intermittently, to work full-time, and to support dependents, often as single parents. In the technology-filled classroom, adult learners may feel far inferior to their traditionally-aged fellow students who seem to have been born with a computer in their hands. They may make more inadvertent plagiarism mistakes because they are not familiar with Internet research.

Adults may take their classroom experiences more personally than traditional students, according to Zemke and Zemke (1988): "Self-esteem and ego are on the line when they are asked to risk trying a new behavior in front of peers and cohorts. Bad experiences in traditional education, feelings about authority and the preoccupation with events outside the classroom affect in-class experience" (p. 610). They may be embarrassed to ask for help from the teacher, especially in front of their classmates.

Adults who have worked in business before coming back to the community college for their first or second degree are familiar with the "just-in-time" system of inventory. Most businesses cannot stay profitable if they must store unneeded inventory. Many adult students transfer this idea to their learning and ask difficult questions of teachers. Exactly why do I need to learn this material? Exactly how will this class help me in

131

my job and my life? According to Ryan (2004), "A just-in-time theory of knowledge says that it's actually a waste of effort to learn things that can be easily referenced. And as time becomes a premium commodity in our society, this may be an attractive concept" (p. 64). Ryan continues, "Yet educators know that the life-changing effects of thinking require introspection and examination, neither of which can be achieved through just-in-time knowledge acquisition" (p. 64).

Although this discussion has given examples of adult characteristics and reasons why adult students could be tempted to plagiarize intentionally, there is no evidence that adult learners would be more likely to do so than traditional college students. In fact, most evidence is to the contrary. Ercegovac and Richardson (2004) cite a large-scale study of students in the United Kingdom that found that cheating declines with age. Unintentional rather than intentional plagiarism may be the bigger problem for adult students because they have been out of school for several years and may not be aware of academic conventions.

TIME MANAGEMENT

One of the most common excuses students use for intentionally plagiarizing is lack of time (Breen & Maassen 2005, WPA Statement on Best Practices). According to the American Association of Community Colleges (2006), 80 percent of community college students work full or part-time jobs, and work often interferes with study time. The National Center for Education Statistics Report, "Special Analysis 2002: Nontraditional Undergraduates," states that 46 percent of students who worked found that working limited their class schedule, 39 percent thought that working limited the number of classes they could take, and 30 percent found that working limited their access to the library. Almost half of the students reported that working has a negative effect on their grades.

Many students do not intend to plagiarize. Those who do usually have run out of time for their school work, and because of pressures from scholarships, family, or work, or because of unrealistic goals, they see plagiarizing as a better choice than failing the assignment (Pearson, 2004; WPA Council). It often does not occur to them that the penalties for being caught plagiarizing can be much greater than failing a paper or even a class. Teachers who have not built contingencies into deadlines may actually be inviting plagiarism. A more balanced approach might be to give students who have a reasonable excuse an extension or to deduct points for late assignments, but still allow them to be turned in. This approach may encourage students to complete their assignments successfully rather than being tempted to plagiarize.

Many community college students lack time management skills. They are not just students; they are workers, husbands and wives, parents, volunteers, and daughters and sons, with tremendous responsibilities and real-life problems outside the classroom. Many community college advisors notice that students want to schedule their classes back-to-back, with no times for study or meals. Students try to squeeze every available second into attending class before they rush off to jobs, pick up children from school, or take care of aging parents. First generation or underprepared students may not have thought about the possibility of attending part-time to keep their grades high because they are so eager to complete a degree and move on with their lives and careers. Advisors could encourage students to schedule study time on campus. The campus library, computers, access to tutors, and technology access at most colleges is superior to what students have at home at their disposal, so students who stay on campus to study can do so without worrying about children's needs, the doorbell ringing, and the pull of household chores.

Two-day-a-week classes are popular on community college campuses, especially with rising gas prices. Since most community colleges are commuter campuses, rising gas prices have hurt those students who have no options for public transportation or reasonably-priced dorms. Many community college students take a full load of classes on two days a week so they can attend school full time and still work the other three days and weekends. First generation students may be unaware of the amount of studying time that college faculty expect, not taking seriously the statement in their class syllabus that two hours study is expected for every hour of class. They often slide by, attending class but not truly digesting material, until the results of first test confirm that they did not spend the appropriate amount of time outside of class studying.

Faculty who schedule more frequent assignments and tests help their students by making the amount of material that must be learned smaller and more concentrated. Boylan's (2002) *What Works: Research-Based Best Practices in Developmental Education* lists frequent testing as one of the most valuable study aids teachers can provide, a key component being testing over each unit of instruction (p. 78). Frequent testing can include paper and pencil tests, computer tests, practice tests, pre-post tests, quizzes, verbal questioning, recitation, group and individual projects written papers, reports, class presentation, or completion of exercises (p. 79). Another way teachers can help students with time management is for faculty to use a class discussion to take their students through a personal day by day calendar, having students input the number of hours per week they must attend classes, commute, work, and sleep to give students a picture of the requirements of their daily lives. Then students must include study, time with family, recreation, as well. The Academic Advancement Center at Ohio University has a useful exercise on their Web site called "The 168-Hour Exercise: How Do I Use My Time Now?" Students enter the number of hours they spend in class, in study, on personal care, on meals, on commuting, at work, and at sleep to get their total fixed hours. The computer will calculate how much flexible time they have left over and students can evaluate the results.

Many underprepared students have unrealistic goals. Giving them research projects that are set up in small steps—turning in a topic, then a working bibliography, then notes, then a rough draft, then a peer-reviewed draft, then a final copy—helps them avoid procrastination. In addition, focusing on the process of writing a paper rather than the finished product means that students are less likely to buy a paper off the Internet and then backtrack to complete the required steps. Helping students manage their time is an important way faculty can reduce the possibility of plagiarism.

CRITICAL THINKING

Writing is thinking, so many of the problems community college students have with writing and research are actually critical thinking problems. Chaffee (1992) states that critical thinking is essential for college success, but few students are taught these skills in high school. In order to bridge the gap, problem solving and critical thinking should be taught as a part of each college course. Articles, research, resources, and conferences about critical thinking can be found at the Critical Thinking Community Web site. Boylan (2002) cites the model used by La-Guardia Community College in New York City which emphasizes the following skills: to solve challenging problems; to analyze complex issues and arrive at reasoned conclusions; to establish appropriate goals and design plans for action; to analyze complex bodies of information and make informed decisions; to communicate effectively through speaking, discussing, and writing; and to critically evaluate the logic, relevance, and validity of information (p. 96).

Students who are taught how to think logically and critically will be more ready to tackle writing and research projects with confidence and not be as tempted to plagiarize. Professors can use time at the beginning of the semester to suggest study strategies in their particular discipline, leading a class discussion about individual preferences and examples of students' successful or unsuccessful research attempts. Students might fill out a study inventory with questions such as: what time of day do I study best? Do I prefer a quiet atmosphere? Does music help me study? What kind/s? How do my study techniques differ from course to course? Where do I like to study? Do I like to study alone or in a group?

Another helpful technique at the beginning of the semester would be to encourage students to take one or more of the dozens of online learning style inventories and write a short response paper about the results so that they may more completely understand their own learning preferences. A good source is Community College's Web site "How to Study," which has a list of learning styles sites (MacDonald, 2007).

MORE ACCESS TO TECHNOLOGY

Because one of the missions of community colleges is to provide career training, computers and technology are an integral part of many classrooms. However, this easy access to computers and the Internet may invite copy and paste plagiarism, which concerns teachers and administrators "who want students' work to represent their own efforts and to reflect the outcomes of their learning" (WPA Council). Scanlon (2003) states: "In the not-so-distant past, plagiarism at least required time-consuming physical work: going to the library, searching, reading, and copying. Now a student can cobble together a paper from online sources literally in minutes" (p. 164). Georgetown University's Web site confronts the copy and paste syndrome this way:

The trouble comes when you start to use someone else's words all throughout your paper. Pretty *soon your paper looks like nothing but a field of quotation marks with a few country roads in between (your few sentences) connecting them. This does not represent very much intellectual work on your part. You have assembled a paper rather than writing one.*

Technology has also meant that online classes have made higher education more accessible for students, especially for those who work swing shifts, are disabled, must take care of dependents at home, or have transportation problems. Enrollment in these classes is growing. However, faculty witnessing student plagiarism problems in the traditional classroom wonder if those problems are compounded by online classes because of the lack of face-to-face contact. Additionally, underprepared students may have particular problems with online classes since many of these students lack academic reading experience. Online classes demand a higher level of reading comprehension than traditional classes as well as careful time management, computer expertise, organizational expertise, and critical thinking skills, areas underprepared students may not have mastered. Without a face-to-face teacher to provide quick answers to the dozens of questions underprepared students might face in a typical research or writing assignment, inadvertent plagiarism should probably be expected.

Scanlon (2003) cites recent studies that suggest that instances of plagiarism have not necessarily grown because of easy access of the Internet. A study by Scanlon and Neumann in 2002 found the same levels of copy and paste plagiarism occurred as were found by a 1996 survey by McCabe and Trevino, approximately 25 percent. "Of course, no one should be happy that 'only' a quarter of college students surveyed self-reported Internet plagiarism, even if this number argues against popular notions of an epidemic of online cheating" (p. 162).

ADJUNCT FACULTY

Depending on adjunct faculty is one way community colleges fulfill their mission to connect education and the work world, and a high percentage of adjuncts teach developmental classes. Boylan (2002) cites a study by the American Association of Community Colleges that found that over 65 percent of developmental faculty is part-time, and there is no evidence that adjunct teachers are any less successful than full-time teachers (Boylan, Bonham, Claxton, & Bliss, 1992). Many adjunct faculty members work full-time in business or industry and teach night or weekend classes, bringing the relevancy to the classroom that community college students demand. In addition, relying on adjunct faculty helps keep costs down for community college students. However, adjunct faculty, who are paid a fraction of the salary that full-time faculty receive and who may only be on campus for three hours a week, may not have the same kind of time or the same kind of academic bent that full-time faculty have, which could include trying to keep plagiarism issues at the forefront. Sterngold (2004) states, "Planning, managing, and evaluating research assignments are difficult tasks, and having to worry about plagiarism only adds to the burden" (p. 17). In addition, industry boilerplates and ghost writing are common occurrences in the business world, so some adjunct teachers may not be overly concerned by seemingly slight offences.

Because some adjuncts may not have taken education courses or may not be able to attend in-service professional development opportunities at the college, they may rely on the teaching methods that were used when they were in college, some of which Sterngold says, "invite cheating" (p. 16). He elaborates:

The traditional paradigm favors lecture-based courses, orderly classroom environments, and limited interaction between professors and students. . . [and] in the absence of strong institutional incentives to adopt learning-centered methods, many instructors rationally choose to continue using familiar, lecture-based teaching methods that are easier, safer, and less time-consuming to practice. (p. 17)

Most adjunct faculty are highly qualified, caring individuals who teach for little compensation because they have altruistic motives: they want to share their expertise with others. However, they probably cannot be expected to direct the same kind of attention to plagiarism problems as full-time faculty. Community colleges must provide adjunct faculty with the same kinds of in-service training about plagiarism issues that they provide full-time faculty, as well as giving information on the institution's Web page or in an adjunct handbook so that all instructors know the institution's stand on plagiarism and where to go for help if needed. Boylan (2002) states that adjunct faculty should be invited to attend faculty meetings, social activities, and professional development workshops. In staffing developmental classes, he suggests that institutions should only hire adjuncts who have a desire to teach those classes and that mentoring of adjuncts is important.

RESEARCH ACROSS A THE CURRICULUM

Many community college students arrive on campus with preconceived notions about plagiarism. Having an institutional policy that is clear and understandable for students is a beginning, but much more is needed. Discussing how the research process takes place in a particular discipline is every content teacher's responsibility, and no faculty member should assume that students know how to conduct research. Students in a history class need to know ethical ways to conduct ethnography research and students in a biology class need to know ethical ways to conduct scientific research. A Research Across the Curriculum emphasis is just as important at community colleges as a Writing Across the Curriculum emphasis because composition courses cannot possibly include all the ways different disciplines conduct research. When students hear about how to gather evidence, organize findings, write a report, and cite sources ethically from all their professors, not just from their English instructors, they will realize that proper research is an issue that is important in their future jobs.

SOLUTIONS

In helping diverse community college students learn the writing and research process, no one teaching method has emerged as the best. Instead, faculty should use as many different kinds of methods as possible (Boylan, 2002). Although many community college teachers still use the lecture method followed by drill work, best practice institutions use a variety of methods including: distance learning, self-paced instruction, individualized instruction, peer review of student work, collaborative learning, computer-based instruction, mastery learning, small-group work, and other active learning techniques (Boylan, 2002, p. 73). Group projects and collaborative writing are methods many business, science, health, and agriculture faculty use to mirror real-world work practices. Faculty can give students information about learning styles, helping them understand their own preferences and perhaps experiment with different learning approaches. Many community college students are visual or kinesthetic learners, so the lecture method may not be the best way for them to learn. They should have the opportunity to use manipulatives, videotapes, computer graphics, models, labs, and field trips (Boylan, 2002, p. 75). The key is diverse teaching methods for diverse students.

Most sources agree that faculty should be proactive rather than reactive in their efforts to teach research and writing skills to students by

using pedagogically sound course and assignment design rather than punitive after-the-fact methods (Akers, 2002; Bloomfield, 2004; Carbone; Davis, 1993; Ercegovac & Richardson, 2004; Harris, 2004; Martin, 1994; McDonnell, 1999; Pearson, 2005; Scanlon, 2003). For Ercegovac & Richardson, 2004, "It is simply not enough to define plagiarism, distribute neatly prepared citation templates for different formats, and say that plagiarism is wrong, punishable, easily detectable, and against honor code." Some sources suggest taking most of the punishment away from plagiarism. Martin (1994) states that plagiarism

is given too much attention and condemned in far too extreme terms. Given the pervasiveness of plagiarism, it should be treated as a common, often inadvertent problem rather like speeding on the road or cheating on income taxes. Most cases should be dealt with as matters of etiquette rather than 'theft'. (p. 44)

In his Web article, "Talking About Plagiarism," Carbone begins the plagiarism dialog with his syllabus. He disagreed philosophically with the typical syllabus in his course, which had a brief definition of plagiarism that concluded with the punishment a plagiarist would receive if caught. "My conflict here is that I don't lead any other discussion with threats, so why one on plagiarism? Why start off scolding? Why build anxiety and fear when I know that I'll be asking students to learn complex literacy skills, writing skills, and academic conventions?" He suggests that plagiarism is a matter of Dos and Don'ts in a list for students that he uses in class discussions throughout the semester.

McDonnell (1999) also suggests faculty use a proactive approach to plagiarism. He lists the following suggestions: 1) create and/or find assignments so unique to your teaching style that they can not be duplicated outside it; 2) use authentic assignments based on experiential learning such as service learning, writing for action, or writing for the community; 3) stress collaborative learning; 4) use the writing process and become involved in all five steps: prewriting, writing, evaluation, rewriting, and editing; and 5) include primary research in as many projects as you can such as interviews, telephone calls, or family documents.

The "Preventing Plagiarism" Web site from the University of Alberta Libraries suggests that plagiarism be discussed as a moral issue: "The relationship between faculty and students is based on trust; teach students the value of academic honesty and outline the responsibilities of being a junior member of the academic community." In addition, this site suggests that faculty discuss the benefits of citing: "proper attribution shows that the student has done thorough research and that the student has been exposed to a diverse range of thought and opinion. As a result, the paper will likely be stronger."

In her chapter "Preventing Academic Dishonesty," Davis (1993) lists general strategies faculty should start with to help students understand academic conduct; defines plagiarism, paraphrasing, and direct citation; discusses how to pick appropriate paper topics; and lists ways faculty can provide students with help during the writing process.

Harris (2004) has a very helpful Web site for faculty, discussing the reasons why students cheat, strategies for prevention, and strategies for detection. Suggestions that Harris gives to help teachers prevent plagiarism include: make the assignment clear and specific; provide a list of specific topics and require students to use one of them; require specific components such as one or more sources written within the past year or incorporation of information the teacher provides; require a metalearning essay—an in-class essay about what students learned from the assignment. He also gives a list of detection strategies.

Coastal Carolina University's Web site "Cheating 101: Easy Steps to Combating Plagiarism" suggests that the writing or research topic be tied into class experiences.

- Have writing assignments that have students analyze classroom activities or discussions in light of the text.
- Use local issues as topics.
- Ask students to include a section in their term paper that discusses their topic in light of what was covered in class.
- On the final exam, ask students to summarize the main points of their research paper.

The Electronic Plagiarism Seminar from Lemoyne College (2005) by Gretchen Pearson, Public Services Librarian, also has good suggestions for faculty. Her list includes: talk about plagiarism, focus on research skills, lower the stakes so that a single paper is not the entire grade, require primary research, think about the primary purpose of the assignment, and be wary of the request for a last-minute change in a topic. She also has suggestions for using the writing process to prevent plagiarism and detect plagiarism.

Bloomfield (2004) reminds us that in order to prevent plagiarism,

...students need to be taught that the act of writing is intrinsically valuable to them. It crystallizes one's thoughts in a way that nothing else can. As a physicist, I find that I often learn more from writing papers and proposals that I do from working in the laboratory. I rarely find writing easy, but I always find it rewarding.

ACTIVE LEARNING TECHNIQUES AND THE LEARNING COLLEGE

A radical educational shift from a focus on teaching to a focus on learning has motivated community college leaders in the past decade, a shift championed by the League for Innovation in the Community College. The Learning College is one which "places learning first and provides educational experiences for learners anyway, anyplace, anytime." This emphasis on cultivating an organizational culture that supports learning as the major priority has as one of its project goals "to create or expand learning-centered programs and strategies to ensure the success of underprepared students."

Sterngold (2004) refuses to agree that plagiarism is a product of "students' laziness, lax morals, or ignorance of the rules ... Before placing all the blame on students, we should consider how conventional teaching methods invite cheating, and how strategies designed to improve student learning can prevent it" (p. 16). He continues:

It turns out that many of the learning-centered teaching practices reformers have been advocating for years can help deter plagiarism as a by product of improving student learning and performance....These strategies discourage plagiarism by making it difficult for students to cheat and also by eliminating many of the incentives to cheat. At the same time, these strategies allow instructors to treat most instances of plagiarism as fixable errors rather than fatal violations of academic policies. (p. 17)

Johnson (2004) also gives strategies for combating plagiarism in his article, "Plagiarism-Proofing Assignments" by listing Low Probability of Plagiarism (LPP) assignments. He states that LPP projects:

1.   Have clarity of purpose and expectations
2.   Give choices to students
3.   Are relevant to students' lives
4.   Ask students to write in a narrative rather than an expository style
5.   Stress high-level thinking skills and creativity
6.   Answer real questions
7.   Involve a variety of information-gathering activities
8.   Tend to be hands-on
9.   Use technology to spur creativity
10.   Use formats that engage multiple senses
11.   Can be complex but can also be broken down into manageable steps
12.   Are often collaborative and can produce better results than individual work
13.   Share results with people who care and respond
14.   Are authentically assessed
15.   Allow learners to reflect, revisit, and improve their final projects
16.   Are encouraged by adults who believe that, given enough time, resources, and motivation all students are capable of original work

Scanlon (2003) suggests that using plagiarism checker software is not necessarily a good teaching strategy because the software could cloud whether the plagiarism was inadvertent and could "introduce an element of distrust" which turns faculty into "detectives with new—and as yet unproven—high-tech tools at their disposal, rather than teachers instructing students in what, for many of them are baffling principles and techniques" (p. 165). He suggests using mechanical means of detection during the writing process rather than afterwards "as a teaching tool...to provide an opportunity to discuss the proper handling of sources" (p. 165). Other examples of using well-designed assignments and topics to prevent plagiarism are discussed by Bolkan (2006), Carbone's "Thinking About Plagiarism," Fister, (2001), Leland (2002), McCullen (2003), McKenzie (1998), and Murray (2002). Fister lists a useful bibliography that includes general discussions of student research processes and problems as well as sources for specific assignments. Ercegovac and Richardson (2004) use Kohlberg's States of Development in Moral Reasoning to chart how research can be put into practice at all educational levels.

PORTFOLIOS

Portfolios have been defined as a collection of student work (O'Malley & Pierce, 1996), so portfolios can be used effectively to collect all of the information gathered in the research process. One method is to divide the research process into sections: topic selection, working bibliography, copies of source materials, first draft, peer-reviewed draft, final draft, and evaluation. The sections may have distinct due dates and may be kept together in a large mailing envelope, so the teacher can judge whether the student is making adequate progress or needs further instruction. Portfolio criteria often include a metacognitive essay in which the student evaluates his or her progress, learning process, goal achievement, and other categories. O'Malley and Pierce (1996) consider this self assessment to be the "key" to the portfolio process, so students are urged to become "independent evaluators of their own progress" (p. 38).

In his article "Using Portfolios to Avoid Plagiarism in Your Class," Carbone lists several ways that portfolios can benefit students: they help students manage time and set smaller goals and deadlines; teachers can tie the portfolio into issues of plagiarism; teachers can see how students research; teachers can see student work from the start; teachers can identify struggling students; failure to do a portfolio can result in the final paper graded as incomplete. Carbone also states that portfolios can also give students the opportunity to write before researching, which "helps avoid the get-a-stack-of-sources-cobble-quote-cite-and-then-patch-a-paper-together-thing that often results in voiceless, bland, unengaged research writing." Carbone suggests that the portfolio begin with a "knowledge of inventory: a list of everything [students] think they know about their given topic" which lets students "get their voice on paper."

LOWER CLASS SIZE

Community college faculty may be able to react to plagiarism problems more readily than four-year faculty because their class size is often smaller, making it possible for them to know their students by name and by their writing style. Knowing their students means that community college faculty, who have more required office hours than four-year faculty, can personally meet with students who might be having problems with research. Trust builds between community college faculty and students, enabling faculty to deal with plagiarism problems "as educators first" (Scanlon, 2003). Large classes are listed as a factor that was positively correlated with academic cheating and plagiarism according to a study of nineteen colleges in the U.K. by Ashworth, Bannister, and Thorne (1997).

CONCLUSION

Although technology has made plagiarism easier than ever, educators have many strategies to combat both intentional and unintentional plagiarism. Bolkan (2006) says, "The final deterrent strategy, solid assessment and good teaching, can't be over emphasized....Motivation, of course, is the key. Motivated and engaged learners are much less likely to take shortcuts. If they're only in your classroom to get a grade and move on, the potential for plagiarism will be greater" (p. 12). Intentional plagiarism can be addressed by restructuring assignments, helping students develop better time management skills, and using learner-centered teaching methods. Unintentional plagiarism can be addressed using student/teacher conferences, portfolios, peer and self evaluations. Writing and researching are critical thinking skills that should be incorporated in every class. To Sterngold, "Indeed, acquiring strong research and writing skills may be more important to students' future careers than acquiring subject-matter expertise that may become outdated soon after the students graduate or that may become irrelevant when students switch jobs and careers."

REFERENCES

Akers, S. (2002). Deterring and detecting academic dishonesty: Suggestions for faculty. Office of Student Rights and Responsibilities Web Site, Purdue University. Retrieved August 8, 2006 from http://www.purdue.edu/ODOX/osrr/academicdishonesty.htm

American Association of Community Colleges (2000). National profile of community colleges: Trends and statistics. Retrieved August 12, 2006 from http://www.aacc.nche.edu

Ashworth, P., Bannister, P., & Thorne, P. (1997). Guilty in whose eyes? University students' perceptions of cheating and plagiarism in academic work and assessment. *Studies in High Education, 22*(2), 187-203.

Bloomfield, L (2004). The importance of writing. *Philadelphia Inquirer,* April 4. Retrieved August 8, 2006 from http://plagiarism.phys.virginia.edu/essays/The%20Importance%20of%20Writing.html

Bolkan, J. V. (2006). Avoid the plague. *Learning and Leading with Technology, 33*(6),10-13.

Bombak A. (2005). Guide to plagiarism and cyber-plagiarism. May 2005. Retrieved August 8, 2006 from http://www.library.ualberta.ca/guides/plagiarism

Boylan, H. R. (1999). Developmental Education: Demographics, outcomes, and activities. *Journal of Developmental Education, 23*(2), 2-8.

Boylan, H. R. (2002). *What works: Research-based best practices in developmental education.*

National Center for Developmental Education: Boone, NC.

Boylan, H., Bonham, B., Claxton, C., & Bliss, L. (1992). *The state of the art in developmental education: Report of a national study.* Paper presented at the First National Conference on Research in Developmental Education, Charlotte, NC.

Breen, L. & Maassen M. (2005). Reducing the incidence of plagiarism in an undergraduate course: The role of education. In *Issues In Educational Research, 15*(1), 1-16. Retrieved August 14, 2006 from http://www.iier.org.au/iier15/breen.html

Carbone, N. Thinking about plagiarism. From Bedford St. Martin's Strategies for Teaching with Online Tools. Retrieved August 8, 2006 from http://www.bedfordstmartins.com/technotes/hccworkshop/plagiarismhelp.htm

Carbone, N. Using portfolios to avoid plagiarism in your class. From Bedford St. Martin's Strategies for Teaching with Online Tools. Retrieved August 8, 2006 from http://bedfordstmartins.com/technotes/hccworksohp/avoidplagiarism.htm

Carnevale, A. P. (2001). Community colleges and career qualifications. Educational Testing Service, Washington, DC. Retrieved August 12, 2006 from http://www.aacc.nche.edu/Content/NavigationMenu/ResourceCenter/Projects_Partnerships/Current/NewExpeditions/IssuePapers/Community_Colleges_and_Career_Qualifications.htm

Chaffee, J. (1992). Critical thinking skills: The cornerstone of developmental education. *The Journal of Developmental Education, 15*(3), 2-8, 39.

Coastal Carolina University Kimbel Library: Presentations. Cheating 101: Easy steps to combating plagiarism. Nov 05, 2004. Retrieved August 8, 2006 from http://www.coastal.edu/library/presentations/easystep.html

The Council of Writing Program Administrators. Defining and avoiding plagiarism: The WPA statement on best practices. Retrieved August 8, 2006 from http://www.wpacouncil.org/node/9

The Critical Thinking Community. Retrieved December 15, 2006 from http://www.criticalthinking.org

Davis, B. G. (1993). *Tools for teaching.* Jossey-Bass Publishers: San Francisco.

Edlund, J. R. (2000). What is "plagiarism" and why do people do it? Retrieved August 8, 2006 from http://www.calstatela.edu/centers/write_cn/plagiarism.htm

Ercegovac Z. & Richardson, J. V. (2004). Academic Dishonesty, plagiarism included, in the digital age: A literature review. *College & Research Libraries, 65*(4), 301-18.

Fister, B. (2001). Reintroducing students to good research. Lake Forest College. November 7, 2001. Retrieved August 8, 2006 from http://homepages.gac.edu/~fister/LakeForest.html

Furedi, F. (2004). Cheats are having a field day on campus. *Telegraph.* March 17, 2004. Retrieved August 8, 2006 from http://www.telegraph.co.uk/education/main.jhtml?xml=/education/2004/03/20/tefcheat17.xtml

Georgetown University Honor Council Web Site. What is plagiarism? Retrieved on August 8, 2006 from http://gervaseprograms.georgetownledu/hc/plagiarism.html

Harris. R. (2004). Anti-Plagiarism strategies for research papers. November 17, 2004. Retrieved August 8, 2006 from http://www.virtualsalt.com/antiplag.htm

Horne, L. J. & Carroll, D. C. (1996). *Nontraditional undergraduates: Trends in enrollment from 1986 to 1992 and persistence and attainment among 1989-90 beginning postsecondary students.* Washington, DC: National Center for Education Statistics, U.S. Department of Education. (ED 402 857)

Howard, R. M. (2001). Forget about policing plagiarism. Just teach. *The Chronicle of Higher Education,* B24. November 16, 2001. Retrieved August 15, 2006 from http://chronicle.com/weekly/v48/i12/12b02401.htm

Howell, C. L. (2001). Facilitating responsibility for learning in adult community college students. ERIC Digest. Retrieved August 12, 2006 from www.eric.ed.gov (ED 451 841)

Johnson, D. (2004). Plagiarism-proofing assignments. *Phi Delta Kappan, 85*(7), 549-52.

Kasper, H. T. (2002-2003). The changing role of community college. *Occupational Outlook Quarterly, 46*(4), 14-21. Winter 2002-2003. Retrieved August 14, 2006 from http://vnweb.hwwilsonweb.com/hww/results/results_single_fulltext.jhtml

Knopp, L. (1996). Remedial education: An undergraduate student profile. *American Council on Education: Research Briefs, 6*(8), 1-11.

Knowles, M. S. & Associates (1984). *Andragogy in action.* San Francisco: Jossey-Bass.

Laden, B. V. (2004). Serving emerging majority students. *New Directions for Community Colleges,* (127), 5-19.

Lamkin, M. D. (2004). To achieve the dream, FIRST look at the facts. *Change 36 (6),* 12-15. Retrieved on August 14, 2006 from http://vnweb.hywilsonweb.com/hww/results_single-fulltext.jhtml

League for Innovation in the Community College. "The learning college project." Retrieved on September 30, 2006 from http://www.league.org/league/projects/lcp/index.htm

Leland, B. H. (2002).Plagiarism and the web. January 29, 2002. Retrieved August 8, 2006 from http://www.wiu.edu/users/mfbhl/wiu/plagiarism.htm

MacDonald, L. T. (2007). Learning styles sites. *How To Study.* Chemeketa Community College.

Retrieved January 2, 2007 from http://www. howtostudy.org/resources_skill.php?id=5

Martin, B. (1994) Plagiarism: A misplaced emphasis. *Journal of Information Ethics, 3*(2), 36-47. Retrieved on August 8, 2006 from http://www. uow.edu.au/arts/sts/bmartin/pubs/94jie.html

McCullen, C. (2003) Tactics and resources to help students avoid plagiarism. *Multimedia Schools, 10*(6), 40-43.

McDonnell, C. (1999). *Proactive pedagogy: Limiting student plagiarism through course design.* Presentation at the Teaching English in the Two-Year College Southeast Convention, Memphis, Tennessee. February 19, 1999.

McKenzie, J. (1998). The new plagiarism: Seven antidotes to prevent highway robbery in an electronic age. *From Now On: The Educational Technology Journal, 7*(8). Retrieved August 15, 2006 from http://fno.org/may98/cov98may.html

McLemee, S. (2004). What is plagiarism? *The Chronicle of Higher Education, 51*(17), A9-D17.

Merriam, S. B., & Caffarella, R. S. (1999). *Learning in adulthood: A comprehensive guide. 2ⁿᵈ Edition.* San Francisco: Jossey-Bass.

Murray, B. (2002). Keeping plagiarism at bay in the Internet age. *Monitor, 33*(2)..Retrieved August 8, 2006 from http://www.apa.org/monitor/feb02/plagiarism.html

National Center for Education Statistics. (2002). Special analysis 2002: Nontraditional undergraduates. Retrieved August 21, 2006 from http://www.bedfordstmartins.com/technotes/hccworkshop/plagiarismhelp.htm

Nordstrom, A. D. (1997, September 15). Adult students a valuable market to target. *Marketing News, 31*(19), 20-21.

Ohio University Academic Advancement Center. The 168-hour exercise: How do I use my time now?

Retrieved August 21, 2006 from http://studytips.aac.ohiou.edu/?Function=TimeMgt&Type=168hour

O'Malley, J. M. & Pierce L. V. (1996). *Authentic assessment for English language learners: Practical approaches for teachers.* Addison-Wesley.

Pascarella, E. T., Whitt, E. J., Nora, A., Edison, M., Hagendorn, L. S., & Terenzini, P. T. (1996). What have we learned from the first year of the national study of student learning? *Journal of College Student Development, 37*(2), 182-192.

Pearson, G. (2005). Preventing plagiarism: General strategies. Electronic Plagiarism Seminar of Lemoyne College, Syracuse, NY. Retrieved on August 8, 2006 from http://www.lemoyne.edu/library/plagiarism/prevention_strategies.htm

Phillippe, K. A. (ed.). (2000). *National profile of community colleges: Trends and statistics 3ʳᵈ edition.* Washington, D. C.: American Association of Community Colleges. (ED 440 671)

Plagiarism.org. (2005). Retrieved August 8, 2006 from http://www.plagiarism.org/plagiarism.html

Rocklin, T. (1998). Downloadable term papers: What's a prof. to do? Retrieved on August 15, 2006 from http://www.uiowa.edu/%7Ecenteach/resources/ideas/term-paper-download.html

Roueche, J. E., & Roueche, S. D. (1999). Keeping the promise: Remedial education revisited. *Community College Journal, 69*(5), 12-18.

Ryan, J. (2004) Stealing from themselves. *ASSEE Prism 13,*(5), 64.

Sampson, Z. C. (2004). Demand for community colleges tests resources. *Community College Times,* September 7.

Scanlon, P. M. (2003). Student online plagiarism: How do we respond? *College Teaching, 51*(4), 161-5.

Shemo, D. At two-year college, students eager but unready. *New York Times* online. Retrieved on September 6, 2006 from http://www.nytimes.com/2006/09/02/education/02college.html?ex=1157860800&en=d5cfaff8cdeb31bb&ei=5070&emc=etal

Standler, R. B. (2000). Plagiarism in colleges in USA. Retrieved August 8, 2006 from http://www.rbs2.com/plag.htm

Sterngold, A. (2004). Confronting plagiarism: How conventional teaching invites cyber-cheating. *Change, 36*(3),16-21.

Stolley, K. (2006). Avoiding plagiarism. The Online Writing Lab at Purdue. May 12, 2006. Retrieved on August 8, 2006 from http://owl.english.purdue.edu/owl/printable/589

University of Alberta Libraries Web Site. Why students plagiarize. Retrieved August 8, 2006 from http://www.library.ualberta.ca/guides/plagiarism/why/index.cfm

Whisnant, W. T., Sullivan, J. C., & Slayton, S. L. (Summer, 1992). The "old" new resource for education: Student age. *Catalyst 22(*3). Retrieved May 20, 2005 from http://scholar.lib.vt.edu/ejournals/CATALYST/V22N3/whisnant.html

Zemke, R., & Zemke, S. (1988). Thirty things we know for sure about adult learning. In J. Gordon, R. Zemke, P. Jones (Ed.) *Designing and Delivering Cost-Effective Training, 2nd Ed.* Minneapolis: Lakewood Books.

Chapter X
The Phenomena of Contract Cheating

Thomas Lancaster
Birmingham City University, UK

Robert Clarke
Birmingham City University, UK

ABSTRACT

This chapter discusses the issue of contract cheating. This is where students have work completed on their behalf which is then submitted for academic credit. A thorough background to this phenomena is presented, and a list of the main contract cheating Web sites is given. These contract cheating sites are placed into four classifications: auctions sites, discussion forums, essay mills, and feed aggregators. Approaches are proposed for tutors to set assigned work that is less susceptible to contract cheating than standard assessments. The chapter concludes by arguing that urgent attention needs to be paid to contract cheating to avoid it becoming an educational problem of the same scale as plagiarism.

INTRODUCTION

The sheer volume of information that is conveniently accessible to students has grown dramatically in recent years. The Internet provides educators with new opportunities to innovate with the instruction and assessment methods they use. The Internet also offers students new opportunities to commit academic dishonesties, such as plagiarism. It appears that the educational community is starting to take the plagiarism issue seriously as it grapples with the necessity to ensure the maintainability of academic integrity for all.

The same level of publicity and understanding has not yet hit the related phenomena of contract cheating. First publicised by Clarke and Lancaster (2006), contract cheating refers to the outsourcing of assignments by students to have work produced on their behalf. As was the case for plagiarism, it is the availability of an online world which provides students with easier opportunities to commit contract cheating than they may have had in the past. Unlike plagiarism the area of contract cheating is still only loosely defined, meaning that standard prevention and detection techniques are neither widely known, nor easily applicable.

The work submitted by contract cheaters has been produced exclusively for them. This means that sources for their submissions will not usually be found on the Internet. This immediately eliminates the use of plagiarism detection engines or the technique of searching the Web for unusual phraseology.

The presentation of this chapter may be considered non-standard. The primary objective is not to present new results, even though advice about contract cheating has not been published in this depth before. Instead, the aim is to publicise a growing area of concern. The authors believe strongly that more tutors need to be made aware that some original coursework submitted by their students will not be the results of the labour of those students.

A number of smaller objectives exist within this primary aim of publicity. The small amount of existing contract cheating research is discussed. An initial attempt is presented to classify the type of online sources that students can use to contract cheat. Methods are proposed that can, ideally, prevent students from contract cheating, but, if necessary, enable this cheating to be detected. This approach can be considered as an analogy to the way that the anti-plagiarism movement has evolved with its two pronged approach of prevention and detection. The chapter considers ways in which an individual contract cheater within a larger cohort can be identified or made identifiable. This is a problem when a tutor knows that their assignment has been placed on an auction outsourcing site, but not who the originator is. The chapter concludes by discussing the future

direction that the anti-contract cheating movement should be taking and detailing the need for a community based approach of prevention and monitoring.

BACKGROUND

The issue of students plagiarising materials from the Web is a key theme of this book. From the early reporters (Austin & Brown, 1999), to the key issue reviews (Carroll & Appleton, 2001; Culwin & Lancaster, 2001) and the advice manuals (Lathrop & Foss, 2000), it can be noted that a comprehensive set of literature exists, detailing how to prevent and detect those items that students use without acknowledgments. These sources offer a number of standard suggestions for tutors to employ. To prevent plagiarism these include requiring tutors to regularly generate new assignments for which model answers cannot be retrieved from the Web. To detect plagiarism these advocate the use of anti-plagiarism services, such as the self-professed world leader in Web database scanning software TurnItIn.com (Turnitin, n.d.). This chapter assumes that the reader has a working knowledge of the plagiarism problem and potential solutions.

The literature devoted to contract cheating is only in its infancy. The newer discipline of study, popularised by Clarke and Lancaster (2006) and covered in the media (Cheating students put homework to tender on Internet, 2006; Lightfoot, 2006; Morton & Tarica, 2006; Student cheats contract out work, 2006) specifically covers the submission of work that has been produced on behalf of a student, whether for money or not. It can be inferred that such a submission is original; however the work is not by the claimed author. This originality means that a standard plagiarism detection engine, such as TurnItIn.com will not detect this style of cheating, as a source for the work cannot be found.

Clarke and Lancaster (2006) produced an initial study of the extent of this type of cheating. The investigation analysed student use of the RentACoder.com (Rent A Coder: how software gets done, n.d.) auction site. RentACoder is advertised as a site on which computer contractors can find work. An individual or company requiring a solution, for instance a Web presence for their business, places a bid request detailing their requirements. Contractors bid for the opportunity to complete the work in a process that could be described as a reverse auction. The buyer may then choose to accept one of the bids, which is the usually the lowest. The buyer pays for the solution, and RentACoder.com holds the money in escrow. The money is released to the contractor when the solution is completed to the buyer's satisfaction.

Although RentACoder.com is consider primarily for business use, Clarke and Lancaster exposed a trend of use of the site by students looking to have assignments completed for them. A number of findings were presented, of which three are worthy of particular highlighting:

1. Of all bid requests placed on the site, 12.3 percent represented attempts by students to solicit contract cheating materials. This was based on a three week exhaustive study of all bid requests placed on the site, identifying those that were assignments.
2. The majority of students (over 50 percent) had placed between two and seven bid requests on the site. This result was found by looking at the historical use of all students who had placed a bid request identified as contract cheating across a two-month period. Clarke and Lancaster suggested that these students could be described as "habitual cheaters."
3. Six out of 236 users had previously placed more than 50 bid requests in this same study. One out of 236 placed more than 100 bid requests. An initial analysis of this corpus

revealed that many of these were non-originality agencies, as identified by Lancaster and Culwin (2007). Clarke and Lancaster suggested that these users may be soliciting requests to complete work for students through other channels. They may then be submitting these assignment specifications to RentACoder.com for profit without completing the work for themselves.

Clarke and Lancaster noted that this analysis, although involving a labour intensive study, only included one contract cheating site. Many other auction sites suitable for contract cheating exist on the Web and can be assumed to be being used by students in this manner. Later in this chapter a number of these will be categorised.

A further analysis on a sample of the Clarke and Lancaster data completed for the benefit of this chapter reveals that 98 percent of the bid requests are likely from computing students, leaving approximately 2 percent from other disciplines. This suggests that these technically minded students are best placed to cheat in this manner. However, it would be unfair to suggest that it is solely or primarily computing students who are contract cheating. The data set collected is slowly becoming dated. Recent publications in the media may mean that other types of students are now more widely engaging in contract cheating.

Other sites exist which more closely provide standard essay based assignments, such as Elance. com (Outsourcing to Freelance Programmers, Web & Logo Designers, Writers, Illustrators on Elance, n.d.). Although no comprehensive studies of this or other sites have yet been completed, it is possible that less technical students may be using contract cheating auction sites to write their assignments.

Little investigative work has yet been done on the quality of work provided by these sites. Levinson (2005) reported on a UK study commissioned by the BBC and carried out by Professor Charles Oppenheim. In this study three students each purchased custom written 1500 words essays on copyright law at prices between £135 and £205. Oppenheim graded these at between 42 and 58 percent, relatively poor marks under the UK marking system, suggesting that the custom written essays represented poor value for money.

A similar study carried out by Jenkins and Helmore (2006) revealed a far more cost effective way for students to contract cheat. In their study Jenkins and Helmore purchased solutions to first year degree computing assignments from auction style sites including RentACoder.com and competitor GetACoder.com (GetACoder—Quick and easy project outsourcing. Outsource your project today, n.d.). Using this source of cheating, assignments were found to cost between $10 and $25, far cheaper than in the study reported by Levinson. Jenkins and Helmore stated that this work would have received "very good marks." This suggests that the use of coding auction sites could be good value for students wanting to contract cheat, certainly when compared with essay mills.

A number of worldwide media sources have used the results by Clarke and Lancaster (2006) and by Jenkins and Helmore (2006) as a basis for their own studies, often going further than could be ethically attempted within an academic setting. Gusmaroli (2006) reported on using RentACoder. com to request urgently needed English Literature essays. Gusmaroli's request received 16 offers from worldwide bidders within a day, offering to ghost write the essay for between $20 and $100. Gusmaroli stated that these prices are negotiable and included offers to write the assignment in the student's usual style, something that may allay one of the most basic indicators to tutors that the work was not produced by the student.

Kom (2006) produced a similar investigation, using not only RentACoder.com, but also GetACoder.com and Elance.com. Kom again noted the ease by which original work could be sourced from these sources. Kom's article includes correspondence from some of the agencies using RentACoder to outsource work. It is also the first to have received comments from representatives of RentACoder.com and Elance.com. The piece produces a contract cheating success story, with Elance.com, but not RentACoder.com, agreeing to monitor use of their sites by students seeking to outsource work in order to cut down on the practice. The successfulness of the Elance.com policy is not yet known.

It is clear that the media continues to perceive contract cheating as a concern. It is also evident that few formal contract cheating studies exists within the literature. With the exception of the data presented by Clarke and Lancaster (2006), most of the other literature exists only as publicity pieces. Publicity is a key aim of this chapter. There is also an aim to more formally present and classify contract cheating problems and possible solutions. It is within this frame of reference that the remainder of the chapter is presented.

CLASSIFICATIONS OF CONTRACT CHEATING SITES

Contract cheating, loosely defined as the external outsourcing of work by students for completion on their behalf, is wide ranging. The description covers the use of a multitude of different types of online services. A key observation that cannot be stressed enough is that contract cheating produces original work for students; this would not be detected by standard plagiarism detection engines.

There is no equivalent definition of a contract cheating Web site. An inference could be that a contract cheating Web site is an online source used by students for the purpose of outsourcing assignment specifications to be completed for them.

A more general set of classifications of the types of sites used by contract cheating students is of interest. These are presented as initial groupings of the unattributed sources that students are using. The classifications are not guaranteed to be complete. Despite this, the authors currently do not have any examples of sites that do not fit into these classifications. The range of online sources continually is changing. This means that the classifications and inherent Web site examples only can be taken as a real time contract cheating snapshot. A longer term view would need to anticipate the changes in the arms race between tutors and students. Were this possible, contract cheating could be completed eliminated.

The contract cheating sites used by students fall into four proposed categories: auction sites, discussion forums, essay mills, and feed aggregators.

The classification known as auction sites covers those contract cheating sites that work on the principle of an auction. Examples include RentACoder.com and GetACoder.com. These usually are sites with a legitimate business model, rather than existing solely to encourage students to cheat.

Discussion forums can be loosely defined as sites open for users to discuss a shared topic of interest. An example is CodingForums.com (CodingForums.com - Web coding and development forums. Get help on JavaScript, PHP, CSS, XML, mySQL, ASP, and more!, n.d.). Since community discussions produce original words and ideas they can be misused by contract cheaters even if this is not a forum's intent. Since many discussion forums are closed to external viewing, students can solicit help that is not easily detected, either blatantly, or sneakily without revealing their intent, from fellow contributors.

Essay mills are sites existing primarily to supply assignment solutions to students, such as ProfEssays.com (*Custom Essays Writing Service*—ProfEssays, n.d.), a definition largely equivalent to Lancaster and Culwin's definition of non-originality agencies (Lancaster & Culwin, 2007). Some companies advertise that they will write material for students only to be used as a "model answer." Despite this the key motivation for these services is clear. Of most interest to

contract cheaters are those essay mills writing to order, as opposed to those distributing "off the shelf" solutions for which the detection of plagiarism is more susceptible.

The final proposed classification is that of feed aggregators. These are not sites providing new sources of contract cheating opportunities as such; rather they are ways of collecting existing materials for wider distribution. For instance, a feed aggregator may combine bid requests from several auction sites as they arrive, but in a common format. Alternatively, it might present headlines from a number of forums. Such sites legitimately can be used by contractors looking for work opportunities. As the contents may be filtered, these aggregators cannot be considered as complete a record of contact cheating opportunities as the original sites from which they derive their contents.

The existing literature on contract cheating and the wider area of plagiarism focuses solely on the areas of auction sites and essay mills. There are no known studies of the use of discussion forums or feed aggregators within the contract cheating process.

The auction site classification contains the focus of much of the existing contract cheating literature. This includes the primary usage study (Clarke & Lancaster, 2006) and an attempt to purchase programming solutions to order (Jenkins and Helmore, 2006).

The auctions appear to work along the following lines. A buyer, looking for a contract cheating solution, posts a bid request. The bid request is offered to contractors for a finite length of time. During this time contractors make offers to complete a solution for a specified financial incentive. The buyer selects a contractor, who then is expected complete the work and receive the agreed amount. The exact financial and logical operation of sites differs, but sites such as RentACoder.com will hold the funds in escrow until this work is completed to a satisfactory standard. RentACoder.com will also take a commission percentage off the agreed bid amount. Other sites may require buyers and sellers to make their own financial arrangements or charge a subscription charge for their use.

Recent developments have seen students starting to place private bid requests within the auction sites, limiting those who can view or bid on their requests. This element of privatisation can make tracing offenders difficult. Additionally, some bid requests have started to become restricted by geographical area, for instance Eastern Europe or Asia. Viewers outside those areas find details of the requests hidden, limiting their opportunities to detect cheaters.

The use of essay mills pre-dates the Internet, but the ease by which students can purchase custom writing is purely a product of the online world. Oppenheim's experiment puts doubt on the quality of this work (Levinson, 2005). Despite this the ease through which solutions can be retrieved, especially when students feel they are too time-limited to wait for auction bids to be returned, suggests that these will have a continued usage by contract cheaters. The use of these paper mills is difficult to detect, since no evidence trail is generated. Hence it is necessary for tutors to consider alternatives to assessment methods that make such cheating unsustainable.

There are no known studies of the use of discussion forums in contract cheating. Unlike both essay mills and auction sites, students can use most discussion forums without direct payment, giving them access to free information. The potential for money to change hands is also there. A student might make use of private subscription sites. They might also make an individual arrangement with another forum user to supply a solution for a cash incentive. Many discussion forums now require users to register an account before they can view or post discussions. This has a by-product of hiding their content from search engines. When hidden discussion sources are used by students the material they contain is unlikely to be detected by an online search.

The discussions that can be viewed demonstrate some of the types of users. Many requests are short and focused, along the lines of "how can my program be fixed?" or "can someone point me on the correct path?" These may be being made by students who are looking for assistance rather than explicit contract cheating solutions. Such requests can still lead to unacceptable behaviour, for instance where a student asks a number of questions in turn sufficient to develop a complete solution to an assessment. This approach is comparable with the offline activity where a student visits a series of tutors in order to receive, piecemeal, a complete solution to an assignment. More blatant approaches are also possible.

There is anecdotal evidence of a link between discussion forums and auction sites, where requests originally placed on a discussion forum have subsequently been found on an auction site. The exact reasoning behind this is unknown. A couple of best guesses are presented. Some students may try and get help for free, fail, and then choose the paid option. Others may agree to pay someone in the forum to complete the work for them, who then subcontracts the work to an auction site. This might be unknown to the student. The number of buyers observed on RentACoder.com by Clarke and Lancaster who had requested assignments from multiple institutions suggests that a recruitment method similar to this is used.

Examples of contract cheating sites within the different classifications are useful. Table 1 shows a snapshot of many of the sites in use. The number of discussion forums and essay mills on the Internet appear almost limitless and their existence can be fluid. This means that it is not possible to give a complete list of such sites for all subjects and domains of interest. The table is intended to give tutors an opportunity to reflect on their discipline by showing the wide range of contract cheating sites in the online world.

The spectrum of contract cheating sites identified is wide. This suggests that any form of direct monitoring of sites would be difficult, although

Table 1. Example categorisations of identified contract cheating sites

Site url	Categorisation of site			
	Auction Site	Discussion Forum	Essay Mill	Feed Aggregator
www.academicdb.com			X	
www.justanswer.com	X			
forums.belution.com		X		
www.brainmass.com			X	
cboard.cprogramming.com		X		
codercc.com	X			
www.codingforums.com		X		
computing.net		X		
www.coursework.info			X	
www.coursework4you.co.uk			X	
www.dbforums.com		X		
forums.devshed.com		X		
news.devx.com		X		
www.elance.com	X			
www.essayrelief.co.uk			X	
freelancecontests.com/fc	X			
freepint.willco.com		X		
www.getacoder.com	X			
www.getafreelancer.com	X			
www.gidforums.com		X		
answers.google.com/answers			X	
www.icq.com		X		
www.ifreelance.com	X			
www.jiskha.com		X		
www.kasamba.com			X	
www.listbid.com	X			
www.netskool.com/index.html			X	
www.oppapers.com			X	
www.professays.com			X	
www.programmingtalk.com		X		
p2p.wrox.com		X		
www.programmersheaven.com		X		
www.projectspring.com/freelance	X			
www.projectslist.biz	X			
www.rentacoder.com/RentACoder	X			
www.rssmad.com				X

(continued on next page)

Table 1. continued

Site url	Categorisation of site			
	Auction Site	Discussion Forum	Essay Mill	Feed Aggregator
www.seofeeds.org				X
www.technical-outsourcing.com	X			
www.thestudentroom.co.uk		X		
www.unix.com		X		
www.weblogalot.com/Dir/Computers				X

smaller scale monitoring may be possible. Without complete coverage it is necessary for tutors to seriously consider methods of designing opportunities for contract cheating out of the assignment specifications that they set.

CONTRACT CHEATING SITE MONITORING AND ITS ASSOCIATED DIFFICULTIES

One method of stopping contract cheating is simply to find all those students using such sites and put them through university disciplinary procedures. A few successful prosecutions may be enough to stop other students who are thinking of following in the footsteps of their peers.

If the academic actions of students were an open book, it would be straightforward to monitor the contract cheating sites that they visited and collect evidence that they were being academically dishonest. This often is not the case. In order to successfully stop students making unfair use of such resources it is necessary to know not only what sites they are using, but also which of those of a cohort of students are involved.

Monitoring sites is a labour intensive process and its success largely dependent on a tutor being in the right place at the right time. The choice of sites used by students can be subject and location specific. Here the localised subject knowledge

of tutors may be sufficient to suggest to such tutors where they need to look. A search for key terminology on likely auction and forum sites may be enough to detect the most blatant cases. However, there is a danger of such an approach being rather scattergun in nature. An alert cheater quickly would realise not to use the common keywords most associated with their topic. They also may learn other methods of disguising their intent. More sophisticated cheaters may start to take their business to sites less directly associated with their academic subject, hence reducing the likelihood of their being caught.

A related approach is to use a search engine such as Google.com (Google, n.d.) to search a wide range of sites. This method is only as successful as the keywords used to search. Content hidden from the Google.com database is unlikely to be found. One small advantage of this approach is that Google.com creates a regular cache of Web sites. This means that an assignment specification placed on an auction site, but then subsequently removed or hidden can still sometimes be indirectly assessed.

A purely systematic approach involves manually visiting and exhaustively checking the many sites. On an auction site this would require checking each bid request as it is placed and approved. Such checks can be made directly, or perhaps through a feed aggregator service or a Real Simple Syndication (RSS) feed reader application program. The big downside of this is the time consuming nature required for any guaranteed level of coverage. The experience of the authors has shown that an RSS feed reader can prove useful, especially if the highlighting of likely keywords is used. But as an RSS feed only contains the first section of the file this means that keywords later in the posting, or in attached files, would not be flagged.

There are advantages to tutors of monitoring the types of sites that their specific students may be using. Experience of cheating techniques is important intelligence when trying to design out the problem from assignment specifications.

Monitoring contract cheating sites does not have to be an individual affair. In the spirit of cooperation some academics take the time to police contract cheating sites at the same time as looking for work of their own students. As an example MacLeod (2006) describes attempts by Robert Clarke to notify other tutors when it has been detected that one of their assignments is being contracted out. More cooperation is needed across the academic community to ensure that a wide range of sites can be monitored without the duplication of efforts, although the practicalities of such an approach would require a great level of planning. The automation of this process to as great an extent as possible would also be beneficial, so long as student motives are not prejudged. This could be supported by a standard format for traceable assignment specifications across the education sector.

TRACEABILITY OF ASSIGNMENTS

Catching a cheat using a contract cheating site is difficult. There are often four stages to doing so. First, it is necessary to identify the institution from which an assignment specification is posted. Next, the tutor associated with the assignment specification has to be identified. Third, it is necessary to identify which student, often not going by their real name, has put the assignment specification on the site. Finally, the burden of proof is on the tutor to demonstrate that the student has submitted work that is not theirs.

This multi-stage process usually requires cooperation from a number of academics across multiple institutions. Even when a cooperative fellow tutor does the legwork of pointing out the existence of a contract cheating attempt there is still detective work required at the final institution to work out which student it is.

This chapter will not go in depth into the forensic methods that can be used to identify from where students have cheated or who the students are. To do so would be exposing many of the tools available to a tutor and this could render them ineffective. Suffice to say that many student postings can be traced to a source, even when a student has made an attempt at disguise, for instance removing a module code or tutor name.

Many assignments do prove untraceable to everyone but the tutor who originally set them. This does not need to be the case. There are simple recommendations that tutors can follow to make their assignments more traceable and hence contract cheats more likely to be detected.

The key is to ensure that accurate information about the tutor, their modules and their assignments are made available on search engines such as Google.com. This includes a contact e-mail address so that the tutor can be informed when their assignment specification is found. All these details need to be embedded within an assignment specification. They also need to exist elsewhere on the Web so that some traceability is possible if a student tries to remove them from the specification. Many institutions place assignment specifications on a local intranet. Such specifications are not accessible outside the institution and do not appear when searching the Web. This makes identifying and contacting a tutor concerned very difficult.

The ideal situation is to place the whole assignment specification on the indexed Internet. It is understood that in some cases this is difficult. Such availability allows fragments of text in an assignment specification to be directly searched for. At the very least a summary of the assignment requirements and details of modules and tutors need to be available on the Internet.

The plagiarism prevention guidelines recommend setting original assignments. This is equally crucial when making an assignment traceable. Some tutors, particularly those involved with technical and mathematical subjects, set standard exercises to be completed that come straight from a commonly used text book. If a standard exercise is found on a contract cheating site it is nearly impossible to trace the correct institution. Model answers for these exercises may also be accessible on the Web. Tutors setting written work are prone to a similar concern. They risk sample essays being available from students who have taken the subject at other institutions, or, where a subject is reused in the same institution, in previous sittings of the same subject.

Assignment specification traceability is a particular problem for institutions that provide large online courses. Contact with a tutor can be hidden inside a private intranet. Attempts to warn staff by using a generic contact option often fail to illicit a response. The geographically widespread nature of students on online courses can also make it difficult to identify an institution. With such courses many other methods of identification and contact need to be left accessible.

Making an assignment specification both original and traceable through embedding multiple pieces of traceable information is the best way of ensuring that cheating students can be traced. However this method is not foolproof. Students can still slip through the safety net or may succeed in keeping all their cheating attempts hidden away from public view, for instance by using the services of an essay mill. The need to design out contract cheating opportunities when setting assessment tasks still remains.

ASSESSMENT REDESIGN

The plagiarism literature almost inevitably recommends a multi-directional approach to eliminating plagiarism. One direction requires the compulsory application of plagiarism detection techniques, both to find cheaters and also as a deterrent to stop those who may otherwise be tempted to indulge. Many departments announce when a student has been caught cheating. If local policies allow this it is a valid method of showing students that if they plagiarise they are taking a risk.

The complementary direction for eliminating plagiarism is to design out the opportunities. This direction asks tutors to consider ways in which they can ensure that students will find plagiarism opportunities very difficult.

A similar analogy of detection and prevention should be applicable for contract cheating. Detection, where possible, is a valid solution, but the threat to students of being caught plays an equally important role. Letting students know that their work is monitored for contract cheating will deter some students. Prevention, through assessment redesign, is also vital. Making contract cheaters able to pass only a small section of an overall assessment procedure should be a deterrent.

Redesigning assessment techniques is as vital for combating contract cheating as it was for avoiding plagiarism. Some, although not all, anti-plagiarism redesign techniques can be directly applied. The methods suggested here are all intended for the prevention of both plagiarism and contract cheating and are as follows.

Eliminate coursework: A possible solution is to consider how important coursework is to an individual subject or module. If it is not important then it could be avoided. Such a step would likely eliminate both contract cheating and plagiarism. However, there are also contract cheating dangers to this approach. Some recent auction bid requests have been observed asking for a contractor to be available at a set time to communicate answers to computerised examinations. An examination only strategy, as well at being at the extreme end of the assessment spectrum, requires careful monitoring during examinations and for anti-cheating techniques to be in place.

Base an examination on the coursework: A less extreme solution to eliminating assignments entirely is to base an examination on the coursework produced. That is, to set an examination that, in some way, requires a student to amend, reflect on or improve work that was originally completed in their own time. One example is a laboratory based programming exam (Cutts, Barnes, Bibby, Bown, Bush, Campbell, Fincher, Jamieson, Jenkins, Jones, Kazatov, Lancaster, Ratcliffe, Seisenberg, Shinner-Kennedy, Wagstaff, White, & Whyley, 2006). In this the students are required to make a small change to a program that they have already written. This could be very simple if the student has produced the program themselves, but difficult if they have not done so. An appropriate marking strategy should ensure that only students who have not outsourced pass a subject overall.

The approach is also applicable to non-technical subjects. One example is the use of the Cloze procedure (Taylor, 1953) where the student's work is presented back to them with words removed for them to replace. The premise is that a student who wrote the work themselves should be able to replace most words successfully. The student's level of success can determine their final mark.

Viva-voce examinations: A good way to guarantee that work is that of student is for the tutor to have a structured discussion about the submission with the student. Any marking scheme associated with a viva needs to substantially penalise students who cannot suitably discuss the work that they claim to have produced. A downside of this oral examination approach is its labour intensive nature; even restricting vivas to 15 minutes per student can be time consuming for large cohorts.

To ensure fairness and the same level of detection and deterrence, all students need to receive a viva and to be asked equivalent questions. This requires some control over students to ensure that the questions are not leaked after students timed in earlier viva slots have taken them.

Some institutions recommend a sampling approach for vivas. Although there are cases where this may be suitable many faculty assessment policies require all students to be treated equally. In such cases sampling may not be permitted.

Setting original assignments: The anti-plagiarism literature constantly recommends that new assessment tasks are set for students at each sitting. In popular subjects that are delivered more than once every year or where there are multiple opportunities for students to retake a failure this means that many different assignment specifications need to be written. Any lack of originality can create a local market for old solutions. An entrepreneuring contract cheating company could operate based solely on rewriting paraphrased versions of such solutions. The requirement for originality is also important for traceability reasons if work is submitted to contract cheating sites.

One method advocated when setting multiple assignments is to use variations on a theme. This can allow reuse of elements of the assignment briefing and marking criteria, whilst ensuring that the student tasks are sufficiently different each time the module is run. One recent example used by the authors originally asked students to write a simulation to meet the specifications of the local UK version of an internationally franchised TV game show involving contestants trying to sell the contents of their case or box. Retake versions have asked for simulations of the US and Australian versions of the game show. If extra retake opportunities become needed this approach leaves many more localised versions to consider requiring less effort to amend an assignment specification than would be required to write one from scratch. Such an approach could be tweaked for other subject areas.

Creating individualised versions of assignments: Variations can be created within an assignment specification to ensure that each student is working on a unique version of the same assignment. This is said to allow students some element of ownership of the material and ensures traceability of any attempt by them to cheat (Fincher, Barnes, Bibby, Bown, Bush, Campbell, Cutts, Jamieson, Jenkins, Jones, Kazatov, Lancaster, Ratcliffe, Seisenberg, Shinner-Kennedy, Wagstaff, White, & Whyley, 2006). Individualisation can be simpler to understand where there are numeric underpinnings to an assignment, for instance a randomised data set for each student, a process advocated by Blayney and Freeman (2004). For more traditional assignment specifications consider splitting these into distinct and combinable components. Different variants on a theme can be generated for each component. These can be merged to create unique combinations. Alternatively student could each be allocated a different unique subset of tasks out of a larger selection, again allowing an individual student to be traced and meaning that students cannot directly collude.

There are some complications that a tutor generating individualised assessments needs to consider. It is necessary to ensure that they are all generated to the same level of difficulty. The generation process can also be involved, although some automated solutions are available or in development (Keating, 2005). When students submit work this needs to be carefully checked against their original requirements to ensure that the student has met their own requirements and not those of an acquaintance. This can add to the marking overload.

On the positive side, individualisations made up of unique combinations can be used to conclusively identify miscreants posting on a contract cheating site. This can aid dramatically at this late stage of the contract cheating detection process.

Supervised coursework: The UK Government has announced that coursework is to be removed from some GCSE examinations and to be supervised for others (Maths GCSE coursework is dropped, 2006; Move to end more GCSE coursework, 2006). Such an approach could work at all levels, where coursework is required to be completed in class time or under recognised supervision.

There are considerations about how complex a subject can be covered in this way, and how logical problems, such as staffing and monitoring, can be solved. However, there also are benefits: primarily that if student activities were carefully observed during these times it would ensure that students were not able to contract cheat.

Log books: It is difficult to fake accurate narrative records of tasks completed, particularly if these are regularly checked by tutors during the assessment period. Such provision for forward planning should also ensure that students do not leave work until the last minute and run out of time, something that students have been known to claim when posting their work on contract cheating Web sites. There are also pedagogic advantages to requiring students to regularly reflect on their work.

Modern log books need not be onerous for tutors to collect. Electronic versions exist, for instance e-LogBook (Kammering, Hensler, Petrosyan, & Rehlick, 2003) and some are integrated into Virtual Learning Environments such as Moodle (Moodle - A Free, Open Source Course Management System for Online Learning, n.d.). There is however a requirement for tutors to regularly monitor these diaries and provide feedback, which can be difficult if they are already working under time pressures. It is also vital that marking schemes take into account the meeting of these interim deadlines, otherwise there is little incentive for some students to take part.

CONCLUSION

There is no doubt that students are taking advantage of the new contract cheating opportunities that the online world has provided them with. It is hoped that this chapter has given an overview of the current state of contract cheating research and suggested some practical steps that tutors can take to reduce the impact of this type of cheating.

Existing anti-plagiarism techniques, such as TurnItIn.com are not sufficient to ensure that original work submitted by students is their own. Tutors must continue to innovate. They also need to develop and publicise techniques to stop contract cheating and ensure that the research community continues to build.

It is necessary to ensure that the prevention measures do not cause assessment techniques to become draconian and that by obtaining a qualification a student still has the skills that an employer wants them to have. The UK seems to be moving towards the elimination of coursework as a way to ensure that work submitted by students is their own (Maths GCSE coursework is dropped, 2006; Move to end more GCSE coursework, 2006). It is not clear that exams alone can test all the qualities that are required of students. The plans of the UK Government at present have only been announced for the General Certificate in Secondary Education (GCSE). Experience with past innovations suggests that this will be extended to higher level students. This could mean students arriving at university level education with no experience of completing coursework. Such students are clearly at risk of succumbing to using external agencies to have their work completed.

There also is a concern that many institutional cheating policies have not yet caught up with opportunities introduced by the online world. Many regimes depend on evidence showing, word for word, where a student has copied work from. With contract cheating, where the work submitted is, by all accounts, original, the collection of this form of evidence is not possible. Instead regulations need to be moving towards a system where the onus is placed on the student to be able to prove that work is their own. This may require a student to be asked to undertake a viva about any

coursework they have submitted, with a student being required to show that they understand it in order to receive academic credit.

Continuing to educate tutors about contract cheating is necessary. It also is sensible to educate students. Some tutors do not realise that many students feel strongly that their peers should not cheat. If nothing else, cheating by their peers devalues these students' own academic achievements through association. If tutors are seen to be strongly tackling contract cheating this can raise morale amongst the student body and perhaps contribute to a greater level of deserved academic achievements for all.

The honour code, often used by US institutions and faculties, can contribute. Here students are expected to subscribe to an honourable policy when joining a course of study. This is something that can be used to show to students that cheating is not a victimless crime. By spreading the onus of reporting these incidences amongst a wider set of people, it could be argued that contract cheaters are more likely to be caught. Alongside such policies, a wider range of penalties should become available for those students who are involved with cheating.

Academics need to seriously consider a community anti-contract cheating approach. A central repository of assignment specifications should be established, so that tutors can be contacted when their work is outsourced. This would make partially automated searching of contract cheating sites for suspect postings possible. Searches would need to look at both the words of the posting and the contents of attachments where many crucial assignment details are hidden. A central service could also capture immediate evidence of potential wrongdoing. Such regular captures are crucial if a student places a bid request on an auction site and subsequently privatises it. A community of volunteers monitoring such a service could make significant headway into the contract cheating concern.

The ongoing monitoring of the RentACoder. com auction site, carried out by the authors in tandem with this research, has led to the contacting of many academic departments to inform tutors that their students are likely cheating. The most common response from staff contacted is that they were unaware of this activity being carried out by their students. It is hoped that this chapter will provide a guide to such tutors about how to approach the problem. Some tutors have had success at getting assignments removed from cheating sites by claiming breach of their copyright, but this is only a stop gap solution, potentially driving cheats further underground. It would appear that ensuring that students do not benefit if they cheat is a more practical way forwards.

The techniques presented here can only be considered as a starting point against contract cheating, plagiarism and collusion. It is hoped that interested tutors will take the matter up in their own academic disciplines and help to publicise the need for an integrated approach. Only a community attack on cheating can make the online world an asset to tuition once again and ensure that all students get the results that they deserve.

REFERENCES

Austin, M., & Brown, L. (1999). Internet plagiarism: Developing strategies to curb student academic dishonesty. *The Internet and Higher Education, 2*(1), 21-33.

Blayney, P., & Freeman, M. (2004). Automated formative feedback and summative assessment using individualised spreadsheet assignments. *Australasian Journal of Educational Technology, 20*(2), 209-231.

Carroll, J., & Appleton, J. (2001). *Plagiarism a good practice guide*. Retrieved February 20, 2007, from http://www.jisc.ac.uk/uploaded_documents/ brookes.pdf#search=%22carroll%20plagiarism% 20good%20practice%20jiscpas%22

Cheating students put homework to tender on Internet. (2006, June 13). *Daily Mail, 21.*

Clarke, R., & Lancaster, T. (2006). Eliminating the successor to plagiarism? Identifying the usage of contract cheating sites. In *Proceedings of 2nd International Plagiarism Conference*. Gateshead, UK: Northumbria Learning Press.

CodingForums.com—Web coding and development forums. Get help on JavaScript, PHP, CSS, XML, mySQL, ASP, and more! (n.d.). Retrieved February 20, 2007, from http://www.codingforums.com

Custom Essays Writing Service—ProfEssays. (n.d.). Retrieved February 20, 2007, from http:// www.professays.com

Cutts, Q., Barnes, D., Bibby, P., Bown, J., Bush, V., Campbell, P., Fincher, S., Jamieson, S., Jenkins, T., Jones, M., Kazatov, D., Lancaster, T., Ratcliffe, M., Seisenberg, M, Shinner-Kennedy, D., Wagstaff, C., White, L., & Whyley, C. (2006). Laboratory exams in first programming courses. In *Proceedings of 7th Annual Conference for Information and Computer Sciences* (pp. 224-228). Dublin, Ireland: Higher Education Academy.

Culwin, F., & Lancaster, T. (2001). *Plagiarism, Prevention, Deterrence and Detection.* Retrieved February 20, 2007, from http://www.heacademy. ac.uk/resources.asp?process=full_record&sectio n=generic&id=426

Fincher, S., Barnes, D., Bibby, P., Bown, J., Bush, V., Campbell, P., et al. (2006). Some good ideas from the Disciplinary Commons. In *Proceedings of 7th Annual Conference for Information and Computer Sciences* (pp. 153-158). Dublin, Ireland: Higher Education Academy.

GetACoder—Quick and easy project outsourcing. Outsource your project today. (n.d.). Retrieved

February 20, 2007, from http://www.getacoder.com

Google. (n.d.). Retrieved February 20, 2007, from http://www.google.com

Gusmaroli, D. (2006, June 17). The Cybercheats making a small fortune. *Daily Mail,* 12-13.

Jenkins, T., & Helmore S. (2006). Coursework for cash: The threat from online plagiarism. In *Proceedings of 7th Annual Conference for Information and Computer Sciences* (pp. 121-126). Dublin, Ireland: Higher Education Academy.

Kammering, R., Hensler, O., Petrosyan, A., & Rehlick K. (2003). Review of two years experience with an electronic logbook. *Proceedings of ICALEPCS 2003.* Gweongju, Korea: Pohang Accelerator Laboratory.

Keating, E. (2005). *Individualized assignment generation and grading system.* Retrieved February 20, 2007, from http://www.provost.harvard.edu/it_fund/moreinfo_grants.php?id=131

Kom, J. (2006, September 25). Cheating students outsource to lowest bidder. *The Ottawa Citizen.*

Lancaster, T., & Culwin, F. (2007). Preserving academic integrity—fighting against non-originality agencies. *British Journal of Educational Technology, 38*(1), 153-157.

Lathrop, A., & Foss, K. (2000). *Student Cheating and Plagiarism in the Internet Era—A Wake Up Call.* Libraries Unlimited Inc.

Levinson, H. (2005). *Internet essays prove poor buys.* Retrieved February 20, 2007, from http://news.bbc.co.uk/1/hi/education/4420845.stm

Lightfoot, L. (2006, June 13). Cheating students put assignments out to tender on the Internet. *Daily Telegraph,* 1.

MacLeod, D. (2006, June 13). Publish and be damned. *The Guardian, Education Supplement,* 10.

Maths GCSE coursework is dropped. (2006). Retrieved February 20, 2007, from http://news.bbc.co.uk/1/hi/education/5385556.stm

Moodle—A Free, Open Source Course Management System for Online Learning. (n.d.). Retrieved February 20, 2007, from http://www.moodle.org

Morton, A., & Tarica, E. (2006, September 9). Web offers cheats tailor-made assignments. *The Age.*

Move to end more GCSE coursework. (2006). Retrieved February 20, 2007, from http://news.bbc.co.uk/1/hi/education/5411350.stm

Outsourcing to Freelance Programmers, Web & Logo Designers, Writers, Illustrators on Elance. (n.d.). Retrieved February 20, 2007, from http://www.elance.com

Rent A Coder: how software gets done. (n.d.). Retrieved February 20, 2007 from http://www.rentacoder.com

Student cheats contract out work. (2006). Retrieved February 20, 2007 from http://news.bbc.co.uk/1/hi/education/5071886.stm

Taylor, W. (1953). Cloze procedure: A new tool for measuring readability. *Journalism Quarterly, 30,* 414-438.

Turnitin. (n.d.). Retrieved February 20, 2007, from http://www.turnitin.com

Section V
Prevention is Better than Cure

Chapter XI
Prevention is Better than Cure:
Addressing Cheating and Plagiarism Based on the IT Student Perspective

Martin Dick
RMIT University, Australia

Judithe Sheard
Monash University, Australia

Maurie Hasen
Monash University, Australia

ABSTRACT

This chapter adopts a four-aspect model to address cheating and plagiarism in universities: education, prevention, detection, and consequence. The research focussed on the two aspects of education and prevention as the authors feel that this area has not been considered in detail by the research. Building on past research, a series of eight focus groups (72 students) were conducted with students from information technology degrees at an Australian university. The students were asked to comment and discuss the phenomenon of cheating from their perspective. The chapter presents in detail the responses of the students as analysed by the researchers and then builds a set of guidelines for educators to use in the areas of education and prevention in relation to student cheating.

INTRODUCTION

The problem of cheating is a long-standing one. Despite recent claims that the Internet and a decline in moral standards has caused a large increase in cheating, the evidence is that cheating has been a problem in universities over many decades (see for example: Bowers, 1964; Hetherington & Feldman, 1964; Stern & Havlicek, 1986). Yet most universities have not seriously addressed the problem unless forced to by events. The WIRA incident at the University of Newcastle in Australia where a blatant cheating situation was ignored by senior management as long as was possible is an exemplar of this approach and which led to an inquiry by the New South Wales Independent Commission against Corruption and the condemnation of the relevant senior management (Cripps, 2005; Longstaff, Ross, & Henderson, 2003).

Where universities have addressed the issue of cheating, the predominant approach has been one of punishment. Taking a broader view, we see the process of addressing cheating as having four aspects:

- **Education:** putting in place educational processes that provide students the necessary skills and knowledge to allow them to avoid cheating and to understand why cheating is undesirable. It also covers the education of academics to ensure that they understand the processes of the university in relation to cheating and that they implement good educational practice that will reduce cheating.
- **Prevention:** designing assessment so that cheating is both difficult to do and counterproductive for the student to attempt.
- **Detection:** establishing processes that allow academics to detect cheating when it occurs and also establishing processes for students to identify problems with their work prior to submission, for example, allowing students to submit work to a plagiarism detection service.
- **Consequence:** creating fair and equitable processes for dealing with cheating situations appropriate to the circumstances of individual cases.

We believe that in order to properly address these four areas, it is necessary to have a good understanding of the major actors in the situation, that is, the students, the academics and the uni-

versity. We address in detail only the first group of actors, the students, as this chapter intends to provide assistance to individual academics in their approaches to reducing cheating as opposed to the development of general university policy. Subsequently, the chapter examines the aspects of *education* and *prevention* because the aspects of *detection* and *consequence* have been covered in detail in previous work (see Jude Carroll's work [Carroll & Appleton, 2001] for an excellent and comprehensive discussion of the policy issues surrounding cheating and plagiarism). The aspects of *detection* and *consequence* are more appropriate to the strategic approach needed in the policy area as opposed to the tactical approach needed in the teaching area. In addition, dealing with cheating once it has been detected is both time-consuming and difficult in the best of situations. By focusing on *education* and *prevention*, the overall time and effort required to manage cheating is reduced.

Education and *prevention* are not sufficient lenses in themselves to understand the student perspective. It is also necessary to determine the student's understandings of, and motivations for cheating. From this framework we aim to develop guidelines for educational curriculum and for designing assessment for academic programs.

BACKGROUND

This section addresses four questions that are raised by the current discussions of cheating in the community and which are necessary to inform our understanding of the student perspective:

1. What is cheating?
2. Should we be concerned about cheating in the university sector?
3. What influences students to engage in cheating?
4. How are universities currently addressing this problem?

What Is Cheating?

There are many ways that tertiary students may cheat, making it difficult to arrive at a simple definition of cheating. A search of the literature has shown that cheating is often defined using multiple dimensions. These typically are described by sets of practices that encompass illegal, unethical and immoral behaviours, and behaviours that are against generally accepted institutional codes of practice. In some cases, however, whether a practice is cheating or not can depend on the rules set by an educator within a particular educational environment or for a particular task. For example, students may be encouraged to collaborate on a particular task but instructed to work individually on another. Cheating is a complex concept to define, leading to confusion as to what constitutes cheating (Ashworth, Bannister, & Thorne, 1997). We have defined a behaviour to be *cheating* if it violates the rules that have been set for an assessment task or it violates the accepted standard of student behaviour at the institution (Sheard, Markham, & Dick, 2003).

Why Is It A Concern?

A long history of studies indicate alarmingly widespread and high rates of cheating in universities (Bowers, 1964; Franklyn-Stokes & Newstead, 1995; Marsden, Carroll, & Neill, 2005; McCabe, 2005; Sheard et al., 2003)). Of further concern is that there are indications that the incidence of cheating is possibly increasing (Cole & McCabe, 1996; Diekhoff, LaBeff, Clark, Williams, Francis, & Haines, 1996). Major factors in this trend are changing assessment practices (e.g., online tests) and the increased use of technology enhanced teaching and learning environments (such as WebCT, Blackboard, and Moodle), which allow students more opportunities and a greater variety of ways to engage in cheating behaviour.

Levels of cheating and the changes in cheating patterns form a complex picture that needs to be viewed in light of changing educational practices, new learning environments and changing student work practices. Cheating can have many harmful consequences, but for the authors cheating is fundamentally about failing to learn. As educators we find that unacceptable and therefore a major concern.

Influences on Cheating Behaviour

When investigating cheating behaviour, it is important to determine the reasons why students cheat and the factors that prevent them from cheating. A number of studies of tertiary students have found that the most common reasons for cheating are time pressures and the need to pass or gain better grades (Davis & Ludvigson, 1995; Franklyn-Stokes & Newstead, 1995; Sheard & Dick, 2003). These studies also found that a commitment to learning and a desire not to engage in unethical or dishonest behaviour influenced students not to cheat. The comparative study of undergraduate and graduate students by Sheard, Markham, and Dick (2003) found that the reasons for cheating were the same for both groups of students; however, the reasons were rated more strongly for the undergraduate students and, in most cases, these were significant. In contrast, the factors that influenced students not to cheat were higher for the graduate students. A consistent finding across many studies is that fears of detection and punishment were not rated highly as factors that would prevent cheating.

Addressing the Problem

As stated in the introduction, the four major aspects for addressing cheating have been education, prevention, detection and consequence. Our particular focus on the education and prevention fronts has been predated by many studies and a brief review should provide a sense of development in both areas.

The establishment of honour codes has addressed both issues of education and prevention and seems to offer a reliable level of ensuring cheating is minimised, at least within the North American experience (McCabe & Trevino, 1993). Peer disapproval was assessed as having the greatest effect on cheating levels (McCabe & Trevino, 1997). Particular success seems to be found in the US, in smaller or military based colleges and universities where students share common values (Maramark & Maline, 1993). But as the size of classes and institutions rises, so too does student anonymity and the honour code loses its potency (McCabe, 2005). Honour codes have also not been part of the largely non-residential university population in Australia, and therefore have not been used in the local response to cheating practices.

Davis and Ludvigson (1995) are also sceptical about external deterrents and emphasise the importance of students learning to take greater responsibility. They posit that it is "…only when students have developed a stronger commitment to the educational process and an internalized code of ethics that opposes cheating will the problem be eradicated" (p. 121).

A sophisticated concept that would have IT students taking on more responsibility over unethical practices both at university and in the workplace, can be found in the model proposed by Greening, Kay, and Kummerfeld (2004). Their proposition suggests an integration of scenario-based ethical problems into the computing curriculum as a means of institutionalising ethical study as core content. The authors would use a survey as a teaching implement rather than a research one, to spark interest and engagement, and in so doing, enhance student awareness of a vast array of questionable practices.

Plagiarism detection programs such as Turnitin which might otherwise cause fear and loathing can be used as educational tools to inform students of accepted academic practice (Barrett & Malcolm, 2006). In such programs, students are encouraged to scan their work until the program indicates it is clear of plagiarism.

In a similar attempt to allay student anxiety about inadvertent plagiarism, McGowan (2005) maintains that students must begin their academic careers with an appreciation of the conventions and values of academic inquiry. If the university can achieve this objective, then students will be far more positive in their approach to learning and less concerned with plagiarism and its detection; as McGowan puts it: "plagiarism minimisation."

Reynard (2000) is mindful of both the unintentional and deliberate cheater and the efforts required to reveal and prosecute them. Her response is to bypass that process and design "Cheat-Resistant Assignments." Usually these tasks involve contributing something of one's own experience. Therefore, she suggests that an assignment that might typically ask for an analysis of the plot of *The Odyssey* could be framed as an exposition of a student's life journey, and how it might share some qualities with that of Odysseus. Reynard identifies several critical elements that help to cheat-proof a paper. For example, changing topics from year to year, being more specific when choosing topics for assignments, and monitoring all the stages of the writing process, are some of the many helpful suggestions.

Zobel and Hamilton (2002) address specific IT issues by recommending "verifiable submission" which involves presenting assignments electronically so that each will be identified by a user-name and a date-stamp. They suggest that students be required to submit draft submissions as well as source archives that will allow tracking the development of the assignment. This would overcome the last minute panic phenomenon that might otherwise encourage desperate responses.

In their comprehensive and insightful guide to dealing with plagiarism, Carroll and Appleton (2001) echo Reynard's suggestions, and add,

...reconsider the learning outcomes for the course and decrease those that ask for knowledge and understanding, substituting instead those that require analysis, evaluation and synthesis... (p. 10)

Perhaps Carroll and Appleton's most significant contribution is their emphasis on changing the atmosphere of the learning environment to one of engagement and commitment. This notion of cultural change is by no means new, with studies such as that by Dick, Sheard, Bareiss, Carter, Joyce, Harding and Laxer (2003) suggesting the provision of orientation programs for new students, as well as programs designed for academics to embrace cultural change.

RESEARCH METHODOLOGY

The goal of the research was to obtain a deeper understanding of the student perspective in relation to student cheating and plagiarism. In order to do that, we concentrated on the following issues with the students:

- Understandings of cheating and plagiarism
- Motivations for cheating and plagiarism
- Methods by which the university can reduce cheating and plagiarism

While survey research has been the mainstay of most cheating and plagiarism research, there have been exceptions (for example, Carter, 1998). In our study, we saw the need to extend the sources of data beyond that provided by surveys. A qualitative approach was used to provide a richer level of detail than that provided by the authors' past survey research. Observational techniques were considered to be impractical in this area, so this led us to the decision to use interview techniques. While individual interviews could have been used, it was felt that the interactive nature of focus groups led by a trained facilitator would be more likely to surface valuable material from the students than interviewing individual students in isolation.

Students were recruited to the study via announcements in a number of lectures. One of the authors presented the research process to the students and answered any questions. Students then nominated via a form, to participate in the focus groups. Students then were contacted and asked to attend one of the groups.

The distribution of students in the focus groups was stratified. Firstly, it was decided that it would be useful as well as practical to be able to distinguish between the traditional campus students and the technology campus students as there may be differences in the culture at the two campuses. This was considered likely, not only due to the different backgrounds of the campuses (traditional campus – originally a traditional university, technology campus – originally an institute of technology), but also because the students are enrolled in different degrees. Traditional campus students are enrolled in either a three-year bachelor of computer science or a four-year bachelor of software engineering. Technology campus students are enrolled in a three-year bachelor of computing. Our previous research had also indicated that there were some differences in levels of, and attitudes to, cheating at the different campuses.

Secondly, full-fee students were separated from Higher Education Contribution Scheme[1] (HECS) students for two reasons. Full-fee students are nearly entirely international in the student body and in the focus groups there were no domestic full-fee students. The first reason was that we felt that international students may feel freer to talk if there were no domestic students present. The second reason was the belief amongst some academics (Dick et al., 2003) and also in the general community that international students are more likely to cheat than Australian students. Our previous research does not support this belief, but we felt that it was worthwhile to explore the differences in opinion between international and domestic students. Our belief is that if there is any difference between international and domestic students, it is more likely to arise from the economic imperatives of full-fees than cultural differences.

Finally, the focus groups were divided on the basis of year level. Second and third year students were grouped together as they had both had significant experience of the university environment, and our previous research had shown little difference between the two year levels. First year students have had less experience of the university environment, therefore it seemed likely that separating them from the other year levels would be useful. No fourth year students from the bachelor of software engineering were involved in the focus groups.

The eight focus groups were organised on the basis of campus, fee status, and year level. Table 1 shows the profile of the focus groups that took place.

The gender balance of the focus groups approximates the gender balance of the student populations in the relevant degrees.

The interviews were conducted in an open manner with the facilitator directing the discussion in a light way. The students were free to range around the general issues introduced by the facilitator. The focus group discussions were audio-taped and then transcribed. Transcriptions of the focus group interviews were analysed with the NVivo tool using a grounded theory approach (Strauss & Corbin, 1998).

Ethical Issues

In conducting the focus groups it was inevitable that examples and possibly even admissions of cheating would occur. In order to ensure that no harm came to the participants in the focus group in the event that they admitted to cheating, a variety of measures were undertaken. An independent

Table 1. Focus group profiles

Focus Group	Campus	Fee Status	Number of 1st Year Students	Number of 2nd Year Students	Number of 3rd Year Students	Male	Female	Total
1	Technology Campus	Full Fee	8			2	6	8
2	Technology Campus	HECS	9			7	2	9
3	Technology Campus	Full Fee		3	4	5	2	7
4	Technology Campus	HECS		5	3	6	2	8
5	Traditional Campus	Full Fee/HECS (6/2)	8			8	0	8
6	Traditional Campus	HECS	10			7	3	10
7	Traditional Campus	Full Fee		6	5	7	4	11
8	Traditional Campus	HECS		6	5	8	3	11
		Totals	35	20	17	50	22	72

facilitator with no links to the university was hired to conduct the focus group; none of the academics who had any connection with the students was involved. The audiotapes were then transcribed by another independent person in such a way that students were only identified by their gender and it was not possible to attribute any statement to a particular student. Students also were advised of the process prior to participating in the focus groups to ensure that they were fully informed.

A final ethical issue was that the students were paid for their participation in the focus groups. As students were spending one to two hours in the focus group, the authors felt that it was appropriate to reimburse them for their time participating in the study. Students were paid a fee of Aus$30.00 to participate. The research was approved by the Monash University ethics committee (Application number 2004/494).

THE STUDENT PERSPECTIVE

This section details the results of the analysis of the focus groups based on the framework presented in the introduction. This framework consists of the four concepts of:

- Understandings of cheating and plagiarism
- Motivations for cheating and plagiarism
- Education to prevent cheating and plagiarism
- Prevention of cheating and plagiarism

In each section, the dominant concepts that arose from the focus groups will be presented with quotes to illustrate them.

Understandings

Student understanding of cheating phenomena is overall shallow and literal, as will be seen from the following concepts which arose from the analysis of the focus groups. As opposed to this shallow conceptual understanding, students displayed a sharp understanding of the practicalities of cheating when asked about the cheating methods that they were aware of.

Cheating is About Plagiarism

The first concept to arise from the interviews was that "Cheating is about plagiarism." At the start of each interview, the facilitator asked the students to indicate what their understanding of the purpose of the focus groups was. The great majority of students indicated that the purpose was to address the issue of plagiarism, for example "It's a focus group about plagiarism" or:

Facilitator: *Thanks all for coming. Do you all know why you're here? Do you know what we're talking about?*
Student: *Plagiarising.*

The university's educational emphasis has been on plagiarism as opposed to other forms of cheating and students have taken this attitude on board. Further probing by the facilitator was usually able to elicit more broad understandings of cheating from the students, but it was clear that for many students their salient understanding of cheating was restricted to plagiarism.

Cheating is Easy

One of the clear statements from students that arose out of the focus groups was that students believe that it is easy to cheat. A perception that cheating is not difficult is highly likely to encourage cheating amongst the student population.

It's pretty easy especially with IT, the technology, just copy and paste from other files. A lot easier than pen and paper where you have to read it and then copy it.

Cheating is Inevitable

Many of the students saw cheating as the natural way of things and that it was inevitable. Exemplars of this attitude were:

For example, if you can get the material from someone else it's easy. You can see it everywhere. It's kind of like a human network. You know this person, you know another one. And if you can cheat you take the opportunity to cheat.

Seriousness of Different Types of Cheating

One of the understandings that arose from the focus groups was that they saw cheating as a range of behaviours and that the seriousness differed depending upon the type of behaviour. The most serious form of cheating was that done in exams as the students exhibited some trust in the exam to assess them fairly, despite as we will see later on, their considerable knowledge of ways around exam protocols.

I think we all trust the exam process though.

Overall, students reported that they considered exam cheating to be a "bad thing."

But like if you go into an exam and you pull out cheat notes or something like that, I think that's much worse than just copying an assignment and then not referencing it properly.

Literal copying was also considered to be serious by many students:

Unacceptable, I think, would be like direct copy.

Though quite a few students did not find literal copying to be a particularly serious matter:

See if a friend of mine wanted to copy off me I wouldn't be too impressed. But it would only bother me in terms of not giving him the work if I thought there was a chance of getting caught. Otherwise I'd be happy for him to just take it

What was considered to be significantly less serious, was assistance for the purpose of learning, even where this might be considered by lecturers to be cheating. For example, the student above who referred to copying a substantial portion of a program extended his comment:

I've got no problem with someone looking at my program even if they look at every line of it and ask me why do you do this. …I've got no problem with it because they've learnt that and the next time they do that it wouldn't be considered cheating.

This student amongst others made a clear distinction between copying where the purpose was to learn as opposed to just completing an assessment task without attempting to understand the material. The following student made a similar point:

It also depends on what people classify cheating as. Like if you look at someone else's work because you don't understand something and you write it down and then you learn from it well then do you call that cheating? If you're learning from something that you've been given by someone else…

6 Words or More

In several courses in the degrees, students are provided with the following rule:

Six words or more in a row without quotes or references is plagiarism!

The aim of the lecturers in these courses is to provide students with a clear, objective measure of plagiarism and thereby allow the students to easily avoid it. Unfortunately, the student response is that they are far from reassured that this assists them to avoid plagiarism. In fact, it seems to create significant stress for the students with its arbitrary size:

If you get like 6 words the same you get caught and some people would do it by accident.

Boundaries of Cheating

The students were clearly confused about where the boundaries of cheating were, especially in the area of collaboration (acceptable) versus collusion (unacceptable). In all the degrees these students were enrolled in, many courses emphasized to the students that they should share ideas and work with other students. This was not always the case though, in some courses, the rule was that all work must be done by the individual and no collaboration was allowed.

I guess copying so much isn't so good but often lecturers will say it's good to try and teach other people. Because it helps reinforce the knowledge and I agree. I think to try and help somebody do the problems is the best way as well no, you got to write, it helps you know as well.

The lines are fuzzy. It's not defined really.

Pointlessness of Cheating

A key point for many students was that they considered cheating to be a pointless activity for two reasons. Firstly, cheating prevented them from learning and secondly they would be unprepared for their future careers.

What's the point of cheating if you don't learn anything.

I don't understand why you do it. ... Like when you get out of here you don't know anything and

you pay this money you might as well learn it and understand it or change courses or do something else. Cheating is a waste of time.

Motivations

In attempting to reduce cheating in the classroom situation, it is important to understand the perceptions of students in relation to their and other student's motivations to cheat. It is also important to listen to what students say about what motivates them to choose not to cheat. The previous section on Understandings overlaps with student motivations in two areas. One of the reported motivations for cheating which has already been mentioned in the section on Understandings, is the inevitability of cheating. Where students believe that cheating is inevitable, it becomes a motivation for them to cheat themselves. On the other hand, clearly the student's understanding of cheating as pointless provides us with information as to the motivation for not cheating. Students who value learning will be far less likely to cheat. Other motivations that were presented by the students are reported in the following sections.

Laziness

The most commonly raised reason for cheating by the students was that cheating students were lazy. This is a rather damning statement about their fellow students but it was consistently raised without any prompting by the facilitator.

Some people are just lazy and they just want to get by without doing anything.

I think what leads to cheating is just some people are lazy.

If students perceive other students as lazy, they are less willing to collude in cheating with their fellow students by providing assistance.

It depends why they need it as well. If somebody who really doesn't understand ... has been going to lectures and doesn't understand and they've got a prac coming up and they need help with something its different from if somebody is just ...they know what they're doing but they're just lazy and haven't done it and they just want to copy you because they couldn't be bothered.

Financial Pressure

Both local and international students reported that financial pressures can be a factor in causing students to cheat.

And with international students they have like ...not all of them, but some of them have a financial burden. Like they got to look after their rent. Their general fees. They don't get concession on buses and trains and stuff and it all adds up in the end and they need to work for it. Do you know what I mean.

With HECS as much as it is people are under a lot of pressure. They don't want to fail. It'll cost you about $800 to repeat a subject. And it's just not something most people can afford.

Family Expectations

It was mentioned several times that if students are under significant pressure from their family to perform well at university, then this can create a strong temptation to cheat.

I guess it's also the pressure from parents who push their children

The first time I brought home a C my mum flipped. I've never seen her so angry at me. And I know some parents are like that. Even when you're at uni. They can see how, but when it comes to grades they seem pretty harsh. And you get scared and you get desperate and...

Peer pressure

Far more commonly reported than family pressure was peer pressure to assist other students in their cheating. This took two forms: the first form was pressure from friends to assist them and the difficulty of refusing the friend because of the relationship.

I just reckon probably the top reason is like some people are pressured into cheating like giving their work to others.

Student: *Also that could be your friend who asks you. And you just don't want to ...*
Facilitator: *...so you collude in their cheating because you can't get out of it.*
Student: *Yes*

The second form is where students feel an obligation to assist their friend when they have suffered some form of setback and that not helping causes the student to feel guilty.

When someone is under pressure or something you kind of feel bad and you want to help them out.

No Connection to the Degree

A motivation that was strongly supported by the students was that many students felt no real connection to the content of the degrees that they were studying and that many students had enrolled in the degree by default, rather than because they felt a passion for an IT career.

Some people do a course just to get the certificate, the degree. They just want a pass.

I know people that are doing the course just because they got into it. They put it on their VTAC[2] and they got in and they're stuck here.

Doing the stuff that you enjoy doing so that's probably a deterrent to cheating itself because if you're enjoying it you want to understand.

Lack of Relevance or Importance

Assignments where the students felt that the material was irrelevant or of little value to their final mark were likely to encourage cheating according to a number of students.

I personally take a fairly laid back approach and my style of thinking is if I need to cheat to get to a near pass or just to get a pass mark then I shouldn't be cheating, ... And the only exception is when you have a subject you don't feel it has any relevance, the core subject doesn't lead onto anything else and its just an addition.

The exams seem to be worth a lot sort of 80% so that's why it doesn't bother me that people cheat on assignments cause they're going to make up maybe 5% of their mark.

High Stakes/Failing Hurdles

Related to the issue of work that was irrelevant or unimportant in the student view, were assessments that were high stakes in terms of the result, but did not have a major effect on the final mark. In this case, students felt that it was a reasonable response to collaborate/collude with other students.

There is this particular subject where in the pracs, it's either pass or fail so you finish the mile stones ... and you understand them and explain them and everything is there so you pass. So only 2 grades. Pass or Fail. But I remember it was so hard as they say you can't really finish it because you have like 10 milestones and no matter how early you started the prac, still until the end you can't finish it because it's that hard. Then suddenly what people started doing is okay I do the first 3 and then the last 4 and will explain to each other and

you take part of mine and I take part of yours and we will work it out from there. Make it different or anyhow. So what do you call that, cheating as well. Or cooperating or helping.

In uni there's very strict conditions about hurdles and all that sort of stuff. So basically what they say is you failed 2 pracs. You failed a prac hurdle. You failed a unit. You know you're going to have to catch up in summer which is quite scary for some people. So they're willing to cheat just so they don't have to do that

Status with Peers

At the traditional campus, many computer science students feel that there is a real division in the student body between those who are good at programming and those who are not:

You'll assimilate in the first year, like computer programming, computer science, either you will get 50% of people getting HDs and 50% of people getting passes.

Students in the lower performing group, then feel a social pressure to improve their results and see cheating as one way of doing this.

... and what I was saying about stigma. If you get lower marks or whatever. There seems to be this thing you've got to be a star student or you're nothing. You know hero or zero.

Availability of Support

Students reported that the level of availability of support from tutors and lecturers influenced the likelihood of students cheating. When students were unable to access help, they felt that it justified cheating to some extent.

Like there's not enough time for the prac person to go around and help everybody. Like you ask them [the tutor] for help and they go oh it's prac, I can't help you with that.

Poor Time Management

A reason commonly put forward by students in the focus groups was that an inability by students to manage their time often led to the necessity of cheating.

Sometimes people do cheat. Like I've seen my friends because 3 assignments are due on Friday so what do you do? And the assignment they are carrying like 15% of the assessment. You have to do all 3 and if you're not catching this stuff as quickly as other people are, then you have to resort to other measures.

Sometimes you get stuck in some way and you will be very tempted to refer to someone else.

Internal Conscience

The reason that students most commonly put forward as a motivation for not cheating was that it would be a burden on their conscience to have cheated.

So I need something internal that will tell me the reason for every movement I make or everything I do and say ah, this is not good, even if I really need it and I have to cheat in this situation but it's no good, the consequences will be worse.

I could never fathom it. I'd just have too much of a guilty conscience.

Other Motivations

A number of motivations that had been indicated in our earlier research as impacting on the decision to cheat were not strongly supported by the students in the focus groups. Language difficulties as a motivation to cheat was only raised by one

student and received little if any support from the other members of their focus group. As well, there was little support for the theory that cheating was a matter of misunderstanding, except in the case mentioned earlier of the confusion between collusion and collaboration. Fear of failure and the fear of getting caught had weak responses in the survey (Sheard et al. 2003) as reasons not to cheat. Focus groups supported this result, barely mentioning these fears.

Education

This section on the student perspective addresses two issues. First, how do students perceive the educational instruction that they have received about cheating? Second, what education should be provided to them to help them understand cheating?

Awareness of Education Efforts

In general, students clearly knew of the educational efforts made by the university to inform them about cheating and plagiarism. Nearly all the students acknowledged that the university provided some education in courses about these issues.

I guess this university makes a start when at the beginning of each lecture or lecture of each subject the lecturer tells you that plagiarism is not allowed. In tutorials they say you're not allowed to plagiarise or cheat or anything like that.

In the first semester we had something in class which was about how to cite stuff and how to quote it and what plagiarism was

Impact of Educational Efforts

However, while students were aware of the education efforts made by the university, the impact of those efforts was clearly marginal. A strong consensus from the students was that these efforts were not very effective. They perceived the educational efforts as perfunctory and paid little attention to them.

Student: Yeah. Every subject has like a lecture dedicated to try and scare you into not doing anything at all, ever.
Facilitator: Okay. But the rest of you did it scare you? What was the impact of that? Those lectures.
Student: I kind of zoned out.

Student 1:   I'm just saying generally I just don't read anything that's got to do with cheating. Just because I couldn't be bothered with reading it.
Student 2:   We've heard it so many times.

Some students who were studying double-degrees contrasted the educational effort in their IT courses unfavourably with the effort in their non-IT courses.

I think it was definitely helpful like as you were saying in Law like at the start of the year in our lectures they actually...when you had an assignment coming up they actually sat down and spent 15 minutes going through what plagiarism is and what does actually constitute cheating and plagiarism and what you can do and what you can't do. Where as with computer science ... that was just give you a piece of paper that has rules on it and nobody actually explains anything.

Clear Definitions

When asked about ways to improve the education provided on cheating and plagiarism, one issue came up again and again; the need for the university to provided clear definitions. This supports the findings on confusion regarding collaboration and collusion we saw earlier.

I think student need to be explained clearly what is cheating and what is plagiarism really.

They should say exactly what you shouldn't do or say anything that's not expressly permitted is forbidden. Something like that.

Where as they say how big they are on referencing but they don't fully explain what they mean. So they'll give a student a P and say yeah you didn't reference properly but there've never really sat down and explained to people what is plagiarism. How even if you paraphrase you still need to reference.

Education Won't Work

A common, but not universal, attitude expressed by the students in the focus groups was that regardless of the efforts the university might make, it will not be able to eliminate cheating.

I don't think telling people would make a difference.

A lot of...like if you try to tell people what cheating is I think a lot of people just find it boring and don't...like when I put on the cheating paragraph to my projects or I read it or whatever I have to ... I just ignore it. I copy, paste and put my name in, that's it. I don't read anything to do with cheating.

Suggestions for Improvement

A variety of suggestions were received from students about measures the university could use in their educational efforts to reduce cheating. One suggestion was to provide examples to help students understand what cheating and plagiarism really meant.

Maybe if they gave examples. Like just made it kind of more interactive when they explained it instead of read this.

Another suggestion was to ensure that students were informed about the sources of help available to them, so that cheating became less necessary. It follows from this that the provision of adequate help systems is a necessary first step.

How to get help and where you get the help from and having lecturers tell you constantly this is a point...

Other issues raised were educating students on how to handle situations where they know of other students cheating or when they are pressured to assist students to cheat.

Students aren't told how to deal with other people plagiarising.

Facilitator:	*Do you think you should be told how to deal with other people plagiarising?*
Student:	*Yeah. Cause they say don't plagiarise and you don't plagiarise. You need to know what to do if someone is plagiarising or cheating on your work.*

Finally, a common suggestion was to focus the educational efforts on why cheating is a bad thing, by pointing out that by cheating, the student reduces their learning to a minimal level and that this will impact upon their ability to perform in industry when they graduate.

Well you'd have like associate it to life experience. For example if you just cheated your way through university and then towards the end like you get out of university and you get a job like 6 months later, you have no clue what to do.

Prevention

This section looks at the student perspective in terms of how cheating may be prevented from occurring or at least reduced.

Interviews

A common practice at the technology campus was the use of oral exams to assess the assignment work of students. Students in the focus groups were strongly in favour of this approach as a means of preventing cheating.

I don't know if its done in other code classes but with the Java [a programming course] that we're talking we're actually tested on whether our work is ours by taking it in there and reviewing. So I think that's a good way of dealing with it.

And after each assignment and stuff like they should like in one of our subjects the first year after you did the assignment a few weeks down the track or whatever they mark you and they have a mark on the side but they interview as well. Interview you to make sure that you know the stuff that you wrote down. Like that was a pretty good system

Teacher Approachability

A very common issue raised by the students was that lecturers and tutors needed to be approachable. If a student felt that they could not approach a teacher for help, they were more likely to cheat as they had no alternative.

I think somebody raised about the tutors. The fact that some tutors are unapproachable or some people are to scared to ask questions. If we could somehow encourage more interaction between students and tutors and student groups and whatever, whoever is responsible I think that would sort of alleviate the problem with plagiarising.

Student 1:   ...well they tell you that you can ask any question they want. The silly question or whatever. But when you start asking them that's when the reaction is not all that good.

Student 2:   They're always getting frustrated with the questions you're asking.

Caring

Students in the focus groups were very quick to categorise lecturers and tutors according to whether they felt they cared or not. When teachers were considered to be uncaring, it was felt that this encouraged students to cheat.

That can be difficult to when the lecturers are swapping around. Especially if the lecturer has gone overseas ... and the replacement guy comes in and he just says well I'm here for a fortnight. I really don't care about you guys.

The ones who don't make it look like they're just doing it because they're getting paid. Like the ones who look like they actually want to teach something and they interact with you well.

Levels of Interaction

Students felt that high levels of interaction in the course were one means of preventing cheating from occurring.

The other thing is I think the best place for all these things to start solving all these problems is in a tute where you feel friendly. I mean free to talk with the tutor and some tutors are not all that experienced. They've just done their degree. They know their subject but then you also you should know how to get those student to interact with you on a really friendly basis. I think if you have that you learn. Anyone would ask questions and they learn.

But before the exam it's just that we have [consultation sessions] ...but if we have them throughout the whole semester it will reduce the number of cheaters.

Relevance of Work

In situations where students couldn't see the relevance of an assessment item, they felt that this heightened the incidence of cheating.

Where I've seen more occurrence of cheating is where people feel the topic is irrelevant to them on the assignments and they don't see where they all contribute to their final goal.

Positive Teaching Approach

A strongly held attitude expressed by the students in the focus groups was that teachers that had a positive approach to students really discouraged students from cheating.

Because he gave me that good help which is here a positive attitude. Instead of pushing me down when I'm already down. Instead of pushing me down again because it seemed to be a very stupid question.

I remember I had this particular tutor, demonstrator, I really couldn't do anything in my first 2 pracs and he just started talking positive to me and he knew that I couldn't do it and he just went I know you are smart, you can do it, you can do it, you are smart, and that helped me to revive myself from the incident and I knew I could do it.

Poor Teaching Practices

Students were particularly scathing of teachers that used poor teaching practices and felt that this was likely to increase the amount of cheating.

We've got a programming [course]. We've got Lecturer 1 and Lecturer 2 and I find that Lecturer 1 is like he's good. Interesting. Talks through his stuff. He's really that involved with people making sure everyone understands. Explains. Does plenty of examples. And then you've just got the other one Lecturer 2, that's just like wave after wave waiting for information.

One tutor is like really shy so she wouldn't ask anybody to...she'll just stand there waiting for someone to put their hand up.

Dobbing In

While honour codes have had some success in the United States as was mentioned in the Background section of this chapter, students reacted quite negatively to the idea that they might report cheating by their fellow students. It was only raised as a possibility where another student had stolen their own work.

Facilitator:	*Would you ever dob anyone in?*
Student 1:	*No.*
Student 2:	*Not a chance.*
Student 3:	*Unless it was really blatantly obvious and bad.*
Student 4:	*Unless they copied you, you didn't know, they just stole your work.*

Facilitator:	*If you know of someone who doesn't have that motivation and has cheated what do you do? How do you deal with it?*
Student:	*I don't care.*
Facilitator:	*You don't care.*
Student:	*Firstly I wouldn't report them.*

Group Work

A positive idea presented by the students in the focus groups as a means to prevent cheating was to use group work, so as to avoid situations where a student feels the need to cheat to cope with the work.

I think if a person just by themselves and they're trying to work it out then that's where they're going to feel oh no I can't do this. If they're in a group that's very, I mean it's not like 5 people are all not going to be able to do the problem. Because they can think together. Bounce ideas off each other. If you've just got one person and they can't do it well then there's going to be a high chance of them cheating.

An interesting accommodation to the reality of cheating was noted by one student in relation to group work.

Actually had an occasion last semester where one of the guys in our group assignment we knew that he plagiarised in a previous assignment so we sort of just...we actually limited the amount of work that he did. Don't know if that was the right way to go about it.

Exam Cheating

While as we saw earlier, many students have a belief that the use of exams prevents cheating, a belief accepted by many academics, students were well aware of methods to cheat in the exam environment.

I think in major exam it's easy to cheat. The thing is the individual privacy and the cheat has no conflict. For example if the person wants to cheat, the toilet during exam you can't supervise them in the toilet. Some students maybe have some notes and look at notes in the toilet.

Student 1:	*You can send in like mobile SMS. By the choice answer, multiple choice.*
Student 2:	*From someone outside of the uni.*
Student 1:	*Yeah. otherwise you finish first and*

then turn on my mobile and then he send me the SMS and look at....

Student 2:   *...actually cool.*

If you're going to bring your mobiles into the exams ..., there's nothing to stop you from storing everything in your mobile.

Examples

A suggestion to reduce the need for cheating and assist in learning was that lecturers should provide examples of the assessment items that they wish students to produce.

...because I know in one course the lecturer I had he actually provided past assignments you know this is what we're looking for. Like it was a totally different case study but he goes oh okay you have to do diagrams that look like this. We have to produce documentation though. We knew what was required of us. So if they don't know what's required of them they're more likely to go and ask someone else and then take the easy way which is just copy most of it.

I think as she said, give the examples to the student. I'm thinking give the student past student assignment example when the student is doing the assignment

Access to Help and Facilities

An issue that arose very commonly in the focus groups was that cheating is often caused by a lack of access to help and facilities. If a student is unable to access the relevant computer facilities for example, or unable to talk to a tutor about their assignment, then cheating becomes a more attractive option.

Student 1:   *...and just knowing there's going to be computers available at any time that you require it.*

Student 2:   *Its not just access to facilities and access to tutors and access to lecturers.*

Student 3:   *More consultation time with tutors.*

well you don't tend to get help [in pracs]. And you have to finish it. You didn't have enough time to ask the tutor because everyone else needs the tutor as well. It's not just you. It's like there's not enough resources in that way. Like the classes need to be a bit smaller maybe.

Staged Assessment

Another idea that students felt assisted in the effort to reduce cheating was that assignments could be submitted in stages rather than in one single submission.

I have a subject which the assignment it's based on stages and it progresses all the time so rather than submitting the whole thing at the end of the week you actually have to show to the tutor what you have done and you know for stages and I find that useful.

There's another way to do it. Put something to submit every week. It will be a big job. It will be possible to finish it like in one or two days and then submit it each week and you definitely wouldn't have [to cheat]

Repeated Assignments

One practice that students felt increased the likelihood of cheating was the repetition of assignments from one year to the next.

Facilitator: *Okay so you're saying it's easy to cheat from other people's work or from X. How do you get hold of work from previous semesters?*

Student 1:   Your friends.
Student 2:   Networking.

APPROACHES TO ADDRESS CHEATING

In this section, we examine the approaches in the areas of education and prevention that we feel arise out of the information provided by the students in the focus groups.

Education

Analysis of the focus groups' responses indicate that students are in need of education about cheating and plagiarism. Looking at this information provided by the focus groups, the curriculum of an effective educational program to reduce cheating and plagiarism would have these characteristics.

1. Some aspects of cheating are well understood by students to be unacceptable, for example, cheating in exams or the wholesale copying of material from other students, books and the Internet and therefore these don't need to be addressed in detail in the curriculum.

2. Students are clearly confused about the difference between collusion and collaboration. Any curriculum about cheating should concentrate on distinguishing between these two concepts. The line between collusion and collaboration varies from class to class, course to course, and university to university, so no single definition suffices. From our perspective, collusion is where the level of collaboration exceeds that which is permitted for a particular assessment task. It follows that the acceptable level of collaboration needs to be clearly set out for each assessment task.

3. Students are uncertain about what constitutes plagiarism and how they should handle references in their work. Simple mantras such as "No more than six words" are in some ways counter-productive. The curriculum needs to ensure that students have a deep understanding of the issue as opposed to trying to inculcate simple rules into the students.

4. Simple statements and definitions of what constitutes cheating are insufficient for students to understand the issues of cheating and plagiarism. Curriculum needs to be example-driven so that students can place cheating behaviours into a concrete context that they can relate to their own experiences as a student.

5. Students are easily bored by the repetition of statements about cheating and educational efforts in this area must be interactive and not be routine announcements. The curriculum must be placed so as to be distinguishable from the normal classroom activities.

6. The curriculum should not over-emphasise the issue of plagiarism in comparison with other forms of cheating.

7. It is highly recommended that the curriculum focuses on the long-term impacts of cheating on a student's career, rather than presenting cheating as simply something that is wrong to do and that will be penalised if caught.

8. It also is recommended that the curriculum addresses the issues of the impact on learning of cheating and the need to have a moral compass on this issue. Overall, the curriculum should get students to examine their own reasons for why they might cheat or not cheat and thereby raise their consciousness about the issue.

9. The concept that "cheating is inevitable" and therefore students shouldn't worry about the issue needs to be addressed in the curriculum.

10. The issue of time management skills needs to be addressed in any educational program that wishes to reduce cheating.

11. The curriculum needs to provide students with methods to handle the pressures from the peers to assist them in their cheating. It is not reasonable to expect students at this stage of their life to easily resist peer pressure.

12. The curriculum should not attempt to scare students or use fear of consequences to motivate students to not to cheat. Students are well aware that cheating is easy and unlikely to be caught, so scare tactics will for most students be ineffective. This is not to say that the consequences of being caught should not be discussed.

13. Educational programs about cheating need to emphasise the sources of assistance that are available to students to aid them in their studies.

Prevention

A variety of methods have been proposed in the literature to prevent cheating, as earlier sections have discussed. In addition, the students in the focus groups have raised significant issues with regards to prevention. This section looks at both sources of data and applies the information from the student perspective to present a critical analysis of the various methods proposed to prevent cheating. It should be understood that we are not presenting any of these methods as a panacea for cheating or even all of them in concert as the solution. As the students made clear, there will always be cheating in university courses, but these ideas seem likely to assist in the ongoing process of reducing cheating.

Caring and Being a Good Teacher

One of the methods of preventing cheating that arises from the research is that having academics who clearly care about the students and their course and who apply good teaching practices to their courses is likely to reduce the level of

cheating. Students clearly respond well in this situation. Students also appear to respond well in this area to increased levels of interaction in the classroom. The provision of high levels of interaction has been recognised as an indicator of good teaching practice for many years. Poor teaching practices such as repeating assignment material from year to year or presenting voluminous quantities of material in lectures without providing interaction opportunities is likely to increase cheating.

Interviews and Presentations

The practice of assessing student work via oral exams is seen by the students as being highly effective in reducing cheating. In an oral exam students need to be able to demonstrate mastery of the material and this is significantly less likely if the student has copied the material or received excessive assistance. It should be noted that it is not impossible for a student who has copied from other students to do well in an interview situation. Two of the authors who regularly use this technique have seen several examples of this happening (Dick, 2005).

Presentations can achieve similar results to an interview as the presentation of material also relies to some extent on the student's mastery of it. However, it is probably less effective as it is not the one-on-one environment of the interview and the level of interaction is reduced.

Set Literature

One possible method to reduce plagiarism has been the use of a set reference list for an essay. By limiting the possible references to be used by the students in a piece of work, it reduces the likelihood that they will plagiarise material. In such a situation students will still be able to gain the capability of synthesising a body of literature into a cohesive whole; however, it downplays the learning of skills such as gathering and evaluating literature. To some extent, it sidesteps the issue of developing the student's understanding of plagiarism and does not equip them for handling such issues in the future. We believe that this method is of limited utility in an overall degree, though it may be of some use in particular circumstances. An example might be where the major learning objective is for the students to master a particular body of knowledge embedded in the set reference list.

Individual Assignment Specification

Students are confused about the difference between collaboration and collusion and find it difficult to resist allowing their peers to copy from their assignments. A method of prevention that addresses this issue is to provide each student with an individual assignment. If each student is required to solve a different problem, then the solutions they propose must inherently be different and it thereby makes copying, to a large degree, pointless. In many technical subjects, a simple program can be used to generate many individual assignments, alternatively the techniques proposed by Reynard (2000) can be used in non-technical subjects. Another alternative is to allow students to set their own question with guidance from the teacher and thereby ensure minimal collusion and copying. In multiple-choice assessment, the development of question banks can allow individualised tests. One drawback is that this often can require extra effort on the part of the academic to develop and/or to mark. The use of individual assignments may not be suitable in all circumstances, but a wide range of assessments may benefit from their use in relation to reducing cheating.

Peer Assessment

Peer assessment has many positive aspects and theoretically should be effective in preventing cheating as students are far more likely to be aware of the cheating of their peers than the teacher. The results of the research reveal a problematic aspect to peer assessment. Many students don't seem to care if other students cheat unless they are directly involved. Given this attitude, it is likely that students will not punish their peers for cheating and the possible deterrent effect of peer assessment may not exist. Of course there are many other good reasons to use peer assessment, but reducing cheating is probably not one of those reasons.

Monitored Assessment

The classic case of a monitored assessment is the traditional exam with invigilators, silence and strict rules, yet along with previous research, the focus groups reveal that students are well aware of how to subvert exam protocols. Academics would be well advised not to place too high a reliance on the use of exams and other forms of monitored assessments to control and reduce cheating. Universities need to consider measures to handle cheating practices in exams, for example deploying mobile phone jammers in exam venues.

Continuous Assessment

One method that seems to have promise, according to the focus groups, is assessment that is not concentrated into one or two major submissions, but instead has many submissions throughout the semester. A continuous assessment regime provides incentives to students to manage their time better and possibly reduces the stress associated with assessment. Both of these effects would be likely to reduce the possibility of a student cheating.

Relevant Assessment

When designing assessment, the relevance of the assessment to the students should always be considered by the academic. It should also be made explicit to the students. Academics should not assume that the relevance of an assessment or indeed of course material is obvious to the students. By avoiding assessment that the students see as irrelevant to them, the incidence of cheating on the piece of assessment is likely to be reduced.

Clarity and Consistency of Assessment Rules

Students can easily be confused if the assessment rules for an item of work are not made clear. If a piece of work must be worked on by a student alone, then this must be made very clear, as well the rationale for this approach to the assessment also should be made explicit to the students. The rules for assessment for a specific piece of work or a specific course should also take in to consideration the general rules of assessment used in that degree. If most other assessments in the degree encourage collaboration between students, a piece of assessment that insists on no collaboration often will find this assessment rule breached. Rules for assessment that are inconsistent with norms the student expects must doubly be emphasised.

Inappropriate Student Attitudes

Two of the major issues raised in the focus groups were that cheating is often motivated by laziness and/or students having no interest in the content of their degree. There is little that any one course can do to address large personal issues for a student like this. One possible solution at a higher level is different selection practices to try and ensure that commencing students have a genuine interest in the degree, rather than just rely on the ENTER[3] score of applicants. A related solution is for universities to ensure that transfer between degrees is easy. It is difficult for a student at the

end of their secondary education to be sure as to what path they want their career to take. Many students will pick the wrong degree, so within reason, it should be made possible for students to transfer to a different degree with minimal penalties and hurdles. Of course, there would need to be measures to ensure that this transfer mechanism was not used to bypass ENTER score requirements for a degree.

Honour Codes

While honour codes have met with some success in the USA, they rely on a culture amongst the students that places honesty and integrity above peer pressure and apathy. The results of the focus groups indicate that this culture currently does not exist amongst the students and that it would require long-term and large-scale efforts by the university to develop that culture.

CONCLUSION

We have examined the IT student perspective on cheating in order to generate ideas about education and prevention. It is clear that the traditional concentration of universities on detection and punishment is an insufficient response to cheating and plagiarism and that individual academics must take responsibility for their teaching and use a wide variety of techniques to reduce student cheating. It is the opinion of the authors that the application of many of these techniques will not only reduce student cheating but also result in increased student learning. If we can prevent students from cheating in the first place, through improved education and prevention techniques, many students and academics will be spared a discipline process that is traumatic for both and a more positive learning environment established.

REFERENCES

Ashworth, P., Bannister, P., & Thorne, P. (1997). Guilty in whose eyes? University students' perceptions of cheating and plagiarism in academic work and assessment. *Studies in Higher Education, 22*(2), 187-203.

Barrett, R., & Malcolm, J. (2006). Embedding plagiarism education in the assessment process. *International Journal for Educational Integrity, 2*(1).

Bowers, W. J. (1964). *Student dishonesty and its control in college* (No. CRP-1672). New York: Columbia University.

Carroll, J., & Appleton, J. (2001). *Plagiarism: A good practice guide.* Oxford Brookes University.

Cole, S., & McCabe, D. L. (1996). Issues in academic integrity. In *New Directions for Student Services* (pp. 67-77). Jossey-Bass Publishers.

Cripps, J. (2005). *Independent commission against corruption's report on investigation into the University of Newcastle's handling of plagiarism allegations*: NSW Independent Commission Against Corruption.

Davis, S. F., & Ludvigson, H. W. (1995). Faculty forum: Additional data on academic dishonesty and a proposal for remediation. *Teaching of Psychology, 22*(2), 119-121.

Dick, M. (2005, June 27-29). *Student interviews as a tool for assessment and learning in a systems analysis and design course.* Paper presented at the 10th Annual SIGCSE Conference on Innovation and Technology in Computer Science Education, Monte de Caparica, Portugal.

Dick, M., Sheard, J., Bareiss, C., Carter, J., Joyce, D., Harding, T., et al. (2003). Addressing student cheating: Definitions and solutions. *ACM SIGCSE Bulletin, 35*(2), 172-184.

Diekhoff, G. M., LaBeff, E. E., Clark, R. E., Williams, L. E., Francis, B., & Haines, V. J. (1996). College cheating: Ten years later. *Research in Higher Education, 37*(4), 487-502.

Franklyn-Stokes, A., & Newstead, S. E. (1995). Undergraduate cheating: Who does what and why? *Studies in Higher Education, 20*(2), 159-172.

Greening, T., Kay, J., & Kummerfeld, B. (2004). *Integrating ethical content into computing curricula.* Paper presented at the Sixth Australasian Computing Education conference, Dunedin, New Zealand.

Hetherington, E. M., & Feldman, S. E. (1964). College cheating as a function of subject and situational variables. *Journal of Educational Psychology, 55*(4), 212-218.

Longstaff, S., Ross, S., & Henderson, K. (2003). *St James Ethics Centre Report. Independent inquiry: Plagiarism policies, procedures & management controls* (Commissioned report). Newcastle, New South Wales, Australia: St James Ethics Centre.

Maramark, S., & Maline, M. B. (1993). *Academic dishonesty among college students. Issues in education.* (Information analyses No. OR-93-3082). Washington, DC: Office of Educational Research and Improvement (ED).

Marsden, H., Carroll, M., & Neill, J. (2005). Who cheats at university? A self-report study of dishonest academic behaviours in a sample of Australian university students. *Australian Journal of Psychology, 57*(1), 1-10.

McCabe, D. L. (2005). Cheating among college and university students: A North American perspective. *International Journal for Educational Integrity, 1*(1).

McCabe, D. L., & Trevino, L. K. (1993). Academic dishonesty: Honor codes and other contextual influences. *Journal of Higher Education, 64*(5), 522-538.

McCabe, D. L., & Trevino, L. K. (1997). Individual and contextual influences on academic dishonesty: A multicampus investigation. *Research in Higher Education, 38*(3), 379-396.

McGowan, U. (2005). *Plagiarism detection and prevention: Are we putting the cart before the horse?* Paper presented at the Higher Education Research and Development conference (HERD-SA), Sydney, Australia.

Reynard, L. (2000). Cut and paste 101: Plagiarism and the Net. *Educational Leadership, 57*(4), 38-42.

Sheard, J., & Dick, M. (2003). *Influences on cheating practice of IT students: What are the factors?* Paper presented at the Innovation and Technology in Computer Science Education (ITiCSE 2003), Thessaloniki, Greece.

Sheard, J., Markham, S., & Dick, M. (2003). Investigating differences in cheating behaviours of IT undergraduate and graduate students: The maturity and motivation factors. *Journal of Higher Education Research and Development, 22*(1), 91-108.

Stern, E. B., & Havlicek, L. (1986). Academic misconduct: Results of faculty and undergraduate student surveys. *Journal of Allied Health, 5,* 129-142.

Strauss, A. L., & Corbin, J. M. (1998). *Basics of Qualitative Research* (2nd ed.). Thousand Oaks, California, USA: Sage Publications Inc.

Zobel, J., & Hamilton, M. (2002). Managing student plagiarism in large academic departments. *Australian Universities Review, 45*(2), 23-30.

ENDNOTES

[1]   The Higher Education Contribution Scheme is where Australian students must make a contribution of several thousand dollars per year to their university education but are able to postpone payment until they have completed their degree. The payments are then collected through the Australian income tax system when the student surpasses a threshold income level.

[2]   VTAC is the Victorian Tertiary Admissions Centre. During their final year of secondary schooling, students submit a list of the nine degrees they wish to apply for in order of their preference.

[3]   Equivalent National Tertiary Entrance Rank—used to determine entry to undergraduate degrees in Australian universities.

Chapter XII
Plagiarism, Instruction, and Blogs

Michael Hanrahan
Bates College, USA

ABSTRACT

This chapter takes as its point of departure the Colby, Bates, and Bowdoin Plagiarism Project (http://ats. bates.edu/cbb), which sought to approach the problem of undergraduate plagiarism as a pedagogical challenge. By revisiting the decision to publish the project's content by means of a weblog, the article considers the ways in which weblogs provide a reflective tool and medium for engaging plagiarism. It considers weblog practice and use and offers examples that attest to the instructional value of weblogs, especially their ability to foster learning communities and to promote the appropriate use of information and intellectual property.

INTRODUCTION

Alarmist news accounts of student dishonesty and cheating abound. More often than not, such stories describe how universities, colleges, and even high schools have resorted to plagiarism detection services to fight a veritable epidemic of student cheating. The preferred method of combating academic dishonesty, after-the-fact detection, is not the only and is perhaps not the best way to address the problem of student plagiarism. Instead of fighting the lost cause of plagiarism retroactively, technologists and librarians at Colby, Bates, and

Bowdoin colleges (CBB) collaborated to develop a program of instruction to educate students about the principles of academic honesty. The resulting plagiarism resource site (http://ats.bates.edu/cbb) includes an introduction to plagiarism, an online tutorial that tests one's understanding of plagiarism and that provides guidance in the conventions of citation, and a dedicated weblog that publishes links to newsworthy articles, notices, and projects dedicated to plagiarism.

Conceived as a case study, this chapter discusses and evaluates the project's reliance on a weblog to develop, manage, and publish learning resources dedicated to plagiarism. In the matter of technical choices, the project developers were influenced by their commitment to Open Source Software as well as Creative Commons licensing. The former influenced the choice of weblog software, Drupal (http://www.drupal.org), and the latter informed the decision to make all of the project's learning objects and resources available under an "Attribution-Non-Commercial-Share-Alike" Creative Commons license. These decisions, it turns out, have allowed the project to model the appropriate use of online materials and have retrospectively provided an occasion to reflect on weblogs as an effective medium for engaging plagiarism.

BACKGROUND

Over the past several years, national, regional, local, and campus newspapers across the globe have regularly featured articles on student cheating. While academic dishonesty takes any number of forms (using a PDA, cell phone, or crib notes during an exam; submitting unoriginal work copied from an existing publication, cut and pasted from an online source, or purchased from a paper mill; or simply peering over a classmate's shoulder during a quiz), plagiarism has emerged as the most visible form of student cheating. In many ways, the term threatens to subsume all other categories of academic dishonesty. A passing visit to the statistics page at Turnitin's Web site (plagiarism.org) reinforces this tendency. Turnitin, the world's leading plagiarism detection service, claims that "A study by The Center for Academic Integrity (CAI) found that almost 80 percent of college students admit to cheating at least once." Besides generalizing and rounding up the center's published summary ("On most campuses, over 75 percent of students admit to some cheating"), Turnitin's claim isolates a common tendency to conflate a number of dishonest "behaviors" with plagiarism. Donald McCabe

(personal communication, August 4, 2004) explains that the 75 percent figure published by the CAI "represents about a dozen different behaviors and was obtained in a written survey." Plagiarism is certainly one form of cheating, but not all cheating is plagiarism.

Reports of plagiarism in the media tend to indulge in hyperbole: it is consistently described as nothing less than an epidemic on campuses. McCabe (1996), who conducted extensive surveys between 1996 and 2003, repeatedly found that the facts do not correspond with "the dramatic upsurge in cheating heralded by the media." McCabe (2000) has elsewhere observed: "Even though I've stated on previous occasions that I don't believe these increases have been as great as suggested by the media, I must admit I was surprised by the very low levels of self-reported Internet-related cheating I found." McCabe has subsequently further qualified his view of the problem: "Although plagiarism appears to have remained relatively stable during the past 40 years, . . . it is actually far more prevalent today because many students don't consider cut-and-paste Internet copying as cheating" (Hansen, 2003, p. 777). More recently, McCabe's evaluation of his 2002-2003 Survey of U.S. Colleges and Universities identifies an increase in certain kinds of cheating and a continued misunderstanding of plagiarism among undergraduates: "The past few decades have seen a significant rise in the level of cheating on tests and exams. . . . While the data on various forms of cheating on written assignments do not reflect the same trend, this may be due to a change in how students define cheating" (2004, p. 127).

To complicate matters further, statistical estimates of academic dishonesty seem to vary due to contexts (including education level and geography). For example in a recent survey of graduate students enrolled in 32 business programs in the United States and Canada, McCabe, Butterfield, and Treviño (2006) have reported that business students tend to cheat more than other graduate students: "Fifty-six percent of graduate business students, compared to 47 percent of their nonbusiness peers, admitted to engaging in some form of cheating . . . during the past year" (p. 299). The level of self-reported cut-and-paste plagiarism in this survey, in turn, was "33 percent of the graduate business students . . . compared to 22 percent for nonbusiness students" (p. 300). A recent study conducted by the University of Guelph and co-administered by McCabe and Christensen Hughes (2006) has estimated that 53 percent of Canadian undergraduate students engage "in serious cheating on written work" (Gulli, Kohler & Patriquin, 2007). According to Christensen Hughes, "Serious cheating on written work includes copying a few sentences without footnoting, fabricating or falsifying a bibliography, or turning in a paper that someone else has written" (Cooper, 2007). To help put matters in a global perspective, a recent survey of British higher education conducted by Freshminds.co.uk (with the assistance of the JISC's Plagiarism Advisory Service and the Center for Academic Integrity) found that "75 percent of respondents have never plagiarized." This figure in turn approximates what Turnitin representatives have elsewhere estimated: in an interview for the student newspaper at University of California, Santa Barbara, Paul Wedlake, director of sales for iParadigms, the parent company of Turnitin.com, is reported to have claimed that "approximately 30 percent of all students in the United States plagiarize on every written assignment they complete" (Ray, 2001).

Regardless of the figures and statistics, the Internet very much lies at the center of the current fascination with plagiarism. As a result, the fundamentally ethical nature of the offense often gets confused with a technological one. As Patrick Scanlon of the Rochester Institute of Technology has acknowledged: "'Plagiarism is not a technological problem—it's a problem that has to do with ethical behavior and the correct use of sources. And it existed long before the advent of the Internet'" (Hansen, 2003, p. 791).

Whether attributed to hype or misperception, plagiarism and the Internet remain entangled in the popular and the academic imaginations. The association is further reinforced by student study habits, especially their research practices. A recent Pew report found that "nearly three-quarters (73 percent) of college students" in the United States claim to "use the Internet more than the library" (Jones, 2002, p. 3). An even greater percentage of students no doubt resorts to the Internet for leisure—to game, surf, IM, and share music files. This reliance on the Internet for study and entertainment has blurred the lines between appropriate and inappropriate cyberpractice and has promoted the intentional as well as unintentional misuse of intellectual and creative property.

The Internet is not the sole source of undergraduate plagiarism. The current manifestation of the problem also can be attributed to non-technological developments, including the increased tendency among students and their parents (at least in the English-speaking world) to perceive higher education as a service industry. That is, the relegation of higher education to a service for which one pays has created a scenario in which students-as-consumers readily expect performance (in the form of good grades) as something to which they are entitled. This sense of entitlement, in turn, overrides concerns about academic honesty. Plagiarism, in this light, emerges as symptomatic of wide-ranging cultural shifts that are not simply or easily reducible to technological shifts and developments. Recent commentary on student plagiarism has provoked observations on this phenomenon. For example, Frank Furedi, professor of sociology at the University of Kent, has observed that "In the 'customer-client culture', degrees are seen as something you pay for rather than something you have to learn. It's the new ethos of university life" (A Quarter of Students Cheating, 2004). This cultural shift and attendant "ethos" may very well lie at the root of the misrecognition of plagiarism among undergraduates that McCabe has observed (Hansen, 2007, p. 777; McCabe, 2004, 127).

Another significant contributing factor to the rise of plagiarism is an educational culture that resists adapting its instructional methods in the face of advances in technology. This resistance is forcefully demonstrated by the widespread adoption of plagiarism detection services. In an ostensible attempt to counter technology with technology, schools have settled for a punitive solution to what is a basically an instructional problem, and in doing so have escalated rather than engaged the problem. Turnitin, for example, adds each assignment submitted to its service to its databases. This ethically questionable practice of collecting content has been widely criticized as ignoring the intellectual property rights of students: the issue was raised several years ago by Howard (2001); it surfaced in 2003 at the center of a controversy at McGill University (McGill Student, 2006); more recently Mount Saint Vincent University in Halifax, Nova Scotia, has banned Turnitin for this reason (MSVU bans anti-plagiarism software, 2006); and high school students in suburban Washington, D.C., have protested their school's subscription to Turnitin on the same grounds (Glod, 2006). In most of these cases, iParadigms has defended its product against this allegation. In a surprising move, however, the company recently took the issue into account when renegotiating its contract with the University of Kansas: "Because Turnitin.com retains student papers, the service has raised intellectual property and copyright issues … Turnitin.com addressed the issue by agreeing to remove papers from the database if requested by the KU Writing Center, which administers the service for KU" (Maines, 2006).

Intellectual property matters aside, the discourse of combating and surveillance that commonly attend the use and promotion of plagiarism detection technology seems ill-suited in an instructional setting. Colleges and universities, after all, have the luxury of privileging learning

in their approach to problem solving. Recognizing that after-the-fact detection of plagiarism is a lost cause, faculty, educational technologists, and librarians at Colby, Bates, and Bowdoin jointly developed a plagiarism resource site that attempts to discourage student plagiarism through a program of instruction.[1] The project takes for granted that plagiarism is an inescapable condition of learning. Such a view is by no means unique: Howard (1999, p. xviii), who has published widely on the subject, likens plagiarism to imitation: that is, while trying to find their own voices as writers, inexperienced students invariably adopt and imitate the voices of others and rarely in accordance with the scholarly conventions of attribution. With this view of the problem in mind, instruction would seem to be the desirable as well as the necessary solution to plagiarism. Many educators share this view, and few have been more vocal over the years than librarians, including Burke (2004).

Plagiarism certainly has caught the attention of instructors, librarians, and administrators, but students by-and-large continue to have a vague grasp of it. As Jackson (2006) recently discusses, "there is clearly evidence to support the notion that students, in fact, do not understand plagiarism and lack the necessary skills to avoid it … Many authors agree that students lack understanding of what constitutes plagiarism, how to properly paraphrase, what needs to be cited, and how to cite sources" (p. 420). The many acts of negligence or ignorance that constitute plagiarism also vary in degrees of magnitude: failure to observe accurately the rules for citing sources, for example, is a different order of offense than the inadvertent, unattributed incorporation of another's language or ideas into a written assignment. These lapses, in turn, are potentially more easily remedied than the conscious, pre-meditated submission of another's work or ideas as one's own.

With this range of plagiaristic practices in mind, Howard (1995, pp. 799-800) has usefully identified three categories: outright cheating; non-attribution as a result of unfamiliarity with the conventions of citing sources; and "patch-writing," or stringing together someone else's language or ideas without proper attribution. The CBB plagiarism project seeks to promote instruction as the best remedy to help teachers and librarians prevent the last two categories of plagiarism, which inexperienced students are especially prone to commit. Based on responses to the project's instructional materials, these goals are being met. For example, Suffolk Community College has used the project's online tutorial in library workshops on Understanding Plagiarism and Documenting Sources. Students there have found the tutorial helpful, and "they are always particularly interested to learn about the need to cite paraphrases" (Beale 2006). In a recent survey of an online tutorial on plagiarism, *Plagiarism: The Crime of Intellectual Kidnapping,* created by San Jose State University, Jackson (2006) has produced convincing evidence that "students need more instruction and practice with proper paraphrasing" (p. 426).

To achieve its goal of providing an instructional solution to plagiarism, the project takes full advantage of the Internet and responsible cyberpractice: its developers chose an open source content management system to store, manage, and publish resources; and its resources are freely available not only to be viewed and used via the WWW, but also to be shared, adapted, and re-published under a Creative Commons copyright license.[2] The resources include a general overview of academic honesty, an introduction explaining different kinds of plagiarism, an online tutorial for testing one's understanding of the various practices that constitute plagiarism, and dynamic examples of citations and paraphrasing. The project's Web site also boasts a dedicated weblog that serves as a clearinghouse on all matters plagiaristic, including news items from around the world and notices on resources, tools, activities, and events concerning plagiarism in higher education. Taking advantage of Web syndication, the project's weblog makes its content available via RSS feeds.

As a result, anyone can import the project's news updates into individual, departmental, or institutional Web sites or weblogs by means of prepared JavaScripts.[3]

The CBB Plagiarism Project promotes the responsible use, re-use, and re-purposing of its resources so instructors and librarians can address the problem of plagiarism at the level of local institutional practices, values, and concerns. While plagiarism undoubtedly is a global problem, its solution might best be sought at the local level, where definitions, policies, and expectations vary widely. The decision to publish content by means of a weblog has in retrospect leveraged a technology that has unexpectedly provided a reflective tool and medium for engaging plagiarism. A consideration of weblog practice and use, guided by the concept of plagiarism, provides a framework for understanding the instructional value of weblogs, especially their ability to foster and promote learning communities that discourage plagiarism.

ISSUES, CONTROVERSIES, AND PROBLEMS ASSOCIATED WITH WEBLOGS

Weblogs basically aggregate meta-data: that is, they compile information about information in the form of chronological postings and do not generally publish original content per se. More often than not, weblogs refer and link to other weblogs or Web sites, and the result is a highly interconnected network of communication. The resultant mode of disseminating information has reinforced certain practices that are commonly understood as plagiaristic. Researchers at Hewlett-Packard (HP) Labs have tracked the flow of information in what they call "blogspace" and have identified how ideas, regularly unattributed, spread among blogs (Asaravala 2004). The RSS feeds, moreover, that enable blogs to publish content in various ways are often understood as contributing to plagiarism because they allow unscrupulous users to capture content (specifically textual data) and re-purpose it without attribution. Dishonest practices aside, the HP researchers assert that the dynamic flow of information in blogspace has a generative function: individual weblogs "link together" to create "a complex structure through which new ideas and discourse can flow." The HP researchers, Adar, Zhang, Adamic, and Lukose (2004), conceive of the circulation of information among blogs as ultimately creative rather than iterative and original rather than plagiaristic. This interpretation of blogs isolates tensions that have attended the reception of the World Wide Web from its earliest days. Such tensions similarly inform cultural perceptions of our students' use of the Internet. Their habitual cutting and pasting and sampling and repurposing are commonly dismissed as purposeless, narcissistic self-expression and are censoriously viewed as indicative of their disregard for intellectual and creative property rights and laws. In a recent article, Ellis (2003) productively has situated youth culture's creative as well as plagiaristic practices in contemporary contexts.

High school and college students operate with the conscious or unconscious understanding (based on a lifetime of practice) that any content available on or accessible via the Web is public property and free. By re-using and re-purposing what they find online, students not only contribute to and reproduce a sub-culture founded on pastiche, but they also develop and acquire the transferable skills that Ellis (2003) suggests will enable those interested to join "the ever-growing ranks of knowledge workers in post-industrial economies." There are drawbacks as well as benefits to what Ellis envisions as the evolving "new knowledge environment … chunks up human experience into multiple, cross-referenced nuggets dispersed in oceanic cyberspace. Stripped of our distinctively human purposes, the new knowledge environment is what George Trow famously called 'the context of no context.'"

This cutting adrift of knowledge results in its circulation without respect to historical or cultural contexts and creates a number of potential abuses and ethical problems—plagiarism among them. According to Ellis (2003), however, the "new knowledge environment" has some potential benefits that he describes in terms similar to the HP researchers' description of blogspace: "This environment favors those who can apprehend the interconnectedness of things, create bridges and connections, spark associations and create the éclat of montage. . . . Social network analysis, network topology and other new perspectives are being framed to help us understand the 'natural' dynamics of this new environment."

The dynamics of the blogosphere represent potentially exciting developments in cyber-communication, but they simultaneously revisit many of the criticisms commonly invoked to condemn the WWW. The Web is many things to many people: a commerce tool for business; a recruitment tool for new religions; a protest space for political activism; a play space for dedicated gamers; and so on. Regardless of its intended use or unintended abuse, the WWW has provided interested parties with a readily available means to publish content of all sorts, and its users have responded by taking advantage of its publishing capabilities: according to a recent Pew report, practically half (or 44 percent) of adult users of the Internet in the United States have created and published content (*Online Activities and Pursuits*, 2004). The value, usefulness, and originality of that content are an endless source of debate, and the popularity of weblogs has provided additional fodder for critics who question the informational and instructional value of the WWW.

Weblogs tend to promote a confessional mode of discourse that celebrates self-referentiality (McDonald 2004). This tendency has fueled the criticism that blogs have ushered in a new era of navel-gazing. The form and content of many personal blogs reinforce this view, but virtual personal diaries do not exhaust the uses and applications of blogs. Adar and Adamic (2005) have suggested that "beyond serving as online diaries, weblogs have evolved into a complex social structure, one which is in some ways ideal for the study of the propagation of information." Their observation posits an interrelationship of information and its circulation that previous scholars have variously noted—from McLuhan's "The Medium is the Message" to Clanchy's *From Memory to Written Record* to Brown and Daguid's "The Social Life of Documents."

In their approach to the interconnectedness of information and its circulation, Brown and Daguid (1996) have considered the ways in which "developing technologies" have historically "supported social relations in new ways." A wide range of disciplines and historical examples inform their understanding. Enlisting Anselm Strauss's notion of "'social worlds,'" Brown and Daguid (1996) describe a dynamic of group formation that can further the understanding of the culture of weblogs. Following Strauss, Brown and Daguid (1996) observe that "once formed, social worlds continually face disintegration (as dissenting members split off into 'sub-worlds')." The blogosphere seems largely populated by such sub-worlds that all too often appear to celebrate a community of one; that is, if one is viewing weblogs as repositories of content rather than as nodes within a network. The flow of information that populates many weblogs, as tracked by the HP researchers, establishes a social matrix that assumes both implicit and explicit communities. Dedicated weblog writers can be roughly divided into two main types: political bloggers and techno-bloggers. This overly simplistic distinction falls short of capturing the full range of representative blogging sub-worlds (edubloggers, for examples), but it conveniently describes two influential communities of bloggers.

Drawing on the theory of the "imagined community" proposed by political scientist Anderson (1991), Brown and Daguid (1996) further consider the ways in which "'popular' cultural items, such as journals, novels, pamphlets, lampoons, ballad sheets, and so forth" contributed to the formation of national identity in the American colonies leading up to the Revolution. Citing daily newspapers, in particular, they point out that it was their widespread circulation and not just their content that helped foster Colonial America's sense of nationhood. The similarities between newspapers and weblogs are instructive. Many observers have noted that blogs have greatly contributed to if not forever changed journalism. McDonald (2004), for example, understands blogging to be "a genuinely positive development in mass communication, and particularly in publishing and journalism." He attributes the popularity of weblogging to its adoption by "the journalistic establishment." I would attribute their popularity to their embrace by alternative journalists, especially the proliferation of "warblogging" in the aftermath of 9/11 and the subsequent events leading up to the U.S. invasion of Iraq in 2003.

Weblog pioneer and advocate Dave Winer, moreover, has speculated that newspapers will ultimately be replaced by weblogs as news sources in the not too distant future. This prediction is based in no small part on the publishing ability of weblogs, which has greatly extended the publishing capacity of the WWW. According to Winer, "In a Google search of five keywords or phrases representing the top five news stories of 2007, weblogs will rank higher than *The New York Times'* Web site" (*Long Bet*).

SOLUTIONS AND RECOMMENDATIONS: BUILDING LEARNING COMMUNITIES VIA WEBLOGS

Blogs are powerful and flexible publishing tools: they publish content rapidly and easily; they provide an archive for content that is readily searchable by date, subject, or keyword; and they can also publish their content in a number of ways, including dedicated Web sites as well as RSS feeds that can populate other Web sites, weblogs, aggregators, e-mail clients, and Web browsers. That which has secured their popularity and wide reception (the rapid creation, publication, and circulation of information) also represents their greatest potential for instruction. Librarians, technologists, and instructors can capitalize on blogs for making available a range of resources and information to targeted users—students, staff, faculty, and colleagues—both on their own as well as on other campuses. They can do so, moreover, with their own content or with content developed entirely by other institutions. This latter ability, importing content from elsewhere, demonstrates how blogs can reinforce the responsible and productive use and circulation of information.

The hallmark features of weblogs (the rapid creation and dissemination of content) are extremely useful for fostering learning communities whose members resort to various methods and media for instruction and information. Certain integral aspects of weblogs further promote their instructional potential. Weblogs have not only made publishing content easier but more social—they open content development up to a group by means of their ability to allow various levels of access to different groups of users; and they invite dialogue between creators and readers of content by permitting the exchange of comments within the blog as well as between blogs. Weblogs are dynamic in a couple of ways: the content posted on them changes as information is added and they allow users to interact by carrying on a dialogue. This dialogic aspect of blogs enables content developers to work towards breaking down the distinction between the creator and the user of content. This feature of blogs participates in the trend already discerned by Pew: that the consumers of Web content are also largely the producers of it.

FUTURE TRENDS: ENGAGING PLAGIARISM VIA MULTIMEDIA

The controlled dissolution of boundaries between producers and users of content (or between instructors and students, for that matter) has emerged as a valuable lesson of the CBB project's use of a weblog. Successful instruction in plagiarism must strive to increase the awareness of the difference between the creation of new and the appropriate use of existing content. The project has sought to promote this awareness in practice by example and in theory by instruction. The content is freely available to be used and re-purposed according to an "Attribution-Non-Commercial-ShareAlike" Creative Commons Deed. The project developers have also sought to create learning objects that help socialize students into the culture of academics, which is founded on what Green (2002, p. 171) has described as the "norm of attribution." Most teachers take for granted the scholarly conventions used to avoid plagiarism. Recognizing the profound difference that exists between the initiated and the uninitiated, the CBB Plagiarism Project has set out to provide students with guidance and instruction in the standards of academic integrity. In doing so, it strives to facilitate our students' initiation into the norms and practices of the academic community.

Looking ahead to further development, the project's next phase will involve creating a more adaptive learning environment for engaging plagiarism. While the weblog provides a valuable means to deliver, create, and respond to content, the text-based nature of that content may reinforce some of the limitations of online tutorials as instructional resources. Jackson (2006, pp. 423-26) has recently considered the effectiveness of plagiarism instruction online. By developing media-rich content about the subject (including audio, video, and animation), the project would create a range of resources that better suit diverse learning styles. In doing so, the project would be more responsive to the needs of its users and would further realize its goal of helping to integrate students into academic cultural practice.

CONCLUSION

An increased use and understanding of media in the curriculum, moreover, may very well allow faculty to harness the creative energies of students in a way that deals with plagiarism in both practical and theoretical terms readily understood by students. Current wisdom on how to avoid plagiarism has emphasized the need to rethink written assignments—for example, essays should be conceived of as ongoing processes consisting of specific, discrete stages or components, all of which are submitted for review, evaluation, and assessment, rather than a single finished product submitted in its entirety only once. In rethinking assignments, instructors may also want to begin to rethink what writing is and to encourage non-traditional forms of writing. I have in mind here the creation of fictional and non-fictional narratives, reports or accounts by means of multimedia—digital video and audio or computer animation and graphics or any combination of these and other media. Just as the weblog has emerged as a reflective tool for considering plagiarism, a media-rich learning environment would allow students to begin to understand plagiarism in new and perhaps more compelling ways. In a recent essay on plagiarism, the novelist Jonathan Lethem (2007) describes what it is like to be cut adrift in our contemporary media environment:

The world is a home littered with pop-culture products and their emblems. I also came of age swamped by parodies that stood for originals yet mysterious to me … I'm not alone in having been born backward into an incoherent realm of texts, products, and images, the commercial and cultural environment with which we've both supplemented and blotted out our natural world. I can no more claim it as "mine" than the sidewalks and forests of the world, yet I do dwell in it, and for me to stand a chance as either artist or citizen, I'd probably better be permitted to name it.

In the academy, students are encouraged to name and when appropriate cite their sources, influences, and inspirations. However, finding themselves, like Lethem, in a world already created and populated with signs, they need to learn how to negotiate the conventions and practices of that world and to decode its constituent signs. Educators should begin to make use of the multitude of media that figures our manifold experiences of the world. The energy and creativity generated by such a diversely constituted learning environment would permit powerful models for rethinking our engagement of plagiarism.

REFERENCES

Adar, E. & Adamic, L. A. (2004). Tracking information epidemics in blogspace. Retrieved October 5, 2006 from http://www.hpl.hp.com/research/idl/papers/blogs2/index.html

Adar, E., Zhang, L., Adamic, L. A., & Lukose, R. M. (2004). Implicit structure and the dynamics of blogspace. Retrieved October 2, 2006 from http://www.hpl.hp.com/research/idl/papers/blogs/index.html

Anderson, B. (1991). *Imagined communities: Reflections on the origin and spread of nationalism.* London: Verso.

Asaravala, A. (2004). Warnings: Blogs can be infectious. *Wired News.* Retrieved October 2, 2006 from http://www.wired.com/news/culture/0,1284,62537,00.html

Beale, P. (2006). E-mail, October 6.

Blog Epidemic Analyzer. Retrieved October 5, 2006 from http://www.hpl.hp.com/research/idl/projects/blogs/index.html

Brown, J. S. & Daguid, P. (1996). The social life of documents. *First Monday, 1*(1). Retrieved October 2, 2006 from http://www.firstmonday.dk/issues/issue1/documents/index.html

Burke, M. (2004). Deterring plagiarism: A new role for librarians. *Library Philosophy and Practice, 6*(2), 1-9.

Center for Academic Integrity. Retrieved October 2, 2006 from   http://www.academicintegrity.org/cai_research.asp

Clanchy, M. T. (1979). *From memory to written record, England, 1066-1307.*   Cambridge: Harvard University Press.

Cooper, L. (2007). Cheating a big problem. *At Guelph.* Retrieved February 22, 2007, from http://www.uoguelph.ca/atguelph/06-10-25/featurescheating.shtml

Ellis, L. (2003). MP3s, Plagiarism, and the Future of Knowledge. *The ClickZ Network.* Retrieved October 2, 2006, from http://www.clickz.com/showPage.html?page=3080961

Freshminds.co.uk. Retrieved October 2, 2006, from http://www.freshminds.co.uk/FreshMinds_plagiarism_survey.pdf

Glod, M. (2006). Students rebel against database designed to thwart plagiarists (p. A01). *Washington Post.* Retrieved October 2, 2006 from http://www.washingtonpost.com/wp-dyn/content/article/2006/09/21/AR2006092101800.html

Green, S. (2002). Plagiarism, norms, and the limits of theft law: Some observations on the use of criminal sanctions in enforcing intellectual property rights. *Hastings Law Journal. 54*(1), 167-242

Gulli, C., Kohler, N., & Patriquin, M. (2007). The great university cheating scandal. *MacLeans.* Retrieved February 22, 2007 from http://www.macleans.ca/homepage/magazine/article.jsp?content=20070209_174847_6984

Hansen, B. (2003). Combating plagiarism: Is the Internet causing more students to copy? *The CQ Researcher, 13*(32), 773-796.

Howard, R. M. (1995). Plagiarisms, authorships, and the academic death penalty. *College English, 57*(7), 788-806.

Howard, R. M. (1999). *Standing in the shadows of giants.* Stanford, CT: Ablex.

Howard, R. M. (2001). Point of view: Forget about policing plagiarism. Just teach. *The Chronicle Review.* Retrieved October 2, 2006 from http://chronicle.com/prm/weekly/v48/i12/12b02401.htm

Jackson, P. A. (2006). Plagiarism instruction online: Assessing undergraduate students' ability to avoid plagiarism. *College and Research Libraries, 67*(2), 418-427.

Jones, S. (2002). *The Internet goes to college: How students are living in the future with today's technology.* Washington, DC: Pew Internet and American Life Project.

Lethem, J. (2007). Ecstasy of influence: A plagiarism. *Harper's Magazine.* Retrieved February 22, 2007 from http://www.harpers.org/TheEcstasyOfInfluence.html

Maines, S. (2006). KU renews anti-plagiarism software subscription. *LJWorld.com.* Retrieved October 7, 2006 from http://www2.ljworld.com/news/2006/oct/04/ku_renews_antiplagiarism_software_subscription/?ku_news

McCabe, D. L. (2000). *New research on academic integrity: The success of "Modified" honor codes.* College Administration Publications. Asheville, NC. Retrieved October 2, 2006 from http://www.collegepubs.com/ref/SFX000515.shtml

McCabe, D. L. (2004). E-mail August 4, 2004.

McCabe, D. L., Butterfield, K. D. & Treviño, L. K. (2004). Academic integrity: How widespread is cheating and plagiarism? In D. R. Karp & T. Allena (Eds.), *Restorative justice on the college campus: Promoting student growth and responsibility, and reawakening the spirit of campus community* (pp. 124-35). Springfield, IL: Charles C. Thomas.

McCabe, D. L., Butterfield, K. D. & Treviño, L. K. (2006). Academic dishonesty in graduate business programs: Prevalence, causes, and proposed action. *Academy of Management Learning & Education, 5*(3), 294-305.

McCabe, D. L. & Christensen Hughes, J. (2006). Understanding academic misconduct. *The Canadian Journal of Higher Education, 36*(1), 49-63.

McCabe, D. L. & Treviño, L. K. (1996). What we know about cheating in college. *Change, 28*(1). Academic Search Premier.

McDonald, N. (2004). The future of weblogging. *The Register.* Retrieved October 2, 2006, from http://www.theregister.co.uk/2004/04/18/blogging_future

McGill student continues fight against anti-plagiarism Web site. (2003). *CBC.com.* Retrieved October 6, 2003 from http://www.cbc.ca/news/story/2003/12/27/plagiarism031227.html

McLuhan, M. (1964). The medium is the message. *Understanding Media: The Extensions of Man.* New York: McGraw Hill.

MSVU bans anti-plagiarism software. (2006). *CBC.com.* Retrieved October 2, 2006, from http://www.cbc.ca/canada/nova-scotia/story/2006/03/08/ns-msvu-plagiarism20060308.html

Online Activities and Pursuits. (2004). Retrieved October 2, 2006, from http://www.pewinternet.org/report_display.asp?r=113

Plagiarism.Org. Retrieved October 2, 2006, from http://www.plagiarism.org/plagiarism_stats.html

A Quarter of Students Cheating. (2004). *BBCNews.* Retrieved February 16, 2007 from http://news.bbc.co.uk/2/hi/uk_news/education/3852869.stm

Ray, D. (2001). Web site may catch, deter plagiarized work. *Daily Nexus Online: UC Santa Barbara's Student Newspaper.* Retrieved October 3, 2006 from http://www.ucsbdailynexus.com/news/2001/1252.html

Winer, D. *Long Bet.* Retrieved October 2, 2006 from http://www.longbets.org/

ENDNOTES

[1] Original project members included Judy Montgomery and Sue O'Dell, Bowdoin College; Zach Chandler and Marilyn Pukkila, Colby College; and Thomas Hayward, Bates College. Jim Hart at Bates College served as a technical consultant from the project's inception and generously provided extensive support by administering the Linux server that hosted the project's weblog and resources.

[2] The site is driven by Drupal, a PHP-MySQL-based open-source content management system, which is freely available to download at http://www.drupal.org. For further details on Creative Commons, see http://creative-commons.org.

[3] See http://leeds.bates.edu/cbb/rss/rss.html for instructions and guidelines. For an example of the feed in action, see the Missouri State University Libraries, http://library.missouristate.edu/resources/cheating.shtml.

Chapter XIII
Minimizing Plagiarism by Redesigning the Learning Environment and Assessment

Madhumita Bhattacharya
Athabasca University, Canada and Massey University, New Zealand

Lone Jorgensen
Massey University, New Zealand

ABSTRACT

In this chapter we have raised a number of questions and made attempts to respond. These questions are: Can plagiarism be stopped? Should we stop students from using the information available on the Internet? Is it enough if the students just acknowledge the sources in their work? What action is required to minimize the harmful, and maximize the useful, aspects of Internet use in the educational setting? We want our students to learn and demonstrate their learning with honesty and integrity. In the institutions of higher education, student learning is judged through assessment tasks in the form of assignments, tests, and examinations. We have to ensure that high stakes assessments do not act as an inspiration to cheating in the form of plagiarism. We have provided arguments in support of the integration of process approach with deliverables at the end of the course for assessment of students learning.

INTRODUCTION

In the 21st century, it is difficult to think about life without the Internet. In the past there has never been such free and easy access to information. This may be considered both a blessing and a curse. On one hand, information and communication technologies have provided us with the advantages associated with this open information market. On the other hand, it has raised issues and concerns about the usage of materials gained from this source (Sterngold, 2004, as quoted in Warn, 2006). Not least of these is plagiarism. Although plagiarism is not a new phenomenon, it has become a much more discussed and seemingly problematic issue based on the accessibility of information and the ease with which it can be "lifted" from Internet sources (Baggaley & Spencer, 2005). In addition to the potential for copying material from unacknowledged sources, students often do not distinguish between academic and non-academic sites and seem to have become uncritical consumers of all knowledge. While such naïve use is of concern for all educators, the issue of plagiarism has become the most worrying aspect of academic student outputs to teachers and educators all over the world. This concern is reflected in the thousands of sites on the Internet on this issue and availability of a number of electronic tools for detection of plagiarism. In this chapter, the authors discuss various possible reasons for plagiarism and try to identify the underpinning causes which foster this. The ethical and moral issues associated with plagiarism and its detection are also discussed briefly. The authors argue that teachers will need to change their approach to assessment in view of the ever changing challenges of the Internet/information age. We will have to assess both process and the product in order to ensure the authenticity of students work. The authors propose a model for design and development of assessment tasks and learning environment for prevention of plagiarism.

BACKGROUND AND ASSOCIATED ISSUES

To plagiarise is to use the writings or ideas of another in an unacknowledged way (Schwarz, 1992). This is a difficult term to "pin down" in terms of teaching and assessed outputs and often confuses rather than enlightens as to just what it

is, its causes, and how to alleviate it (Chandrasoma, Thompson & Pennycook, 2004). The art of teaching and learning is rooted in the principle of mimicry, or mimesis (imitation or representation in art, the rhetorical use of a person's supposed or imaginable words [Schwarz, 1992]). The level of cognitive development of the learner and/or the type of subject being studied determines the level of mimicry required and tolerated. Where the student is at the first three stages of Bloom's Taxonomy of cognitive development (Knowledge, Comprehension and Application), "memory" or "recall" will constitute the majority of assessed output. Thus, teachers using "role play" utilize this mimicking to enable the student to scaffold and practise the concept taught. Cognitive apprenticeships and mastery learning are traditionally used by the "Masters" in traditional apprenticeship relationships, to encourage the students to emulate "good practice" before becoming Masters themselves. In these cases, mimicking is encouraged to enable the student to "practise" the skills desired. The term "plagiarism" would be unsuitable to cover the outputs at this level as "recall" constitutes a plagiarizing of others' work. For example: a request to recite the poem by Wordsworth "I wandered lonely as a cloud/ that floats on o'er Vales and Hills" (Wordsworth, 1807), will usually not be considered a plagiarism, especially when the poet's name is referenced. If the task, however, is to show understanding of the sentiment and the technique used in the poem, by writing a poem to show this, the student will copy the verse rhythm, the syntax and the vocabulary to emulate the writer's style as closely as possible. A teacher of students at this level will accept this and no accusations of plagiarizing will arise. Once a student reaches tertiary level, however, such tolerance is no longer to be expected. Even paraphrasing will be considered a form of plagiarism if executed without appropriate citations. Teachers concerned with the scholarship of their students initially may allow heavy reliance on such tactics in the unsophisticated students but will discourage excessive paraphrasing as they develop (Orlans, 1999).

As the seedling in the forest grows straight and tall amongst other trees to get to the sunlight, so our students may use the teachers' and other students' knowledge for support and protection when young and vulnerable, but they must learn to operate individually and with intellectual originality as they grow scholastically. In an electronic culture of "remixing" of music for new effects and the use of artistic imagery to inspire new pieces of work, it may be very difficult for students to understand the concept of "plagiarism" of the written word (MacDonell, 2005) and "borrow" more than they acknowledge. The concept of "common vs. plagiarized knowledge" is an issue that needs teasing out as to clarify the debate around plagiarism. The statement, traditionally attributed to Isaac Newton, that: "if I have seen further than other men, it is because I have stood on the shoulders of giants" (Horn, 1998), is relevant in trying to define which knowledge is "common knowledge," and which is "plagiarized knowledge." Common knowledge is that set of shared ideas and background knowledge that defines a demographic group. Plagiarized knowledge is knowledge defined as belonging to another person and used without that person's permission and without acknowledging that person. Within a student setting, however, what constitutes common knowledge to one student may not be so to another (Chandrasoma et al., 2004). The complexity of this issue increases when students come from many different cultures, and with languages other than English. Where texts are constructed from commonly shared knowledge, students may fail to recognize that they are practising plagiarism. Such "popular plagiarism" is unconscious and non-malicious (ibid). Students can be excused for being further confused as it seems "old ideas" are acceptable to use when they have entered our common language usage. For example, if a student is on a "slippery slope," is he/she required to

reference this term or is it all right to just use it? If the student describes a "eureka moment," will this have to be referenced to its Greek author? If a student discusses health and disease in a general setting, does the student have to reference this discussion on par with a discussion quoting particular research papers? What about common issues discussed in the media, such as global warming or ozone depletion? All these ideas are based on initial scientific publications, but have since entered the realms of "shared knowledge." As lecturers we also emphasise collaborative knowledge construction, distributed cognition and social constructivism in our teachings. This further complicates the definition of what are acceptable outputs from our students.

The commodification of knowledge and the idea that knowledge belongs to individuals and can be "ring-fenced" and sold, was a 20th century phenomenon (John Codd—personal comment, 2006). This means that knowledge takes on an economic importance and becomes a commodity in its own right. Copyrights protect such knowledge, but also restrict access to it. The open publication of knowledge on the Internet counters this (e.g., the human genome) but introduces other skills required by the students. For example, to be able to tell copyrighted from copyright-free material, to distinguish high quality information from low quality, and to understand something about the lifespan of copyrights, requires knowledge many, or perhaps most, students cannot reasonably be expected to have, especially where the student comes to the tertiary institution from another culture.

The distinction of "ownership" in the setting of studies and student outputs, should be a clear and defined concept, delimited by the students' level, language background, and subject. Many students do not fully understand the limits of plagiarisation versus mimesis. The guidelines set out in study guides and on institutional Web sites appear to presume that the students in general have this knowledge (Massey University, 2006).

Such presumptions are flawed and raise ethical, as well as educational issues the tertiary educators need to address. The limits need to be discussed at each paper/course level, and the students need to be encouraged to examine what constitutes valid use of knowledge versus "plagiarism."

Educators encouraging international students to participate in the tertiary sector of their nation need to have a clear understanding that students from different cultures, rooted in different educational principles (Wu & Singh, 2002) and with high personal investments in the qualification sought, may find the concept of plagiary as cheating difficult on so many levels: One of these is the style of learning within a student's own culture which values recitation and copying of the tutor's style and knowledge. Pecorari (2001 quoted in Sowden, C., 2005) reports a conversation with a group of Japanese students in which a tutor questions their failure to cite an author whose arguments they had used in their assignments. They replied that since what the author said was obviously true, his name did not need to be mentioned. In other words, the author's insights, having achieved the status of common sense, had thereby entered the field of common knowledge and no longer belonged to him exclusively. A second level is the language available to the student. He/she may be unable to express the knowledge in language other than that given in papers/texts they have read. The student may not consciously be plagiarizing the information, but the use of the language. A third level may be that the "Notion of Success" may drive the student's choices (Wu & Singh, 2002). This means that failure in a paper/course is not an option because of cultural/family expectations, and the student will "cheat" to get the grades required for a pass. This is an ethical issue which involves a personal choice to do "the wrong thing," and is at the extreme of the levels discussed above. The conditions that lead students to choose to plagiarize might be located in a broad cultural climate that privileges an unhealthy competitiveness and the results that it garners as the means to the limited opportunities and material wealth by which success is measured (Willen, 2004). A fourth level influencing plagiarism may be the time pressures arising from assessment requirements, the knowledge and information explosion making it necessary to sift through much more material and financial pressures requiring students to work to support their tertiary studies.

As tertiary education in English-speaking countries is becoming more and more commodified, with students being charged for attendance and funding to the institutions becoming dependent on proven research outputs, there is a greater risk that plagiarizing "pays off" if it remains undetected (Saltmarsh, 2004). Since the mid 1980s universities became required to find funds from student fees. Competition in the market for international students is a result of this commercialisation of tertiary education as institutions look overseas for a source of such funds. This has moved the tertiary sector from a "teaching and learning" place to an economic market, with students designated as "consumers" rather than learners (ibid). Plagiarism, seen in this light becomes a "consumptive practice" driven by a desire for "success" at the lowest price, rather than learning for its own sake (ibid). We have to ensure that high stakes assessments do not act as an inspiration to cheating in the form of plagiarism.

PLAGIARISM DETECTION: IS THAT THE END?

There are a number of electronic tools around for detection of plagiarism namely, Turnitin (can be integrated with WebCT, Blackboard, Moodle, Angel learning, etc.). Moss (an automatic system for determining the similarity of C, C++, Java, Pascal, Ada, ML, Lisp, or Scheme programs), WCopyfind (examines a collection of document files), Scriptum (content of students work is compared with material on the Internet), EVE 2, My DropBox,

JPlag, and so on (Academic Computing Center (AAC), 2007). Although the routine checking of all assignments appears to signal an institutional distrust, this strategy is unsustainable on a large scale. Checking every report for originality has the same effect as checking every coin or cheque for authenticity—the system simply grinds to a halt (Evans, 2006).

Recent evidence of an emerging backlash against plagiarism detection (Levin, 2003) demonstrated that the introduction of online detection needs to be sensitively handled to avoid building up a culture of resentment among students. Plagiarism detection software also can have a negative effect on learning. If used on a blanket basis, the presumption is that every student is a potential cheat. This can discourage an openness to learning and instead foster an attitude that whatever gets through the system, such as plagiarism of ideas, is okay (Martin, 2004).

Ethical, moral, and legal issues arising from the issue of plagiarism are too many and far reaching which are difficult to identify, categorize, or classify. According to L. Rooker, director of the U.S. Department of Education's Family Policy Compliance Office, "You can hire a vendor to check for plagiarism," he says. "But once they do that, they can't then keep that personally identifiable document and use it for any other purpose" (in Foster, 2002). The over arching dilemma is, should we forget about the problem of plagiarism (we could if we think that detection tools are getting better every day and using these tools will allow us to detect students' cheating) or should we see the problem in the new light. It has been pointed out that plagiarism is more often a factor of misunderstanding rather than misconduct (Emerson, Rees, & Mackey, 2005). The discussion of plagiarism impacts students from diverse cultures in different ways. Students that have traditionally learnt by rote and imitation, and never been taught critical thinking and analysis skills, are likely to plagiarise unintentionally (Leask, 2006).

THE DEFINITION OF KNOWLEDGE IN THE STUDENT ENVIRONMENT

As mentioned earlier any group of students in the tertiary sector can be thought of as being embedded in the "presumed knowledge" within the community hosting the tertiary institution. While this knowledge is specific to the host community and very pervasive it is indefinable and amorphous and can be referred to as "the Soup of Knowledge" (Figure 1) Within this soup/environment a paper/course will prescribe the new/academic knowledge required for the student output, referred to as Institutional Knowledge in Figure 1. This knowledge is determined by the academic staff. Each student arrives at the academic institution with his/her own knowledge set. Within a group of students from the same cultural background this individual knowledge set will overlap to a large extent. Students from different cultural groups will have quite divergent sets. Thus, a student group fits into the various subsets of knowledge in such a way that some students have shared knowledge, some share the knowledge of the community group and some the knowledge of the academic group. This is illustrated by the use of arrows in Fig.1. The shared knowledge of the academic/institutional knowledge has always been considered to give students an advantage and is referred to as "cultural capital" of those students (Brown, 1995). The heterogeneous background of the student body renders the validity of the tasks for assessing the academic knowledge suspect, unless the lecturer incorporates the potential for "short-cuts" in the assessment task and provide tasks rich in process and not in recall (Fig. 2 & 3). The use of exemplars to encourage high academic standards and excellence should be expanded to also illustrate what constitutes plagiarism and what does not.

Students immersed in the electronic world of computers and the Internet traverse knowledge in a much more open fashion than in the past,

Figure 1. The definition of knowledge in the student environment

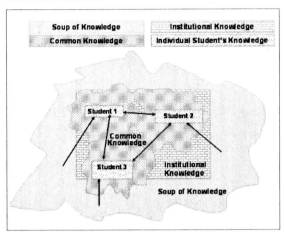

Figure 2. Attributes of meaningful learning

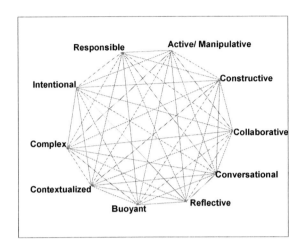

and lecturers of such students need to teach their students about plagiarism by providing them with examples of plagiarism and how to avoid it when paraphrasing (Landau, Druen, & Arcuri, 2002). Further confusion can be introduced when using exemplars for excellence. These frequently are used by teachers to introduce students to the idea of what constitutes levels of achievement. The overall results are often an improvement in performance, but how far does "inspiration" stretch from "plagiarism" when students use exemplars to do this?

Learning Environment and Assessment Design

In the institutions of higher education, students' learning is judged through assessment tasks in the form of assignments, tests, and examinations. In a climate of internal assessment tasks and a move away from external examinations, the risk of plagiarism may increase. In formal tests and examinations, plagiary should be minimized as they are conducted under conditions where there is no access to outside material and

questions cannot, in theory, be prepared for. In reality, this too depends on the teacher's ability to create new questions from year to year, and it is a naïve student who does not understand the advantage of access to old test and exams papers for practice. In tertiary institutions assessment is not only about what a student can/cannot *do*; it is also about what it *means* he or she can/cannot do (adopted from Ramsden, 1992, p.182). Educators in the tertiary sector tend to measure "assessment of learning" (summative) and do not use "assessment for learning" (formative) to any great extent. In the majority of the cases, tertiary students are not made aware of the learning objectives and expected learning outcomes of their course. In the tertiary sector, summative assessments tends to be normative which serves the function of ranking students rather than teaching them. This increases the stakes of the assessment as it determines the individual's position in the system and may restrict his/her access to funding or to courses. If the assessment is designed to help students to learn through diagnosing their errors and misconceptions and reinforcing their correct understanding, then assessment becomes a tool for learning and progression. When students are given more au-

Box 1. Assessment Task A

Discuss ONE of the following statements. Your discussion should show familiarity with research related to your chosen statement and the implications this has for teaching "early number." It is expected that you will include references to at least six articles.

    1.   Children need to understand place value if they are to use the number system accurately and efficiently.

    2.   Number sense in young children should be seen as more than the ability to count. Discuss.

    3.   How can the teachers support and build on children's intuitive, verbal based strategies as a basis to encourage them to develop as competent mathematicians?

Box 2. Assessment Task B

Learning Outcome: Demonstrate knowledge about and appraise critically teaching methods and learning activities used in the teaching of Biology in years 11, 12, and 13.

Task: Plan three of the lessons out in full. One MUST be the introductory lesson. One clearly must reflect planning for students with special needs. One must plan around untilising cooperative group activities. You must annotate your plans to indicate points of transition. Each plan must have the length of the period indicated and the length of each episode within the lesson.

Critically appraise and reflect on the choice of teaching methods and learning activities you have planned for in your lesson. Comment on whether this could be taught using other methods. Justify your choice of methods for this plan.

---

tonomy in the choice regarding the methods of assessment, then assessment encourages greater responsibility for self-directed learning. This, in turn, minimizes cheating, including plagiarism, copying, and collusion, even in assessments based on work done in the student's own time. In the remainder of this section the authors will discuss and critically evaluate different types of assessment tasks, and show how the degree and chances of plagiarism reduce as the assessment tasks correspond more with the attributes of meaningful learning (Bhattacharya, 2004 adapted from Jonassen, 2001). Ensuring that these are present in course design and development, the principles of online development should ensure maximum value for the learner.

Assessment tasks that are open-ended and use ambiguous language are vulnerable to plagiarism. Ill-defined assignments that are descriptive rather than analytical in nature afford greater chances for cheating than very specific, thought-provoking assignments (Davis, 1994). This is particularly important in summative, norm-referenced assessment tasks where students are ranked against each other. Positions in schools and scholarships can hinge on this ranking. Thus students have a vested interest in scoring as highly as they can in this ranking system. Teachers have a strong responsibility to minimize the effect of this. The structure of the assessment task and the language used will have a large influence on how effective this will be. For example in the essay question in Box 1, the term "discuss" leaves the naïve student with the impression that all the referencing that needs to be done is to the six articles. If other material is paraphrased or borrowed that may be OK.

Assessment task A could easily be changed to minimize plagiarism by introducing a sentence or two, for example, critically review and reflect on your personal experience. If the task is changed to a standards-based assessment where students are required to demonstrate mastery, the task will be spelt out more narrowly and better defined, associated with expected learning outcomes defining the limits of the mastery required.

In Assessment Task B, the students are presented with a clear learning outcome and clear tasks required to reach that learning outcome. The verbs: critically appraise, reflect, justify, aim at

Box 3. Assessment Task C

ASSESSMENT ONE	**(20 marks)**
ESSAY	

Focus statement:

The "focus statement" will be given to you at the end of the first week.

In writing your essay, you will be required to use references from the readings provided and other sources if appropriate. Do ensure that the references are in the appropriate format. The maximum word limit is around 1500 words. Quality, not quantity, is the key to success.

Date Due: **End of Week 4 in the course.**

The assessment of your essay will use the following assessment criteria indicators:

• Ability to answer the *focus statement*
  (8 marks)
  - with a focus on curriculum integration and
  - a focus on technology investigations and
  - a focus on science investigations

• Application of the readings and other sources   (4 marks)
  - which is (are) appropriate for the context(s)
  - which provide support for the statements written
  - which demonstrates a willingness to read beyond the set readings

• Inclusion of an evaluation/reflection   (4 marks)
  - which demonstrates higher order thinking
  - which demonstrates metacognition
  - that considers the value of the set readings which support this essay

• Inclusion of a concluding paragraph   (4 marks)
  - which demonstrates what you have learnt

the higher cognitive skills and reduces the options for plagiarizing. In Assessment Task A, only the verb "discuss'" is used. Discussion can occur at many levels and students may present a variety of interpretations of this term.

Another example using essay on curriculum integration provided students with a short description of the assessment task and the marking criteria in the course material. In this example, the task is broken down into required steps with clear mark allocation to each task. It is noticeable that the tasks most vulnerable to plagiarism also are the tasks allocated the lowest marks. Students are also provided with a set of readings where each reading has a set of questions to be discussed in

the class/online forum within a group following a reading schedule.

On the first day of the course, students offer individual responses to the following two questions. These are written down and submitted to the teacher.

1. You have studied Science Curriculum I and Technology Curriculum I in previous years. We would like you to share your understanding about Science and Technology. Particularly, we would be interested to know what do you think are the similarities and differences between these two subject areas/disciplines (Science and Technology).

Box 4. Example of focus statement

Focus statement:

Use your current understanding of curriculum integration and its relationship to *science and technology* to (a) **critique your original understanding** provided on the first day of class and (b) **construct** a robust *"personal subject construct."* You might want to use your previous teaching experiences when developing your essay.

Please support your essay with references from the readings provided and/or other sources. Ensure that the references are in the appropriate format. The maximum word limit is **around** 1500 words.

---

2. Provide your views on "Curriculum Integration." Write about your understanding of "Curriculum Integration." Acknowledge if you have done the readings for 210.210. Mention how these readings have influenced you thoughts on "Curriculum Integration."

At the end of first week in the course, students are given back their responses to the questions mentioned above. A copy of the students responses are kept by the lecturer for cross referencing. At the same time students are provided with the focus statement for the assignment in Assessment Task 3.

From the example in Box 4, it is clear that it is not only the design of the assessment but also the design of the learning environment and the scheduling of the activities, facilitating learning, and providing feedback to the students that contribute to learning for understanding. Personalisation of the assessment tasks reduces stress, provides ownership of learning, and encourages an authentic and honest response and provides almost no opportunity for plagiarism. Instead of calling for discussion of an extant, outside body of knowledge, essays need to promote the active involvement of students by having them solve problems, analyse issues, and/or make decisions (McKenzie, 1998). Marsh, Landau, and Hicks, 1997 (in Landau et al., 2002) reported some preliminary evidence from work done by instructional groups of undergraduates who were asked to brainstorm to produce solutions to everyday problems. Participants returned one week later

and generated new solutions under the admonition that the ideas not come from the first session. Approximately 20 percent of these "new" solutions were from the first week. However, instructions to carefully review the solutions from week one drastically reduced the level of plagiarism. This finding indicates that people can; in fact, avoid plagiarism if they are cautious and conscious. In the following three figures we will elaborate on assessment design to minimize plagiarism.

Figure 3 demonstrate the relationship between the levels in cognitive domain of learning, the levels in affective domain of learning and the complexity of assessment tasks as three axes. It is clearly visible in Figure 3 that assignment tasks set for higher levels of learning become more complex and challenging.

In Figure 4, P_1, P_2 and P_3 represent particular points in the three dimensional space of all the three axes. The dotted lines represent the co-ordinates of the point. By joining these points we can visualize the process of learning and increasing levels of learning as we move from one point to another. It is apparent that students can go from either P_1 to P_3 or via P_2. Students' progress depends on his/her own knowledge and ability. Teachers can support students to progress through by designing appropriate assessment tasks.

Figure 5 describes how the increase in the complexity of the assessment task and aiming at higher levels of learning can contribute to a decrease in plagiarism and enhance the quality of learning outcomes. Where the three axes of the cognitive, affective, and assessment domains

Figure 3. Levels of cognitive and affective domains of learning and complexity of assessment task

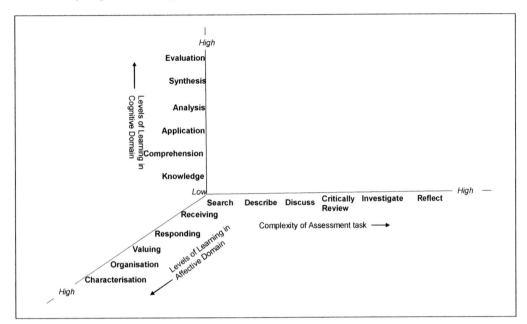

Figure 4. Levels of learning represented in a three dimensional space

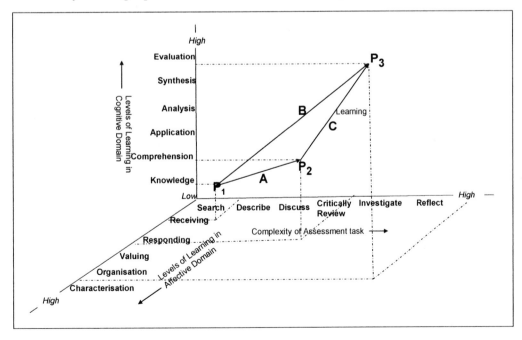

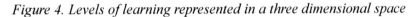

Figure 5. Graphical representation of orientation of assessment task vs degree of plagiarism

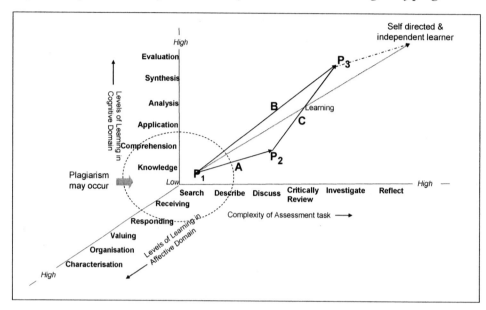

intercept, the skills required of the students are low and the learning dependent on mimesis. Plagiary may be tolerated close to this source. The degree of tolerance of plagiarism diminishes as we move away from the origin, that is, we have a greater risks of plagiarism if our assessment tasks are not complex and challenging enough and are oriented towards the lower levels of cognitive and affective domains of learning. This graph shows that the awareness about moral and ethical values, and judging and decision making abilities can minimize the degree of plagiarism. The region under the curved dotted line indicates that plagiarism of some sort could be acceptable at the lower levels of learning.

Process approaches to teaching, learning, and assessment and formulating objectives and designing activities oriented to development of specific skills can reduce plagiarism. For example, in Figure 4, Line A represents a learning task where students have started at point P_1 but then engaging through various activities students' progressively move towards point P_2. In the

same paper/course, one could give another set of activities for the students to accomplish which can be represented by Line B (from P_1 to P_2) or Line C (from P_2 to P_3) depending on the learning objectives, students' abilities, and allocated time for course completion. The assessment tasks and activities are designed in way that leads students to become self directed and independent learners. It is possible for a student to start at P_1 and progress through a different path and became a self directed independent leaner where the dotted line represents the journey in the process of learning.

CONCLUSION

It is obvious that we cannot and should not stop students from using the information available on the Internet, but we do have control over how students could use the information for meaningful learning. Although students rightly are encouraged to take advantage of the Internet as a source of information, academics must ensure, through their own actions, that students realize that "learning requires more than high-speed connections and a good search engine" (Carnie 2001, quoted in Park, 2003, p. 481).

If assessment is done in a formative way with specific milestones at different stages of students progression, then we could do justice to the proposition of Ramsden (1997, p. 186): assessment of students is above all about *understanding the processes and outcomes of student learning, and understanding the students who have done the learning.* Establishing a relationship of trust, giving emotional support, and knowing the student beyond an ID number will definitely ease our stress about students' plagiarism. Approaches such as problem-based learning (Bhattacharya, 2004), project-based learning, inquiry-based learning, and development of integrated electronic portfolios (Bhattacharya, 2006) provides the opportunities for accomplishing higher order learning and development of interpersonal, self organization, problem solving, and other life long learning skills, thereby reducing plagiarism. Working in collaboration with colleagues, designing and developing courses together, team teaching approaches, and carefully prepared assessment tasks can minimize cheating (copying, collusion, plagiarism, etc.). It is clearly the concern of many tertiary educators to "stamp out" plagiarism, but the authors of this chapter maintain that prevention is far better than a cure. The real culprits should, of course, be detected and stopped, but let us not make criminals out of the naïve and/or the culturally diverse students.

ACKNOWLEDGEMENT

Authors would like to thank their colleagues, Mr. Bill Macintyre & Ms. Ngaire Davies (School of Curriculum and Pedagogy, College of Education, Massey University) for their cooperation.

REFERENCES

Academic Computing Center (AAC). (2007). Electronic Plagarism: Anti-Plagarism Tools. *American University of Beruit.* Retrieved October 15, 2006, from http://wwwlb.aub.edu.lb/~eplagio/Anti_plag.htm

Baggaley, J., & Spencer, B. (2005). The mind of a plagiarist. *Learning, Media and Technology, 30*(1), 55-62.

Bhattacharya, M. (2004). Conducting problem-based learning online. In E. McKay (Ed.), *International Conference on Computers in Education 2004 (*pp. 525-530). Melbourne, VIC: RMIT University.

Bhattacharya, M. (2006). Introducing integrated e-portfolio across courses in a postgraduate program in distance and online education. In R.C. Sharma & S. Sharma (Eds.), *Cases on global e-learning practices: Successes and pitfalls.* Chapter 7. Hershey, PA: Information Science Publishing.

Brown, P. (1995). Cultural capital and social exclusion: Some observations on recent trends in education, employment and the labour market. *Work, Employment & Society, 9*(1), 29-51.

Carnie, A. (2001). How to handle cyber-sloth in academe. *Chronicle of Higher Education, 47*(17), B14. Retrieved October 15, 2006 from http://chronicle.com/weekly/v47/i17/17b01401.htm

Chandasoma, R., Thompson, C., & Pennycook, A. (2004). Beyond plagiarism: Transgressive and nontransgressive intertextuality. *Journal of Language, Identity, and Education, 3*(3), 171-193.

Codd, J. (2006). Personal Comment. Palmerston North: Massey University College of Education.

Collier, H., Perrin, R., & McGowan, C. (2004). Plagiarism: Let the policy fix the crime. *Faculty of commerce papers*. Woollongon: University of Woollongon.

Davis, S. J. (1994) Teaching practices that encourage or eliminate student plagiarism. *Middle School Journal, 25*(3), 55-8.

Emerson, L., Rees, M., & MacKay, B. (2005). Scaffolding academic integrity: creating a learning context for teaching referencing skills. *Journal of University Teaching & Learning Practice, 2*(3a), 1-14. Retrived October 15, 2006 from http://jutlp.uow.edu.au/

Evans, R. (2006). Evaluating an electronic plagiarism detection service: The importance of trust and difficulty of proving students don't cheat. *Active Learning in Higher Education, 7*(1), 87-99.

Foster, A. L. (2002). Plagiarism-detection tool creates legal quandary. *The Chronicle of Higher Education, May 17*. Retrieved October 15, 2006 from http://chronicle.com/free/v48/i36/36a03701.htm

Jonassen, D. H. (2001). Design of constructivist learning environments. Retrieved October 15, 2006 from http://www.coe.missouri.edu/~jonassen/courses/CLE/index.html

Horn, D. (1998). The shoulders of giants. *Science 29, 280*(5368), 1354-1355.

Landau, J. D., Druen, P. B., & Arcuri, J. A. (2002). Methods and techniques: Method for helping students avoid plagiarism. *Teaching of Psychology, 29*(2), 112-115.

Leask, B. (2006). Plagiarism, cultural diversity and metaphor-implications for academic staff development. *Assessment & Evaluation in Higher Education, 31*(2), 183-199.

MacDonell, C. (2005). The problem of plagiarism. Students who copy may not know they've committed an offence. *School Library Journal, 54*(1), 35.

Marsh, R. L., Landau, J. D., & Hicks, J. L. (1997). Contributions of inadequate source monitoring to unconscious plagiarism during idea generation. *Journal of Experimental Psychology: Learning, Memory and Cognition, 23*, 886-897.

Martin, Brian. (2004). Plagiarism: policy against cheating or policy for learning. *Nexus 16(2) 15-16*. Retrieved October 15, 2006, from http://www.uow.edu.au/arts/sts/bmartin/pubs/04nexus.htm

Massey University, (2006). Policy on plagiarism. Palmerston North: College of Education.

McKenzie, J. (1998). The new plagiarism: Seven antidotes to prevent highway robbery in an electronic age. *From Now On-The Educational Technology Journal, 7*(8). Retrieved October 15, 2006 from http://fno.org/may98/cov98may.html

McKeever, L. (2006). Online plagiarism detection services-saviour or scourge? *Assessment & Higher Education, 31*(2), 155-165.

Orlans, H. (1999). Fair use in US scholarly publishing. *Learned Publishing, 12*(4), 135-244.

Park, C. (2003). In other (people's) words: Plagiarism by university students—literature and lessons. *Assessment & Evaluation in Higher Education, 28*(5), 471-488. Retrieved October 15, 2006 from http://www.lancs.ac.uk/staff/gyaccp/caeh_28_5_02lores.pdf

Pecorari, D. (2001). Plagiarism and international students: How the English-speaking university responds. In D. Belcher & A. Hirvela (Eds.), *Linking literacies: Perspectives on L2 reading-writing connections* (pp. 229-245). Ann Arbor, MI: University of Michigan Press.

Ramsden, P. (1992). *Learning to teach in higher education*, London: Routledge.

Saltmarsh, S., (2004). Graduating tactics: Theorizing plagiarism as consumptive practice. *Journal of Further and Higher Education, 28*(4), 445-454.

Schwarz, C. (Ed) (1992). *Maxi paperback dictionary.* Edinburg: Chambers Harrap Publishers Ltd.

Sowden, C. (2005). Point and counterpoint: Plagiarism and the culture of multilingual students in higher education abroad. *ELT Journal, 59*(3), 226-233.

Sterngold, A. (2004). Confronting plagiarism. How conventional teaching invites cyber-cheating. *Change, 36*(3), 16-21.

Szabo, A. & Underwood, J. (2004). Cybercheating: Is information and communication technology fuelling academic dishonesty? *Active Learning in Higher Education*, *15*(2), 180–199.

Walden. K., & Peacock, A. (2006). The i-Map: a process-centered response to plagiarism. *Assessment & Evaluation in Higher Education, 31*(2), 201-214.

Warn, J. (2006). Plagiarism software: no magic bullet! *Higher Education Research & Development, 25*(2), 195-208.

Willen, M.S., (2004). Reflections on the cultural climate of plagiarism, *Liberal education,* 55-58.

Wu, J., & Singh, M., (2002, July). *Wishing for dragon children: An educational tradition in China that is influencing families ant home and abroad.* Paper presented at the Ninth International Literacy and Education Network Conference on Learning. Beijing, China.

Chapter XIV
Expect Originality!
Using Taxonomies to Structure Assignments that Support Original Work

Janet Salmons
Vision2Lead, Inc., USA

ABSTRACT

The online world offers opportunities to appropriate others' work, while simultaneously offering opportunities for valuable research and creative exchange. The use of secondary research materials in academic writing can be represented as a continuum, with "plagiarism" on one end and "original work" on the other. Educators can take steps to prevent plagiarism by designing assignments that expect learners to respect others' ideas and strive toward creating their own original work. Educational taxonomies, including the Cognitive and Affective Domains of Bloom's Taxonomy, and the author's Taxonomy of Collaborative E-Learning, can serve as conceptual frameworks for designing assignments that (1) expect learners to present original work; (2) provide opportunities for learners to develop new ideas through meaningful online interaction; and (3) value learners' ideas while respecting published authors' intellectual property.

INTRODUCTION

While plagiarism involves ethical dilemmas in regard to misrepresentation of work and/or violation of copyright rules, it also involves dilemmas for teaching and learning. When learners represent others' ideas as their own, they are not developing their own ideas. When learners plagiarize, they are not developing the thinking, research, and writing skills necessary to successfully achieve the learning outcomes of a course and to prepare for professional life.

The online world offers easy access an extensive array of work by other writers. Learners no longer need to re-type material; they can easily find writings in electronic format on any subject, select, copy, and paste it, and call it their own. The same technologies that make it easy to plagiarize also facilitate a rich culture of free exchange emerging in the online world. Sharing, forwarding, linking, and blending information and media are intrinsic to life in the online world. Participants in this culture do not see use of materials they find online as stealing someone else's intellectual property. Similarly, learners who make free use of materials they find online for academic work do not see it as plagiarism (Kraus, 2002; Madden & Rainie, 2003, 2005; Renard, 2000; Wood, 2004, p. 299). Since learners tend to study in an academic context using the same processes they use in informal interactions, it is not surprising that practices used to complete their assignments are similar to those they use in everyday interactions with friends (Crook & Light, 2002). Clearly, approaches being used to address plagiarism must take into account profound changes to the world of information and the ways it is accessed and used.

This chapter proposes a model for thinking about use of resources in academic work as a continuum, with "plagiarism" on one end and "original work" on the other. Strategies for addressing the issues at each point on the continuum are discussed. While achieving proper attribution of sources represents success in terms of academic honesty, other steps are needed to ensure that higher order thinking and learning occurs. This chapter focuses on ways educators can plan and facilitate learning assignments that discourage cheating by encouraging learners to aim for original work.

The chapter explores ways that educators can support the positive aspects of learners' use of the Internet to locate diverse materials and exchange ideas with peers within an academic culture that respects intellectual property. In particular, this chapter shows how educators can used Bloom's Taxonomies together with the Taxonomy of Col-

laborative E-Learning as a framework for designing learning activities that make productive use of online materials and peer collaboration.

BACKGROUND

Four broad strategies to combat plagiarism are frequently mentioned in the literature:

- Having, promoting, and administering clear, institution-wide policies for academic honesty.
- Using electronic detection tools such as Turnitin.com or using a search engine to find sources of suspicious phrases.
- Teaching the proper use of sources by defining plagiarism and educating learners in methods for citation.
- Designing meaningful and unique assignments to minimize the opportunity for cheating.

Educational institutions widely recognize the need for policies on academic honesty. An institutional approach should ideally be embedded into academic rules and regulations and promoted throughout the institution (Park, 2004). The Center for Academic Integrity suggests four stages for developing academic honesty policies and diffusing them into campus life. At the first stage, no policy is in place. The next stage involves building faculty and student awareness of academic honesty issues and options. At the third stage, the institution has policies that are widely known but not fully supported. At the fourth stage, policies are widely understood and students are involved in development and implementation of academic honesty policies (Drinan, 2006).

At best, policies alone are an imperfect solution for addressing plagiarism. One study, based on an experiment with two large undergraduate classes, found that "warning students not to plagiarize, even in the strongest possible language, appears not to have had any effect whatsoever. Revealing the use of plagiarism-detection software to the student…on the other hand, seemed to be a remarkable strong (though not perfect) deterrent" (Braumoeller & Gaines, 2001, p. 835). Similar results were found in a study conducted at Murray State University in Kentucky: students "who have a stronger belief that plagiarism will be detected will be less likely to plagiarize" (Martin, 2005, p. 152). Electronic detection services such as Turnitin.com, and the use of search engines to locate copied text are becoming popular deterrents.

At the same time, many educators voice concerns about widespread use of electronic detection and the perceived role for instructors as enforcers. Martin represents the viewpoint of many instructors who believe that "the policing approach is educationally counterproductive" (Martin, 1992). Some fear that routine plagiarism checks might breed an atmosphere of suspicion and mistrust, and undermine the intellectual fabric of the academy. The unintended consequence they fear is that "rather than being mentors to students; we are replacing the student–teacher relationship with the criminal–police relationship" (Howard, 2002, p. 47; Park, 2004). Renard (2000) states the concern bluntly: "catching cheaters is not the best answer. It's a lot like doing an autopsy. No matter how terrific the coroner is at determining how or why a person died, the damage has been done" (p. 41). She points out that "our interest lies in helping students learn to document sources, not in prosecuting cheaters" (p. 40).

It is not surprising that, while educators believe blatant cheaters should be punished, they prefer instructional approaches to punitive ones. As Purdy (2005) observes, "rather than panic that students are now rampantly plagiarizing at numbers never known before, we must take a step back to consider the role the writing technologies they use play in their writing processes and consider how we as teachers—rather than hunters, police officers, or super sleuths—can pedagogically address these technologies" (p.

291). Howard (2002) similarly advocates changes to curriculum, even when that implies a major change to an instructor's approach to curriculum development. She states, "we risk categorizing all of our students as criminals. Worst of all, we risk not recognizing that our own pedagogy needs reform. Big reform" (p. 47).

One way instructors can change curricular approaches to prevent plagiarism is by clearly defining plagiarism and teaching learners appropriate methods to give credit for ideas they quote or paraphrase. *The Good Practice Guide to Plagiarism* recommends that colleges and universities offer compulsory teaching sessions on academic writing and citation skills (Carroll & Appleton, 2001). The online Kaplan University has implemented this approach, with a three-unit segment in the required *Effective Writing I* class covering: (1) citations, (2) APA style and (3) plagiarism. "The order is intentional; plagiarism is a scary word, and if they are thinking about it before they learn citation, they don't learn citation as well. If they learn citation first, then once they get to plagiarism, they already have the skill set to avoid it" (VanDam, personal communication, September 26, 2006). An example of non-compulsory instruction in proper techniques is the use of online writing centers. Such centers can offer faculty and learners alike information and skills-development in all areas of academic writing.

Many instructors feel that improved teaching of citation protocols needs to be part of a broader set of changes to instruction and assignments for the Internet age. "Conventional teaching invites plagiarism," is the premise stated by Arthur Sterngold (2004), who recommends "learner-centered approaches such as hands-on, active and collaborative learning methods" (p. 18). John Moye, Director of Curriculum Development at Capella University, points to educators' responsibilities: "If a learner can plagiarize, something was wrong with the assignment" (Moye, personal communication, September 15, 2006). Moye describes a framework for assignments that requires integration of the learner's explanation of external information (instructional messages, readings, etc.), internal reflection on relevant experiences, and discussion of new understandings that emerge from this synthesis of internal and external information. Each learner's assignment will necessarily be unique, because no two learners could identically process internal and external information. He recommends that instructors keep learners engaged in the process of learning and encourage them to continually re-evaluate previously held ideas.

High school principal Mitchell Shron also suggests that curricular approaches can minimize plagiarism. He states that: "Interesting assignments will result in interesting responses; rote responses will result in rote responses" (Shron, personal communication, September 18, 2006). He also says:

Don't keep the [review] process secret—pull back the curtain. Give the students tools to critique, so it is no surprise. Use Bloom's Taxonomy as a lesson. Share with students the meaning of metacognition. Make it clear: we expect synthesis. In assignments ask students: 'can you create something original?' Not every student will hit the high point, but some will. (M. Shron, personal communication, September 18, 2006)

Other suggestions include avoiding broad, fact-based assignments, discussing research with learners, and including information gathering as an outcome in its own right (Carroll & Appleton, 2001; McLafferty & Foust, 2004). *The Good Practice Guide to Plagiarism* recommends instructional practices that provide learners with opportunities for discussion, practice and feedback (Carroll & Appleton, 2001).

Bruner's (1977) pre-Internet observations support the arguments made in contemporary literature: "The best way to create interest in a subject is to render it worth knowing, which means to make the knowledge gains usable in one's thinking beyond the situation in which the learning has occurred" (p. 31). Many educators still believe that when learners perceive a subject as "worth knowing" and relevant to their own inquiries, life, and work, they will be engaged in the learning process enough to contribute their own insights. As Park (2004) suggests, a balanced and positive approach to plagiarism would emphasize prevention and improved attention to instruction and education, backed up by robust and transparent procedures for detecting and punishing plagiarism. "If successful, such an approach would create a level playing field on which staff and students can operate, to the benefit of all stakeholders" (p. 299).

PLAGIARISM: IT IS NOT BLACK AND WHITE

What is *plagiarism*? The college Writing Program Administrators Council says that "in an instructional setting, plagiarism occurs when a writer deliberately uses someone else's language, ideas, or other original (not common-knowledge) material without acknowledging its source" (*Defining and avoiding plagiarism*, 2003). Whether the thoughts of another author are used directly or are imitated, it is plagiarism. The *Publication Manual* of the American Psychological Association states that plagiarism includes ideas as well as specific text (APA, 2001).

Plagiarism issues are too complex for a simplistic right and wrong assessment. Plagiarism may occur intentionally or inadvertently. In an educational context, these are important distinctions because dishonesty generally requires administrative repercussions whereas careless attribution generally entails response from the instructor. A continuum provides a way to look at purposeful plagiarism at one end of the spectrum, and original work at the other end.

Figure 1. Plagiarism as a continuum

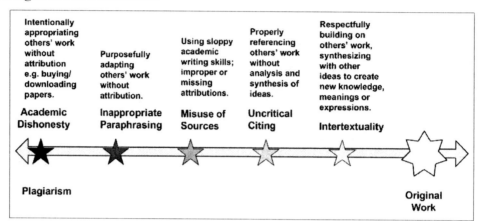

Points on the Continuum: Definitions

Academic Dishonesty: When learners purposefully appropriate all or part of an assignment from another source and represent it as their own, they do not benefit from the learning intended for the assignment. This kind of intentional plagiarism constitutes academic dishonesty.

Inappropriate Paraphrasing: When learners simply rearrange the order of words in sentences or change words to synonyms, they may present their own words but not their own ideas (APA, 2001; Share, 2006). This type of paraphrasing is a purposeful misrepresentation of someone else's work.

Misuse of Sources: When learners do not use proper citation protocols, they may inadvertently plagiarize another's work. Learners may cite the source material somewhere in the assignment, but it is not clear which passages are original and which are not (Braumoeller & Gaines, 2001). While this may be less critical in terms of academic honesty, the learner is not achieving learning objectives (*Defining and avoiding plagiarism*, 2003).

Uncritical Citing: Even when students use proper citation techniques and avoid plagiarism, they may still achieve limited learning outcomes when their work lacks analysis and synthesis of main ideas from the sources they are referencing.

Intertextuality: The term "intertextuality" can be used to describe an educationally productive process of building on or synthesizing others' ideas, and adding new perspectives or interpretations. The term was coined by Julia Kristeva in the context of literary analysis. She proposed that "any text is constructed of a mosaic of quotations; any text is the absorption and transformation of another..." (Kristeva, 1980). The dictionary definition of the term is: "Relating to or deriving meaning from the interdependent ways in which texts stand in relation to each other" (*American Heritage Dictionary*). The important principle here is that learners "derive meaning" from the sources they reference. Intertextuality, then, is a term that can be used to define practices whereby learners use other sources as a springboard for new connections, and derive meaning from the process.

Original Work: At the other end of the spectrum from plagiarism, learners create their own original work with new discoveries and innovations. Proper citations are used for any foundational ideas or arguments not original to the student (Braumoeller & Gaines, 2001).

MATCHING PROBLEM TO STRATEGY

The four most common strategies for combating plagiarism are: (1) enforcing academic honesty policies; (2) using electronic detection to identify plagiarized text; (3) instructing learners to use protocols for citation of sources; and (4) designing learning activities that cannot be easily copied from other sources. Comprehensive approaches integrate all four strategies through administrative and instructional policies and practices—throughout the institution and within the classroom. All of the strategies are needed in combination, because each addresses particular issues in ways that are not interchangeable with the others.

Academic honesty policies are needed to inform learners of the ethical and legal issues, and to clearly state implications for breaking the rules. But policies alone are not enough; instructors need detection tools so they can readily identify sections or entire papers drawn from other sources.

Teaching proper citation protocols and requiring submissions in academic style can help to prevent careless copying or adapting others' writings. If successful, such instruction can mo-

tivate learners to accomplish assignments using proper attributions. While positive in light of honesty and ethical practice, papers that draw on other sources with proper citations may still be inadequate in terms of the potential for learning from and building upon the ideas contained in resource materials.

The fourth strategy, designing learning activities that cannot be easily copied from other sources, is the focus of the rest of this chapter. As noted earlier, when learners represent others' ideas as their own, they are not developing their own ideas. The converse statement is equally important: when students develop their own ideas, they are not representing others' ideas as their own. Curriculum and teaching methods must support the goal of students developing their own ideas. Learner-centered pedagogical approaches help learners to develop critical thinking abilities, to contribute to fruitful collaborations, to give appropriate credit for others' contributions and to strive for originality. Educational taxonomies can help educators design and plan such learning activities.

Figure 2. Appropriate strategies

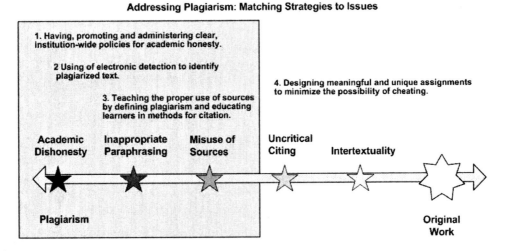

213

TAXONOMIES: BLOOM AND COLLABORATIVE E-LEARNING

"A taxonomy is a system of categories or classifications that are used for purposes of organization, conceptualization, and communication" (Gilbert, 1992). Benjamin Bloom observed that, beyond just classifying observations, a taxonomy should clarify the relationships among classes of phenomena. "While a classification scheme may have many arbitrary elements... a taxonomy must be so constructed that the order of the terms must correspond to some 'real' order among the phenomena represented by the terms" (Bloom, Engelhart, Furst, Hill, & Krathwohl, 1956). Taxonomies can facilitate communication among educators by providing a common language for discussing ways to address various educational dilemmas.

Bloom's Taxonomies

The materials known as "Bloom's Taxonomy" actually are the product of a team of five researchers: Max Engelhart, Edward Furst, Walker Hill, David Krathwohl, and Benjamin Bloom. In acknowledgement of the many ways people learn, they identified three domains: Cognitive, Affective and Psychomotor. The Cognitive and Affective Domains are relevant to the present study.

The *Taxonomy of Educational Objectives for the Cognitive Domain* is a framework that shows six levels of thinking, from knowledge through evaluation. The Taxonomy for the Cognitive Do-

Table 1. Bloom's Taxonomy and revision

Bloom's Cognitive Taxonomy (1956)	Revised Taxonomy (2000)
Knowledge: • Recall information; bring to mind the appropriate material.	Remember • Recognizing • Recalling
Comprehension • Understand what is being communicated; able to grasp the meaning of material presented.	Understand • Interpreting • Exemplifying • Classifying • Summarizing • Inferring • Comparing • Explaining
Application • Use abstractions in particular and concrete situations.	Apply • Executing • Implementing
Analysis • Break down material into its constituent parts or elements; recognize organizational structure.	Analyze • Differentiating • Organizing • Attributing
Synthesis • Assemble elements or parts to form a whole.	Evaluate • Checking • Critiquing
Evaluation • Make a judgment about the value of material or methods for a given purpose or situation.	Create • Generating • Planning • Producing

main focuses on development of critical thinking skills, beginning with the ability to retain terminology and basic concepts of a subject, and moving toward the ability to use, critically evaluate, and ultimately improve upon the concepts through synthesis with new ideas (Bloom et al., 1956).

The *Taxonomy of Educational Objectives for the Affective Domain* is a framework that shows five levels of development of attitudes and values (Krathwohl, Bloom, & Masia, 1964). The Taxonomy for the Affective Domain begins by describing the ability to receive experiences or information, through the development of values, and the internalization of those values. At level five, behaviors are consistent with values.

Forty-five years after Bloom's team put together the Taxonomies, a group of people went through a similar process of meetings and discussions in an effort to update the work. Lorin Anderson, a former student of Bloom, and one of the original team members, David Krathwohl, led the revision team. The team was made up of experts from the fields of cognitive psychology, curriculum theory, and testing and assessment. The result of their work is published as *A Taxonomy for Learning, Teaching and Assessing: A Revision of Bloom's Taxonomy of Educational Objectives* (Anderson, Bloom, Krathwohl, & Airasian, 2000).

The explanation of the "Knowledge" category in the original version states: "By knowledge, we mean that the student can give evidence that he remembers, either by recalling or by recognizing, some idea or phenomenon" (Bloom et al., 1956 p. 28). In the revision, the action of "remembering" is at the foundational level. The Taxonomy is described as two-dimensional with a "Cognitive Process" and "Knowledge Dimension." The Cognitive Processes are organized from simple to complex, based on the assumption that to Remember requires a simpler cognitive process than to Apply. The Knowledge Dimension is organized from concrete to abstract. The Revision includes a new area, Metacognitive Knowledge, which reflects cognitive psychology findings made since the original Taxonomy. The term is used to describe two aspects: (1) knowledge about cognition and (2) control, monitoring, and regulation of cognitive processes. (Anderson et al., 2000)

Educators across disciplines and from K-12 through graduate level use Bloom's Taxonomies for the Cognitive and Affective Domains. These educators want to do more than teach content, they also want to foster development of critical thinking skills They understand that it is not enough for learners to acquire information; learners also need to know how to use, apply and evaluate information, and how to create new knowledge. In the process, learners develop the affective qualities and internalize and act on values that include academic honesty. These are precisely the skills that

Table 2. Knowledge dimensions in Bloom's Taxonomy revision

Knowledge Dimensions
Factual Knowledge: The basic elements that students must know to be acquainted with a discipline or solve problems in it.
Conceptual Knowledge: Interrelationships among the basic elements within a larger structure that enable them to function together.
Procedural Knowledge: How to do something; methods of inquiry, and criteria for using skills.
Metacognitive Knowledge: Knowledge of cognition in general as well as awareness and knowledge of one's own cognition.

motivate learners to draw on the work of others constructively and to contribute their own value to an assignment rather than plagiarize.

COLLABORATIVE E-LEARNING

Bloom's Taxonomies provide useful frameworks for design of assignments that encourage individual learners to acquire critical thinking skills. The Taxonomy of Collaborative E-Learning offers a new conceptual framework for understanding levels of collaboration and for organizing assignments so that participants learn to work together and achieve unique collective outcomes. Learners must analyze each other's work and synthesize key ideas in order to produce outcomes that represent the diverse inputs of participants.

Collaborative learning can complement individual study and leverage the power of learner-learner interaction. Interaction is intrinsic to collaboration (Gray, 1989; Wood & Gray, 1991). While not all interaction is collaborative, all collaboration builds on interaction among participants. Educators since John Dewey have pointed to interaction as intrinsic to education. Constructivists and social constructivists believe that learning occurs when learners interact with each other and their environment (Jonassen, 1994; Vygotsky, 1978, 1987; Weil & Joyce, 1978).

Learners can benefit from purposeful collaboration, whether the class is taught online, face-to-face, or in a blended combination. Renard points out that educators can try vainly to make [students] do things the traditional way—or we can capitalize on digital technologies to help students learn and grow. We can find ways to combine the newer, faster technology with more traditional methods (Renard, 2005 p. 45) In an era where text-messaging, e-mail, and blogging are common ways learners interact socially, collaborative e-learning encourages learners to apply these practices to educational tasks.

The Taxonomy of Collaborative E-Learning is grounded in the results of a qualitative study, which explored an in-depth view of instructors' perceptions of teaching with online collaborative methods, and descriptive examples of their approaches. Phenomenological research methodology provided a structured approach for inquiry into the perceptions of success factors for collaborative e-learning of a purposeful sample of 12 experienced online educators from five countries. Study findings were used to refine and build on the author's original model for the Taxonomy of Collaborative Learning.

For the purpose of this study, collaborative e-learning was defined as:

constructing knowledge, negotiating meanings, and/or solving problems through mutual engagement of two or more learners in a coordinated effort using Internet and electronic communications.

"Mutual engagement" means all are participating in shared, reciprocal work. "Two or more learners" means these are activities that engage pairs or groups of learners. Others also may be a part of the collaborative e-learning activity including the instructor or those involved in applied or service-learning projects. "Coordinated effort" means the project is purposeful and meshes with curricular goals. "Construct knowledge, negotiate meanings, and/or solve problems" means learning together in meaningful ways that use and develop higher order thinking skills. "Internet and electronic communications" means learners use synchronous or asynchronous tools such as e-mail, Web conferencing, instant messaging, wikis, or threaded discussion forums.

By this definition, while learners may complete parts of a project independently, when they integrate their efforts into one outcome, we can describe their work as "collaboration." Collaboration provides opportunities for people to learn from each other or transfer knowledge. Together

Figure 3. Salmons' Taxonomy of Collaborative E-Learning

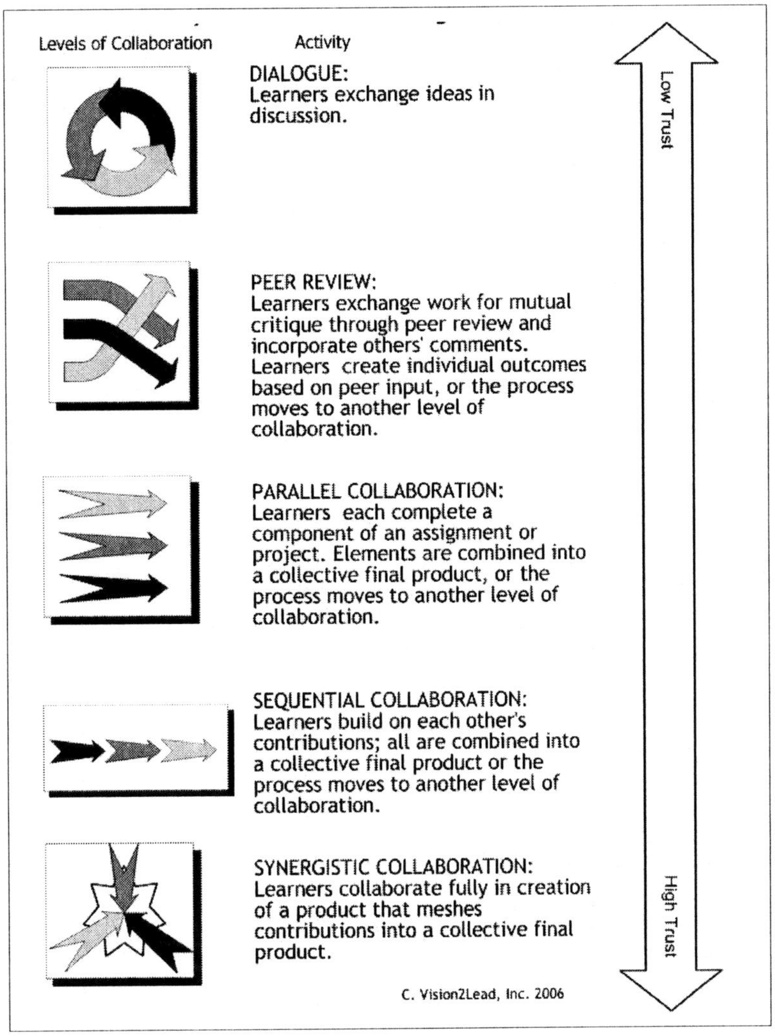

they can generate innovative new ideas or approaches, or new applications for best practices.

Elements of the Taxonomy of Collaborative E-Learning

The Taxonomy of Collaborative E-Learning contains three key elements: the Levels of Collaboration, Learning Activities and Trust Continuum.

1. Levels of Collaboration

Levels of Collaboration lists progressively more collaborative styles of working in a group. One level is not better than another in absolute terms, but one may be better than another in relation to the learning goals, the configuration or social stage of the group, timing or other issues. The five levels are: dialogue, peer review, parallel, sequential, and synergistic collaboration. Arrows in the diagrams represent process, and the stars represent outcomes.

Levels of Collaboration can be ordered or combined in various ways to organize multi-stage projects. In the process of completing projects organized with this system, participants can gain the skills needed to lead, organize and participate in collaborative projects.

Dialogue

 The foundational level of collaboration is Dialogue. This term is used to describe a shared, mutually-responsive discussion. Dialogic teaching draws from Socrates and Plato, who encouraged active learning through self-examination, intelligent dialogue and interactive communication. In *Discussion as a Way of Teaching*, Brookfield and Preskill (2005) define the purpose of dialogue to help learners: reach a more critically informed understanding of the topic, become more appreciative of diverse opinions, enhance learners' capacity for self-awareness and self-critique, and to act as a catalyst for action. Philosopher Matthew Lipman (1993) argues, "The skills needed for good thinking are bred by the dialogue itself. The dialogue elicits, draws out, the cognitive performances of the students" (p. 10).

In the context of this model, Dialogue is a catalyst for collaboration, a means for learners to find coherence in the ideas, plans, and/or tactics needed to coordinate their efforts. While Dialogue is a foundational step, it is assumed that it will be an essential part of any collaborative process at all stages.

Peer Review

 The second level is Peer Review. This term is used to describe a process of critique and feedback between learners. Giving and receiving feedback allows learners to practice elements essential to leadership develop-ment—assessment, challenge, and support (Mc-Cauley & Douglas, 2005). When Peer Review is structured with mutually acceptable boundaries and set criteria, learners can provide objective perspectives and learn from each other (Guthrie & King, 2004).

Parallel

 The third level is Parallel collaboration. When an assignment is completed by a group of learners using a Parallel struc-ture, components of the assignment are allocated among learners. Parallel collaboration typically involves individual work and a process of Dialogue and Peer Review to integrate contributions into a final product.

Sequential

 The fourth level is Sequential collaboration. When an as-signment is completed by a group of learners using a Sequential structure, components of the assignment are organized into a series of progressive steps and results are com-bined into one collective product. Each component depends on successful completion of another in the series of steps. Each step typically involves individual work and a process of Dialogue and Peer Review to integrate contributions into a final product.

Synergistic

 The fifth level is Synergistic collabo-ration. When a group of learners uses a Synergistic structure, they work to-gether through all steps and synthesize their ideas to plan, organize, and complete the assignment together. Their contributions are fully meshed into collective final product.

2. Learning Activity

The Learning Activity column includes simplified descriptions of the kinds of actions learners take in each corresponding level.

3. Continuum of Trust

The continuum illustrates a relationship between trust and the level of collaboration. As illustrated here, as collaboration increases, so does the need for trust. Charles Handy (1995) observed the need for more attention to trust in the virtual world in his predictive article, "Trust and the Virtual Organization." He defined trust as "the confidence that a person is competent to reach a goal and is committed to reaching it," and observed that the practice of trust "implies reciprocal loyalty" (pp. 7-8). Collaboration means reliance on others' abilities and integrity and confidence that the other learner(s) can and will share your commitment toward meeting the learning goal of the assignment. The reciprocal loyalties and common purpose among learners involves trust not only among the learners, but also between the instructor and the learners.

Instructional Approaches: Findings from the Collaborative E-Learning Study

Research participants reported on the use of cognitive processes and multiple knowledge dimensions in each stage of the collaborative process. While Peer Review exchanges described in the data typically asked learners to organize and integrate information into a classification scheme provided in the assignment, activities conducted at the Parallel, Sequential, or Synergistic levels usually required learners to create their own classification schemes and protocols for organizing, managing, and integrating information from multiple inputs. To do so, they had to do more than discuss what to do; they had to think together about how to do it (London, 2005). At the Dialogue and Peer Review levels the focus was on communicating, and on giving and receiving constructive criticism. At the Parallel level, learners created agreements, developed mutual accountability and dealt with under-performing team members. Kantner (1994) called this process learning to collaborate.

Nearly half of the research participants describe some kind of individual metacognitive, reflective process as part of the collaborative activity.

At the Parallel, Sequential, and Synergistic levels, learners were typically engaged in activities that invited them to generate new information or knowledge by adapting and integrating multiple parts into a collective whole.

At the Sequential level, learners worked out ways to build shared commitment to a goal, and how to coordinate a multi-step process. For effective collaborative learning, there must be a balance between "group goals" and "individual accountability," with individual learning success as part of the group task (Slavin, 1989). At the Synergistic level they learned to interact with partners at all stages of the project. At these higher levels of collaboration they practiced participatory decision-making and learned to balance individual interests with group purpose.

Research participants described learning experiences that correspond to each level of the Taxonomy of Collaborative E-Learning. As instructors, research participants were actively involved in every step of the process. Research participants were in agreement that, regardless of the design and planning carried out prior to the class, there is no substitute for active involvement by instructors during the class.

Figure 4. Salmons' and Bloom's Taxonomies

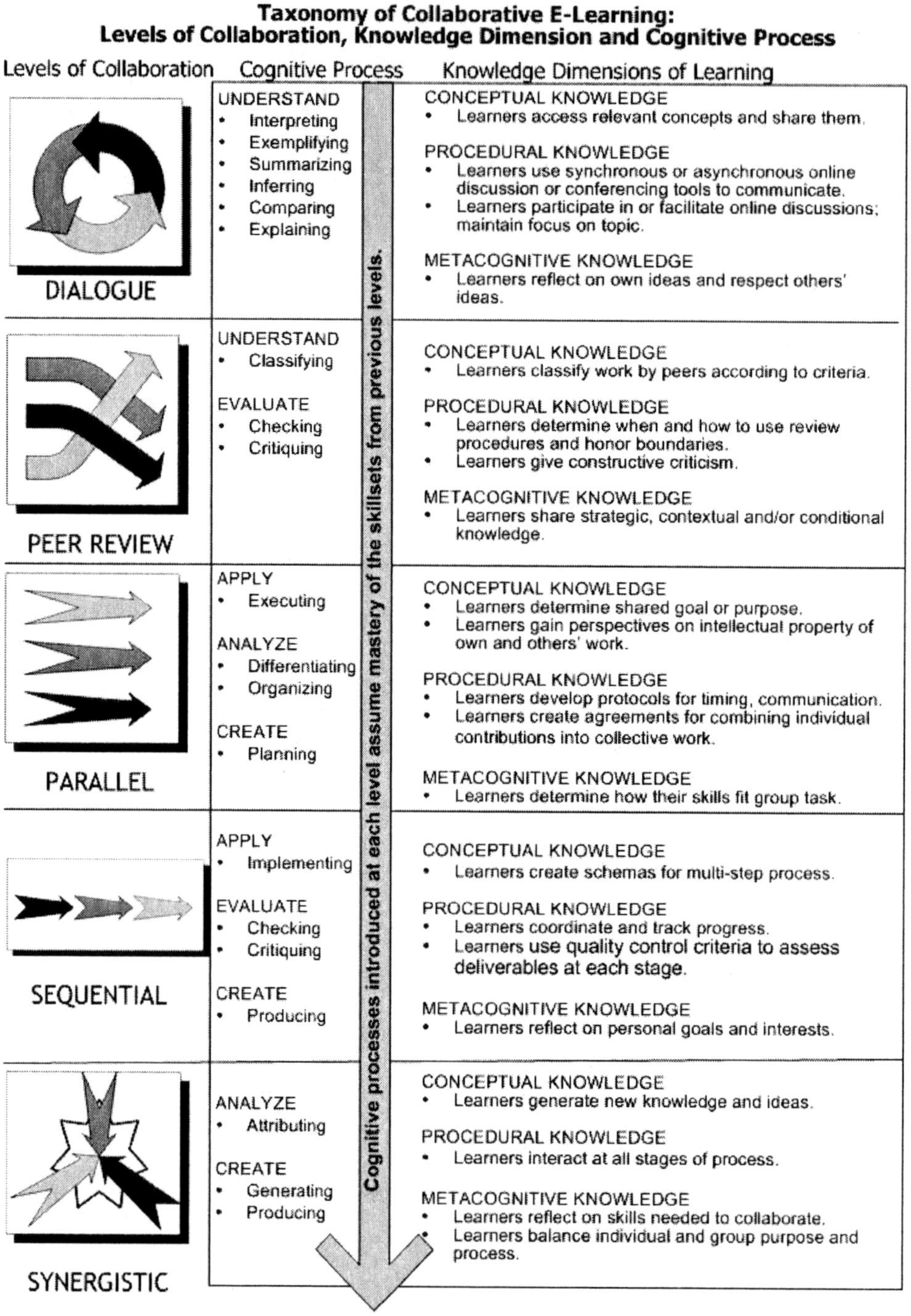

Taxonomy of Collaborative E-Learning:
Levels of Collaboration, Knowledge Dimension and Cognitive Process

Levels of Collaboration	Cognitive Process	Knowledge Dimensions of Learning
DIALOGUE	UNDERSTAND • Interpreting • Exemplifying • Summarizing • Inferring • Comparing • Explaining	CONCEPTUAL KNOWLEDGE • Learners access relevant concepts and share them. PROCEDURAL KNOWLEDGE • Learners use synchronous or asynchronous online discussion or conferencing tools to communicate. • Learners participate in or facilitate online discussions; maintain focus on topic. METACOGNITIVE KNOWLEDGE • Learners reflect on own ideas and respect others' ideas.
PEER REVIEW	UNDERSTAND • Classifying EVALUATE • Checking • Critiquing	CONCEPTUAL KNOWLEDGE • Learners classify work by peers according to criteria. PROCEDURAL KNOWLEDGE • Learners determine when and how to use review procedures and honor boundaries. • Learners give constructive criticism. METACOGNITIVE KNOWLEDGE • Learners share strategic, contextual and/or conditional knowledge.
PARALLEL	APPLY • Executing ANALYZE • Differentiating • Organizing CREATE • Planning	CONCEPTUAL KNOWLEDGE • Learners determine shared goal or purpose. • Learners gain perspectives on intellectual property of own and others' work. PROCEDURAL KNOWLEDGE • Learners develop protocols for timing, communication. • Learners create agreements for combining individual contributions into collective work. METACOGNITIVE KNOWLEDGE • Learners determine how their skills fit group task.
SEQUENTIAL	APPLY • Implementing EVALUATE • Checking • Critiquing CREATE • Producing	CONCEPTUAL KNOWLEDGE • Learners create schemas for multi-step process. PROCEDURAL KNOWLEDGE • Learners coordinate and track progress. • Learners use quality control criteria to assess deliverables at each stage. METACOGNITIVE KNOWLEDGE • Learners reflect on personal goals and interests.
SYNERGISTIC	ANALYZE • Attributing CREATE • Generating • Producing	CONCEPTUAL KNOWLEDGE • Learners generate new knowledge and ideas. PROCEDURAL KNOWLEDGE • Learners interact at all stages of process. METACOGNITIVE KNOWLEDGE • Learners reflect on skills needed to collaborate. • Learners balance individual and group purpose and process.

Cognitive processes introduced at each level assume mastery of the skillsets from previous levels.

USING TAXONOMIES TO STRUCTURE MEANINGFUL ASSIGNMENTS

The following examples are drawn from the author's study on collaborative e-learning. They illustrate ways that instructors can adapt learning activities in an existing course or design activities for new course. These activities expect learners to interact with others in the class and the community, then to integrate multiple inputs into unique outcomes.

Example 1: Collaborative E-Learning in an Online Doctoral Course

The first example describes collaborative learning in an advanced quantitative research doctoral course: "Applied Multivariate Modeling." The design of this course includes two components that are typical for online courses: 1) a unit-by-unit discussion, which requires learners to answer questions and comment to other learners, and 2) a research paper or project completed by learners individually. In addition, the instructor added some creative elements by integrating opportunities for collaborative and original work.

Applied Multivariate Modeling is sequentially organized with a series of assignments throughout the twelve-week term and a final project. Assignments include individual work, group participation and collective work. The collaborative e-learning project for the course is creation of a *Decision Makers' Guide to Application of Multivariate Statistical Analysis* by the class.

For each of the Units 3 through 9, one or two learners in the class lead a discussion thread on pragmatic applications of a particular technique or techniques which were explored in a previous unit. These assigned learners each work individually to prepare for the discussion, then work together to construct proposed applications for the *Guidebook*. The whole class discusses the proposed

applications. The outcomes of the discussions are the basis for the *Decision Makers' Guide to Application of Multivariate Statistical Analysis*. So, this final product is crafted synergistically, with input from individual learners and from the class acting together.

Assignments for a mathematics course could consist of a series of problems to solve with each problem requiring a short answer that is either right or wrong. Such an assignment could be vulnerable to cheating. In this course, the instructor utilized several preventative practices to design multiple assignments that ask learners to make original contributions. The instructor created individualized tasks, instead of expecting all learners to fulfill the same requirements (Carroll & Appleton, 2001). The project—creation of a guidebook—asked the learners to explore real questions in the discipline (Procter, 2006). This kind of project asks learners to discuss their understanding of course material and relate it to life or professional experiences (McLafferty & Foust, 2004). The project expected learners to value the quantitative methods as essential decision-making tools in professional settings. The instructor assessed multiple kinds of assignments, including those that focused on process—facilitating class dialogue (Procter, 2006).

Learning activities in this course used multiple levels of collaboration. Learners alternated between individual preparation, Dialogue and Peer Review throughout the course, then worked Synergistically to create the final project deliverable. Learners were expected to use an intertextual approach to respectfully synthesize multiple perspectives. To accomplish these learning activities, learners used diverse cognitive processes and knowledge dimension:

- **Understand:** Learners construct meaning from instructional messages exchanged instructor-learner and learner-learner. They interpret and clarify quantitative research theories and models (Conceptual Knowledge). Learners summarize and explain techniques and procedures for an anticipated audience of practitioners who will use the *Guidebook* (Procedural Knowledge).

- **Apply:** Learners applied multivariate statistical analysis to both familiar and unfamiliar tasks (Procedural Knowledge).
- **Analyze:** Learners differentiated and organized statistical analysis techniques for users of the *Guidebook*.
- **Evaluate:** Learners checked and critiqued each other's work through Peer Review (Conceptual and Procedural Knowledge). Learners reflected on their own abilities to carry out complex statistical analyses (Metacognitive Knowledge).
- **Create:** Learners planned and produced a collective outcome for the course, the Decision Makers' Guide to Application of Multivariate Statistical Analysis.

Example 2: Collaborative E-Learning in a Blended Learning Undergraduate Course

The second example describes collaborative learning in a blended undergraduate course: "Advanced Business Writing." Business writing is a topic area with high potential for blatant plagiarism, since the Internet is full of examples that could be adopted or adapted for assignments. In this example, the instructor created a course design that defies either purposeful or inadvertent plagiarism.

Advanced Writing for Business is designed not only to help learners write effectively in a business environment, but also to improve the ability to research and analyze complex ideas, to appreciate and develop the skill of effective argumentation, and to write clear, grammatical, well-structured communications. With some emphasis on ethics and issues of public concern, coursework is designed to increase learners' capacity to analyze audiences and tailor content and style to produce written presentations that communicate with confidence.

A semester-long field project with a local non-profit organization provides teams of learners with real-world application where learners craft memos, press releases, reports, and other kinds of business writing. This sequentially organized project involves a series of incremental, interdependent steps throughout the semester. These steps include both individual writing and collective work in teams. Members work in parallel to research non-profit agencies as potential partners with whom to conduct the project. Learners have ongoing online and face-to-face dialogue about the research. Team members and instructor work synergistically to accomplish several key steps: determine their criteria, select a non-profit agency setting, and develop interview questions to ask the agency staff in order to assess the needs. After developing an internal proposal memo to communicate decisions and plans to the agency and the instructor, learners comment on at least one other team memo (via the weblog) and choose the best one. The final report is crafted synergistically, using deliverables created individually and collectively, and presented to the agency and the instructor.

The structure of Advanced Writing for Business and the organization of learning activities throughout the term demonstrate high expectations for learners. It would not be possible to use the more blatant forms of plagiarism, since a paper of this kind could not be copied or bought.

The instructor used a number of recognized preventive strategies. Instead of asking for one big paper at the end of the term, she broke the assignment into parts with discrete deadlines (McLafferty & Foust, 2004; Sterngold, 2004). By reviewing work throughout the process, the instructor became familiar with the writing styles and of her students, so she would be sensitive to student writing, style, and content that is out of character (Thomas, 2004, p. 428). The nature of the assignment compelled students to analyze and integrate data from multiple sources (Sterngold, 2004, p. 18). The collaborative process included ongoing peer review, which serves a preventative purpose since students are often tougher on cheaters than instructors (Martin, 1992). She discussed research with learners in required meetings to converse about findings (Sterngold, 2004, p. 18).

Learning activities in this course used all levels of collaboration and encouraged learners to use higher order cognitive processes and multiple knowledge dimensions. Learners exchanged, reviewed, analyzed, and reflect on each other's writing. They developed affective qualities through dialogue about ethical issues and values with their respective non-profit partners. The final team deliverable was an intertextual synthesis of learners' research, interviews, fieldwork, and discussions with the instructor. To accomplish these learning activities, learners used diverse cognitive processes and knowledge dimensions:

- **Understand:** Learners construct meaning from instructional messages exchanged instructor-learner, learner-learner, and learner-field placement supervisor. They infer and summarize communications needs in the field placement settings (Factual and Conceptual Knowledge). Learners determine criteria to use to determine when to use appropriate business writing approaches (Procedural Knowledge).
- **Apply:** Learners apply business writing strategies to both familiar and unfamiliar tasks (Procedural Knowledge).
- **Analyze:** Learners distinguish between various communication needs in the field placement agency to determine a project focus; learners organize their collaborative writing work (Conceptual and Procedural Knowledge).
- **Evaluate:** Learners check and critique each other's work through Peer Review (Conceptual and Procedural Knowledge). Learners reflect on their own writing and collaboration skills (Metacognitive Knowledge).
- **Create:** Learners plan and produce collective outcomes for the course in the form of

business materials tailored to the needs of their respective field placements.

SUMMARY: USING TAXONOMIES TO STRUCTURE MEANINGFUL ASSIGNMENTS

When an educator creates a learning experience with Bloom's Taxonomy as a guide, learners are encouraged to pursue two goals through that experience: acquiring competencies in the content area and learning how to learn through critical thinking. When an educator creates a learning experience with the Taxonomy of Collaborative E-Learning as a guide, learners are encouraged to pursue three goals through that experience: acquiring competencies in the content area, skills in team and group process, and proficiency with Internet and communications technologies (ICT).

NEXT STEPS

The author's study supports the conclusion that the Taxonomy of Collaborative E-Learning is useful for expressing patterns of instructional design and pedagogy that have proven effective in practice. The research of others cited in this article makes it clear that collaborative practices that the taxonomy are designed to foster increase the original contributions of learners and reduce plagiarism. This strongly suggests that research to directly evaluate the relationship between using the taxonomy and reducing plagiarism would be fruitful.

Recommendations for faculty development generated from the author's study include:

1. Allow curricular and instructional flexibility, so instructors can adopt learner-centered approaches to respond to the characteristics and needs of their students.
2. Offer classes or workshops for faculty through the same course management platform and features that the learners use.

Instructors can benefit from the experience as a 21st century learner.

3. Encourage peer learning among faculty. This recommendation corresponds to Reilly's findings that show advantages for having experienced "faculty peers" conduct workshops to show how to utilize new pedagogies and new technologies in the context of their shared discipline, instead of workshops by technology trainers (Reilly, 2005).

4. Fund and encourage faculty to participate in online conferences or events where they can interact with other educators. Faculty will benefit from the experience of diverse online interactions, as well as from the exchange of ideas and practices with others.

Sterngold (2004) echoed the recommendation for increased faculty development—and preparation of the next generation of faculty members.

Persuading professors to use the kinds of learning-centered practices that deter plagiarism will require major changes in faculty development, evaluation and promotion systems, so that instructors are trained and rewarded for adopting these methods. Accelerating the shift from an instruction-based to a learning centered paradigm will also require changes in how we train and prepare doctoral students for academic careers (p. 21).

CONCLUSION

The proposals here are aimed not to "stamp out" plagiarism but rather to create the sort of educational environment where it is rare because both students and staff expect the highest standards in each other. The aim should be to develop a culture of respect for quality work. (Martin, 1992)

This chapter focused on two inter-related ways to create the educational environment and culture described by Martin. One is to teach with a learner-centered pedagogy. Learner-centered pedagogy offers learners the opportunity and encouragement to create meaningful, unique assignments. The other is to teach with purposeful awareness of the information-rich online world. Kraus (2002) asks us to consider "what happens when students learn to use—in contrast to misuse—the Web. The more they prepare legitimate material to post online, the more they participate in the largest collective intellectual undertaking in the history of the world." When learners use the web to research and/or conduct collaborative projects they can make respectful use of diverse resources through intertextual synthesis of others' work and their own. By using Bloom's Taxonomy in conjunction with the Taxonomy of Collaborative E-Learning, educators can create assignments that encourage learners to use online interactions and information as the springboard for their own original work.

REFERENCES

American Heritage Dictionary. Retrieved October 4, 2006 from http://www.bartleby.com/61/91/I0199150.html

Anderson, L., Bloom, B. S., Krathwohl, D., & Airasian, P. (2000). *Taxonomy for learning, teaching and assessing: A revision of Bloom's Taxonomy of Educational Objectives.* New York: Allyn & Bacon, Inc.

APA. (2001). *Publication manual* (Fifth ed.). Washington, DC: American Psychological Association.

Bloom, B., Engelhart, M., Furst, E., Hill, W., & Krathwohl, D. (1956). *Taxonomy of educational objectives: Book 1, Cognitive domain.* New York: David McKay and Company.

Braumoeller, B. F., & Gaines, B. J. (2001). Actions do speak louder than words: Deterring plagiarism with the use of plagiarism-detection software. *Political Science and Politics, 34*(4), 835-839.

Brookfield, S. D., & Preskill, S. (2005). *Discussion: Tools and techniques for democratic classrooms* (Second ed.). San Francisco: Jossey Bass.

Bruner, J. (1977). *The process of education* (Second ed.). Cambridge: Harvard University Press.

Carroll, J., & Appleton, J. (2001). *Good practice guide to plagiarism.* London: Oxford Brookes University.

Crook, C., & Light, P. (2002). Virtual society and the cultural practice of study. In S. Woolgar (Ed.), *Virtual society? Technology, cyperbole, reality* (pp. 153-175). London: Oxford University Press.

Defining and avoiding plagiarism: The Writing Program Administrators' statement on best practices (2003). Retrieved October 12, 2006 from http://www.ilstu.edu/~ddhesse/wpa/positions/WPAplagiarism.pdf

Drinan, P. (2006). *Institutional stages of development.* Retrieved October 13, 2006 from http://www.academicintegrity.org/resources_inst.asp

Eanes, R. (2004). *Task oriented question construction wheel based on Bloom's Taxonomy.* Retrieved November 13, 2005 from http://www.stedwards.edu/cte/resources/bwheel.htm

Gilbert, S. W. (1992). Systematic questioning: Taxonomies that develop critical thinking skills. *Science Teacher, 59*(9), 41-46.

Gray, B. (1989). *Collaborating: Finding common ground for multiparty problems.* San Francisco: Jossey Bass.

Guthrie, V. A., & King, S. N. (2004). Feedback-intensive programs. In C. D. McCauley & E. V. Velsor (Eds.), *Center for Creative Leadership handbook of leadership development* (2nd ed.). San Francisco: Jossey Bass.

Handy, C. (1995). Trust and the virtual organization. *Harvard Business Review.*

Howard, R. (2002). Don't police plagiarism: just teach! *Education Digest, 67*(5), 46-50.

Jonassen, D. (1994). Thinking technology: towards a constructivist design model. *Educational Technology* (April), 34-37.

Kanter, R. M. (1994). Collaborative advantage: The art of alliances. *Harvard Business School Press, July-August* (Reprint 94405), 96-108.

Krathwohl, D., Bloom, B., & Masia, B. B. (1964). *Taxonomy of educational objectives: The classification of educational goals Book 2: Affective domain.* New York: David McKay and Company.

Kraus, J. (2002). Rethinking plagiarism: What our students are telling us when they cheat. *Issues in Writing, 13*(1), 80-95.

Kristeva, J. (1980). *Desire in language: A Semiotic approach to literature and art.* New York: Columbia University Press.

Lipman, M. (1993). Promoting better classroom thinking. *Educational Psychology, 13*(3/4).

London, S. (2005). Thinking together: The power of deliberative dialogue. In R. J. Kingston (Ed.), *Public Thought and Foreign Policy.* Dayton: Kettering Foundation Press.

Madden, M., & Rainie, L. (2003). *Music downloading, file-sharing and copyright*: Pew Internet and American Life Project.

Madden, M., & Rainie, L. (2005). *Music and video downloading moves beyond P2P*: Pew Internet and American Life Project.

Martin, B. (1992). Plagiarism by university students: the problem and some proposals. *Tertangala* (July 20-August 3).

Martin, D. (2005). Plagiarism and technology: A tool for coping with plagiarism. *Journal of Education for Business,* (January/February), 149-152.

McKenzie, J. (1999). The Research cycle 2000. *From Now On: The Educational Technology Journal, 9*(4).

McLafferty, C. L., & Foust, K. M. (2004). Electronic plagiarism as a college instructor's nightmare—Prevention and detection. *Journal of Education for Business, 79*(3), 186-189.

Park, C. (2004). Rebels without a clause: Towards an institutional framework for dealing with plagiarism by students. *Journal of Further and Higher Education, 28*(3), 291-306.

Procter, M. (2006). *Deterring plagiarism: Some strategies.* Retrieved October 10, 2006 from http://www.utoronto.ca/writing/plagiarism.html#3

Purdy, J. (2005). Calling off the hounds: Technology and the visibility of plagiarism. *Pedagogy: Critical Approaches to Teaching Literature, Language, Composition, and Culture, 5*(2), 275-295.

Reilly, C. (2005). Teaching by example: A case for peer workshops about pedagogy and technology. *Innovate: Journal of Online Education, 1*(3).

Renard, L. (2000). Cut and paste 101: Plagiarism and the Net. *Educational Leadership, 57*(4), 38-42.

Scott, J. (2002). *Using technology wisely.* Retrieved July 7, 2004 from http://www.wmich.edu/imi/teaching/blooms-pyramid.html

Share, P. (2006). *Managing intertextuality: Meaning, plagiarism and power.* Paper presented at the 2nd International Plagiarism Conference 2006, Newcastle Gateshead, UK.

Slavin, R. E. (1989). Research on cooperative learning: An international perspective. *Scandinavian Journal of Educational Research, 33*(4), 231-243.

Sterngold, A. (2004). Confronting Plagiarism: How conventional teaching invites cybercheating. *Change, 36*(3), 16-21.

Thomas, D. A. (2004). How educators can more effectively understand and combat the plagiarism epidemic. *Brigham Young University Education & Law Journal,* (2), 421-430.

Vygotsky, L. (1978). *Mind and society: The development of higher mental processes.* Cambridge: Harvard University Press.

Vygotsky, L. (Ed.). (1987). *Thinking and speech: The collected work of L.S. Vygotsky.* New York: Plenum.

Weil, M., & Joyce, B. (1978). *Social models of teaching.* Englewood Cliffs: Prentice Hill.

Wood, D., & Gray, B. (1991). Toward a comprehensive theory of collaboration. *The Journal of Applied Behavioral Science, 27*(2), 139-162.

Wood, G. (2004). Academic original sin: Plagiarism, the Internet, and librarians. *Journal of Academic Librarianship, 30*(3), 237-242.

Section VI
Two Looks to the Future

Chapter XV
Substantial, Verbatim, Unattributed, Misleading:
Applying Criteria to Assess Textual Plagiarism

Wilfried Decoo
Brigham Young University, USA and University of Antwerp, Belgium

ABSTRACT

This chapter examines how to measure textual plagiarism more precisely, using as basis the four criteria of the American-based Office of Research Integrity's definition of plagiarism: to what extent is the reuse of someone else's text substantial, (nearly) verbatim, unattributed, and misleading? Each of these criteria is studied in its variables, leading to the proposal of a scale. Next, the implications for the verdict are discussed. This criterion-based approach does not claim to offer an easily workable solution in all cases, but at least stresses the need to achieve greater consensus and impartiality in assessing alleged plagiarism. Indeed, such cases are often handled very differently in terms of disclosure, assessment, and decision-making. For the sake of fairness, an allegation as serious as plagiarism requires the establishment and acceptance of more solid criteria.

INTRODUCTION

Dictionaries give closely resembling definitions of plagiarism, in essence the copying of someone else's words or ideas while pretending you are the author. By such definitions, some cases seem to require only a short assessment. A student who hands in a paper which has been copied verbatim from a published source, giving the impression it is his/her own work, is considered guilty of plagiarism. A student who fills major parts of a thesis with sentences written by someone else, without proper quotation marks and attribution, is prone to deserve the same label.

Nevertheless, even in such obvious cases, legal inventiveness may deny the charge of plagiarism. It suffices to add to the definition facets such as the element of monetary profit, the requirement that the copier explicitly claim that the work is his/her own, and/or proof of damage to the original author. If the accused did not make money from his/her work, if he/she did not overtly state that he/she created that particular text, or if the original author did not suffer, the verdict might be, not plagiarism, but the far more innocuous "failure to cite the source properly" or "inaccurate processing of information" or "improper delineation of citations." More than one case of alleged plagiarism has been defused that way, even in jurisdiction. It shows the complexity of defining plagiarism for assessment purposes. This chapter, however, is not about the way cases of alleged plagiarism have been or can be handled in judicial contexts (Dijkhuis, Heuves, Hofstede, Janssen, & Rorsch, 1997; Green, 2002; Kamvounias & Varnham, 2006; Saunders, 1993; Standler, 2000; Taubes, 1995).

Besides the obvious cases where extensive verbatim copying is involved, without any required personal input, there are also the more confusing and more numerous marginal situations that fall in a variety of gray areas. In such cases, the defense of the accused is predictable: there are "significant" differences in wording, the overlap is minimal, it is impossible to express a truism in completely original language, a word-processing glitch mixed up copied material with original, the document actually cites the source—perhaps not completely, correctly, or in the correct location—still, it is there, and so on. And, indeed, the convicting term *plagiarism* may have been used too quickly in view of the seriousness of such an allegation and the dramatic consequences it often entails, as cases in academia show (e.g. Bottum, 2004; Fox, 2004; Jansen, 1996; Kirkpatrick, 2002; Leatherman, 1999).

What should strike us as teachers and scholars as we thoughtfully consider various cases of al-

leged or proven plagiarism is the wide range of evaluations and subsequent verdicts. A trivial instance, if highly publicized, may destroy a student's career, while a case of extensive copying for a thesis may be kept quiet and end in tacit exoneration. A graduate student who plagiarizes a paper will, at one institution, gently be reprimanded in a private meeting with a professor, while the same offense at another institution will mean expulsion from the program. An author may be publicly exposed as a plagiarizer because two or three sentences are ambiguously referenced while, at the same time, an academic institution handles a "plagiarism" case behind closed doors even though the accused researcher has published under his own name a work that uses whole pages out of an article in another language that is hardly known in his field. The school, concerned about damage to its reputation, handles the matter within a small circle of insiders, with no publicity at all, and administers only a discreet verbal rebuke.

In our sometimes over-regulated society, it is surprising to see how much vagueness still prevails in the identification of student plagiarism once we take into account more variables. It is equally surprising to see Web services advertising to detect student plagiarism, but without offering advice or warnings on how to handle alleged findings. Moreover, those services usually work with massive databases of potential source texts, that is, student papers handed over by professors, often without the consent of their students, thus raising already for the professors themselves intellectual-property issues.

This chapter probes into criteria that can help us assess alleged plagiarism more consistently, especially once we leave the relatively simple case of verbatim copying of a full text or of large extracts without any citation of the source. I limit the discussion here to textual plagiarism, omitting such areas as the complex theft of ideas or methods, the plagiarism in music or visual arts, or software plagiarism, which belongs to the realms of "look and feel" controversies and of "software forensics." For the purposes of this discussion, I am also assuming that the sources of the alleged textual plagiarism have already been identified and analyzed. I have discussed elsewhere the detection and analysis of textual plagiarism (Decoo, 2002, pp. 42-51, 63-99).

THE ORI'S DEFINITION OF "PLAGIARISM"

As my basis for discussion, I quote the definition of the Office of Research Integrity (ORI) of the U.S. Department of Health and Human Services (1994):

As a general working definition, ORI considers plagiarism to include both the theft or misappropriation of intellectual property and the substantial unattributed textual copying of another's work ... Substantial unattributed textual copying of another's work means the unattributed verbatim or nearly verbatim copying of sentences and paragraphs which materially mislead the ordinary reader regarding the contributions of the author. ORI generally does not pursue the limited use of identical or nearly-identical phrases which describe a commonly-used methodology or previous research because ORI does not consider such use as substantially misleading to the reader or of great significance.

This definition, the result of several years of experience with controversial cases and intensive professional examination, provides us, for the aspect of textual plagiarism, with essential terms: "substantial," "verbatim" and "nearly verbatim," "unattributed" and "materially mislead the ordinary reader." Each of these terms forms the basis for our subsequent discussion in an effort to clarify their range and specify their variables. Thus, four criteria stand out—substantial, verbatim, unattributed, misleading—which could lead to a scale. It is remarkable that nearly all definitions of

plagiarism in dictionaries and honor codes follow the same basic terms—copying someone else's work and then passing it off as one's own—without further nuances as to quantity, degree of textual similarity and effect on the reader.

Substantial

The ORI states that only "substantial" copying warrants a conclusion of plagiarism. This characteristic is clearly meant to rule out minor, trivial, or accidental cases. But when is the amount of copied sentences "substantial" enough? Opinions will differ greatly from the standpoint of the accuser or from the defendant. Some persons start whistle-blowing at the level of a few sentences, while for others, the minimum threshold is one or two paragraphs. Though there is no way one can justify or allow any such copying, "plagiarism" is a serious allegation. In the world of writing, it may have a comparable gravity as felonious burglary in the legal realm. However, a one-time shoplifting of a package of chewing gum is not the same as breaking and entering into a private residence and removing stocks and bonds from a wall safe. Both are forms of theft, but the strength of our judicial system is that it can differentiate between minor offenses and crimes. Precisely that proportionality forms the basis of our sense of justice. This comparison with the legal realm does not imply that plagiarism belongs by definition to the realm of jurisprudence. Still, cases of alleged plagiarism deserve a similar differentiation from triviality to seriousness.

A Lexical Quandary

The problem with plagiarism, however, is that we do not have a range of terms to differentiate between levels of improper copying. In the legal world of theft, the lexical array is extensive, not only for the form—shoplifting, pickpocketing, purse-snatching, mugging, burglary, robbery, fraud, scam, racket, extortion, embezzlement, looting, pillage, and so on—but also for the legal weight as expressed in degrees of larceny, for example, in the U.S., from a Class C misdemeanor to a Class B felony, depending on the amount of stolen property involved.

Part of the uneasiness caused by cases of alleged plagiarism thus stems from our lexical poverty. Any copying, whether one sentence or a whole book, is commonly called "plagiarism." Nor is it helpful to differentiate between "minor plagiarism" and "substantial plagiarism," for only "substantial" plagiarism is plagiarism if we take the ORI's definition as our starting point. Moreover, "minor" also includes various degrees. There is a need for more terms to identify such shades. Though I suggest a few words in this chapter, like sentence-lifting and phrase-mugging, my purpose is not to define them with mathematical precision, but to launch some lighter terms than the often inappropriate "plagiarism" and to initiate further discussion on the lexical quandary.

How Do We Count?

To establish a somewhat measurable criterion as a starting point, I have suggested elsewhere a minimum average of one sentence per page (Decoo, 2002, p.129). This is not meant as a mathematical cutoff point, but as an incentive to first search for more occurrences after the first copied sentences have been discovered. The sheer requirement of establishing a numerical rate of occurrence will curb the tendency to use the word "plagiarism" precipitately. Whatever the amount an investigator next discovers, those numbers need to be nuanced and refined according to other criteria discussed below. However, if the author is meeting or exceeding this average of one sentence per page, we safely can say that we are dealing with an ingrained attitude of disrespectful usage of source material.

Two nuances immediately can be added. First, the quantification through sentences and pages is a raw one. A more precise quantification would require us to work with the number of words in obviously reused strings. If this figure is easily possible to establish, for example, through computerized routines, all the better. In such cases, it would be helpful to stipulate comparable proportions, for example, a minimum of 4 or 5 percent of the text. By using automated devices, one can even go further in the establishment of precise mathematical ratios of overlap. I refer to the work of my colleague Jozef Colpaert on string-matching algorithms in the program Cerberus (described in Decoo, 2002, pp. 207-234). But even such accurate quantitative results should be only a provisional indicator, not the basis for a stringent separator between plagiarism and nonplagiarism.

Second, determining the "average" for a whole text makes the most sense if the copied sentences are fairly equally dispersed as single items throughout the whole text. In the case of the copying of a lengthy passage, preceded and followed by "clean" pages, the matter may have to be assessed differently. If, for example, 10 sentences in a row have been copied, and the whole paper is 20 pages long, the conspicuous concentration of those 10 sentences would make it necessary to count those sentences in relation to that one page where they appear, thus leading to a "substantial" finding. If measured against the whole text, those 10 sentences would account for only half a sentence per page, whereby the infraction could be considered minor. The numerical criterion of "a minimum average of one sentence per page" thus needs corrective considerations in view of particular circumstances. If in a 200-page dissertation, a passage of 199 sentences appears to have been copied verbatim without attribution, it is obvious that such an infraction could not be minimized simply because it is less than an average of one sentence per page. In that case the entity to be considered can be the chapter or section and the average of copied sentences is counted from there.

One senses the ambiguities to be faced in marginal cases, but, again, this counting is only part of the preparatory process obliging us to investigate quantity, while formal assessment must occur at a later stage when all variables have been considered.

A practical hint for counting sentences: Microsoft Word contains the feature "Show readability statistics," as part of the options of "Spelling and grammar." Running this feature displays the number of sentences in a text.

How to Weigh Small Amounts Against Motives and Circumstances?

As mentioned above, I am not out to justify unsubstantial copying, but it is important to have some basis for determining whether such copying can be attributed to accident, ignorance, special circumstances, or malice. A look at various profiles, in which cases only a few copied sentences are involved, will illustrate this. In order to do this, I need to expand the topic beyond student plagiarism only, and include other academic levels.

Is the writer a prolific professional of generally good reputation, writing under some or all of the following conditions? (1) Was he/she experiencing deadline pressures from his/her publisher? (2) Did he/she employ a secretary, research assistant, or pre-publication editor? (3) Was this work produced under circumstances that differed in significant ways from the author's usual mode of proceeding? (4) Does a spot-check of other works reveal a similar pattern? The purpose of asking and answering such questions is that even an excellent and conscientious researcher and writer can make an occasional error of transcription when dealing with complex sources, miss a reference, or omit quotation marks. Even if the error comes from a secretary or assistant, the author is, of course, responsible and does him/herself credit if he/she does not attempt to shift the blame.

Is the writer a fairly young researcher with a still low publication record who, under pressure to publish but swamped by a teaching workload, turns in a proposed article of 20 pages contain-

ing a small number of copied sentences scattered over the text? Some questions here are: (1) What penalties might the researcher accrue by failing to produce the article, for example a promotion/tenure decision; an editor exasperated by missed deadlines for a special issue; the potential of a research grant being cancelled or not renewed? (2) Does the topic deal with a significantly different subject than the researcher's earlier work? (In other words, is he/she writing outside his area of expertise?) (3) Was the researcher experiencing personal/professional problems that made it unlikely that he/she would do his/her best work? (4) Does his/her academic and professional training make it clear that he/she knows that such copying violates the ethical norms of the profession? (5) Does a spot-check of other works reveal a similar pattern? In other words, are there extenuating circumstances?

Is the writer a student submitting the paper for a class, with less than one copied sentence per page? This situation is, in some ways, the easiest of all to deal with since it can usually be handled according to already established norms in the department or college, and the writer is young enough to quickly learn a better way of behaving. It is crucial that the behavior be confronted and corrected, however, since it signals a cheating attitude that cannot be tolerated for the sake of the individual, the academic discipline, and the institution.

Obviously other cases can add other complexities, but these examples show a range of offenses that are comparatively minor and comparatively easy to correct without requiring publicity or severe punishment. The accidental sentence-lifting of the established author, the malicious but probably not yet habitual sentence-lifting of the young, pressured researcher, and the probably ignorant (or at least experimental) sentence-lifting of the student all fall within the realm of what we could call "painful learning experiences." The author will certainly self-correct his/her working methods in the future, the researcher and the student will decide that the disadvantages heavily outweigh the benefits, and the professional fields or institutions to which they belong will not suffer since these lapses occur within boundaries that can be identified and tolerated, as long as the corrections are, in fact, made.

Although I have positioned the discussion of motive and circumstances as part of the context that must be considered, a comparison with jurisprudence teaches us the following: while motive and circumstances can be considered in determining the sentence, they are never an excuse or justification for breaking rules. The same applies to the ethical realm of plagiarism.

The bottom line, however, is that *substantial* copying leaves little doubt as to the malicious motive of such an action. In that sense ORI's definition provides a boundary shielding less guilty persons from an ordeal.

What If No (Complete) Source Can Be Found?

As mentioned before, all the preceding assumes that the sources of the alleged textual plagiarism already have been identified and analyzed. A particular problem in counting copied sentences arises when it is virtually impossible to screen a complete text, such as a thesis or dissertation, and to identify the potential sources behind every sentence. Unless we deal with a verbatim copy of a (nearly) complete text (such as may occur in student papers), the detection of possible plagiarism usually starts with the fortuitous discovery of a single copied sentence or small paragraph. Suspicion arises and detection procedures, either manual or electronic, are put to work to discover more. But a deliberate and clever plagiarist will have obfuscated his/her sources by an astute selection of sources, by lingual alterations, and by mixing various sources. It usually is not possible to identify 100 percent of the sources a clever plagiarist has used; furthermore, disentangling

intricate textual assemblages will require much more effort than the plagiarist used in making them. Therefore, even if common sense tells us that a certain text "must" have been copied from somewhere (as when a weak student suddenly hands in a perfect essay), we must accept as a standard of proof that no plagiarism exists if the source has not been identified. We may hope with some confidence, however, that the development of stronger automated detection techniques and the growing databases of potential source material will enable quicker and more effective identifications, simultaneously deterring plagiarizers.

Can Unintentional Plagiarism Exist?

The question of "how much" is crucial in dealing with the oft-used defense that the plagiarism is accidental or unintentional because of the genuine possibility of some error in word processing, the mixing of data gathered long ago with one's personal notes, confusion in typesetting after proofreading, and so on. Such an explanation can be perfectly true; however, by ORI's inclusion of "substantial" in the definition, "unintentional plagiarism" is a contradiction in terms. If a person walks out of a shop with an overlooked and unpaid-for item still in his shopping cart, this is not "unintentional shoplifting." It's simply a mistake. But if he walks out with 10 unpurchased items, or repeatedly with one unpurchased item, it is not accidental. Similarly, a writer cannot credibly continue to claim inadvertence for a series of unattributed copied parts. No writer, not even an untrained amateur, could copy 10 sentences unwittingly. The same principle applies to the sometimes-used defense that the writer read the copied sentences long ago and internalized them, forgetting their source. Although this phenomenon of reuse does happen, it never produces several sentences or whole paragraphs in the same pattern as the original. See the discussion of cryptomnesia in Brown & Halliday, 1991; Brown &

Murphy, 1989; Marsh & Bower, 1993; Marsh & Landau, 1995; Tenpenny, Keriazakos, Lew, & Phelan, 1998.

In sum, the need to quantify the amount of material that can clearly be identified as copied is crucially important to determining whether a case actually qualifies as plagiarism. Yet even when the average falls below a minimum criterion, the question of the significance and gravity of the copying must be considered. We now turn to those considerations.

Verbatim, Nearly Verbatim

A writer, whether student or not, defending him/herself against an accusation of plagiarism nearly always points to differences in wording. This opens a large area of potential controversy. What are the boundaries between "verbatim reproduction," "nearly verbatim imitation," and "non-verbatim alteration?" How do we define paraphrasing in this realm and when does that become allowed?

The starting point "verbatim" poses no problem for assessment if the reuse of text is also substantial, because such evidence is decisive. "Nearly verbatim" falls under the ORI's definition of plagiarism, meaning we can apply the same criteria and variables as for verbatim copying. We can understand "nearly verbatim" as a minimal change in wording whereby the origin of the source still seems undisputable. Such "nearly verbatim" material will be especially visible if the suspect sentence is part of a larger sequence drawing from the same source.

However, it is important to quantify, as much as possible, a "minimal change." What criteria will differentiate between the levels of copying that move from "nearly verbatim" to "non-verbatim alteration?" Moreover, at what point do such alterations become permissible in the light of other criteria, such as originality?

How Much is Altered?

Language, as a malleable and stochastic mechanism, lends itself admirably to manipulation. The first and easiest technique is the replacement by synonyms. For example, if I apply this very principle to a sentence illustrating a form of this technique, the result could be similar to what is illustrated in Box 1.

From the point of view of language, the altered sentence is not "nearly verbatim." But from the point of view of idea, it is the direct transposition of the original. If the source is cited, such altered sentences would be considered allowable "paraphrasing." This situation usually occurs in indirect speech. If the sentence on the left were written by Johnson, the paraphrase would become "Johnson has explained that by applying the glossary function…" However, if I do not cite Johnson and pretend the sentence is my own, did I cross the line of acceptability? Indeed, would I say in my defense, it is not "nearly verbatim?"

Next to synonyms, a whole range of syntactic permutations allows changes in word order, thus further obscuring the origin. Participial phrases can become independent ones, subordinate clauses can be changed into gerund phrases, the subject

Box 1. Example of alterations

By using the thesaurus-key in word-processing, anyone can now quickly change all the significant words in a sentence to produce a different one, which moreover dodges the detection routines of traditional search engines.	By applying the glossary function in text processing, any person can now promptly modify every single notable term in a phrase to construct a dissimilar one, which additionally avoids the recognition procedures of conventional search routines.

and predicate of linking verbs can be swapped, passive constructions can be converted into active ones, long sentences can be split, short sentences can be combined, and so on. In fact a grammar checker will suggest a number of these transformations and the user has only to confirm them to have them implemented. In the extensive analysis of a dissertation I have given numerous examples of linguistic manipulation techniques in the context of plagiarism (Decoo, 2002, pp. 71-84). See also Clough, n.d.; Damashek, 1995; Helfman, 1993; and Roig, 2001.

These linguistic considerations make the concept of "nearly verbatim" slippery. It is impossible to establish a quantitative threshold—for instance, that a maximum of 10 percent change in a copied sentence would keep it in the range of "nearly verbatim" while additional changes would place it beyond that boundary and make it therefore acceptable. The spirit of ORI's statement, which includes "nearly verbatim" as plagiarism, points rather to a "still obvious" degree of unacceptability in reusing material. If a whole page follows the original data and content development from a certain source, without attribution, even if most of the language has been altered, it should probably be considered as plagiarized. In fact, we then enter the realm of the first part of ORI's definition of plagiarism, which is the "theft or misappropriation of intellectual property." An obvious example would be translating material that appeared first in another language. Much plagiarism, indeed, occurs as translation. Literal translation would be verbatim, while less literal translation would be nearly verbatim. But since good translation is never literal and may depart significantly from the original, even the criterion "nearly verbatim" would not apply. Still, if the use of the source is substantial, it would be considered plagiarism.

But what if such altered sentences or parts of sentences appear only occasionally in a text without proper citation? Also here we may be in need to create an appropriate term. Perhaps *phrase-mugging?* It would emphasize the dubious nature of the operation, whereas *paraphrasing* can be perfectly justified if accompanied by a proper citation.

The matter of the alteration of sentences also raises pedagogical questions as to how students are taught how to avoid plagiarism. Instructions such as "read the passage and then express it in your own words" may encourage forms of paraphrasing that are still forms of plagiarism, because students may think that it is not intellectual theft to express someone's concept without attribution as long as the packaging words are different. A profitable study would be a comparison of antiplagiarism warnings given to students—many found on the Web sites of educational institutions—with the intention of identifying the ambiguities students face and of clarifying the guidelines.

How Original is the Copied Expression?

An important variable affecting the seriousness of the copying, both in verbatim or nearly verbatim forms, is the commonality or originality of the copied expression. The ORI's definition excludes from plagiarism "the limited use of identical or nearly identical phrases which describe a commonly used methodology or previous research." This criterion could be broadened to include what we may call "common knowledge." Examples would be biographies of celebrities, important historical events, basic descriptions of famous inventions, and so on—information on which can be found in numerous locations. It is a common and valid defense that there are only a limited number of ways for conveying some types of specific information—for example: "George Washington was born into a Virginia farming family in 1732" or "John F. Kennedy was assassinated in Dallas in November 1963." Although what makes up "common knowledge" and whether a particular use is "reasonable" both are subjective criteria, expertise in a particular field develops an awareness of what constitutes both categories.

But even in common knowledge, the style may be distinctive and personal, using a rich lexis and style (metaphor, simile, colloquial expression, classical or poetic allusion, folk comparison, etc.). Copying the same unique combination of imaginative words and structures without attribution should be considered unacceptable. Indeed, the birth of George Washington, common knowledge, also could be expressed: "How could Benjamin Franklin have known, while at work on his newspaper in 1732, that in a Virginia farming family a boy was born who was one day to become the first president of the United States?"

The same weight in offense should be attributed to the appropriation, even in the most altered form, of a sentence containing unique and original information which is the result of personal efforts, through creation, discovery, or analysis.

The assessment of the level of originality of a copied sentence, both in terms of content and of style, needs additional study, for often we do not deal with a clear-cut contrast, but with a range taking us from common knowledge to more unique information, and from flat sentences to more stylish creations. Moreover, it may well be that for certain audiences some metaphors are so well known that their use does not require attribution. Further research and experience should refine the criteria to differentiate between those shades.

What is the Level of the Student's Own Originality in the Problematic Document?

Does the student's work containing copied sentences contribute something new and valuable of its own? If so, this of course does not justify the lack of proper quotation or citation for the copied parts, but it gives at least a raison d'être for the paper, thesis, or dissertation. Proper assessment would require gauging the value of the author's original contribution compared to what he/she improperly copied. If that personal contribution is still overwhelming and the copied part quite small, we should concede that such situation is much less serious than a reverse situation where nearly everything is improperly used and nothing original is contributed.

For example, a lack of any personal contribution may be rather common in student papers, research reports, masters' theses and even doctoral dissertations when such work does nothing more than reproduce what others have said. This lack of originality is not inherently wrong (it may even be valuable as in extended literature searches for a status quaestionis), unless it is undermined by faltering quotation and citation.

Unattributed

This criterion seems obvious: Either the text contains a reference to the source or it does not. However, the reality is that many plagiarism cases grow out of ambiguities in handling references. Indeed, a common defense against an accusation of plagiarism is that the author has indeed cited the source but it does not appear directly attached to the disputed sentences or passages. If the copying is substantial, this defense usually is not a successful one, since the literature on plagiarism leaves no doubt that this procedure is not acceptable: "A plagiarist might paraphrase from a source for three paragraphs before or after a direct quotation properly attributed, giving the impression that all but the quotation itself is original material" (Watkins, 1994; p. 26). Equally, the American Historical Association (1986, amended 2002) condemns the "reference to a borrowed work in an early note and then extensive further use without attribution." In both cases, Watkins and AHA assume that the intent is to deceive the reader into thinking that the author has created original material when he/she in fact has not.

I have called this phenomenon extended pre-use (extensive material already used before the reference appears) and extended post-use (extensive material used after the reference appears) (Decoo, 2002, pp. 84-88, 133-134).

How Clearly are the Boundaries Delineated?

If the disputed passage contains an embedded sentence or sentences in which quotation marks are properly used, it is easy to demonstrate the deceit of the additionally copied material, as the author him/herself has indicated where correct usage begins and stops (although it certainly was not his/her intention that the copying would be uncovered).

In cases where source material is copied, in altered forms, without quotation marks, but is still accompanied by a reference, the matter becomes controversial. Plagiarizers (or, in unsubstantial cases, phrase-muggers) prefer to use this system for it allows them more latitude in claiming that they have in fact cited the reference, should the disputed document be compared to the source. Indeed, if the reference comes at the end of a paragraph, how much of the preceding material is covered by that reference? Only the last sentence would be the normal standard. But the accused will claim that the nature of the text, because it belongs to one concept, makes it clear that also a preceding sentence, or even more, "obviously" is included.

Conversely, if an attribution ("As Johnson points out ...") is given at the beginning, normally only that sentence is covered by the citation. The plagiarizer or phrase-mugger will argue differently on the basis of the nature of the text. However, standard procedure requires that the writer understands how to gracefully cite the name of the original author repeatedly in connection with indirect speech and paraphrases: "Johnson (1996) has shown that ... In the same article she also mentions that ... Her conclusion is that ..." However, when these "reference repeaters" are lacking, the reader will almost certainly assume that only the sentence tied to the reference is Johnson's.

The confusion may become even greater when various references are given at the end of a long paragraph and the reader is left to guess what belongs to the author and what to the cited sources, since it is obvious that these various references apply to more than the last sentence of the paragraph. This consideration is, of course, not valid in cases of a status quaestionis at the beginning of a text where compact sentences summarize previous research, each followed by its appropriate references. Also, when a sentence refers to a specific topic or field of study that various people have contributed to, it is appropriate to add the references to various names.

Finally, the criterion of substantiality, the first ORI-criterion, will be combined with the problem of attribution: what is the amount of such ambiguous occurrences within the whole text? A rare occurrence of extended pre-use and post-use should be considered an accident or "some phrase-mugging," while a recurrent use of the system reveals a pattern of willful deceit.

Misleading the Ordinary Reader

The ORI clearly considers this criterion a relevant one: Does the sentence "materially mislead the ordinary reader regarding the contributions of the author?" The question is also valuable when students accused of plagiarism claim that the origin of copied sentences is perfectly clear to the experts and specialists familiar with the topic—hence, that there is no need to clutter the texts with extra references.

While few plagiarism cases have actually assembled a group of ordinary readers and polled their reactions to the document under discussion, it could be done in highly controversial cases; and this question has the merit of cutting through wrangling about whether a sentence has been correctly attributed to evaluating the effect of the attribution—whatever its form.

Who is an "ordinary reader?" It seems equitable to identify such a person as a native speaker of the language, possessed of sufficient education to read the passage fluently (including access to a dictionary for unfamiliar terms) but without special expertise in the subject. If the topic is written with a high degree of professional jargon or requires an unusually high level of literacy skills, then the "ordinary reader" for that particular document would clearly be another expert or a highly educated reader. In cases of suspected student plagiarism, the professor could submit the text to one or more colleagues of another department or faculty.

However, even in these two situations, it would be important in applying the "ordinary reader" test to identify readers who are not extremely qualified in the topic and/or well acquainted with the writings of the cited authors. Over-qualified readers would judge from foreknowledge. It goes without saying that the selected readers should not be acquainted with the controversy or know the disputants personally. It should be possible for a referee or adjudicating body to empanel such a body, in consultation and mutual agreement with the disputants on the profile of the "ordinary reader;" perhaps following the model of jury empanelling, each could select a given number of readers who correspond to that profile, with the approval of the adjudicator.

The test itself would require those readers to study the disputed pages and indicate which sentences, in their opinion, belong to the student and which are quoted or cited. Their indications, identified with a color or underlining, are next compared to the controversial sentences. Have the ordinary readers been misled as to the origin of these sentences? The test would be quick and the results easy to tabulate.

It is true that such a procedure takes some time and energy but, again, the seriousness of an allegation of plagiarism requires such action if the controversy is ever be put to rest.

TOWARDS A SVUM-SCALE?

SVUM stands for the first letters of the criteria I just discussed and which are based on ORI's definition: substantial, verbatim, unattributed, misleading. In spite of the complexity of the variables which in most cases require a measure of interpretation, it would help assessors to refer to some kind of quantifiable scale based on those criteria. While it will probably never be possible to identify the exact threshold where plagiarism begins, a more detailed protocol which obliges evaluators to collect data systematically and appraise factors according to at least partially objective criteria would avoid overreactions and premature judgments.

Based on the definitions and information-gathering procedures I have suggested up to this point, I would make the following recommendations for criteria that must be met in order to render a more reliable judgment that the accused has committed plagiarism—in case the matter is not immediately obvious in view of the massive amount copied without any attribution:

1. Make a preparatory quantification of the questionable occurrences. This includes all sentences of verbatim or nearly verbatim copying that do not have quotation marks and attribution. This count also includes slightly or moderately altered sentences (synonym substitutions, passive/active verb swaps, etc.). Heavily altered sentences should be counted if they are part of a somewhat larger context which has unmistakably been taken from source material, for example, following a developmental or conceptual sequence that replicates the original. We would also count sentences that are ambiguously attributed in extended pre- and post-use. Sentences that can reasonably be attributed to common knowledge are not taken into account. However, if such common knowledge sentences are part of the verbatim reuse of whole paragraphs, they should be counted.
    This step may be cumbersome and time-consuming in case of longer texts, like a thesis or dissertation, but the quality of the

results depends on the quality of the work done at this stage. Advanced computer-assisted language processing should greatly facilitate this step, even in comparing heavily altered texts.

2. Appraise the quantity, either as an average over the total text in case of dispersed sentences, or as an average over fewer pages in case of longer passages. If electronic screening is available, this result may be rendered as a word-count percentage or as an overlap ratio.

3. Determine whether the level of copying is mainly "verbatim," "nearly verbatim," or "altered," with special attention to a deliberate pattern of deception in the case of alterations.

4. Factor in the level of originality or stylistic distinctiveness in the disputed document compared to the source.

5. Examine occurrences of nonattribution, with special attention to problems of extended pre-use and extended post-use.

6. Test whether the "ordinary reader" is likely to be misled about the authorship of disputed passages.

The application of such a scale is fully dependent on the quality of preceding steps:

- The detection of the source material, which can be cumbersome but should in time profit more and more from advanced computer-assisted language processing in comparing even heavily altered texts.
- The analysis and assessment of all suspect sentences in order to identify, as well as possible, their respective belonging to the various categories discussed above.

The result of such an analysis can lead to this kind of summarized representation, next to a detailed overview of findings as shown in Tables 1 through 3.

Table 1.

The teacher's assignment required a personal analysis of the song "Le p'tit bonheur" by Félix Leclerc. All students had been informed of the university Plagiarism Guidelines. This case reveals:	
Substantial?	83 percent of all the sentences in this paper of 2,124 words were identified as taken from Bégin, Denis. (1993). *Comprendre la chanson québécoise*. Rimouski: Université du Québec à Rimouski, pp. 68-75. No citation, no quotation in the text of the paper.
Verbatim?	Nearly all sentences have undergone slight alterations, more in the first part, less to nothing in the last past. The sequence of sentences and paragraphs is nearly identical to the source, including subtitles. The alterations reveal a deliberate pattern.
Unattributed?	The source is mentioned in the references at the end, between other references. In the paper itself it is not mentioned.
Misleading?	Yes

Table 2.

Chapter 2 of this master's thesis (representing 23 percent of the thesis) on an experiment with multimedia courseware for Japanese describes the history of computer-assisted language learning. The student had signed the honor code for graduate studies, including the rules on plagiarism.	
Substantial?	78 percent of all sentences in this chapter of 4,047 words were identified as taken from Cook, V. J. (1985). Bridging the gap between computers and language teaching. *Computers in English Language Teaching.* ELT Documents 122. Oxford: Oxford University Press, pp. 13-24, and from Wikipedia's article on computer-assisted language learning: http://en.wikipedia.org/wiki/Computer-assisted_language_learning. The rest of the thesis, including the central chapters which describe the experiment and the results, seems genuine.
Verbatim?	82 percent of the sentences in chapter 2 have been copied verbatim. It is telling that the first sentence of a paragraph was nearly always modified.
Unattributed?	Yes. The sources are also not mentioned in the bibliography.
Misleading?	Relative. The material covers historical facts, from 1960 till 2000, without analysis nor interpretation. As such the material is an enumeration of facts, which the student had to find in sources.

Table 3.

The assignment for this essay was: "Reflect on the variables that determine personality and beliefs," based on a number of classroom readings. Rules for quotation and citation had been explained.	
Substantial?	Complex to determine, because of heavily altered sentences, still clearly based on Furnham, Johnson, & Rawles, (1985). The determinants of beliefs in human nature. *Personality and Individual Differences, 6*(6), 675-684. If all sentences are counted, it amounts to 23 percent of the essay of 3,576 words.
Verbatim?	No
Unattributed?	This is a case of frequent extended post-use. The student cites a sentence from Furnham a.o., but continues to borrow from this source in altered sentences.
Misleading?	Yes

THE VERDICT

Who is to Judge?

Anyone accused of plagiarism has the right to a fair evaluation, preceded by careful investigation. Too often, the only judgment is that rendered by quick impressions. Teachers who dislike a student for whatever reason are seldom in a position to assess objectively what they discover and pronounce judgment. Similarly, such decisions cannot be left to institutional representatives when they are more motivated by concern about the institution's reputation or by pressures from the protagonists (think of children of generous donors or influential figures) than by concerns for procedural fairness or upholding the standards of the profession.

Perhaps we should consider the need for a system in which someone who discovers (or thinks he/she discovers) plagiarism is obliged to refer his/her findings discreetly to an official body, without having it trumpeted to colleagues or other insiders. This official body could be a local or regional "Office of Plagiarism Allegations" which can conduct the investigation according to established protocols. In the academic world, allegations of plagiarism could be referred to independent and permanent commissions well-versed in the subject, who can act consistently with precedents established in previous cases. At UC Davis, the faculty in the English writing program is required to refer each suspected case of plagiarism to the Student Judicial Affairs (SJA) for adjudication, and is specifically instructed not to accuse the student of plagiarism. The case is handled by a SJA-officer (Plagiarism Guidelines, n.d.).

If the own accused writer's institution is not the best place for such commissions, inter-school, regional, or national organizations of each discipline or sub-discipline might take more direct responsibility in the matter by instituting their own "Commission for Plagiarism Allegations."

Each case of alleged plagiarism also includes human variables that need to be taken into account when interpreting figures. In courts, juries give heed to elements such as motives, whether the offense is a first occurrence or recurrence, influencing backgrounds, and extenuating or aggravating circumstances. Similar considerations play their role in the ethical realm of plagiarism. In her classic novel, *The Small Room,* May Sarton describes how Lucy Winter, a novice English teacher, has to confront a case of plagiarism and is torn between being just and being caring. Even with a precise, detailed overview of many plagiarized sentences in a student's work, the persons to judge can take into account external factors and the broader context (see also Noddings, 1991).

What Kind of Verdict can be Given?

Unlike most categories of offenses in the legal sphere, procedures for evaluating and punishing plagiarism are murky and unevenly applied. More homogeneous assessment of alleged plagiarism, with due regard to the variants in seriousness, is needed. The lack of proper terms to differentiate between degrees of plagiarism leads to situations where defendants understand a welcome verdict of "no plagiarism" as total exoneration, while their work may still present unacceptable flaws. The whistle-blowers who have drawn attention to what they perceived as plagiarism, are thus put in the wrong. They will carry the stigma of "false accuser" and even suffer retaliation. The fact is, however, that exoneration of plagiarism

seldom means complete innocence. Though I have, more wittily, suggested terms such as sentence-lifting and phrase-mugging, we need researched proposals to make different verdicts related to plagiarism allegations, just as in the legal sphere theft ranges from a Class C misdemeanor to a Class B felony.

One of the most devastating feelings of convicted "plagiarizers" is the realization that similar or much worse cases have ended in exoneration or token punishments. They sometimes feel they have been sacrificed because their case became public or because they were singled out by someone eager to contribute to their downfall. Even if they are correct in identifying differential treatment, it can never be a justification for their own wrongdoings; still, it is unjust for similar cases to receive different treatment. It is the duty of literary, academic, and scientific institutions to come to a consensus about consistent and coherent policies governing such cases, and then apply them evenhandedly.

How do We Keep Track of Verdicts?

From my experience at several universities, cases of alleged student plagiarism are treated on a one-to-one basis, without a central service to document the handling and the verdict. If we want fairness and coherence to prevail, universities need to streamline the reporting of such cases and archive the results in appropriate ways for confidential access. Such an archive also is a source for comparative approaches: how have various cases been handled, which precedents have been set, what verdicts were applied? The existence of such an archive would also be proof of the seriousness with which an institution handles cases. And just like in the judicial system, terms can be set when dossiers need to be discarded. Even a proven case of student plagiarism should not remain indefinitely in the system.

CONCLUSION

All of the preceding, especially the application of the SVUM-scale, may lead one to conclude that assessing plagiarism is always a cumbersome, nearly impossible task. I remind the reader that the more difficult work only starts when we leave the simple cases of verbatim copying of a full text or of large extracts without any citation of the source. Many instances of student plagiarism fall in the simple categories where identification and quantification can be swift, and the reporting on a SVUM-scale would take less than half an hour. But even in those cases, the next steps of referring the final evaluation to a proper entity, weighing the circumstances, and rendering the verdict, deserve the outmost care.

In order not to be misunderstood, I wish to stress again that limited copying, even of one sentence in a whole text, is never an insignificant matter. If done deliberately, taking the chance that no one will ever notice, it reveals duplicity and an unethical disregard for intellectual property. Our standards should not erode to the point where we would consider petty shoplifting inconsequential.

This chapter essentially is about consensus and fairness. I hope it will contribute to a dialogue leading to better institutional responses and clarified standards. In the words of C. Park (2003), there is a growing need "to develop cohesive frameworks for dealing with student plagiarism that are based on prevention supported by robust detection and penalty systems that are transparent and applied consistently" (pp. 483-484).

REFERENCES

American Historical Association. (1986). *Statement on plagiarism and related misuses of the work of other authors*. Section of *Statement on standards of professional conduct*. Amended January 2002.

Bottum, J. (2004). Laurence Tribe and the problem of borrowed scholarship. *The Weekly Standard, 10*(4).

Brown, A. S., & Halliday, H. E. (1991). Cryptomnesia and source memory difficulties. *American Journal of Psychology, 104*(4), 475-490.

Brown, A. S., & Murphy, D. R. (1989). Cryptomnesia: Delineating inadvertent plagiarism. *Journal of Experimental Psychology: Learning, Memory and Cognition, 15*(3), 432-442.

Clough, P. D. (n.d.). *Measuring Text Reuse in a Journalistic Domain*.Unpublished manuscript, Department of Computer Science, University of Sheffield. Retrieved on January 16, 2007 from http://ir.shef.ac.uk/cloughie/papers/cluk4.pdf

Damashek, M. (1995). Gauging similarity with ngrams: Language independent categorization of text. *Science, 267*(February 10), 843-848.

Decoo, W. (2002). *Crisis on campus: Confronting academic misconduct*. Cambridge, Massachusetts: The MIT Press.

Dijkhuis, J., Heuves, W., Hofstede, M., Janssen, M., & Rorsch, A. (1997). *Leiden in last: de zaak-Diekstra nader bekeken* [Dutch. English transl.: *Big troubles in Leiden: A closer look at the case of Diekstra*]. Rijswijk, Netherlands: Elmar.

Fox, R. W. (2004). A heartbreaking problem of staggering proportions. *The Journal of American History, 90*(4), 1341-1346.

Green, S. P. (2002). Plagiarism, norms, and the limits of theft law: Some observations on the use of criminal sanctions in enforcing intellectual property rights. *Hastings Law Journal, 54*(1), 167-242.

Helfman, J. (1993). Dotplot: a program for exploring self-similarity in millions of lines of text and code. *Journal of Computational and Graphical Statistics, 2*(2), 153-174.

Jansen, K. (1996). Grensverleggende stijlen van citeren in ontwikkelingsstudies [Dutch. English transl.: Changing the boundaries in quotation styles in development studies]. *Facta 4*(5), 2-8.

Kamvounias, P., & Varnham, S. (2006). In-house or in court? Legal challenges to university decisions. *Education and the Law, 18*(1), 1-17.

Kirkpatrick, D. D. (2002). As historian's fame grows, so does attention to sources. *The New York Times* (January 11). Retrieved October 5, 2006 from http://www.nytimes.com/2002/01/11/national/11AMBR.html

Leatherman, C. (1999). At Texas A&M, Conflicting charges of misconduct tear a program apart. *Chronicle of Higher Education, 5*(November), A18.

Marsh, R. L., & Bower, G. H. (1993). Eliciting cryptomnesia: Unconscious plagiarism in a puzzle task. *Journal of Experimental Psychology: Learning, Memory, and Cognition, 19*(3), 673-688.

Marsh, R. L., & Landau, J. D. (1995). Item availability in cryptomnesia: Assessing its role in two paradigms of unconscious plagiarism, *Journal of Experimental Psychology: Learning, Memory, and Cognition, 21*(6), 1568–1583.

Noddings, N. (1991). The teacher as judge: A brief sketch of two fairness principles. In David Ericson (Ed.), *Philosophy of Education 1990* (pp. 350-359). Normal, Illinois: Philosophy of Education Society.

Office of Research Integrity. (1994). ORI provides working definition of plagiarism. *ORI Newsletter, 3*(1).

Park, C. (2003). In other (People's) words: plagiarism by university students—literature and lessons. *Assessment and Evaluation in Higher Education, 28*(5), 471-488.

Plagiarism guidelines: Brochure for university writing program faculty. (n.d.). Retrieved February 22, 2007 from http://writingprogram.ucdavis.edu/docs/plagiarism.htm

Roig, M. (2001). Plagiarism and paraphrasing criteria of college and university professors. *Ethics and Behaviour, 11*(3), 307-324.

Sarton, M. (1962). *The small room.* New York: Norton.

Saunders, E. J. (1993). Confronting academic dishonesty. *Journal of Social Work Education, 29*(2), 224–230.

Standler, R. B. (2000). *Plagiarism in colleges in USA.* Retrieved February 25, 2007 from http://www.rbs2.com/plag.htm

Taubes, G. (1995). Plagiarism suit wins; experts hope it won't set a trend. *Science, 268*(May 26), 1125.

Tenpenny, P. L., Keriazakos, M. S., Lew, G. S., & Phelan, T. P. (1998). In search of inadvertent plagiarism. *The American Journal of Psychology, 111*(4), 529-559.

Watkins, E. W. (1994). Plagiarism. In H. A. Christy, J. S. Harrison, & E. W. Watkins (Eds.), *Don't Perish—Publish! Faculty Notebook* (pp. 25–35). Provo, Utah: Scholarly Publications, Brigham Young University.

Chapter XVI
Students and the Internet:
The Dissolution of Boundaries

Jon R. Ramsey
University of California, Santa Barbara, USA

ABSTRACT

This chapter explores the information revolution represented by the Internet. It argues that a number of contemporary debates over the nature of authorship and the ownership of ideas and information present serious challenges to traditional concepts of plagiarism. Especially considered are students' many types of interactions with digital technologies and the effect of a "flat world" on their thinking and information-gathering practices. The author then offers suggestions for improving faculty and student understanding of the new information environment and for sustaining academic integrity in the midst of a knowledge revolution.

INTRODUCTION

We stand amidst the swirling currents of an information revolution, one facilitated by the Internet and contoured by postmodern reassessments of authorship, creativity, and the ownership of ideas. This chapter contemplates some of the sea changes affecting the production and dissemination of knowledge, suggesting a new context in which plagiarism must be understood and addressed. It is possible that our current discussions of plagiarism will be regarded, 10 years from now, as the rearguard defenses of a highly privatized, perhaps Western-world view of the individual's inventiveness and ownership. Perhaps our traditional understanding of original, individual authorship and the criteria we use to teach students about honest intellectual discourse, to warn them against the perils of plagiarism, and to intercept and punish their bad practices are out of touch with a new knowledge paradigm.

These are the concerns explored in this chapter. Let me acknowledge at the outset that I have more questions than answers as I reflect upon such forces as the following:

- The postmodern representations of originality and individual authorship as mythologies born during the Romantic Period and drawn into the service of a capitalist economy.
- The vast and unprecedented resources of the Internet for finding information and ideas, mixing them together, and presenting the "mash-up" results to an individual teacher or, just as easily, to a worldwide audience.
- The debates among university faculty over supposedly oppressive and exclusionary "gatekeeper" pedagogies, as opposed to "facilitative" teaching goals that emphasize "intertextual" and collaborative creation over a privatized model of learning.
- The confusions over boundaries between self and other that seem endemic to the cognitive experience of many young people and characterize a good deal of popular culture.
- The democratizing of ideas and information that informs such movements as The Cultural Commons and Free Culture.
- And the possibility that our students' future careers will reward employees' ability to locate and synthesize digitized information more than their capacity to think in original ways in order to discover and invent.

THE FLAT WORLD OF INFORMATION AND AUTHORSHIP

To take up the first concern, do we face genuine threats to the concept of individual authorship that has been gaining ascendancy at least since the 18th century? In a similar vein, are information and ideas increasingly regarded simply as material held in common by all of us? John Updike (2006)

laments in *The New York Times Book Review* that we are nearing the "end of authorship." Responding to an earlier article by Kevin Kelley of the magazine *Wired*, Updike depicts a world order in which the individual efforts of writers might be Googled into a "universal library" from which anyone can download and synthesize favorite chapters, paragraphs, or smaller textual pieces, then share and swap them with others like "music playlists." Updike foresees, as a consequence of impressive technologies that democratize all information and ideas into a vast digital soup, an invitation for us to ignore authorship and individual endeavor. We risk losing, he asserts, the "intimacy" of true intellectual engagement between author and reader.

Thomas Friedman's *The World Is Flat* (2005) presents the broader picture of a world of international transactions in which information, ideas, and services flow instantly across cyberspace, leading to political and business alliances—indeed, complex knowledge partnerships—that would have been impossible just 15 years ago. This flat world, whether Friedman's or Updike's, does not seem new to our students; it is simply the nature of things. Every time they interact with their computers, BlackBerries, iPods, and Bluetooth-enhanced cell phones, they access an extraordinary range of digital information "out there" for the taking. Many billions of words and extensive data sets can be invoked through the simplest search, and much of this material stands without any obvious authorship or ownership. At yet another level of expediency, students can use even a tiny PDA, from nearly any location, to search almost any topic and find myriad useful answers already assembled. It's usually not a discriminating exploration; nor is it always inventive or challenging. But students' nearly continuous links with the Internet reflect their unquestioned participation in a flat world of information flow. They also routinely download, reassemble, and transmit various portions of what they glean from the Internet.

In a sense, the Internet is the fulfillment, or at least provides the technological infrastructure for, postmodernism. While the postmodern debates over authorship and the integrity of texts rage outside the awareness of most students, many university faculty embrace such perspectives or at least debate their validity. Alice Roy (1999) provides a quick summary of the constructs that tend to destabilize traditional perspectives on authorship:

The postmodern project offers us (or, some would say, burdens us with) a set of questions: Where is the text? Who's got it? Whom does it represent? Who controls it? Who is controlled by it? ... These questions and the act or issue of plagiarism are inextricably linked, since plagiarism assures the concreteness of texts, the reality of authorship, of both words and ideas, and a well-defined role of the reader as receiver of the message. No disappearing subject here, no creative transaction between reader and writer, or reader and text, no negotiation of meaning, no indeterminacy of text. (p. 56)

The postmodern "project," while often provoking a rich re-examination of standard perspectives in many academic disciplines, also fosters uncertainty when we instruct students to distinguish rigorously between their words and ideas and the words and ideas of others.

The tendency to "share" academic materials without regard to authorship and ownership may extend to this recent, curious example: some high school teachers are now selling their lesson plans and notes online to other teachers—through teacherspayteachers.com—who will undoubtedly present the lesson plans to their students without any attribution. I suppose this practice is not much different from what many of us do when we offer information, in class, gleaned from other scholars and from the teachers whom we have admired and now emulate. The assessment of teacherspayteachers.com offered by the president

of the US National Education Association, however, gives the issue a new twist: "This is the new generation of teachers we're talking about. They rely more on technology. If something works, it doesn't matter where it came from" (Feller, 2006, p.20). Caring where information and ideas come from is certainly central to our concerns over scholarly integrity, whether we mean the process of critical inquiry itself or the ways in which a student or scholar benefits from the intellectual efforts of others.

THE INTERNET IS NOT A NEW VERSION OF THE "LIBRARY"

When we focus our concerns, and our research instructions, on students' misuse of the Internet for academic assignments, we are, I think, viewing only a small part of the information revolution seething around us. We essentially are viewing the Internet culture through a lens more appropriate to the traditional library, in which "the best that has been said and thought" (1869, Arnold) is stored for our review, almost always in a particular physical location (less often through digital access from a remote site). This is the library of books and journals (sounds, images, and digitized materials as well, of course) whose physicality, organization of materials, and professional staff announce its special qualifications as a place of learning. It is an institution overseen by professionals who screen, purchase, and arrange materials in various collections and disciplinary hierarchies. Most important for our inquiry into Internet plagiarism, the traditional library is orderly, discriminating, and unmistakably "there" as an entity distinct from the user's own psyche.

How different it is to "browse" in a library in comparison to "surfing" through the huge mélange of materials on the Internet. The Internet is, first of all, vastly bigger than the largest libraries ever assembled. For example, the UC Berkeley Library houses "10 million volumes and 70,000 serials" (Leonard, n.d.), while the US Library of Congress has "130 million items" in its vast collection, including "more than 29 million books and other printed materials, 2.7 million recordings, 12 million photographs, 4.8 million maps, and 58 million manuscripts" (Billington, n.d.). By comparison, the resources on the Internet have proven hard to calculate in a useful way: do we tabulate, for example, terabytes of information, numbers of Web sites, or the number of users around the world? A recent online article by Antonio Gulli and Alessio Signorini (n.d.) provides a sensible approach, suggesting that the Internet contains "at least 11.5 billion [indexable] pages as of the end of January 2005." How much text is included in each site varies widely, of course, and the daily addition of new sites/texts to the Internet undoubtedly surpasses the acquisition capacity of even the most generously funded traditional library.

The size comparison, however, is not the most significant difference. Yes, the Internet provides our students with immediate access to a huge ocean of images, sounds, texts, and data, far more sensory and intellectual information than has ever been assembled, indexed, and made retrievable in all of human history. But the more profound differences are these:

- The Internet is almost completely free of any quality filters or regulations; it serves as a vast, protean repository of anything and everything that can be digitized.
- The digital soup mixes texts, sounds, and images in a thoroughly egalitarian manner: everything is equally deserving, or undeserving, of our consideration.
- In many cases one cannot tell the origins or authorship of the materials posted to the Internet; no human agent stands behind them, and they are there for the taking.
- For our students, the Internet is as much a popular culture phenomenon and resource as

it is a place to look for quotidian or academic information.
- Significant parts of students' social lives are conducted with Internet aid, whether e-mailing or text-messaging a friend, seeking friends or romance on myspace.com, reading one another's blogs and Web pages, sharing gossip, rumors, and celebrity news, or passing on a "mash-up" version of music and video that one has just appropriated from various Internet sites.

The multiple social and practical purposes for which (American) teenagers use the Internet are confirmed by the recent Pew Internet and American Life Project (2005), a survey of young people aged 12-17 years. The survey tells us that 87 percent of teenagers who use the Internet (51 percent on a daily basis) also connect for instant messaging (75 percent of those who go online), for e-mail (89 percent), to access popular culture Web sites (84 percent), to seek information about a college they might like to attend (57 percent), and to find information on current events (76 percent) ("Teens and Technology," pp. i-vi). These levels of activity represent a powerful world of social and informational connections, cyber links that, in many cases, impress the senses and mind more quickly and with greater intensity than does the prose of a printed page. In all of this cyber culture, boundaries, borders, and the ordinary limits of time and place have little significance.

Perhaps most important to our examination of Internet plagiarism is the multitude of purposes for which young people engage the Internet's resources. It becomes easy to imagine how easily distinctions can be blurred between an online chat with a friend or stranger and an e-mail request to a teacher, between a popular song downloaded to an iPod and an authored text saved to a flash drive, or between a blogger's rant and the strong views of a credentialed expert. Everything is just "someone's opinion," our students are inclined to say (and US students will often defend the legitimacy and importance of everyone's opinion), and materials on the Internet are "just there" to be sampled and enjoyed. These and many other Internet activities suggest why the Internet potpourri is extraordinarily more attractive (and, from our perspective, confusing) to the majority of college and university students than was ever true, for most students, of any library of books and periodicals.

It is impossible to know whether student use of the book-centered library constituted better days for genuine intellectual effort, or whether non-digitized copying and paraphrasing were just a less efficient means of doing what can now be accomplished at lightning speed through an Internet search, copy, and paste. The "research" process of years past took a good deal more time, even if one indiscriminately grabbed 10 books from a shelf for use in the paper, then made few distinctions among copying, paraphrasing, and forming one's own perspectives. That being said, one needed to travel to a library and search through physical materials that were not just on-screen versions of one's own words and half-formed thoughts, but rather were more easily recognized as emanating from particular authors, or from identified publishers. We can suggest that it was easier, in the old process, to discern the difference between oneself and the other, between subject and object, even if the lifting of a person's ideas, in contrast to actually stealing the book from the library, was a fairly abstract concept for many students.

Internet resources exacerbate these confusions. How can digitized ideas and information be owned, after all, in the same sense that a person owns a car or a television set? (compare Lessig, 2004, pp. 83-84). What constitutes "theft" when the language on the screen seems to bring the reader's own thoughts into focus, moves a student's fledgling notion about an object of study toward a logical conclusion with inevitability so reassuring and attractive that the words seem an echo of one's own emerging perspectives? Doing

a Google search on virtually any academic topic is likely to yield thousands of Web site hits in a split second, including complete papers available from, for example, answers.com, 123helpme. com, junglepage.com, and eliteskills.com, and a number of student essays published on line for pedagogical purposes in various college courses. It is a matter of a 10-second download to capture a free complete essay, perhaps 15 minutes of work to paste a number of the free sources together in an "original" composition, or a two-minute credit card transaction to purchase a paper composed by another student or a professional writer.

CASES OF ACTUAL AND IMAGINARY PLAGIARISM

While the following examples of plagiarism are not directly related to the Internet, they suggest the psychology at work in a young person's mind as she or he is attracted by materials that speak to personal interests. The first case, a recent one, involves former Harvard sophomore Kaavya Viswanathan, whose first novel contained a number of passages, plot devices, and character situations that echoed novels published by Megan McCafferty (first reported by David Zhou, April 23, 2006). Viswanathan's apology, conveyed through her publisher, Little, Brown, suggested: "When I was in high school, I read and loved two wonderful books by Megan McCafferty … which spoke to me in a way few other books did … I wasn't aware of how much I may have internalized Ms. McCafferty's words … I can honestly say that any phrasing similarities between her works and mine were completely unintentional and unconscious" (Mehegan, April 25, 2006). The claim sounds familiar: the young author found the perfect expression of her own real and imagined life in the books she admired, internalized much of the fiction as part of her own psyche, then merged McAfferty's feelings and insights with her own personal and imagined experiences in a "new" novel. From the standpoint of teenager psychology, it is an understandable, self-referential appropriation. Perhaps the lifting of words and ideas was done without the young author's conscious intent; nevertheless, it was a plagiarism in its impact on the original author, on her imitator, and on all those who had invested their trust (and advance royalties) in Viswanathan.

Consider too how many millions of young people are already "published," so to speak. Their launching an Internet profile of themselves for people all over the world to see, read, and hear tends to complicate the distinctions between themselves and other "authors" of a more traditional sort. Young people create their own Web sites, sometimes just to say "Kilroy is here," more often to set forth their opinions, desires, and struggles, to share music, images, diaries, and photos, to play games online, to pass on rumors and jokes, and to offer links with favorite Web sites. Or, they do some of the same through such commercial forums as myspace.com, facebook. com, and chatroom.org, where they can negotiate hundreds of cyber "friendships" and spend hours each day in conversations with real or fictitious people whom they have no chance of ever meeting in person.

What I think of as the "echoes of oneself" phenomenon is easier to perceive when we consider popular culture, especially its music, which young people may embrace for its expression of their own yearnings and conflicts and their view of the world. There is not one of us who has not felt that various songs embodied our deepest feelings or articulated our aspirations. Professional musicians themselves commonly acknowledge their many borrowings from musicians they admire, often describing their ongoing homage to the many performers and musical styles that they emulated as they composed lyrics and tunes. Thus it is not difficult to understand the temptation, facilitated by technologies unknown to us a few years ago, to sample and download popular songs, often to remix them with friends as one's own interpretive art form and as the currency of social exchange.

The 2004 music industry controversy involving the re-mixed CD by Danger Mouse (Brian Burton) illustrates the leading edge of artistic challenges to a more traditional music production culture. Danger Mouse, clearly driven by a sense of creative challenge and by his deep admiration for The Beatles and for Jay-Z, extensively sampled and remixed the Beatles' *The White Album* and Jay-Z's *The Black Album* to produce *The Grey Album* for free distribution to a few hundred friends. When the new CD was posted on several Web sites for free downloading, both EMI Records and Sony initiated various cease-and-desist orders. The case has many fascinating legal twists and turns and has inspired many defenses of an artist's rights to use and build upon the artistic works of others. My chief interest in this incident is the conviction with which Danger Mouse defends his remix practices as a new and legitimate mode of creativity. Interviewed by MTV, he outlined the technical and creative processes: "'I stuck to those two [albums] because I thought it would be more challenging and more fun and more of a statement to what you could do with sampling alone,' he explained. 'It is an art form. It is music. You can do different things, it doesn't have to be just what some people call stealing. It can be a lot more than that'" (Moss, 2004). There is no pretense here of unconscious borrowing or of a completely independent creative act. We hear instead the full-blown defense of creative interdependence that reshapes the work of others through a complex remixing of pieces already published and owned. This "free culture" view of the materials available from one's predecessors, in any field of endeavor, is already an essential aspect of the Internet milieu, whether the participants borrow things because of a philosophical conviction or simply do so because of the times in which we live.

In Noah Baumbach's *The Squid and the Whale* (Sony Pictures, 2005), we see the threads of popular music production and plagiarism woven together. The film explores issues of originality and ownership through the complications of a family locked in irresolvable conflicts of ego and resentment. Pink Floyd's "Hey You" (from *The Wall* album, 1979) comes to represent the teenage son's isolation and attempts to forge some connection with his estranged father and mother, with potential girlfriends—indeed, with anyone who might break through a wall of pretentiousness and pomposity derived from his father. When the son is caught for presenting "Hey You" in a high school competition as though it were his own song, he tells the counselor whose guidance is mandated by the school principal: "I felt I could have written it." The counselor rejoins that Roger Waters is the actual composer and lyricist, to which the boy responds: "Yes, but I felt I could have. And so the fact that it was already written was kind of a technicality."

The movie adds some delicious complications to the plagiarism at the center of the son's experience. Both parents hold doctoral degrees in literature, the father pontificates on the works of famous authors while his career as a novelist declines and his wife's writing career rises, the father is repeatedly concerned about "his books" that remain captive on the estranged wife's shelves, and the father's most brilliant creative writing student (who briefly becomes the father's live-in girlfriend) acknowledges to the son, "I used to hand in Lou Reed lyrics and pass them off as my own." This intertextual subplot gets even more complicated when the family discusses the "dreamlike" quality of the son's stolen song as an echo of the father's second novel, *End of the Line*, which in turn reminds the son that "the scenes of the baby in the middle [of the novel] are based on me as a baby." When he is eventually confronted with the son's plagiarism, the father tosses back the postmodern rationale, "He made his own interpretation."

PLAGIARISM AND PATCHWRITING

Disagreements in academia over educational philosophies and the nature of the composing process add a further component to the plagiarism conundrum. Such debates, while conducted largely outside students' hearing, do trickle down to the classroom level in important respects. Some relevant faculty discussions—sometimes acrimonious divisions—include:

- Attempts to "decriminalize" plagiarism
- Efforts to distinguish intentional from unintentional plagiarism
- Efforts to expose "original genius" as an outmoded agent of capitalism and patriarchy
- And attempts to champion the benefits of students' "patchwriting," of collaborative composition, and of multiple literacies

There is an extensive literature on all of these topics: books, articles, and blogs that contribute important perspectives to the atmosphere in which faculty members teach and students do their academic work.

The most sophisticated assessment of "plagiarism" within the framework of composition studies is Rebecca Moore Howard's *Standing in the Shadow of Giants: Plagiarists, Authors, Collaborators* (1999). Her special target, Thomas Mallon's *Stolen Words: Forays into the Origins and Ravages of Plagiarism* (1989), takes the high moral ground in tracing a history of academic dishonesty. Mallon charts the emergence of authorship as a profession and the increasing concern of writers, especially in the 18th century and since, to receive credit for and to retain control over the works they produced. He then explores cases of plagiarism in the 19th and 20th centuries, always treating the pilfering as a shocking transgression and taking to task all those who attempt psychological, historical, or other apologetics. Characteristic of Mallon's tone throughout is this early pronouncement: "I was, through my research, eventually, and much more than I expected to be, appalled: by the victims I learned of, by the audacity of their predators, by the excuses made for the latter" (p. xii).

Howard (1999) takes on Mallon directly, acknowledging his insights and verve as a writer but challenging his assumptions at every turn. She marshals many perspectives from current composition theory and practice, from re-examinations of the nature of authorship, and from ontological questions that challenge traditional views of "the text." Howard especially presents a complex picture of the "patchwriting" that students often submit as their own work (that is, the half-conscious incorporation of words and ideas from one or several sources, without understanding the rules of academic discourse). She maintains that patchwriting has its roots in the once-respected traditions of mimesis and is a valuable part of students' emerging literacies and identity formation. Indeed, she claims, "all of us patchwrite all of the time, but we usually cover the trail" (p. 7). She also supports the pedagogical value of patchwriting and of collaborative writing strategies more broadly, and the need to "decriminalize" student patchwriting while taking a fresh look at the customary admonitions and punishments that shadow students' composition efforts. Of the prevailing views on original authorship and ownership she says:

Contemporary scholarship asserts that the premises upon which the modern notion of plagiarism is based—the premises that a writer can and should be autonomous and original, and that as a result the writer can also be deemed moral and accorded ownership of his or her writing—are a fiction, produced by and for a capitalist, patriarchal society. (p. 15)

Thus she throws down the gauntlet to teachers who embrace an older model of authorship, academic politics, and intellectual property.

Howard characterizes the tradition-bound professoriate as "gatekeepers," those who uphold the high standards of the university's professional elite by excluding ill-prepared or under-performing students from the scholars' inner circle until "they have demonstrated the necessary qualifications" for membership (p. 29). By contrast, teachers who are "facilitators" "make sure that students have every chance to meet those qualifications: facilitating teachers are student- rather than discipline-oriented, striving to provide students with the tools requisite to success" (p. 29).

This is one of the more vulnerable distinctions of a very thoughtful argument. Many faculty members who harbor high expectations for students' independent thinking and writing are also passionately committed to helping students participate in, and benefit from, the university's myriad conversations. It is misleading to attribute an exclusionary politics to one set of faculty and a virtuous facilitation of student learning to another. Faculty need to stand together in order to introduce students to the values of both collaborative and individual contributions to the advancement of learning.

FREE CULTURE AND THE CULTURAL COMMONS

This section examines an extraordinarily active area of scholarship, legal disputes, and manifesto proclamations that have emerged alongside the Internet culture. Although plagiarism per se is seldom an explicit part of this discussion, the scholar-activists' fight to protect the knowledge revolution fostered by the Internet carries serious implications for our topic. Their core effort is to ensure that every person has unfettered access to the world's information, data, ideas, sounds, and images, all of which are needed for innovative work (and intellectual and political independence) in the 21st century. The activists provide a counter-thrust to corporate and governmental efforts to oversee, regulate, own, and profit from the Internet's resources.

Consider the battle lines drawn in some recent, provocative book titles: *Freedom of Expression: Overzealous Copyright Bozos and Other Enemies of Creativity* (McLeod, 2005); *Owning Culture: Authorship, Ownership, and Intellectual Property Law* (McLeod, 2001); *Resisting Intellectual Property Law* (Halbert, 2005); *Who Owns Academic Work? Battling for Control of Intellectual Property* (McSherry, 2001); and *Connected Intelligence: The Arrival of the Web Society* (de Kerckhove, 1997). These writers, from communications studies (McLeod), political science (Halbert), literature and language (de Kerchove), and legal practice (McSherry) are charting the impact of an information revolution—and, they would say, the threats to thwart the growth of a "cultural commons."

Among those writing about the friends and foes of the information revolution, Lawrence Lessig, author of *The Future of Ideas: The Fate of the Commons in a Connected World* (2001) and *Free Culture: The Nature and Future of Creativity* (2004), is the voice most likely to be known to at least some university students. Clearly a champion of creativity and originality, and no enemy of intellectual property rights when properly applied and regulated, Lessig is a formidable defender of a free Internet and other sources of information and ideas. Referencing the 2001 Apple Computer advertisement that encouraged consumers to "rip, mix, and burn" (see http://www.theapplecollection.com/Collection/AppleMovies/mov/concert_144a.html), Lessig (2002) defends the need for a creative commons: new technologies "could enable this generation to do with our culture what generations have done from the very beginning of human society: to take what is our culture; to 'rip' it—meaning to copy it; to 'mix' it—meaning to reform it however the user wants; and finally, and most important, to 'burn' it—to publish it in a way that others can see and hear" (p. 9).

Lessig's argument is with the "content" industries that increasingly claim that everything associated with their enterprise has "value" and should thus be protected through extending the laws of property ownership (copyrights, patents, and trademarks, for example). He cites many chilling examples of cease-and-desist actions and law suits that have, in his view, attempted to stifle the conditions necessary to foster both individual and corporate creativity (Lessig, 2002, 2004). He represents the Internet, and digital technologies more generally, as a truly revolutionary force: "For the Internet has unleashed an extraordinary possibility for many to participate in the process of building and cultivating a culture that reaches far beyond local boundaries. That power has changed the marketplace for making and cultivating culture generally, and that change in turn threatens established content industries" (2004, p. 9).

Lessig (2004) is careful to distinguish the types of theft and piracy that truly undermine an artist's or an intellectual's livelihood from a balanced approach to fair use and copyright that "can carry a free culture into the 21st century, without artists losing and without the potential of digital technology being destroyed" (p. 271). When asked about plagiarism in the context of the Creative Commons movement that he founded, Lessig replied:

I see a sharp distinction between the practice of surfing and remixing, and plagiarism. Plagiarism is the failure to acknowledge authorship. In my view, there's no need for that failure. No doubt, the wrong requires intent—sometimes people can forget, or accidentally lose a reference. But the intentional failure to cite has nothing, in my view, to do with the kind of creative practices that I would promote. (e-mail response of October 4, 2006)

Thus, Lessig balances the traditional view of plagiarism as theft with the caution to distinguish a student's ostensible originality from unintentional misuse or forgetfulness. In this realm of academic creativity and authorship, Lessig's focus is not so much on the borrowing itself as on the need to give credit where it is due—a view in line with the creative partnerships he encourages for human culture more broadly.

While no evidence shows that ideas associated with Lessig's Creative Commons (see http://creativecommons.org/) are informing students' intended or unintentional Internet plagiarisms, his ideas about creativity and the less restrictive sharing of ideas and information are having an impact on campuses in the US. Inspired by Lessig's publications and by their successful resistance to Diebold's cease-and-desist orders and copyright claims in 2003, former Swarthmore College students Nelson Pavlosky '06 and Luke Smith '06 co-founded the Free Culture movement. The organization now claims thirty chapters on other campuses and in April 2006 sponsored its "first annual Free Culture summit" (see Sharma, 2006). As their "manifesto" claims, Free Culture celebrates and defends the "new paradigm of creation" fostered by the Internet and related technologies. The larger social and political vision is to "place the tools of creation and distribution, communication and collaboration, teaching and learning into the hands of the common person—and with a truly active, connected, informed citizenry, injustice and oppression will slowly but surely vanish from the earth" (www.freeculture.org/manifesto.php). The manifesto also vows: "We will make, share, adapt, and promote open content ... we will contribute, discuss, annotate, critique, improve, improvise, remix, mutate, and add yet more ingredients to the free culture soup." The most interesting shift in this knowledge paradigm is the conviction that originality and invention require not so much the autonomous activity of an original genius as the democratic and collaborative sharing of a culture's collective brain power.

In a phone interview (Oct. 5, 2006) with Pavlosky, the Free Culture co-founder said that his high school experience with Linux and open source activities stimulated his receptivity to Lessig's ideas. He also referred me to James Boyle's *Shamans, Software, and Spleens: Law and the Construction of the Information Society* (1999), as Boyle's views of authorship are similar to Pavlosky's. Especially important, says Pavlosky, is Boyle's critique of:

the myth of the 'romantic author' who creates new things from thin air: a myth that ignores the creative resources that the author draws from as well as the needs of future creators who also require those resources to create. This certainly argues in favor of citing your sources, but it also calls into question the idea of original authorship ... if we were completely, exhaustively honest (and had a flawless memory), we could track down a previous source for just about everything we've ever thought, said, written, or done, even if we may have put a new spin or twist on it. (e-mail of Oct. 12, 2006)

Pavlosky and his cohorts support the "transformative use" of materials inherited from other thinkers and artists: "Take something, use it, but make something new and different." He admits that the "line between simply copying and making transformative use" can be fuzzy, and he would agree with academics that "credit for a person's contributions is important." He is clearly a strong proponent of critical thinking and original contributions within and beyond the university, but he looks at these issues through the lens of shared, cumulative endeavors undertaken by myriad inventive people over the course of time, and much less from the perspectives of privatization and individual ownership.

The radical reframing of knowledge production represented by Free Culture and its many allied questions and movements may not be on every college and university doorstep. I submit, however, that we need to take such thinking seriously into account as we guide our students through their research and writing tasks. New technologies of inquiry and a collectivist orientation toward ideas and their many manifestations—not to mention the allure and confusions of the cyberspace ocean—stand in competition with the old verities of authorship, individuality, and ownership.

ORDINARY CAMPUS REALITIES

It is not my argument that students who plagiarize do so from a philosophical conviction about community ownership, or the need for creative people to borrow freely from the great reservoir of human culture, or to make a political statement about time-worn university value systems. Over a 23-year period as an administrator at a private liberal arts college, I interviewed several hundred students who had been reported by the faculty for plagiarism. I also acted as "judicial counsel" for perhaps 75 formal hearings, at which a panel of students and faculty thoroughly questioned the "respondent" on motives, methods, and improved practices for the future. Never once did we hear any "philosophical" defense or explanation from the accused student. By far the most common explanation was the pressure of time and a desperate lunge at Internet (or, less often, printed) resources. We also encountered a number of students who feared they simply could not sound like a credible college student in their writing and thus appropriated texts that articulated some of the student's fledgling ideas but in a form that seemed articulate and smart. It is also interesting that nearly all of the students interviewed—even when they acknowledged the plagiarism—claimed they never intended any dishonesty or desired to fool the professor (Ramsey, 2004).

When large numbers of high school and college students acknowledged for Josephson Institute (2006) or McCabe (2004, 2005) surveys that they had "cheated" or "plagiarized" once or more often, the responses affirmed students' conscious

awareness of the dishonesty. In McCabe's 2001 survey of 2294 high school juniors, 34 percent said they had "copied almost word for word from a source;" 52 percent acknowledged they "Copied a few sentences from a Web site;" and 16 percent said they "Turned in a paper obtained in large part from paper mill or Web site" (McCabe, 2005, pp. 238-239). In his focus group interviews with the surveyed students, McCabe found: "Many of these students told me they know cheating is wrong, and they are not proud of their behavior. However, they feel they have to cheat to get the grades they need" (p. 237). The 2002-2003 survey of 18,000 college and university students (McCabe, Butterfield, & Trevino, 2004) also showed 38 to 40 percent of the undergraduates surveyed had "Copied few sentences from Internet w/o citation" or from "written sources"; only 4 percent acknowledged they had "Submitted paper from term paper mill"(p. 125). The students' consciousness of the dishonest activity is telling and casts doubt on recent faculty efforts to characterize plagiarism as largely an unconscious, developmental problem—one requiring better instruction, not punishment.

It is no wonder, then, that a sampling of college and university Web sites suggests that institutional definitions of plagiarism and its consequences retain a traditional stance, despite the thought-provoking re-examinations of authorship and plagiarism undertaken in the past decade by composition theorists and literary scholars. As but one example, the University of Connecticut completed a thorough reassessment of integrity policies and practices in 2004 but left in place the definitions last revised in the year 2000, a description of academic dishonesty that affirms traditional expectations:

A fundamental tenet of all educational institutions is academic honesty; academic work depends upon respect for and acknowledgement of the research and ideas of others. Misrepresenting someone else's work as one's own is a serious offense in any academic setting and it will not be condoned. ("Responsibilities of Community Life: The Student Code 2006-2007," p. 11)

The emphasis remains on the student's obligation to do original work, to assess the value of sources thoughtfully, and to reference them scrupulously. UConn does distinguish, as do many other colleges and universities, between "serious offenses" and "less serious offenses," though in each case some level of academic failure is recommended. UConn has also taken further steps to provide students and faculty with educational tools regarding plagiarism (UConn "Information for Faculty on Internet Plagiarism," n.d.).

Integrity definitions at the University of California, Santa Barbara, reflect a similar emphasis on original authorship and the private ownership of information and ideas. A pamphlet produced by The Office of Student Life, "Academic Integrity at UCSB: A Student's Guide," confirms the generally accepted expectations:

Plagiarism is academic theft. It is the use of another's idea or words without proper attribution or credit. An author's work is his/her property and should be respected by documentation. Plagiarism from the Internet is no different from traditional plagiarism, and is in fact often far easier to catch with the use of technology available to instructors and administrators. ("Academic Integrity at UCSB," n.d.)

The official, online UCSB code also distinguishes the consciously motivated plagiarism from the accidental variety but asserts: "Although a person's state of mind and intention will be considered in determining the university response to an act of academic dishonesty, this in now [sic] way lessens the responsibility of the student" (http://hep.ucsb.edu/people/hnn/conduct/cam_reg_stud_a.html). I have found no evidence that official university

policies have diverged significantly from the integrity codes in place for many years, though certainly the academic conversations (and litigious challenges) of recent years have prompted more thorough definitions of plagiarism and of hearing processes. More importantly, faculty members have been encouraged to make integrity issues an integral part of the teaching process (for example, see Dean of Studies, 1999).

Even if integrity codes reflect traditional expectations regarding student responsibility, national conversations in the US have shifted toward improved pedagogy and away from the older admonitions: warn students, then apprehend and prosecute their transgressions. Chris Anson (2003-2004) is an influential spokesperson for a decriminalized approach:

The fervor over the detection of plagiarism and its accompanying legalistic and punitive apparatus seems antithetical to many educational principles. It subtly begins to wear away at our collective personae as coaches, guides, and mentors, yielding a hardened attitude, detective-like and oppositional. Rows of naïve students begin to look like miscreants ready to dash off and do bad things, deceptive things, things that show blatant disregard for the concepts of copyright, ownership, and individual authorship. Lacking the moral fiber of previous generations, students are to blame. We, the bastions of higher learning, demand honesty and integrity, and our students flaunt them. Our duty then requires us to search and seize, discipline and punish. (third paragraph)

As I noted earlier, Howard (1999) has also been prominent in critiquing the "gatekeepers" of the academy, who mistake students' "patchwriting" for plagiarism, fail to recognize their own inescapable reliance on the ideas and texts of others, and fail to engage students in a more developmental approach to teaching and writing.

Views similar to Anson's and Howard's are echoed in The Council of Writing Program Administrators' (WPA) "Statement of Best Practices" (January 2003) for the avoidance of plagiarism. This document shifts nearly all of its attention from student responsibility to the need for improved faculty understanding and practices (it is a "best practices" document, after all). The WPA distinguishes between intentional plagiarism and the unintentional "misuse of sources" and offers a number of reasons for students' over-reliance on others' work:

- Students' fear of failure
- "Poor time-management skills"
- Student disengagement from the university's or the course's purposes
- Faculty recycling of formulaic and generic writing topics (which invite "canned responses")
- The failure of faculty to report genuine plagiarisms
- Student ignorance of the academy's value system and of research techniques and expectations
- The different academic conventions of some other, especially non-Western, cultures

The WPA document then offers several pages of advice on policy and pedagogy to administrators and faculty, concluding with the curious admonition that our interest in online detection services (such as turnitin.com) "should never be used to justify the avoidance of responsible teaching methods such as those described in this document" (#5 under "best practices"). The WPA teaching recommendations make all sorts of sense, though they might seem daunting even to flexible and creative teachers. One danger is that extensive WPA and similar recommendations could exacerbate the complaint about writing-intensive instruction getting in the way of disciplinary "content."

THE JOB MARKET: BUSINESS AS USUAL?

The ongoing debate over plagiarism and pedagogy in general, and over Internet challenges in particular, raises questions about students' career lives after college. Is it possible that the browsing, gathering, patching, and synthesizing skills that students exercise through the Internet, and often in their "research" for school work, are the abilities that a changing employment market will increasingly value? And what, in contrast, is the employment value currently, and for the future, of originality, creative thinking, and problem solving? Is there any evidence that the more analytical and creative aspects of work might be increasingly consigned to specialists in an organization, while Internet browsing and gathering skills become the more common job expectation? The types of jobs available and the skills expected by employers have often shifted dramatically with the advent of new technologies, and one wonders if the Internet revolution will prompt career-world changes like those inspired by the telephone, television transmission, and the computer.

I posed these questions to the career services directors at a university and at a private college. Micael Kemp, Director at the University of California, Santa Barbara, offered this view on the place of original thinking and creativity in the current and future job market:

I suppose you could say those abilities have been consigned to specialists since the first Ford rolled off the factory line. Research and Development departments have been charged with just this type of work for a hundred years. But I'd argue that originality, creativity, critical thinking, and inventiveness are in demand across departments and job functions. The clerical staff person who created a new and better form has been just as creative as the researcher who found a better way to make a widget, or made the paradigm shift away from widgets to another type of gadget altogether. (Kemp, e-mail of Sept. 25, 2006)

Mike Profita, director of Career Services at Skidmore College, offered a similar perspective:

I haven't seen any literature nor have I noticed anecdotally that employers are placing a higher relative value on the gathering skills you mentioned. Writing, critical thinking, quantitative, analytical skills, integrity, and teamwork still seem to have a higher relative priority. I suspect that job content at the entry level does reflect a greater concentration of activity surrounding Internet research. However, ultimate career advancement is likely still greatly impacted by the ability to analyze data, draw innovative conclusions and represent findings coherently to others (in writing, verbally, and graphically). Employers tend to view Internet research as a very basic skill that most of today's grads possess, so the real long-term value added lies in other skill sets. (Profita, e-mail of Sept. 25, 2006)

Other assessments of the job market appear to confirm Kemp's and Profita's perspectives. The U.S. Department of Labor (2003), for example, forecasts a large increase of jobs in "the information supersector" (p. 3) over the period 2004-2014: "Among all occupations in the economy, computer and healthcare occupations are expected to grow the fastest," with the largest computer growth sector defined as "Network systems and data communications analysts," followed by "Computer software engineers," "Network and computer systems administrators," and "Database administrators" (p. 5). There is no surprise here,

and no doubt that high-level understanding of computer technologies will continue to reward many of our students' career interests.

As for the abilities valued by employers, the "Top 10" or "Top 20" lists generally include "problem-solving" and "information management" (Gale Group, 2003); "troubleshooting skills" (Computerworld, 2003); "problem solving," "team working," and "technical job skills" (Future Skills Wales, 2006); and "Analytical ability," "Computer literacy," "Decision-making," "Problem-solving," "Team-working," and "Written communication" (Loughborough University Careers Centre, 2006). Among the most reliable sources of such information is the US-based National Association of Colleges and Employers (NACE), which publishes the annual *Job Outlook.* The 2006 survey concludes that "employers have consistently cited communication skills (written and verbal) as the most important skill or attribute for job candidates." Other qualities or skills in the survey's top five include "Honesty/integrity," "Teamwork skills," "Strong work ethic," and "Analytical skills." Farther down the list, but still among the top twenty, is "Creativity" (NACE, 2006).

While information gathering through digital and other resources will undoubtedly remain useful to job seekers, it seems safe to conclude that many careers will require more demanding powers of mind to sustain rewarding employment. The individual's ability to think critically and at times independently, to develop new perspectives on an old issue or problem, and to write clearly and persuasively will carry a high value. At the same time, it is clear from employer information that collaborative experience and abilities—a socialized intelligence, so to speak—and proficiency with digital technologies are also of great importance to job success. At least in this respect, no irreconcilable differences need divide the old-guard university goals from the new.

RECOMMENDATIONS FOR AN IMPROVED ENVIRONMENT OF INTEGRITY

From the competing claims and controversies sketched in this chapter, we can derive some areas of agreement. First, the academic advocates for a less punitive response to plagiarism and for a more collaborative approach to teaching and learning also embrace the importance of acknowledging the individuals and groups who inspire our various achievements. Second, there is no reason to fear that the inventiveness, ingenuity, and creativity of extraordinary individuals will be supplanted by more collectivist, more egalitarian perspectives on the advancement of learning. The advocates of Internet access and freedom of use, and the enemies of corporate expansion of copyright and trademark claims, seem equally to champion the rights of individuals to access and make use of information and ideas—and, to a moderated degree, to own what they produce. Indeed, the voices represented in this chapter tend to regard the Internet as a revolutionary opportunity for many more individuals to learn from one another and to make their own contributions to the creative enterprise.

That being said, the arguments I have been exploring make clear that we cannot be complacent about the traditional, time-tested responses to plagiarism. We are simply not winning that struggle, as the statistics on students' Internet (and other) cheating attest. My recommendations below suggest that we need to reframe the typical university model of highly privatized intellectual activity, at least as it pertains to our students. We need to take quite seriously the competing claims of a remarkably intriguing world of shared information and ideas, much of it facilitated by, in some respects inspired by, the Internet and related digital technologies. Especially important is the extraordinary degree to which young people are drawn to this new information culture and make multiple academic, personal, and pragmatic

uses of it. Without our thoughtful engagement with these newer interests and opportunities, my question on the first page of this chapter will be answered in the affirmative: yes, 10 years from now, our traditional modes of addressing plagiarism will look like a futile resistance to the tides of a revolution that we did not quite understand.

The following recommendations, while far from solutions, suggest the broad points upon which faculty especially must win further agreement among themselves and with their students:

1. The traditional view of academic integrity must, I think, be informed by the complex history of originality and authorship and by the knowledge revolution occurring in our time. Without that understanding, we are likely to take a "law and order" approach to students' ignorance, shortcuts, and intentional dishonesty that simply pits us against them—a strategy which seems not to be working, if we take seriously the 60-70 percent of students who acknowledge cheating during their university education (McCabe and Josephson).

2. We should also contemplate the psychology, so to speak, which shapes students' interactions with print and digital forms of information. I have tried in this chapter to describe some ways of thinking about oneself and "the other" that make the Internet highly attractive and tend to obscure the boundaries and distinctions that a faculty value system takes for granted. We don't need to accede to students' modes of thinking, but we must understand them better than we do. We can then, possibly, build some bridges between the cyberspace that fascinates them and the university's educational hopes.

3. To borrow a strategy from Gerald Graff (1993 and 2003), we should be "teaching the conflicts" to our students, not simply recycling traditional perspectives on the

nature of individual authorship, knowledge acquisition, and integrity. These time-honored perspectives are being overwhelmed by our students' attractions to the flat world of the Internet. If we don't study and engage the information revolution as the students are experiencing it daily, we diminish our chances of guiding them toward the excitement and rewards of critical thinking and genuine research. Thus, I recommend that we actually explore with students, and in a serious way, competing views of originality, authorship, shared cultural resources—indeed, the evolving nature of knowledge acquisition, transformation, and dissemination.

4. As many academic reformers have urged, we constantly should explore improved ways for engaging students actively in the learning process. The more they become interested in the information, ideas, methodologies, and questions of the disciplines, the more they are likely to care about the work they produce in their courses. Revitalized pedagogies can help students exercise and build confidence in their own mental capacities, participate in a scholarly conversation with others who have enriched our shared pool of information and ideas, and come to value the written (and other) expressions of their learning as important aspects of who they are and want to become. Their valuing themselves as thinkers, researchers, and authors is especially important to the integrity issues that concern us.

5. The shift, in many academic conversations, from student responsibility for learning with integrity to faculty responsibility for failed practices tends, I submit, to infantilize the students. We do indeed need to take into account their diverse cultural and academic backgrounds, and we should make every effort to provide access to our sometimes mysterious practices and goals. But the students' being strangers in a strange land is also an essential and valuable aspect of human life and of our preparing them for it. Our care for them should suggest pathways to success but not indulge elaborate apologetics for their confusions and mishaps.

6. While faculty consensus on nearly any topic is hard to achieve, we should try to rise above the more divisive critiques of the university's values and practices as they bear upon academic integrity, in particular the distorting schema that divide faculty into pedagogy conservatives and liberals, as it were. A faculty conversation that is united around core assumptions concerning the integrity of student learning is crucial to the students' taking our interests seriously.

7. Although the composition and rhetoric faculty among us have much of great value to suggest to faculty in other disciplines about creative pedagogies and the writing process, the compositionists should also be realistic about the competing epistemologies and teaching demands of other disciplines. It is productive, for example, to encourage faculty toward experimenting with new approaches to research and writing. It is not useful, however, to talk with faculty across the disciplines as though they had only limited insight into student learning processes or were themselves composition specialists. To put this another way, writing-across-the-curriculum initiatives should learn more about the disciplines that are not so centered on text-related research.

8. Faculty members also need to move outside the classroom and work with staff to engage in a broader discussion with student leaders at the university. The more we can enlist students in a serious exploration of the university's values, the more likely we are to influence that huge portion of students' choices that are made outside the classroom.

9. When the best pedagogies, encouragements, informed conversations, and admonitions fail to prevent plagiarism, faculty should respond in a uniform manner to the problem. In my experience, faculty generally want to wink at the plagiarism or "handle it on my own." When they become their own judge and jury, they undercut any semblance of equal justice at the university. The consequence is that students read the value system as personality-dependent, not as a broader set of principles embraced by faculty and by serious students alike. The reported student also loses the potential benefits of a larger conversation, usually with other faculty and students as many integrity systems prescribe. In my experience, students eagerly assume that university processes are arbitrary and capricious, not based on shared values of some importance. The more we play into that perspective, the less chance we have of persuading them toward our versions of intellectual honesty.

The traditional aspirations of academia need not be lost in translation if we look creatively for points of connection with the world in which the students operate daily—in particular, the myriad technological interconnections that increasingly inform students' understanding of information and ideas (and of opinions, social interactions, political perspectives, and popular culture). If it is true that the Internet has become a powerful force for reshaping the nature of knowing, we need to bridge an older generation's allegiance to individual originality and the ownership of ideas, on the one hand, with the cyberspace thrust toward common ownership, syntheses of pre-existing materials, anonymity, and undiscriminating abundance on the other.

In the midst of textual and ethical indeterminacy and destabilizing critiques of university culture and pedagogy, there are still substantial reasons for us to believe in the habits of mind linked with critical thinking and creativity. Teaching should continue to stimulate students' interests in discovering issues and topics on their own as well as collaboratively, in interrogating the objects of study, and in making decisions about context, relevance, and cross-disciplinary and cross-cultural enrichments—in short, demonstrating to students the rewards experienced by a truly inquiring mind.

REFERENCES

Anson, C. (2003-2004). Student plagiarism: Are teachers part of the solution or part of the problem? *The Professional & Organizational Development Network in Higher Education.* Retrieved October 7, 2006 from http://oira.syr.edu/cst12/Home/Teaching%20Support/Resources/Sub

Baumbach, N. (Director). (2005). *The squid and the whale* [Motion picture]. United States: Sony Pictures.

Billington, J. H. (n.d.). *Welcome message from the library of congress.* Retrieved August 26, 2006 from www.loc.gov.about

Council of Writing Program Administrators. (2003). *Defining and avoiding plagiarism: The WPA statement on best practices.* Retrieved August 15, 2006, from http://wpacouncil.org/node/9

Dean of Students, University of Connecticut. (2006). *Responsibilities of community life: The student code 2006-2007*, p. 11. Retrieved September 30, 2006 from http://www.dosa.uconn.edu/student_code.html

Dean of Studies, Skidmore College. (1999, September). *The ethics of scholarship.* Retrieved September 28, 2006 from http://www.skidmore.edu/administration/dean-studies/EthicScholarship

DeKerckhove, D. (1997). *Connected intelligence: The arrival of the Web society.* Canada: Somerville House.

Feller, B. (2006, June 28). Cliff notes for teachers: Educators selling lesson plans online for fee. *Steamboat Today,* p. 20.

Free Culture (2004-2005). *Free culture manifesto.* Retrieved August 8, 2006 from http://freeculture.org/manifesto.php

Friedman, T. L. (2005). *The world is flat.* New York: Farrar, Straus & Giroux.

Future Skills Wales. (2005). *New survey results published.* Retrieved October 14, 2006 from http://www.futureskillswales.com

Graff, G. (1993). *Beyond the culture wars: How teaching the conflicts can revitalize American education.* New York: W.W. Norton.

Graff, G. (2003). *Clueless in academe.* New Haven and London: Yale University Press.

Gulli, A. & Signorini, A. (n.d.). *The indexable Web is more than 11.5 billion pages.* Retrieved August 26, 2006 from www.cs.uiowa.edu/~asignori/web-size

Halbert, D. (2005). *Resisting intellectual property law.* New York: Routledge.

Hoffman, T. (2003, August 25). Job skills: preparing generation z. In *Computerworld Careers.* Retrieved October 14, 2006 from http://www.computerworld.com/action/article

Howard, R. (1999). *Standing in the shadow of giants: Plagiarists, authors, collaborators.* Stamford, Connecticut: Ablex Publishing.

Howard., R. (2005). Plagiarism: What should a teacher do? In A. Lathrop & K. Foss (Eds.), *Guiding students from cheating and plagiarism to honesty and integrity: Strategies for change* (p. 174). Westport, Connecticut: Libraries Unlimited.

Josephson Institute (2006, October 15). *2006 Josephson institute report card on ethics of American youth.* Retrieved October 15, 2006 from http://www.josephsoninstitute.org/reportcard

Leonard, T.C. (n.d.). *Visitor information.* Retrieved August 26, 2006 from http://www.lib.berkeley.edu/AboutLibrary/Visitor_information

Lessig, L. (2002). *The future of ideas: The fate of the commons in a connected world.* New York: Vintage Books.

Lessig, L. (2004). *Free culture: The nature and future of creativity.* New York: Penguin.

Loughborough University, Careers Centre. (n.d.). *Skills employers seek.* Retrieved October 14, 2006 from http://www.lbro.ac.uk/service/careers

Mallon, T. (1989). *Stolen words: Forays into the origins and ravages of plagiarism.* New York: Ticknor & Fields.

McCabe, D., Butterfield, K. & Trevino, L. (2004). Academic integrity: How widespread is cheating and plagiarism? In D. Karp & T. Allena (Eds.), *Restorative justice on the college campus: Promoting student growth and responsibility, and reawakening the spirit of campus community* (pp. 124-135). Springfield, Illinois: Charles C. Thomas.

McCabe, D. (2005). Cheating: Why students do it and how we can help them to stop. In A. Lathrop and K. Foss (Eds.). *Guiding students from cheating and plagiarism to honesty and integrity: Strategies for change* (pp. 237-242). Westport, Connecticut: Libraries Unlimited.

McLeod, K. (2001). *Owning culture: Authorship, ownership, and intellectual property law.* New York: Peter Lang.

McLeod, K. (2005). *Freedom of expression: Overzealous copyright bozos and other enemies of creativity.* New York: Doubleday.

McSherry, C. (2001). *Who owns academic work? Battling for control of intellectual property.* Cambridge, Massachusetts: Harvard University Press.

Mehegan, D. (2006, April 25). After duplicated words, words of apology. *The Boston Globe.* Retrieved September 27, 2006 from http://www.boston.com/ac/books/articles/2006/04/25/after

Moss, C. (2004, May 11). *Grey Album* Producer Danger Mouse Explains How He Did It. *MTV On-Line.* Retrieved February 11, 2007 from http://www.mtv.com/news/articles

National Association of Colleges and Employers (NACE) (2006). *Job Outlook 2006.* Retrieved September 25, 2006 from http://www.naceweb.org

Pew Internet & American Life Project. (2005, July 27). *Teens and technology: Youth are leading the transition to a fully mobile nation.* Retrieved August 22, 2006 from http://www.pewinternet.org

Ramsey, J. (2004). Integrity board case study: Sonia's plagiarism. In D. Karp & T. Allena (Eds.), *Restorative justice on the college campus: Promoting student growth and responsibility, and reawakening the spirit of campus community* (pp. 136-141). Springfield, Illinois: Charles C. Thomas.

Roy, A. M. (1999). Whose words these are I think I know: Plagiarism, the postmodern, and faculty attitudes. In L. Buranen & A. Roy (Eds.), *Perspectives on plagiarism and intellectual property in a postmodern world* (pp. 55-61). Albany, New York: State University of New York Press.

Sharma, T. (2006, April 27). Free culture summit unites movement. *The Phoenix Online.* Retrieved October 8, 2006 from http://phoenix.swarthmore.edu/2006-04-27/news/16199

Thomson/Gale. (n.d.). *Today's must have job skills.* Retrieved on October 14, 2006 from http://www.findarticles.com

University of California, Santa Barbara (n.d.). *Academic integrity at UCSB: A student's guide* [pamphlet]. Santa Barbara, CA: Office of Student Life.

University of California, Santa Barbara (n.d.). *Campus regulations: General standards of conduct* (section A.2.: Academic conduct). Retrieved September 30, 2006 from http://www.sa.ucsb.edu/regulations/index.aspx?page=conduct

University of Connecticut (n.d.). *Information for faculty on Internet plagiarism.* Retrieved on September 30, 2006 from http://www.waterbury.uconn.edu/Plagiarism/index.html

Updike, J. (2006, June 25).The end of authorship. *New York Times Book Review*, p. 27.

U.S. Department of Labor: Bureau of Labor Statistics (2003). *Tomorrow's jobs.* Retrieved October 13, 2006 from http://www.bls.gov?oco/oco2003

Warner, J. (2003, September 16). Clueless in academe: An interview with Gerald Graff. *The Morning News.* Retrieved September 27, 2006 from http://www.themorningnews.org/archives

Young, J. (2006, August 9). U. of California system's 100 libraries join Google's controversial book-scanning project. *The Chronicle of Higher Education.* Retrieved on August 10, 2006 from http://www.chronicle.com

Zhou, D. (2006, April 23). Sophomore's new book contains passages strikingly similar to 2001 novel. *The Harvard Crimson.* Retrieved September 27, 2006 from http://www.thecrimson.com/article.aspx?ref=512968

Compilation of References

A Quarter of Students Cheating. (2004). *BBCNews.* Retrieved February 16, 2007 from http://news.bbc.co.uk/2/hi/uk_news/education/3852869.stm

Abasi, A. R., Akbari, N., & Graves, B. (2006). Discourse appropriation, construction of identities and the complex issue of plagiarism: ESL students writing in graduate school. *Journal of Second Language Writing, 15*, 102-117.

Academic Computing Center (AAC). (2007). Electronic Plagarism: Anti-Plagarism Tools. *American University of Beruit.* Retrieved October 15, 2006, from http://wwwlb.aub.edu.lb/~eplagio/Anti_plag.htm

ACODE. (2005). *Audit of academic integrity and plagiarism issues in Australia and New Zealand.* Retrieved April 30, 2006, from http://www.tlc.murdoch.edu.au/project/acode/

Adar, E. & Adamic, L. A. (2004). *Tracking information epidemics in blogspace.* Retrieved October 5, 2006 from http://www.hpl.hp.com/research/idl/papers/blogs2/index.html

Adar, E., Zhang, L., Adamic, L. A., & Lukose, R. M. (2004). *Implicit structure and the dynamics of blogspace.* Retrieved October 2, 2006 from http://www.hpl.hp.com/research/idl/papers/blogs/index.html

Akers, S. (2002). *Deterring and detecting academic dishonesty: Suggestions for faculty.* Office of Student Rights and Responsibilities Web Site, Purdue University. Retrieved August 8, 2006 from http://www.purdue.edu/ODOX/osrr/academicdishonesty.htm

American Association of Community Colleges (2000). *National profile of community colleges: Trends and statistics.* Retrieved August 12, 2006 from http://www.aacc.nche.edu

American Heritage Dictionary. Retrieved October 4, 2006 from http://www.bartleby.com/61/91/I0199150.html

American Historical Association. (1986). *Statement on plagiarism and related misuses of the work of other authors.* Section of *Statement on standards of professional conduct.* Amended January 2002.

American Psychological Association (2001). *Publication manual of the American Psychological Association* (5th ed.). Washington, DC: Author.

Anderson, B. (1991). *Imagined communities: Reflections on the origin and spread of nationalism.* London: Verso.

Anderson, L., Bloom, B. S., Krathwohl, D., & Airasian, P. (2000). *Taxonomy for learning, teaching and assessing: A revision of Bloom's Taxonomy of Educational Objectives.* New York: Allyn & Bacon, Inc.

Angelil-Carter, S. (2000). *Stolen language? Plagiarism in writing.* UK: Pearson Education Limited.

Angelova, M., & Riazantseva, A. (1999). "If you don't tell me, how can I know?": A case study of four international students learning to write the U.S. way." *Written Communication, 16*(4), 491-525.

Anson, C. (2003-2004). Student plagiarism: Are teachers part of the solution or part of the problem? *The Profes-*

sional & Organizational Development Network in Higher Education. Retrieved October 7, 2006 from http://oira.syr.edu/cstl2/Home/Teaching%20Support/Resources/Sub

APA. (2001). *Publication manual* (Fifth ed.). Washington, DC: American Psychological Association.

Asaravala, A. (2004). Warnings: Blogs can be infectious. *Wired News*. Retrieved October 2, 2006 from http://www.wired.com/news/culture/0,1284,62537,00.html

Ashworth, P. D. (2003). Symposium on academic malpractice among students. In *Improving student learning theory and practice - 10 years on*. Oxford: Oxford Centre for Staff and Learning Development, 363-398.

Ashworth, P., Bannister, P., & Thorne, P. (1997). Guilty in whose eyes? University students' perceptions of cheating and plagiarism in academic work and assessment. *Studies in Higher Education, 22*(2), 187-203.

Atkinson, D. (1999). TESOL and culture. *TESOL Quarterly, 33*(4), 625-654.

Auer, N. J., & Krupar, E. M. (2001). Mouse click plagiarism: The role of technology in plagiarism and the librarian's role in combating it. *Library Trends, 49*(3), 415-432.

Austin, M., & Brown, L. (1999). Internet plagiarism: Developing strategies to curb student academic dishonesty. *The Internet and Higher Education, 2*(1), 21-33.

Australasian Council on Open, Distance and E-learning (ACODE) (2005). *Academic Integrity Project: Audit of Academic Integrity and Plagiarism Issues in Australia and New Zealand*. Prepared by the Teaching and Learning Centre, Murdoch University. Retrieved September 6, 2006, from http://www.tlc.murdoch.edu.au/project/acode/

Australian Government (2004). *International higher education students: How do they differ from other education students?* Department of Education, Science and Training. Retrieved January 15, 2007, from http://www.dest.gov.au/sectors/international_education/publications_resources/profiles/international_higher_education_students.htm

Baggaley, J., & Spencer, B. (2005). The mind of a plagiarist. *Learning, Media and Technology, 30*(1), 55-62.

Bain, A. (2007). *Distribution of International Students*. Paper for the Working Party on Interactions between International and Local Students. South Australia. Adelaide: The University of Adelaide.

Bandura, A. (1986). *Social foundations of thought and action: A social cognitive theory*. Englewood Cliff, NJ: Prentice-Hall.

Bandura, A. (1990). *Multidimentional scales of perceived self-efficacy*. Stanford, CA: Stanford University.

Bao, J. P., Shen, J. Y., Liu, X. D., & Liu, H. Y. (2006). A fast document copy detection model. *Soft Computing, 10*(1), 41-46.

Barrett, R., & Malcolm, J. (2006). Embedding plagiarism education in the assessment process. *International Journal for Educational Integrity, 2*(1).

Baty, P. (2004, May 28). Plagiarist student to sue university. *The Times Higher Education. Supplement*. Retrieved October 15, 2006, from http://www.timesonline.co.uk/article/0,,3561-1126250,00.html

Baumbach, N. (Director). (2005). *The squid and the whale* [Motion picture]. United States: Sony Pictures.

BBC news. (2006). *Net students 'think copying OK.'* Retrieved June 19, 2006, from http://news.bbc.co.uk/go/pr/fr/-/hi/education/5093286.stm

BBC news. (2006). *Students 'admit copying essays.'* Retrieved June 19, 2006, from http://news.bbc.co.uk/go/pr/fr/-/hi/education/4810522.stm

BBC news. (2006). *Maths GCSE coursework is dropped*. Retrieved October 11, 2006, from http://news.bbc.co.uk/1/hi/education/5385556.stm

Bennett, R. (2005). Factors associated with student plagiarism in a post-1992 university. *Assessment & Evaluation of Higher Education, 30*(2), 137-162.

Benos, D. J., Fabres, J., Farmer, J., Gutierrez, J. P., Hennessy, K., Kosek, D., et al. (2005). Ethics and scientific publication. *Advances in Physiology Education, 29,* 59-74.

Bhattacharya, M. (2004). Conducting problem-based learning online. In E. McKay (Ed.), *International Conference on Computers in Education 2004 (*pp. 525-530). Melbourne, VIC: RMIT University.

Bhattacharya, M. (2006). Introducing integrated e-portfolio across courses in a postgraduate program in distance and online education. In R.C. Sharma & S. Sharma (Eds.), *Cases on global e-learning practices: Successes and pitfalls.* Chapter 7. Hershey, PA: Information Science Publishing.

Biggs, J. (1994). Asian learners through Western eyes: An astigmatic paradox. *Australian and New Zealand Journal of Vocational Educational Research, 2*(2), 40-63.

Biggs, J., & Watkins, D. (1996). *The Chinese learner.* Hong Kong: Comparative Education Research Centre.

Billington, J.H. (n.d.). *Welcome message from the library of congress.* Retrieved August 26, 2006 from www.loc.gov.about

Birchard, K. (2006). Cheating is rampant at Canadian colleges. *The Chronicle of Higher Education, 53*(8).

Blayney, P., & Freeman, M. (2004). Automated formative feedback and summative assessment using individualised spreadsheet assignments. *Australasian Journal of Educational Technology, 20*(2), 209-231.

Blog Epidemic Analyzer. Retrieved October 5, 2006 from http://www.hpl.hp.com/research/idl/projects/blogs/index.html

Bloom, B. S. (Ed.) (1956). *Taxonomy of educational objectives: The classification of education goals: Handbook I, cognitive domain.* New York, Toronto: Longmans, Green.

Bloom, B., Engelhart, M., Furst, E., Hill, W., & Krathwohl, D. (1956). *Taxonomy of educational objectives: Book 1, Cognitive domain.* New York: David McKay and Company.

Bloomfield, L (2004). The importance of writing. *Philadelphia Inquirer,* April 4. Retrieved August 8, 2006 from http://plagiarism.phys.virginia.edu/essays/The%20Importance%20of%20Writing.html

Bolkan, J. V. (2006). Avoid the plague. *Learning and Leading with Technology, 33*(6),10-13.

Bombak A. (2005). *Guide to plagiarism and cyber-plagiarism.* May 2005. Retrieved August 8, 2006 from http://www.library.ualberta.ca/guides/plagiarism

Bottum, J. (2004). Laurence Tribe and the problem of borrowed scholarship. *The Weekly Standard, 10*(4).

Bowden, D. (1996, April). Coming to terms. *English Journal,* 82-83.

Bowers, W. J. (1964). *Student dishonesty and its control in college* (No. CRP-1672). New York: Columbia University.

Bowman, V. (2004). Teaching intellectual honesty in a tragically hip world: A pop-culture perspective. In V. Bowman (Ed), *The Plagiarism Plague* (pp. 3–9). New York: Neal-Schuman Publishers, Inc.

Boyer Commission (1998). *Reinventing undergraduate education: A blueprint for America's research universities.* Stony Brook, NY: Carnegie foundation for University Teaching. Retrieved August 15, 2006, from http://naples.cc.sunysb.edu/Pres/boyer.nsf/

Boylan, H. R. (1999). Developmental Education: Demographics, outcomes, and activities. *Journal of Developmental Education, 23*(2), 2-8.

Boylan, H. R. (2002). *What works: Research-based best practices in developmental education.* National Center for Developmental Education: Boone, NC.

Boylan, H., Bonham, B., Claxton, C., & Bliss, L. (1992). *The state of the art in developmental education: Report of a national study.* Paper presented at the First National Conference on Research in Developmental Education, Charlotte, NC.

Braumoeller, B. F., & Gaines, B. J. (2001). Actions do speak louder than words: Deterring plagiarism with the use of plagiarism-detection software. *Political Science and Politics, 34*(4), 835-839.

Breen, L. & Maassen M. (2005). Reducing the incidence of plagiarism in an undergraduate course: The role of education. In *Issues In Educational Research, 15*(1), 1-16. Retrieved August 14, 2006 from http://www.iier. org.au/iier15/breen.html

Brenna, L., & Durovic, J. (2005, December). *"Plagiarism" and the Confucian Heritage Culture (CHC) students: Broadening the concept before blaming the student.* Paper presented at the Australia and New Zealand Marketing Academy Conference, Fremantle, Australia. Retrieved July 3, 2006, from http://anzmac2005.conf. uwa.edu.au/Program&Papers/pdfs/8-Mktg-Edn/8-Brennan.pdf

Brewis, J. (n.d.). *Test your understanding of plagiarism.* Retrieved October 2, 2006, from http://www.essex. ac.uk/plagiarism/test.htm

Briggs, R. (2003). Shameless! *Australian Universities Review, 46*(1), 19-23.

Brin, S., Davis, J., and Garcıa-Molina, H. (1995) Copy detection mechanisms for digital documents. In the *proceedings of the ACM SIGMOD Conference,* pp.398–409.

Brookfield, S. D., & Preskill, S. (2005). *Discussion: Tools and techniques for democratic classrooms* (Second ed.). San Francisco: Jossey Bass.

Brown, A. S., & Halliday, H. E. (1991). Cryptomnesia and source memory difficulties. *American Journal of Psychology, 104*(4), 475-490.

Brown, A. S., & Murphy, D. R. (1989). Cryptomnesia: Delineating inadvertent plagiarism. *Journal of Experimental Psychology: Learning, Memory and Cognition, 15*(3), 432-442.

Brown, J. S. & Daguid, P. (1996). The social life of documents. *First Monday, 1*(1). Retrieved October 2, 2006 from http://www.firstmonday.dk/issues/issue1/documents/index.html

Brown, P. (1995). Cultural capital and social exclusion: Some observations on recent trends in education, employment and the labour market. *Work, Employment & Society, 9*(1), 29-51.

Bruner, J. (1960). *The process of education.* Cambridge, Massachusetts: Harvard University Press.

Bruner, J. (1977). *The process of education* (Second ed.). Cambridge: Harvard University Press.

Bull, J., Collins, C., Coughlin, E., & Sharp, D. (2001). *Technical review of plagiarism detection software report.* Luton, UK: University of Luton and Computer Assisted Assessment Centre. Retrieved October 13, 2006, from http://www.jisc.ac.uk/uploaded_documents/luton.pdf

Burke, M. (2004). Deterring plagiarism: A new role for librarians. *Library Philosophy and Practice, 6*(2), 1-9.

Burke, P. J. & Hermerschmidt, M. (2005). Deconstructing academic practices through self-reflexive pedagogies. In B. V. Street (Ed.), *Literacies across educational contexts: Mediating learning and teaching.* Philadephia: Caslon Publishing.

Carbone, N. *Thinking about plagiarism.* From Bedford St. Martin's Strategies for Teaching with Online Tools. Retrieved August 8, 2006 from http://www.bedfordstmartins.com/technotes/hccworkshop/plagiarismhelp.htm

Carbone, N. *Using portfolios to avoid plagiarism in your class.* From Bedford St. Martin's Strategies for Teaching with Online Tools. Retrieved August 8, 2006 from http://bedfordstmartins.com/technotes/hccworkshop/avoidplagiarism.htm

Cargill, M. (2004).Transferable skills within research degrees: A collaborative genre-based approach to developing publication skills and its implications for research education. *Teaching in Higher Education, 9*(1), 83–98.

Cargill, M., & O'Connor, P. (2006). Developing Chinese scientists' skills for publishing in English: Evaluating collaborating-colleague workshops based on genre analysis. *Journal of English for Academic Purposes, 5*(3), 207-221.

Carliner, S. (2005). Course management systems versus learning management systems. *Learning Circuits: American Society for Training & Development.* Retrieved October 13, 2006, from http://www.learningcircuits.org/2005/nov2005/carliner.htm

Carnevale, A. P. (2001). *Community colleges and career qualifications.* Educational Testing Service, Washington, DC. Retrieved August 12, 2006 from http://www.aacc.nche.edu/Content/NavigationMenu/ResourceCenter/Projects_Partnerships/Current/NewExpeditions/Issue Papers/Community_Colleges_and_Career_Qualifications.htm

Carnie, A. (2001). How to handle cyber-sloth in academe. *Chronicle of Higher Education, 47*(17), B14. Retrieved October 15, 2006 from http://chronicle.com/weekly/v47/i17/17b01401.htm

Carroll, J. (2002) *A handbook for deterring plagiarism in higher education.* Oxford: Oxford Centre for Staff and Learning Development.

Carroll, J. (2002). Suggestions for teaching international students more effectively. Learning and Teaching Briefing Papers Series, Oxford Brookes University, www.brookesac.uk/services/ocsd

Carroll, J. (2003). Deterring student plagiarism: Where best to start. *Improving student learning theory and practice—10 years on* (pp. 365-373). Oxford: Oxford Centre for Staff and Learning Development.

Carroll, J., & Appleton, J. (2001). *Plagiarism: A good practice guide.* Retrieved October 14, 2006, from http://www.jisc.ac.uk/uploaded_documents/brookes.pdf

Carroll, J., & Appleton, J. (2005). Towards consistent penalty decisions for breaches of academic regulations in one UK university. *International Journal for Educational Integrity, 1*(1), No pagination. Retrieved March 23, 2006, from http://www.ojs.unisa.edu.au/index.php/IJEI/issue/view/3

Center for Academic Integrity (1999). *The Fundamental Values of Academic Integrity.* Retrieved September 3, 2006, from http://www.academicintegrity.org/

Center for Academic Integrity. (2007). *CAI Research.* Retrieved February 19, 2007, from http://www.academicintegrity.org/cai_research.asp

Centre for Academic Integrity. (2005). *Levels of Cheating and plagiarism remain high: Honor codes and modified codes are shown to be effective in reducing academic misconduct.* Retrieved October 15, 2006.

Chaffee, J. (1992). Critical thinking skills: The cornerstone of developmental education. *The Journal of Developmental Education, 15*(3), 2-8, 39.

Chandrasoma, R., Thompson, C., & Pennycook, A. (2004). Beyond plagiarism: Transgressive and nontransgressive intertextuality. *Journal of Language, Identity, and Education, 3*(3), 171-193.

Chanock, K. (2004). *Introducing student to the culture of enquiry in an arts degree.* HERDSA Guide. Milparra New South Wales: Higher Education Research and Development Society of Australasia.

Cheating students put homework to tender on Internet. (2006, June 13). *Daily Mail, 21.*

Clanchy, M. T. (1979). *From memory to written record, England, 1066-1307.* Cambridge: Harvard University Press.

Clarke, R., & Lancaster, T. (2006). Eliminating the successor to plagiarism? Identifying the usage of contract cheating sites. In *Proceedings of 2nd International Plagiarism Conference.* Gateshead, UK: Northumbria Learning Press.

Clough, P. D. (n.d.). *Measuring Text Reuse in a Journalistic Domain.* Unpublished manuscript, Department of Computer Science, University of Sheffield. Retrieved on January 16, 2007 from http://ir.shef.ac.uk/cloughie/papers/cluk4.pdf

Coastal Carolina University Kimbel Library: Presentations. *Cheating 101: Easy steps to combating plagiarism.* Nov 05, 2004. Retrieved August 8, 2006 from http://www.coastal.edu/library/presentations/easystep.html

Codd, J. (2006). Personal Comment. Palmerston North: Massey University College of Education.

CodingForums.com—Web coding and development forums. Get help on JavaScript, PHP, CSS, XML, mySQL, ASP, and more! (n.d.). Retrieved February 20, 2007, from http://www.codingforums.com

Cogdell, B., Matthew, B., & Gray, C. (2003). Academic cheating: An investigation of medical students' views of cheating on a problem based learning course. *Improving student learning theory and practice—10 years on* (pp. 384-398). Oxford: Oxford Centre for Staff and Learning Development.

Cole, S., & McCabe, D. L. (1996). Issues in academic integrity. In *New Directions for Student Services* (pp. 67-77). Jossey-Bass Publishers.

Collier, H., Perrin, R., & McGowan, C. (2004). Plagiarism: Let the policy fix the crime. *Faculty of commerce papers.* Woollongon: University of Woollongon.

Conradson, S., & Hernández-Ramos, P. (2004). Computers, the Internet, and cheating among secondary school students: Some implications for educators. *Practical assessment, research & evaluation, 9*(9). Retrieved October 6, 2006 from http://PAREonline.net/getvn.asp?v=9&n=9

Consilio. (2004, October18). Student may sue university for failing to spot plagiarism. *Consilio: The daily online magazine for law students.* London: Semple Piggot Rochez. Retrieved October 15, 2006, from http://www.spr-consilio.com/arteducl.htm

Cooper, L. (2007). Cheating a big problem. *At Guelph.* Retrieved February 22, 2007, from http://www.uoguelph.ca/atguelph/06-10-25/featurescheating.shtml

Cope, B., & Kalantzis, M. (1993). How a genre approach to literacy can transform the way literacy is taught. In B. Cope & M. Kalantzis (Eds.), *The powers of literacy: A genre approach to the teaching of writing* (pp. 1-21). London: Falmer Press.

COPE. (2006). *Cases.* Retrieved October 11, 2006 from http://www.publicationethics.org.uk/cases

Council of Writing Program Administrators. (2003). *Defining and avoiding plagiarism: The WPA statement on best practices.* Retrieved August 15, 2006, from http://wpacouncil.org/node/9

Cripps, J. (2005). *Independent commission against corruption's report on investigation into the University of Newcastle's handling of plagiarism allegations*: NSW Independent Commission Against Corruption.

Crook, C., & Light, P. (2002). Virtual society and the cultural practice of study. In S. Woolgar (Ed.), *Virtual society? Technology, cyperbole, reality* (pp. 153-175). London: Oxford University Press.

Culwin, F., & Lancaster, T. (2001). *Plagiarism, Prevention, Deterrence and Detection.* Retrieved February 20, 2007, from http://www.heacademy.ac.uk/resources.asp?process=full_record&section=generic&id=426

Custom Essays Writing Service—ProfEssays. (n.d.). Retrieved February 20, 2007, from http://www.professays.com

Cutts, Q., Barnes, D., Bibby, P., Bown, J., Bush, V., Campbell, P., Fincher, S., Jamieson, S., Jenkins, T., Jones, M., Kazatov, D., Lancaster, T., Ratcliffe, M., Seisenberg, M, Shinner-Kennedy, D., Wagstaff, C., White, L., & Whyley, C. (2006). Laboratory exams in first programming courses. In *Proceedings of 7ᵗʰ Annual Conference for Information and Computer Sciences* (pp. 224-228). Dublin, Ireland: Higher Education Academy.

Damashek, M. (1995). Gauging similarity with ngrams: Language independent categorization of text. *Science, 267*(February 10), 843-848.

Davies, R. (2006). University catches 237 cheats who trawl the Internet. *The Observer*, September 10, 2006.

Davis, B. G. (1993). *Tools for teaching.* Jossey-Bass Publishers: San Francisco.

Davis, S. F., & Ludvigson, H. W. (1995). Faculty forum: Additional data on academic dishonesty and a proposal for remediation. *Teaching of Psychology, 22*(2), 119-121.

Davis, S. J. (1994) Teaching practices that encourage or eliminate student plagiarism. *Middle School Journal, 25*(3), 55–8.

Dean of Students, University of Connecticut. (2006). *Responsibilities of community life: The student code 2006-2007*, p. 11. Retrieved September 30, 2006 from http://www.dosa.uconn.edu/student_code.html

Dean of Studies, Skidmore College. (1999, September). *The ethics of scholarship.* Retrieved September 28, 2006 from http://www.skidmore.edu/administration/dean-studies/EthicScholarship

Deckert, G. (1993). Perspectives on plagiarism from ESL students in Hong Kong. *Journal of Second Language Writing, 2*(2), 131-148.

Decoo, W. (2002). *Crisis on campus: Confronting academic misconduct.* Cambridge, Massachusetts: The MIT Press.

Defining and avoiding plagiarism: The Writing Program Administrators' statement on best practices (2003). Retrieved October 12, 2006 from http://www.ilstu.edu/~ddhesse/wpa/positions/WPAplagiarism.pdf

DeKerckhove, D. (1997). *Connected intelligence: The arrival of the Web society.* Canada: Somerville House.

Deming, W. E. (1986). *Out of the crisis.* Cambridge, MA: Massachusetts Institute of Technology Press.

Devlin, M. (2006). Policy, preparation and prevention: Proactive minimization of student plagiarism. *Journal of Higher Education Policy and Management, 28*(1), 45-58.

Dick, M. (2005, June 27-29). *Student interviews as a tool for assessment and learning in a systems analysis and design course.* Paper presented at the 10th Annual SIGCSE Conference on Innovation and Technology in Computer Science Education, Monte de Caparica, Portugal.

Dick, M., Sheard, J., Bareiss, C., Carter, J., Joyce, D., Harding, T., et al. (2003). Addressing student cheating: Definitions and solutions. *ACM SIGCSE Bulletin, 35*(2), 172-184.

Diekhoff, G. M., LaBeff, E. E., Clark, R. E., Williams, L. E., Francis, B., & Haines, V. J. (1996). College cheating: Ten years later. *Research in Higher Education, 37*(4), 487-502.

Dijkhuis, J., Heuves, W., Hofstede, M., Janssen, M., & Rorsch, A. (1997). *Leiden in last: de zaak-Diekstra nader bekeken* [Dutch. English transl.: *Big troubles in Leiden: A closer look at the case of Diekstra*]. Rijswijk, Netherlands: Elmar.

DOC Cop. (2007). *Bright Ideas.* Retrieved February 8, 2007, from http://www.doccop.com/

Dodd, T. (2006). Teaching, plagiarism, and the new and improved term paper mill. *Teachers College Record.* Date Published: October 17, 2006. Retrieved February 24, 2007, from http://www.tcrecord.org, ID Number: 12794.

Dougiamas, M. (2006). *About Moodle – background.* Retrieved October 13, 2006, from http://docs.moodle.org/en/Background

Dougieamas, M. (2006). *About Moodle – philosophy.* Retrieved October 13, 2006, from http://docs.moodle.org/en/Philosophy

Dreyfus, H. L. (1992). *What computers still can't do.* Cambridge, MA: Massachusetts Institute of Technology Press.

Drinan, P. (2006). *Institutional stages of development.* Retrieved October 13, 2006 from http://www.academicintegrity.org/resources_inst.asp

Dryden, L. (1999). A distant mirror or through the looking glass? Plagiarism and intellectual property in Japanese education. In L. Buranen & A. Roy (Eds.), *Perspectives on plagiarism and intellectual property in a postmodern world* (pp. 75-85). Albany, NY: State University of New York Press.

Duggan, F. (2006). Plagiarism: Prevention, practice and policy. *Assessment & Evaluation in Higher Education, 31*(2), 151-154.

Eanes, R. (2004). *Task oriented question construction wheel based on Bloom's Taxonomy.* Retrieved November 13, 2005 from http://www.stedwards.edu/cte/resources/bwheel.htm

270

Edlund, J. R. (2000). *What is "plagiarism" and why do people do it?* Retrieved August 8, 2006 from http://www.calstatela.edu/centers/write_cn/plagiarism.htm

Ellis, L. (2003). MP3s, Plagiarism, and the Future of Knowledge. *The ClickZ Network.* Retrieved October 2, 2006, from http://www.clickz.com/showPage.html?page=3080961

Emerson, L., Rees, M., & MacKay, B. (2005). Scaffolding academic integrity: creating a learning context for teaching referencing skills. *Journal of University Teaching & Learning Practice, 2*(3a), 1-14. Retrived October 15, 2006 from http://jutlp.uow.edu.au/

Ercegovac Z. & Richardson, J. V. (2004). Academic Dishonesty, plagiarism included, in the digital age: A literature review. *College & Research Libraries, 65*(4), 301-18.

Eriksson, E. J. (2005). *Plagiarism control: Lectures' attitudes.* Unpublished PhD course paper, Department of Philosophy and Linguistics, Umeå University, Sweden.

Errey, L. (2002). *Plagiarism: Something fishy? ...Or just a fish out of water?* OCSLD

Evans, R. (2006). Evaluating an electronic plagiarism detection service: The importance of trust and difficulty of proving students don't cheat. *Active Learning in Higher Education, 7*(1), 87-99.

EVE2. (2007). *Eve Plagiarism Detection System.* Retrieved February 8, 2007, from http://www.canexus.com/

Feller, B. (2006, June 28). Cliff notes for teachers: Educators selling lesson plans online for fee. *Steamboat Today*, p. 20.

Fincher, S., Barnes, D., Bibby, P., Bown, J., Bush, V., Campbell, P., et al. (2006). Some good ideas from the Disciplinary Commons. In *Proceedings of 7ᵗʰ Annual Conference for Information and Computer Sciences* (pp. 153-158). Dublin, Ireland: Higher Education Academy.

Fister, B. (2001). *Reintroducing students to good research.* Lake Forest College. November 7, 2001. Retrieved August 8, 2006 from http://homepages.gac.edu/~fister/LakeForest.html

Foster, A. L. (2002). Plagiarism-detection tool creates legal quandary. *The Chronicle of Higher Education, May 17.* Retrieved October 15, 2006 from http://chronicle.com/free/v48/i36/36a03701.htm

Fox, R. W. (2004). A heartbreaking problem of staggering proportions. *The Journal of American History, 90*(4), 1341-1346.

Franklyn-Stokes, A., & Newstead, S. E. (1995). Undergraduate cheating: Who does what and why? *Studies in Higher Education, 20*(2), 159-172.

Free Culture (2004-2005). *Free culture manifesto.* Retrieved August 8, 2006 from http://freeculture.org/manifesto.php

Freewood, M., Macdonald, R., & Ashworth, P. D. (2003). Why simply policing plagiarism is not enough. *Improving student learning theory and practice—10 years on* (pp. 374-383). Oxford: Oxford Centre for Staff and Learning Development.

Freshminds.co.uk. Retrieved October 2, 2006, from http://www.freshminds.co.uk/FreshMinds_plagiarism_survey.pdf

Friedman, T. L. (2005). *The world is flat.* New York: Farrar, Straus & Giroux.

Furedi, F. (2004). Cheats are having a field day on campus. *Telegraph.* March 17, 2004. Retrieved August 8, 2006 from http://www.telegraph.co.uk/education/main.jhtml?xml=/education/2004/03/20/tefcheat17.xtml

Future Skills Wales. (2005). *New survey results published.* Retrieved October 14, 2006 from http://www.futureskillswales.com

Gaine, C., Hällgren, C., Domínguez, S. P., Noguera, J. S., & Weiner, G. (2003). "Eurokid": An innovative pedagogical approach to developing intercultural and anti-racist education on the Web. *Intercultural Education, 14*(3), 317–329.

Georgetown University Honor Council Web Site. *What is plagiarism?* Retrieved on August 8, 2006 from http://gervaseprograms.georgetownledu/hc/plagiarism.html

GetACoder—Quick and easy project outsourcing. Outsource your project today. (n.d.). Retrieved February 20, 2007, from http://www.getacoder.com

Gilbert, S. W. (1992). Systematic questioning: Taxonomies that develop critical thinking skills. *Science Teacher, 59*(9), 41-46.

Giles, J. (2005). Taking on the cheats. *Nature, 435,* 258–259.

Gillen, C. M., Vaughan, J., & Lye, B. R. (2004). An online tutorial for helping nonscience majors read primary research literature in biology. *Advances in Physiology Education, 28,* 95-99

Glatt Plagiarism Services Inc. (2007). *Glatt Plagiarism Screening Program (GPSP).* Retrieved February 8, 2007, from http://www.plagiarism.com/

Glod, M. (2006). Students rebel against database designed to thwart plagiarists (p. A01). *Washington Post.* Retrieved October 2, 2006 from http://www.washingtonpost.com/wp-dyn/content/article/2006/09/21/AR2006092101800.html

Goodman, A. (2003, September 24). Scholar Norman Finkelstein calls Professor Alan Dershowitz's new book on Israel a "hoax." *Democracy Now* [News program]. Retrieved February 21, 2007, from http://www.democracynow.org/static/dershowitzFin.shtml

Goodstein, D. (2002). Scientific misconduct. *Academe: Bulletin of the American Association of University Professors.* Retrieved October 11, 2006, from http://www.aaup.org/publications/2002/02JF/02jfgoo.htm

Google. (n.d.). Retrieved February 20, 2007, from http://www.google.com

Graff, G. (1993). *Beyond the culture wars: How teaching the conflicts can revitalize American education.* New York: W.W. Norton.

Graff, G. (2003). *Clueless in academe.* New Haven and London: Yale University Press.

Gray, B. (1989). *Collaborating: Finding common ground for multiparty problems.* San Francisco: Jossey Bass.

Green, S. P. (2002). Plagiarism, norms, and the limits of theft law: Some observations on the use of criminal sanctions in enforcing intellectual property rights. *Hastings Law Journal, 54*(1), 167-242.

Greening, T., Kay, J., & Kummerfeld, B. (2004). *Integrating ethical content into computing curricula.* Paper presented at the Sixth Australasian Computing Education conference, Dunedin, New Zealand.

Gulli, A. & Signorini, A. (n.d.). *The indexable Web is more than 11.5 billion pages.* Retrieved August 26, 2006 from www.cs.uiowa.edu/~asignori/web-size

Gulli, C., Kohler, N., & Patriquin, M. (2007). The great university cheating scandal. *MacLeans.* Retrieved February 22, 2007 from http://www.macleans.ca/homepage/magazine/article.jsp?content=20070209_174847_6984

Gusmaroli, D. (2006, June 17). The Cybercheats making a small fortune. *Daily Mail,* 12-13.

Guthrie, V. A., & King, S. N. (2004). Feedback-intensive programs. In C. D. McCauley & E. V. Velsor (Eds.), *Center for Creative Leadership handbook of leadership development* (2nd ed.). San Francisco: Jossey Bass.

Hacker, D. (1996). *Rules for writer* (3rd ed.). Boston: Bedford/St. Martin's.

Haggis, T. (2003). Constructing images of ourselves? A critical investigation into "Approaches to Learning" research in higher education. *British Educational Research Journal, 29*(1), 89-104.

Halbert, D. (2005). *Resisting intellectual property law.* New York: Routledge.

Hällgren C. (2005). "Working harder to be the same:" Everyday racism among young men and women in Sweden. *Race, Ethnicity and Education, 8*(3), 319-341.

272

Hällgren, C., & Wiener, G. (2003). The Web, antiracism, education and the state in Sweden: Why here? Why now? In N. M. Bloch, K. Holmlund, I. Moqvist, & T. S. Popkewitz (Eds), *Restructuring the governing patterns of the child, education and the welfare state* (pp. 313–333). New York: Palgrave Publishing Co.

Halliday, M.A.K., & Hasan, R. (1985). *Language context and text: Aspects of language in a social semiotic perspective.* Geelong: Deakin University Press.

Halliday, M.A.K., & Martin, J.R. (1993). *Writing science. Literacy and discursive power.* London: Falmer Press.

Handy, C. (1995). Trust and the virtual organization. *Harvard Business Review.*

Hansen, B. (2003). Combating plagiarism: Is the Internet causing more students to copy? *The CQ Researcher, 13*(32), 773-796.

Harklau, L. (1999). Representing culture in the ESL writing classroom. In E. Hinkel (Ed.), *Culture in second language teaching and learning* (pp. 109-130). Cambridge: Cambridge University Press.

Harris, R. A. (2001). *The plagiarism handbook: Strategies for preventing, detecting, and dealing with plagiarism.* Los Angeles: Pyrczak Publishing.

Harris. R. (2004). *Anti-Plagiarism strategies for research papers.* November 17, 2004. Retrieved August 8, 2006 from http://www.virtualsalt.com/antiplag.htm

Harvard University Extension School. (2007). *Statement on Plagiarism.* Retrieved February 19, 2007, from http://cyber.law.harvard.edu/ptc/Statement_on_Plagiarism

Hayes, N. & Introna. L. (2005). Cultural values, plagiarism, and fairness: When plagiarism gets in the way of learning, *Ethics and Behavior, 15*(3), 213-231.

HEA. (2005). Special interest group: Teaching ethics to bioscience students. *The Higher Education Academy: Centre for Bioscience.* Retrieved February 21, 2007, from http://www.bioscience.heacademy.ac.uk/network/sigs/ethics/index.htm

Heintze, N. (1996). Scalable document fingerprinting. In *Proceedings of the Second USENIX Electronic Commerce Workshop,* pp. 191-200.

Helfman, J. (1993). Dotplot: a program for exploring self-similarity in millions of lines of text and code. *Journal of Computational and Graphical Statistics, 2*(2), 153-174.

Hermans, H. J. M., & Kempen, H. J. G. (1998). Moving cultures: The perilous problems of cultural dichotomies in a globalizing society. *American Psychologist, 53*(10), 1111-1120.

Hetherington, E. M., & Feldman, S. E. (1964). College cheating as a function of subject and situational variables. *Journal of Educational Psychology, 55*(4), 212-218.

Hoffman, T. (2003, August 25). Job skills: preparing generation z. In *Computerworld Careers.* Retrieved October 14, 2006 from http://www.computerworld.com/action/article

Högskoleverket (HSV) (2005). Disciplinärenden 2004 vid högskolor och univeristet med statligt huvudmannaskap. *Högskoleverkets rapportserie: 2005:28 R,* Stockholm, Sweden: Högskoleverket. Retrieved December 19, 2005 from http://web2.hsv.se/publikationer/rapporter/2005/0528R.pdf

Horn, D. (1998). The shoulders of giants. *Science 29, 280*(5368), 1354-1355.

Horne, L. J. & Carroll, D. C. (1996). *Nontraditional undergraduates: Trends in enrollment from 1986 to 1992 and persistence and attainment among 1989-90 beginning postsecondary students.* Washington, DC: National Center for Education Statistics, U.S. Department of Education. (ED 402 857)

Howard, R. (1993). A plagiarism pentimento. *Journal of Teaching Writing, 11*(2), 233-245.

Howard, R. (1999). *Standing in the shadow of giants: Plagiarists, authors, collaborators.* Stamford, Connecticut: Ablex Publishing.

Howard, R. (2002). Don't police plagiarism: just teach! *Education Digest, 67*(5), 46-50.

Howard, R. M. (1995). Plagiarisms, authorships, and the academic death penalty. *College English, 57*(7), 788-806.

Howard, R. M. (2001, November 16). Forget about policing plagiarism. Just teach. *The Chronicle of Higher Education.* Retrieved February 21, 2007, from http://leeds.bates.edu/cbb/events/docs/Howard_ForgeT.pdf

Howard., R. (2005). Plagiarism: What should a teacher do? In A. Lathrop & K. Foss (Eds.), *Guiding students from cheating and plagiarism to honesty and integrity: Strategies for change* (p. 174). Westport, Connecticut: Libraries Unlimited.

Howell, C. L. (2001). *Facilitating responsibility for learning in adult community college students.* ERIC Digest. Retrieved August 12, 2006 from www.eric.ed.gov (ED 451 841)

Hull, G. & Rose, M. (1989). Rethinking remediation: Toward a social-cognitive understanding of problematic reading and writing. *Written Communication, 6*(2), 139-154.

Hult, Å., & Hult, H. (2003). Att fuska och plagiera – Ett sätt att leva eller ett sätt att överleva? *Report Centrum för undervisning och lärande, No 6.* Linköping, Sweden: Linköping University.

Hunt, R. (2002). Four reasons to be happy about Internet plagiarism. *Teaching Perspectives.* St. Thomas University, Canada. Retrieved May 25, 2005, from http://www.stu.ca/~hunt/4reasons.htm

Ingleton, C. & Wake, B. (1996). *Literacy Matters.* Adelaide, South Australia: Advisory Centre for University Education, University of Adelaide.

International English Language Testing System (IELTS) (2005). *International English Language Test Score Handbook.* Retrieved September 30, 2005, from http://www.ielts.org/_lib/pdf/1649_IELTShbk_2005.pdf

Introna, L. D., Hayes, N., Blair, L., & Wood, E. (2003). *Cultural attitudes towards plagiarism: Developing a better understanding of the needs of students from divers backgrounds relating to issues of plagiarism.* Lancaster, UK: Lancaster University.

Jackson, P. A. (2006). Plagiarism instruction online: Assessing undergraduate students' ability to avoid plagiarism. *College and Research Libraries, 67*(2), 418-427.

James, R., & Baldwin, G. (2002). *Nine principles guiding teaching and learning in the University of Melbourne.* Centre for the Study of Higher Education. Retrieved June 21, 2005, from http://www.cshe.unimelb.edu.au/pdfs/9principles.pdf

Jansen, K. (1996). Grensverleggende stijlen van citeren in ontwikkelingsstudies [Dutch. English transl.: Changing the boundaries in quotation styles in development studies]. *Facta 4*(5), 2-8.

Jenkins, T., & Helmore S. (2006). Coursework for cash: The threat from online plagiarism. In *Proceedings of 7th Annual Conference for Information and Computer Sciences* (pp. 121-126). Dublin, Ireland: Higher Education Academy.

Jin, L., & Cortazzi, M. (1998). The culture the learner brings: A bridge or a barrier? In M. Byram & M. Fleming. (Eds.), *Language learning in intercultural perspective: Approaches through drama and ethnology* (pp. 98-118). Cambridge: Cambridge University Press.

JISC. (2005). *Institutional issues in deterring, detecting and dealing with student plagiarism* [Electronic Version]. Retrieved October 14, 2006 from http://www.jisc.ac.uk/uploaded_documents/plagFinal.pdf

Johnson, D. (2004). Plagiarism-proofing assignments. *Phi Delta Kappan, 85*(7), 549-52.

Joint Information Systems Committee (JISC) (2005). *Deterring, detecting, and dealing with plagiarism.* Joint Information Systems Committee. Retrieved June 20, 2005, from http://www.jisc.ac.uk/

Jonassen, D. (1994). Thinking technology: towards a constructivist design model. *Educational Technology* (April), 34-37.

274

Jonassen, D. H. (2001). *Design of constructivist learning environments*. Retrieved October 15, 2006 from http://www.coe.missouri.edu/~jonassen/courses/CLE/index.html

Jones, N. L. (2005). A code of ethics for bioscience. In J. Bryant, L. Baggott la Velle, & J. Searle, *Introduction to bioethics*. Chichester: John Wiley & Sons (pp. 217-223).

Jones, S. (2002). *The Internet goes to college: How students are living in the future with today's technology*. Washington, DC: Pew Internet and American Life Project.

Josephson Institute (2006, October 15). *2006 Josephson institute report card on ethics of American youth*. Retrieved October 15, 2006 from http://www.josephson-institute.org/reportcard

Kammering, R., Hensler, O., Petrosyan, A., & Rehlick K. (2003). Review of two years experience with an electronic logbook. *Proceedings of ICALEPCS 2003*. Gweongju, Korea: Pohang Accelerator Laboratory.

Kamvounias, P., & Varnham, S. (2006). In-house or in court? Legal challenges to university decisions. *Education and the Law, 18*(1), 1-17.

Kanter, R. M. (1994). Collaborative advantage: The art of alliances. *Harvard Business School Press, July-August* (Reprint 94405), 96-108.

Kasper, H. T. (2002-2003). The changing role of community college. *Occupational Outlook Quarterly, 46*(4), 14-21. Winter 2002-2003. Retrieved August 14, 2006 from http://vnweb.hwwilsonweb.com/hww/results/results_single_fulltext.jhtml

Katz, R. (2005). In R. Kvavik & J. Caruso, *ECAR Study of students and information technology, 2005*. Retrieved from http://www.educause.edu

Keating, E. (2005). *Individualized assignment generation and grading system*. Retrieved February 20, 2007, from http://www.provost.harvard.edu/it_fund/more-info_grants.php?id=131

Kirkpatrick, D. D. (2002). As historian's fame grows, so does attention to sources. *The New York Times* (January 11). Retrieved October 5, 2006 from http://www.nytimes.com/2002/01/11/national/11AMBR.html

Knopp, L. (1996). Remedial education: An undergraduate student profile. *American Council on Education: Research Briefs, 6*(8), 1-11.

Knowles, M. S. & Associates (1984). *Andragogy in action*. San Francisco: Jossey-Bass.

Kolb, D. A. (1976). *Learning Styles Inventory: Technical manual*. Boston: McBer and Company.

Kolb, D. A. (1984). *Experiential learning: Experience as the source of learning and development*. New Jersey: Prentice-Hall.

Kolich, A. M. (1983). Plagiarism: The worm of reason. *College English, 4*, 141-148.

Kom, J. (2006, September 25). Cheating students outsource to lowest bidder. *The Ottawa Citizen*.

Krathwohl, D., Bloom, B., & Masia, B. B. (1964). *Taxonomy of educational objectives: The classification of educational goals Book 2: Affective domain*. New York: David McKay and Company.

Kraus, J. (2002). Rethinking plagiarism: What our students are telling us when they cheat. *Issues in Writing, 13*(1), 80-95.

Kristeva, J. (1980). *Desire in language: A Semiotic approach to literature and art*. New York: Columbia University Press.

Laden, B. V. (2004). Serving emerging majority students. *New Directions for Community Colleges*, (127), 5-19.

Lamkin, M. D. (2004). To achieve the dream, FIRST look at the facts. *Change 36 (6)*, 12-15. Retrieved on August 14, 2006 from http://vnweb.hywilsonweb.com/hww/results_single-fulltext.jhtml

Lancaster, T., & Culwin, F. (2007). Preserving academic integrity—fighting against non-originality agencies. *British Journal of Educational Technology, 38*(1), 153-157.

Land, R., Cousin, G., Meyer, J. H. F., & Davies, P. (2005). Threshold concepts and troublesome knowledge (3): Implications for course design and evaluation. *Improving student learning - equality and diversity.* Oxford: Oxford Centre for Staff and Learning Development, 53-64.

Landau, J. D., Druen, P. B., & Arcuri, J. A. (2002). Methods and techniques: Method for helping students avoid plagiarism. *Teaching of Psychology, 29*(2), 112-115.

Larkham, P. J., & Manns, S. (2002). Plagiarism and its treatment in higher education. *Journal of Further and Higher Education, 26,* 339-349.

Lathrop, A. (2000). *Student cheating and plagiarism in the Internet era: A wake-up call.* Englewood, CO: Libraries Unlimited.

Lathrop, A., & Foss, K. (2000). *Student Cheating and Plagiarism in the Internet Era—A Wake Up Call.* Libraries Unlimited Inc.

League for Innovation in the Community College. *"The learning college project."* Retrieved on September 30, 2006 from http://www.league.org/league/projects/lcp/index.htm

Leask, B. (2006). Plagiarism, cultural diversity and metaphor—Implications for academic staff development. *Assessment & Evaluation in Higher Education, 31*(2), 183-199.

Leatherman, C. (1999). At Texas A&M, Conflicting charges of misconduct tear a program apart. *Chronicle of Higher Education, 5*(November), A18.

Leland, B. H. (2002). *Plagiarism and the web.* January 29, 2002. Retrieved August 8, 2006 from http://www.wiu.edu/users/mfbhl/wiu/plagiarism.htm

Leonard, T.C. (n.d.). *Visitor information.* Retrieved August 26, 2006 from http://www.lib.berkeley.edu/About-Library/Visitor_information

Lessig, L. (2002). *The future of ideas: The fate of the commons in a connected world.* New York: Vintage Books.

Lessig, L. (2004). *Free culture: The nature and future of creativity.* New York: Penguin.

LeTendre, G. K. (1999). The problem of Japan: Qualitative studies and international educational comparisons. *Educational Researcher, 28*(2), 38-45.

Lethem, J. (2007). Ecstasy of influence: A plagiarism. *Harper's Magazine.* Retrieved February 22, 2007 from http://www.harpers.org/TheEcstasyOfInfluence.html

Levinson, H. (2005). *Internet essays prove poor buys.* Retrieved February 20, 2007, from http://news.bbc.co.uk/1/hi/education/4420845.stm

Li, J. (2003). U.S. and Chinese cultural beliefs about learning. *Journal of Educational Psychology, 95*(2), 258-267.

Lightfoot, L. (2006, June 13). Cheating students put assignments out to tender on the Internet. *Daily Telegraph,* 1.

Lillis, T. M. & Ramsey, M. (1997). Student status and the question of choice in academic writing. *Research and Practice in Adult Learning Bulletin,* Spring, 15-22.

Lipman, M. (1993). Promoting better classroom thinking. *Educational Psychology, 13*(3/4).

LoCastro, V., & Masuko, M. (2002). Plagiarism and academic writing of learners of English. *Hermes, Journal of Linguistics, 28,* 11-38.

London, S. (2005). Thinking together: The power of deliberative dialogue. In R. J. Kingston (Ed.), *Public Thought and Foreign Policy.* Dayton: Kettering Foundation Press.

Longstaff, S., Ross, S., & Henderson, K. (2003). *St James Ethics Centre Report. Independent inquiry: Plagiarism policies, procedures & management controls* (Commissioned report). Newcastle, New South Wales, Australia: St James Ethics Centre.

Loughborough University, Careers Centre. (n.d.). *Skills employers seek.* Retrieved October 14, 2006 from http://www.lbro.ac.uk/service/careers

276

Love, P. G. (1998). Factor influencing cheating and plagiarism among graduate students in a college of education. *College Student Journal, 32*(4), 539-550.

MacDonald, L. T. (2007). Learning styles sites. *How To Study.* Chemeketa Community College. Retrieved January 2, 2007 from http://www.howtostudy.org/resources_skill.php?id=5

MacDonell, C. (2005). The problem of plagiarism. Students who copy may not know they've committed an offence. *School Library Journal, 54*(1), 35.

MacLeod, D. (2006, June 13). Publish and be damned. *The Guardian, Education Supplement*, 10.

Madden, M., & Rainie, L. (2003). *Music downloading, file-sharing and copyright*: Pew Internet and American Life Project.

Madden, M., & Rainie, L. (2005). *Music and video downloading moves beyond P2P*: Pew Internet and American Life Project.

Maines, S. (2006). KU renews anti-plagiarism software subscription. *LJWorld.com.* Retrieved October 7, 2006 from http://www2.ljworld.com/news/2006/oct/04/ku_renews_antiplagiarism_software_subscription/?ku_news

Mallon, T. (1989). *Stolen words: Forays into the origins and ravages of plagiarism.* New York: Ticknor & Fields.

Maramark, S., & Maline, M. B. (1993). *Academic dishonesty among college students. Issues in education.* (Information analyses No. OR-93-3082). Washington, DC: Office of Educational Research and Improvement (ED).

Marsden, H., Carroll, M., & Neill, J. (2005). Who cheats at university? A self-report study of dishonest academic behaviours in a sample of Australian university students. *Australian Journal of Psychology, 57*(1), 1-10.

Marsden, H., Carroll, M., & Neill, J. T. (2005). The contribution of demographic, situational and psychological factors to dishonest academic behaviours *Australian Journal of Psychology, 57*, 1-10.

Marsh, C. & Morris, P. (eds.) (1991). *Curriculum development in East Asia.* London: Falmer Press.

Marsh, R. L., & Bower, G. H. (1993). Eliciting cryptomnesia: Unconscious plagiarism in a puzzle task. *Journal of Experimental Psychology: Learning, Memory, and Cognition, 19*(3), 673-688.

Marsh, R. L., & Landau, J. D. (1995). Item availability in cryptomnesia: Assessing its role in two paradigms of unconscious plagiarism, *Journal of Experimental Psychology: Learning, Memory, and Cognition, 21*(6), 1568–1583.

Marsh, R. L., Landau, J. D., & Hicks, J. L. (1997). Contributions of inadequate source monitoring to unconscious plagiarism during idea generation. *Journal of Experimental Psychology: Learning, Memory and Cognition, 23*, 886-897.

Marshall, S., & Garry, M. (2005, December 3-6). *How well do students really understand plagiarism?* Paper presented at the Annual *ascilite* conference., Brisbane, Australia.

Marshall, S., & Garry, M. (2005, December 2-3). *NESB and ESB students' attitudes and percpetions of plagiarism.* Paper presented at the 2nd Asia-Pacific Educational Conference (Newcastle). Retrieved October 8, 2007, from htp://www.newcastle.edu/au/conference/apeic/papers_pdf/marshall_0519.edd.pdf

Martin, B. (1992). Plagiarism by university students: the problem and some proposals. *Tertangala* (July 20 - August 3).

Martin, B. (1994) Plagiarism: A misplaced emphasis. *Journal of Information Ethics, 3*(2), 36-47. Retrieved on August 8, 2006 from http://www.uow.edu.au/arts/sts/bmartin/pubs/94jie.html

Martin, Brian. (2004). Plagiarism: policy against cheating or policy for learning. *Nexus 16(2) 15-16.* Retrieved October 15, 2006, from http://www.uow.edu.au/arts/sts/bmartin/pubs/04nexus.htm

Martin, D. (2005). Plagiarism and technology: A tool for coping with plagiarism. *Journal of Education for Business*, (January/February), 149-152.

Massey University, (2006). Policy on plagiarism. Palmerston North: College of Education.

Maths GCSE coursework is dropped. (2006). Retrieved February 20, 2007, from http://news.bbc.co.uk/1/hi/education/5385556.stm

McCabe, D. (2005). Cheating among college students. A North American perspective. *International Journal for Educational Integrity*, *1*(1), No pagination. Retrieved March 23, 2006, from http://www.ojs.unisa.edu.au/index.php/IJEI/issue/view/3

McCabe, D. (2005). Cheating: Why students do it and how we can help them to stop. In A. Lathrop and K. Foss (Eds.). *Guiding students from cheating and plagiarism to honesty and integrity: Strategies for change* (pp. 237-242). Westport, Connecticut: Libraries Unlimited.

McCabe, D. L. & Christensen Hughes, J. (2006). Understanding academic misconduct. *The Canadian Journal of Higher Education, 36*(1), 49-63.

McCabe, D. L. & Treviño, L. K. (1996). What we know about cheating in college. *Change, 28*(1). Academic Search Premier.

McCabe, D. L. (2000). *New research on academic integrity: The success of "Modified" honor codes*. College Administration Publications. Asheville, NC. Retrieved October 2, 2006 from http://www.collegepubs.com/ref/SFX000515.shtml

McCabe, D. L. (2001). Cheating in academic institutions: A decade of research. *Ethics & Behavior, 11*(3), 219.

McCabe, D. L. (2003). Promoting academic integrity: A U.S./Canadian perspective in educational integrity: Plagiarism and other perplexities. In H. H. Marsden, M. (Ed.), *Educational integrity: Plagiarism and Other Perplexities, Refereed Proceedings of the Inaugural Educational Integrity Conference*. Adelaide, South Australia: University of South Australia.

McCabe, D. L. (2003). Promoting academic integrity: A US/Canadian Perspective. In *Educational Integrity: Plagiarism and Other Perplexities, Proceedings of the First Australasian Integrity Conference*. University of South Australia, Adelaide.

McCabe, D. L. (2005). Cheating among college and university students: A North American perspective. *International Journal for Educational Integrity, 1*(1). Retrieved October 8, 2007, from http://www.ojs.unisa.edu.au/index.php/IJEI/article/viewFile/14/9

McCabe, D. L., & Drinan, P. (1999). Toward a culture of academic integrity. *Chronicle of Higher Education, 46*(8), B7.

McCabe, D. L., & Trevino, L. K. (1993). Academic dishonesty: Honor codes and other contextual influences. *Journal of Higher Education, 64*(5), 522-538.

McCabe, D. L., & Trevino, L. K. (1997). Individual and contextual influences on academic dishonesty: A multicampus investigation. *Research in Higher Education, 38*(3), 379-396.

McCabe, D. L., Butterfield, K. D. & Treviño, L. K. (2004). Academic integrity: How widespread is cheating and plagiarism? In D. R. Karp & T. Allena (Eds.), *Restorative justice on the college campus: Promoting student growth and responsibility, and reawakening the spirit of campus community* (pp. 124-35). Springfield, IL: Charles C. Thomas.

McCabe, D. L., Butterfield, K. D. & Treviño, L. K. (2006). Academic dishonesty in graduate business programs: Prevalence, causes, and proposed action. *Academy of Management Learning & Education, 5*(3), 294-305.

McCabe, D., Butterfield, K. & Trevino, L. (2004). Academic integrity: How widespread is cheating and plagiarism? In D. Karp & T. Allena (Eds.), *Restorative justice on the college campus: Promoting student growth and responsibility, and reawakening the spirit of campus community* (pp. 124-135). Springfield, Illinois: Charles C. Thomas.

McCullen, C. (2003) Tactics and resources to help students avoid plagiarism. *Multimedia Schools, 10*(6), 40-43.

278

McDonald, N. (2004). The future of weblogging. *The Register*. Retrieved October 2, 2006, from http://www.theregister.co.uk/2004/04/18/blogging_future

McDonnell, C. (1999). *Proactive pedagogy: Limiting student plagiarism through course design*. Presentation at the Teaching English in the Two-Year College Southeast Convention, Memphis, Tennessee. February 19, 1999.

McGill student continues fight against anti-plagiarism Web site. (2003). *CBC.com*. Retrieved October 6, 2003 from http://www.cbc.ca/news/story/2003/12/27/plagiarism031227.html

McGowan, U. (2005). *Plagiarism detection and prevention: Are we putting the cart before the horse?* Paper presented at the Higher Education Research and Development conference (HERDSA), Sydney, Australia.

McGowan, U. (2005). Plagiarism detection and prevention. Are we putting the cart before the horse? In A. Brew & C. Asmar (Eds.), *Higher education in a changing world. Proceedings of the HERDSA Conference* (pp. 287-293). Sydney. Retrieved August 15, 2005, from http://www.itl.usyd.edu.au/herdsa2005/pdf/refereed/paper_412.pdf

McGowan, U. (2005). Does educational integrity mean teaching students NOT to "use their own words?" *International Journal for Educational Integrity, 1*(1), no pagination. Retrieved March 23, 2006, from http://www.ojs.unisa.edu.au/index.php/IJEI/issue/view/3

McGowan, U. (2005). *Educational integrity: A strategic approach to anti-plagiarism*. Paper presented at the 2nd Asia Pacific Educational Integrity Conference (pp. 1-10). Newcastle, Australia, December 1-3. Retrieved January 15, 2007, from http://www.newcastle.edu.au/conference/apeic/papers.html

McGowan, U. (2005). Academic integrity: An awareness and development issue for students and staff. *Journal of University Teaching and learning Practice, 2*(3a), 48-57. Retrieved January 20, 2007, from http://jutlp.uow.edu.au

McGowan, U. (2006). *Plagiarism framework: Student as apprentice researcher*. The University of Adelaide Web site: Resources for Staff. Retrieved December 15, 2006, from http://www.adelaide.edu.au/clpd/plagiarism/staff/

Mckeever, L. (2006). Online plagiarism detection service – Saviour or scourge? *Assessment & Evaluation in Higher Education, 31*(2), 155-165.

McKenzie, J. (1998). The new plagiarism: Seven antidotes to prevent highway robbery in an electronic age. *From Now On: The Educational Technology Journal, 7*(8). Retrieved August 15, 2006 from http://fno.org/may98/cov98may.html

McKenzie, J. (1999). The Research cycle 2000. *From Now On: The Educational Technology Journal, 9*(4).

McLafferty, C. L., & Foust, K. M. (2004). Electronic plagiarism as a college instructor's nightmare--Prevention and detection. *Journal of Education for Business, 79*(3), 186-189.

McLemee, S. (2004). What is plagiarism? *The Chronicle of Higher Education, 51*(17), A9-D17.

McLeod, K. (2001). *Owning culture: Authorship, ownership, and intellectual property law*. New York: Peter Lang.

McLeod, K. (2005). *Freedom of expression: Overzealous copyright bozos and other enemies of creativity*. New York: Doubleday.

McLeod, S. H. (1992). Responding to plagiarism: The role of the WPA. *Writing Program Administration, 15*(3), 7-16.

McLuhan, M. (1964). The medium is the message. *Understanding Media: The Extensions of Man*. New York: McGraw Hill.

McSherry, C. (2001). *Who owns academic work? Battling for control of intellectual property*. Cambridge, Massachusetts: Harvard University Press.

Mehegan, D. (2006, April 25). After duplicated words, words of apology. *The Boston Globe*. Retrieved September 27, 2006 from http://www.boston.com/ac/books/articles/2006/04/25/after

Merriam, S. B., & Caffarella, R. S. (1999). *Learning in adulthood: A comprehensive guide. 2nd Edition.* San Francisco: Jossey-Bass.

Meyer, J. H. F., & Land, R. (2003). Threshold concepts and troublesome knowledge: Linkages to ways of thinking and practising within the disciplines. *Improving student learning theory and practice—10 years on* (pp. 412-424). Oxford: Oxford Centre for Staff and Learning Development.

Meyer, J. H. F., & Land, R. (2005). Threshold concepts and troublesome knowledge (2): Epistemological considerations and a conceptual framework for teaching and learning. *Higher Education, 49,* 373-388.

Moeller, H. (2003). Before and after representation. *Semiotica, 143*(1/4), 69–77.

Moodle—A Free, Open Source Course Management System for Online Learning. (n.d.). Retrieved February 20, 2007, from http://www.moodle.org

Morris, P. & Sweeting, A.(eds.) (1995). *Education and development in East Asia.* New York and London: Garland Publishing Inc.

Morton, A., & Tarica, E. (2006, September 9). Web offers cheats tailor-made assignments. *The Age.*

Moss, C. (2004, May 11). *Grey Album* Producer Danger Mouse Explains How He Did It. *MTV On-Line.* Retrieved February 11, 2007 from http://www.mtv.com/news/articles

Moss. (2007). *A system for detecting software plagiarism.* Retrieved February 8, 2007, from http://theory.stanford.edu/~aiken/moss/

Move to end more GCSE coursework. (2006). Retrieved February 20, 2007, from http://news.bbc.co.uk/1/hi/education/5411350.stm

MSVU bans anti-plagiarism software. (2006). *CBC.com.* Retrieved October 2, 2006, from http://www.cbc.ca/canada/nova-scotia/story/2006/03/08/ns-msvu-plagiarism20060308.html

Mulholland, H. (2006, September 27). Johnson to scrap GCSE maths coursework. *The Guardian.* Retrieved October 11, 2006, from http://education.guardian.co.uk/policy/story/0,,1882294,00.html

Murray, B. (2002). Keeping plagiarism at bay in the Internet age. *Monitor, 33*(2)..Retrieved August 8, 2006 from http://www.apa.org/monitor/feb02/plagiarism.html

MyDropBox. (2007). MyDropBox Suite. Retrieved February 8, 2007, from http://www.mydropbox.com/

Myers, S. (1998). Questioning author(ity): ESL/EFL, science, and teaching about plagiarism. *Teaching English as a Second or Foreign Language, 3*(2). http://www-writing.berkeley.edu/TESL-EJ/ej10/a2.html

National Association of Colleges and Employers (NACE) (2006). *Job Outlook 2006.* Retrieved September 25, 2006 from http://www.naceweb.org

National Center for Education Statistics. (2002). *Special analysis 2002: Nontraditional undergraduates.* Retrieved August 21, 2006 from http://www.bedfordstmartins.com/technotes/hccworkshop/plagiarismhelp.htm

Nature. (1997). Games people play with authors' names. Editorial. *Nature, 387,* 831.

Netskills. (2004, April 7). *Detecting and deterring plagiarism. The Web: hindrance or help?* Workshop held at Leeds Metropolitan University. Netskills, University of Newcastle. Retrieved October 14, 2006, from http://www.netskills.ac.uk/content/about/

Neufeldt, V., & Guralnik, D. B. (Eds.). (1988). *Webster's new world dictionary of American English* (3rd ed.). New York: Simon & Schuster.

Nilsson, L. -E., Eklöf, A., & Ottosson, T. (2005). Copy-and-paste plagiarism: Technology as a blind alley or a road to better learning? *Proceedings of the 33rd congress of the Nordic Educational Research Association (NERA).* Oslo, Norway. March 10 – 12, 2005.

Noddings, N. (1991). The teacher as judge: A brief sketch of two fairness principles. In David Ericson (Ed.), *Philosophy of Education 1990* (pp. 350-359). Normal, Illinois: Philosophy of Education Society.

280

Nordstrom, A. D. (1997, September 15). Adult students a valuable market to target. *Marketing News, 31*(19), 20-21.

O'Connor, S. (2003, May 6-9). Cheating and electronic plagiarism—Scope, consequences, and detection. In *Proceedings EDUCAUSE in Australasia,* Adelaide, (CD-ROM).

O'Donoghue, T. (1996). Malaysian Chinese student's perceptions of what is necessary for their academic success in Australia: A case study at one university. *Journal of Further and Higher Education, 20*(2), 67-80.

O'Malley, J. M. & Pierce L. V. (1996). *Authentic assessment for English language learners: Practical approaches for teachers.* Addison-Wesley.

O'Regan, K. (2006). Policing—or, at least, policing—plagiarism at one Australian university. *Journal of University Teaching and learning Practice, 3*(2), 114-123. Retrieved January 20, 2007, from http://jutlp.uow.edu.au

Oblinger, D. G. & Oblinger, J. L. (2005). Is it age or IT: First steps toward understanding the Net generation. In D. G. Oblinger & J. L. Oblinger (Eds.), *Educating the Net Generation.* An Educause e-book. Retrieved October 10, 2006, from http://www.educause.edu/EducatingtheNetGeneration/5989

Office of Research Integrity. (1994). ORI provides working definition of plagiarism. *ORI Newsletter, 3*(1).

Ohio University Academic Advancement Center. *The 168-hour exercise: How do I use my time now?* Retrieved August 21, 2006 from http://studytips.aac.ohiou.edu/?Function=TimeMgt&Type=168hour

Online Activities and Pursuits. (2004). Retrieved October 2, 2006, from http://www.pewinternet.org/report_display.asp?r=113

Orlans, H. (1999). Fair use in US scholarly publishing. *Learned Publishing, 12*(4), 135-244.

Outsourcing to Freelance Programmers, Web & Logo Designers, Writers, Illustrators on Elance. (n.d.). Retrieved February 20, 2007, from http://www.elance.com

Page, J. S. (2004). Cyber-pseudepigraphy: A new challenge for higher education policy and management. *Journal for Higher Education Policy and Management, 26*(3), 429-433.

Pajares, F., & Schunk, D. H. (2001). Self-beliefs and school success: Self-efficacy, self-concept, and school achievement. In R. Riding & S. Rayner (Eds.), *Perception* (pp. 239-266). London: Ablex Publishing.

Park, C. (2003). In other (people's) words: Plagiarism by university students—literature and lessons. *Assessment & Evaluation in Higher Education, 28*(5), 471-488. Retrieved October 15, 2006 from http://www.lancs.ac.uk/staff/gyaccp/caeh_28_5_02lores.pdf

Park, C. (2004). Rebels without a clause: Towards an institutional framework for dealing with plagiarism by students. *Journal of Further and Higher Education, 28*(3), 291-306.

Pascarella, E. T., Whitt, E. J., Nora, A., Edison, M., Hagendorn, L. S., & Terenzini, P. T. (1996). What have we learned from the first year of the national study of student learning? *Journal of College Student Development, 37*(2), 182-192.

Pearson, G. (2005). *Preventing plagiarism: General strategies.* Electronic Plagiarism Seminar of Lemoyne College, Syracuse, NY. Retrieved on August 8, 2006 from http://www.lemoyne.edu/library/plagiarism/prevention_strategies.htm

Pecorari, D. (2001). Plagiarism and international students: How the English-speaking university responds. In D. Belcher & A. Hirvela (Eds.), *Linking literacies: Perspectives on L2 reading-writing connections* (pp. 229-245). Ann Arbor, MI: University of Michigan Press.

Pecorari, D. (2003). Good and original: Plagiarism and patchwriting in academic second language writing. *Journal of Second Language Writing, 12,* 317-345.

Pecorari, D. (2006). Visible and occluded citation features in postgraduate second language writing. *English for specific purposes, 25,* 4-29.

Pennycook, A. (1994). The complex contexts of plagiarism: A reply to Deckert. *Journal of Second Language Writing, 3*(3), 277-284.

Pennycook, A. (1996). Borrowing others' words: Text, ownership memory, and plagiarism. *TESOL Quarterly, 30*(2), 201-230.

Pew Internet & American Life Project. (2005, July 27). *Teens and technology: Youth are leading the transition to a fully mobile nation.* Retrieved August 22, 2006 from http://www.pewinternet.org

Phillippe, K. A. (ed.). (2000). *National profile of community colleges: Trends and statistics 3rd edition.* Washington, D. C.: American Association of Community Colleges. (ED 440 671)

Plagiarism guidelines: *Brochure for university writing program faculty.* (n.d.). Retrieved February 22, 2007 from http://writingprogram.ucdavis.edu/docs/plagiarism.htm

Plagiarism.org. (2005). Retrieved August 8, 2006 from http://www.plagiarism.org/plagiarism.html

Prensky, M. (2001). Digital natives, digital immigrants. Do they really think differently? *On the Horizen, 9*(6), 1-6.

Prochaska, E. (2001). Western rhetoric and plagiarism: Gatekeeping for an English-only international academia. *Writing on the Edge, 12*(2). 65-79.

Procter, M. (2006). *Deterring plagiarism: Some strategies.* Retrieved October 10, 2006 from http://www.utoronto.ca/writing/plagiarism.html#3

Purdy, J. (2005). Calling off the hounds: Technology and the visibility of plagiarism. *Pedagogy: Critical Approaches to Teaching Literature, Language, Composition, and Culture, 5*(2), 275-295.

QAA. (2002). *Biosciences: Subject benchmark statements.* Gloucester, UK: Quality Assurance Agency for Higher Education.

Ramsden, P. (1992). *Learning to teach in higher education*, London: Routledge.

Ramsey, J. (2004). Integrity board case study: Sonia's plagiarism. In D. Karp & T. Allena (Eds.), *Restorative justice on the college campus: Promoting student growth and responsibility, and reawakening the spirit of campus community* (pp. 136-141). Springfield, Illinois: Charles C. Thomas.

Ray, D. (2001). Web site may catch, deter plagiarized work. *Daily Nexus Online: UC Santa Barbara's Student Newspaper.* Retrieved October 3, 2006 from http://www.ucsbdailynexus.com/news/2001/1252.html

Reilly, C. (2005). Teaching by example: A case for peer workshops about pedagogy and technology. *Innovate: Journal of Online Education, 1*(3).

Rent A Coder: how software gets done. (n.d.). Retrieved February 20, 2007 from http://www.rentacoder.com

Reynard, L. (2000). Cut and paste 101: Plagiarism and the Net. *Educational Leadership, 57*(4), 38-42.

Roberts, P., Anderson, J., & Yanish, P. (1997, October). *Academic misconduct: Where do we start?* Paper presented at the Annual Conference of the Northern Rocky Mountain Educational Research Association. Jackson, Wyoming.

Roberts, T. S. (2007). *Assessment in higher education: Plagiarism.* Retrieved February 19, 2007, from http://ahe.cqu.edu.au/plagiarism.html

Rocklin, T. (1998). *Downloadable term papers: What's a prof. to do?* Retrieved on August 15, 2006 from http://www.uiowa.edu/%7Ecenteach/resources/ideas/term-paper-download.html

Roig, M. (1997). Can undergraduate students determine whether text has been plagiarised. *The Psychological Record, 47,* 113-122.

Roig, M. (1998). *Undergraduates judgements of plagiarism and correct paraphrasing revisited.* Paper presented at the 69th Annual Meeting of the Eastern Pscyhological Association, Boston, MA.

Roig, M. (2001). Plagiarism and paraphrasing criteria of college and university professors. *Ethics and Behaviour, 11*(3), 307-324.

282

Roueche, J. E., & Roueche, S. D. (1999). Keeping the promise: Remedial education revisited. *Community College Journal, 69*(5), 12-18.

Roy, A. M. (1999). Whose words these are I think I know: Plagiarism, the postmodern, and faculty attitudes. In L. Buranen & A. Roy (Eds.), *Perspectives on plagiarism and intellectual property in a postmodern world* (pp. 55-61). Albany, New York: State University of New York Press.

Ryan, J. (2000). *A guide to teaching international students.* Oxford: Oxford Centre for Staff Development, Oxford Brookes University.

Ryan, J. (2004) Stealing from themselves. *ASSEE Prism 13,(5),* 64.

Saltmarsh, S. (2005). "White pages" in the academy: Plagiarism, consumption, and racist rationalities. *International Journal for Educational Integrity, 1*(1), no pagination. Retrieved March 23, 2006, from http://www.ojs.unisa.edu.au/index.php/IJEI/issue/view/3

Saltmarsh, S., (2004). Graduating tactics: Theorizing plagiarism as consumptive practice. *Journal of Further and Higher Education, 28*(4), 445-454.

Sampson, Z. C. (2004). Demand for community colleges tests resources. *Community College Times,* September 7.

Sandberg, G. (online). *Blog.* Retrieved December 19, 2005 from http://www.vk.se/Article.jsp?article=36545&leftmenu =132

Sapp, D. A. (2002). Towards an international and intercultural understanding of plagiarism and academic dishonesty in composition: Reflections from the People's Republic of China. *Issues in Writing, 13*(1), 58-79.

Sarton, M. (1962). *The small room.* New York: Norton.

Saunders, E. J. (1993). Confronting academic dishonesty. *Journal of Social Work Education, 29*(2), 224–230.

Scanlon, P. M. (2003). Student online plagiarism: How do we respond? *College Teaching, 51*(4), 161-5.

Scanlon, P. M., & Neumann, D. R. (2002). Internet plagiarism amongst college students. *Journal of College Student Development, 43*(3), 374-385.

Schleimer, S., Wilkerson, D.,& Aiken, A. (2003, June). Winnowing: Local algorithms for document fingerprinting. In *Proceedings of the ACM SIGMOD International Conference on Management of Data,* 76-85.

Schunk, D. H. (1991). Self-efficacy and academic motivation. *Educational Psychologist, 26*(3&4), 207-231.

Schwarz, C. (Ed) (1992). *Maxi paperback dictionary.* Edinburg: Chambers Harrap Publishers Ltd.

Scollon, R. (1995). Plagiarism and ideology: Identity in intercultural discourse. *Language in Society, 24*(1), 1-28.

Scott, J. (2002). *Using technology wisely.* Retrieved July 7, 2004 from http://www.wmich.edu/imi/teaching/blooms-pyramid.html

Share, P. (2006). *Managing intertextuality: Meaning, plagiarism and power.* Paper presented at the 2nd International Plagiarism Conference 2006, Newcastle Gateshead, UK.

Sharma, T. (2006, April 27). Free culture summit unites movement. *The Phoenix Online.* Retrieved October 8, 2006 from http://phoenix.swarthmore.edu/2006-04-27/news/16199

Sheard, J., & Dick, M. (2003). *Influences on cheating practice of IT students: What are the factors?* Paper presented at the Innovation and Technology in Computer Science Education (ITiCSE 2003), Thessaloniki, Greece.

Sheard, J., Markham, S., & Dick, M. (2003). Investigating differences in cheating behaviours of IT undergraduate and graduate students: The maturity and motivation factors. *Journal of Higher Education Research and Development, 22*(1), 91-108.

Shemo, D. At two-year college, students eager but unready. *New York Times* online. Retrieved on September 6, 2006 from http://www.nytimes.com/2006/09/02/education/02college.html?ex=1157860800&en=d5cfaf f8cdeb31bb&ei=5070&emc=etal

Sherman, J. (1992). Your own thoughts in your own words. *ELT Journal, 46*(2), 190-198.

Shih, H. P. (2006). Assessing the effects of self-efficacy and competence on individual satisfaction with computer use: An IT student perspective. *Computer in Human Behavior, 22*(6), 1012-1026.

Slavin, R. E. (1989). Research on cooperative learning: An international perspective. *Scandinavian Journal of Educational Research, 33*(4), 231-243.

Sowden, C. (2005). Point and counterpoint: Plagiarism and the culture of multilingual students in higher education abroad. *ELT Journal, 59*(3), 226-233.

Standler, R. B. (2000). *Plagiarism in colleges in USA.* Retrieved February 25, 2007 from http://www.rbs2.com/plag.htm

Stanford University (online) *What is plagiarism?* Retrieved December 19, 2005 from http://www.stanford.edu/dept/vpsa/judicialaffairs/students/plagiarism.sources.htm

Stanford University. (2007). *Honor code.* Retrieved April 3, 2007, from http://www.stanford.edu/dept/vpsa/judicialaffairs/guiding/pdf/honorcode.pdf

Stern, E. B., & Havlicek, L. (1986). Academic misconduct: Results of faculty and undergraduate student surveys. *Journal of Allied Health, 5*, 129-142.

Sterngold, A. (2004). Confronting plagiarism. How conventional teaching invites cyber-cheating. *Change, 36*(3), 16-21.

Stoerger, S. (2006). *Plagiarism.* Retrieved February 19, 2007, from http://www.web-miner.com/plagiarism

Stolley, K. (2006). *Avoiding plagiarism.* The Online Writing Lab at Purdue. May 12, 2006. Retrieved on August 8, 2006 from http://owl.english.purdue.edu/owl/printable/589

Strauss, A. L., & Corbin, J. M. (1998). *Basics of Qualitative Research* (2nd ed.). Thousand Oaks, California, USA: Sage Publications Inc.

Student cheats contract out work. (2006). Retrieved February 20, 2007 from http://news.bbc.co.uk/1/hi/education/5071886.stm

Swain, H. (2004). I could not have put it better so I won't. *Times Higher Education Supplement*, June 25, 2004, p.23.

Swales, J. & Freak, C. (1994). *Academic writing for graduate students*, Ann Arbor: University of Michigan.

Swales, J. (1990). *Genre analysis. English in academic research settings.* New York: Cambridge University Press.

Swales, J. (2004). *Research genres. Exploration and applications.* New York: Cambridge University Press.

Swales, J. M., & Feak, C. B. (1994). *Academic writing for graduate students: Essential tasks and skills. A course for nonnative speakers of English.* Ann Arbor: University of Michigan.

Swales, J. M., & Feak, C. B. (1994). *Academic writing for graduate students: Essential tasks and skills.* Ann Arbor, MI: The University of Michigan.

Szabo, A. & Underwood, J. (2004). Cybercheating: Is information and communication technology fuelling academic dishonesty? *Active Learning in Higher Education, 5*(2), 180-199.

Taradi, S. K., & Taradi, M. (2004). Expanding the traditional physiology class with asynchronous online discussions and collaborative projects. *Advances in Physiology Education, 28*, 73-78.

Taradi, S. K., Taradi, M., Radic, K., & Pokrajac, N. (2005). Blending problem-based learning with Web technology positively impacts student learning outcomes in acid-base physiology. *Advances in Physiology Education, 29*, 35-39.

Taubes, G. (1995). Plagiarism suit wins; experts hope it won't set a trend. *Science, 268*(May 26), 1125.

Taylor, W. (1953). Cloze procedure: A new tool for measuring readability. *Journalism Quarterly, 30*, 414-438.

284

Tenpenny, P. L., Keriazakos, M. S., Lew, G. S., & Phelan, T. P. (1998). In search of inadvertent plagiarism. *The American Journal of Psychology, 111*(4), 529-559.

Texas A&M University. (2007). *Aggie honor code.* Retrieved April 3, 2007, from http://www.tamu.edu/aggiehonor/know.html

The Council of Writing Program Administrators. *Defining and avoiding plagiarism: The WPA statement on best practices.* Retrieved August 8, 2006 from http://www.wpacouncil.org/node/9

The Critical Thinking Community. Retrieved December 15, 2006 from http://www.criticalthinking.org

The New London Group (2000). A pedagogy of multi-literacies. In B. Cope & M. Kalantzis (Eds.), *Muliliteracies. Literacy learning and the design for social futures.* Melbourne: Macmillan Publishers Australia.

Thomas, D. A. (2004). How educators can more effectively understand and combat the plagiarism epidemic. *Brigham Young University Education & Law Journal,* (2), 421-430.

Thomson/Gale. (n.d.). *Today's must have job skills.* Retrieved on October 14, 2006 from http://www.findarticles.com

Tiberius, R. G. (1999). *Small group teaching: a troubleshooting guide.* London: Kogan Page.

Tierney, A. M., Brown,.A., & Neil, D. (2006). Tackling plagiarism in the Level One Biology class—A work in progress. *Practice and Evidence of Scholarship of Teaching and Learning in Higher Education, 1*(1), 13-21. Retrieved October 11, 2006, from http://www.pestlhe.org.uk

Turner, Y. (2000). Chinese students: Teaching, learning, and equality in UK higher education. *Higher Education Equal Opportunities Network, National Network Newsletter for Equal Opportunities Practitioners,* Spring, Issue 13, http://www.worc.ac.uk/services/equalopps/HEEON/newsonline.htm#Yvonne%27s

Turnitin. (2007). *Plagiarism prevention.* Retrieved February 8, 2007, from http://turnitin.com/static/plagiarism.html

U.S. Department of Labor: Bureau of Labor Statistics (2003). *Tomorrow's jobs.* Retrieved October 13, 2006 from http://www.bls.gov?oco/oco2003

Umeå University, Department of Applied Physics and Electronics (online). *Studenthandbok.* Retrieved December 19, 2005 from http://www.tfe.umu.se/studieinformation/Studentguide.htm

Umeå University, Faculty of Arts (online). *Plagiatpolicy för den humanistiska fakulteten.* Retrieved December 19, 2005 from http://www.umu.se/humfak/internt/images/plagiatpolicy.pdf

Underwood, J., & Szabo, A. (2003). Academic offences and e-learning: Individual propensities in cheating. *British Journal of Educational Technology, 34*(4), 467-477.

University of Alabama in Huntsville. (2007). *Preventing plagiarism.* Retrieved February 19, 2007, from http://www.uah.edu/library/turnitin/facultypreventplag.htm

University of Alberta Libraries Web Site. Why students plagiarize. Retrieved August 8, 2006 from http://www.library.ualberta.ca/guides/plagiarism/why/index.cfm

University of California, Santa Barbara (n.d.). *Academic integrity at UCSB: A student's guide* [pamphlet]. Santa Barbara, CA: Office of Student Life.

University of California, Santa Barbara (n.d.). *Campus regulations: General standards of conduct* (section A.2.: Academic conduct). Retrieved September 30, 2006 from http://www.sa.ucsb.edu/regulations/index.aspx?page=conduct

University of Connecticut (n.d.). *Information for faculty on Internet plagiarism.* Retrieved on September 30, 2006 from http://www.waterbury.uconn.edu/Plagiarism/index.html

University of Glasgow. (2005). University of Glasgow plagiarism statement. *Senate office.* Retrieved October 2, 2006, from http://senate.gla.ac.uk/discipline/plagiarism/plagstate.html

University of Glasgow. (2006). Student discipline. *Senate office.* Retrieved October 2, 2006, from http://senate.gla.ac.uk/discipline/stats.html

University of Glasgow. (2006). Student numbers. *Facts and Figures.* Retrieved October 2, 2006, from http://senate.gla.ac.uk/publications/factsandfigures/studentnumbers.html

University of Glasgow. (2006c). Moodle adoption. *Learning and Teaching Centre.* Retrieved October 15, 2006, from http://www.gla.ac.uk/services/learn/elearn/moodhis.html

University of Melbourne. (2007). *Academic honesty and plagiarism.* Retrieved February 19, 2007, from http://academichonesty.unimelb.edu.au/plagiarism.html

University of Oxford. (2007). *Plagiarism: Educational policy and standards.* Retrieved February 19, 2007, from http://www.admin.ox.ac.uk/epsc/plagiarism/

University of Wales, *Validation Handbook of Quality Assurance – Policies and procedures* (online) Retrieved on December 19, 2005 from http://www.wales.ac.uk/newpages/external/e612.asp?E,VALQAA

Updike, J. (2006, June 25).The end of authorship. *New York Times Book Review,* p. 27.

Vandello, J. A., & Cohen, D. (1999). Patterns of individualism and collectivism across the United States. *Journal of Personality and Social Psychology, 77*(2), 279-292.

Vygotsky, L. (1978). *Mind and society: The development of higher mental processes.* Cambridge: Harvard University Press.

Vygotsky, L. (Ed.). (1987). *Thinking and speech: The collected work of L.S. Vygotsky.* New York: Plenum.

Walden, K., & Peacock, A. (2006). The i-Map: A process-centered response to plagiarism. *Assessment & Evaluation in Higher Education, 31*(2), 201-214.

Warn, J. (2006). Plagiarism software: no magic bullet! *Higher Education Research & Development, 25*(2), 195-208.

Warner, J. (2003, September 16). Clueless in academe: An interview with Gerald Graff. *The Morning News.* Retrieved September 27, 2006 from http://www.themorningnews.org/archives

Watkins, E. W. (1994). Plagiarism. In H. A. Christy, J. S. Harrison, & E. W. Watkins (Eds.), *Don't Perish—Publish! Faculty Notebook* (pp. 25–35). Provo, Utah: Scholarly Publications, Brigham Young University.

Webeducate. (2006). *Pollster.* Retrieved October 11, 2006 from http://www.webducate.net/pollster.php

Weil, M., & Joyce, B. (1978). *Social models of teaching.* Englewood Cliffs: Prentice Hill.

Whisnant, W. T., Sullivan, J. C., & Slayton, S. L. (Summer, 1992). The "old" new resource for education: Student age. *Catalyst 22(3).* Retrieved May 20, 2005 from http://scholar.lib.vt.edu/ejournals/CATALYST/V22N3/whisnant.html

Willen, M.S., (2004). Reflections on the cultural climate of plagiarism, *Liberal education,* 55-58.

Willison, J. & O'Regan, K. (2007) Commonly known, commonly not known, totally unknown: A framework for students becoming researchers. *Higher Education Research and Development, 26*(4), 393-409.

Willmott, C. J. R., & Harrison, T. (2003). An exercise to teach bioscience students about plagiarism. *Journal of Biological Education, 37*(3), 139-140.

Winer, D. *Long Bet.* Retrieved October 2, 2006 from http://www.longbets.org/

Wingate, U. (2006). Doing away with "study skills." *Teaching in Higher Education, 11*(4), 457-469.

Wood, D., & Gray, B. (1991). Toward a comprehensive theory of collaboration. *The Journal of Applied Behavioral Science, 27*(2), 139-162.

286

Wood, G. (2004). Academic original sin: Plagiarism, the Internet, and librarians. *Journal of Academic Librarianship, 30*(3), 237-242.

Wu, J., & Singh, M., (2002, July). *Wishing for dragon children: An educational tradition in China that is influencing families ant home and abroad.* Paper presented at the Ninth International Literacy and Education Network Conference on Learning. Beijing, China.

Yamada, K. (2003). What prevents ESL/EFL writers from avoiding plagiarism?: Analyses of 10 North-American college websites. *System, 31,* 247-258.

Young, J. (2006, August 9). U. of California system's 100 libraries join Google's controversial book-scanning project. *The Chronicle of Higher Education.* Retrieved on August 10, 2006 from http://www.chronicle.com

Zemke, R., & Zemke, S. (1988). Thirty things we know for sure about adult learning. In J. Gordon, R. Zemke, P. Jones (Ed.) *Designing and Delivering Cost-Effective Training, 2nd Ed.* Minneapolis: Lakewood Books.

Zhou, D. (2006, April 23). Sophomore's new book contains passages strikingly similar to 2001 novel. *The Harvard Crimson.* Retrieved September 27, 2006 from http://www.thecrimson.com/article.aspx?ref=512968

Zimitat, C. (2004, December 5-8). *Changing student use and perceptions of learning technologies, 2002-2004.* Paper presented at the 21st Annual ASCILITE Conference, Perth, WA.

Zimmerman, B. J. (1990). Self-regulating academic learning and achievement: The emergence of a social cognitive perspective. *Educational Psychology Review, 2,* 173-201.

Zobel, J., & Hamilton, M. (2002). Managing student plagiarism in large academic departments. *Australian Universities Review, 45*(2), 23-30.

About the Contributors

Tim S. Roberts is a senior lecturer with the Faculty of Business and Informatics at the Bundaberg campus of Central Queensland University. He has taught a variety computer science subjects, including courses to over 1000 students located throughout Australia and overseas, many of them studying entirely online. In 2001, together with Lissa McNamee and Sallyanne Williams, he developed the Online Collaborative Learning in Higher Education Web site at http://clp.cqu.edu.au, and in 2003, with Joanne McInnerney, developed the Assessment in Higher Education Web site at http://ahe.cqu.edu.au. He was awarded the Bundaberg City Council's prize for excellence in research in 2001, and the Dean's Award for Quality Research in 2002. He has edited three books: *Online collaborative learning: Theory and practice* (Information Science Publishing, 2003), *Computer-supported collaborative learning in higher education* (Idea Group Publishing), and *Self, peer and group assessment in e-learning* (Information Science Publishing).

* * *

Dorothy Aidulis has a BSc (Hons) and PhD in pharmacology, PGCE (secondary science), and moved from scientific research into secondary school science teaching, becoming progressively more interested in the theory and practice of learning and teaching. She has been a teacher at Glasgow University since 2003 and is completing the New Lecturer and Teacher Programme, leading to membership of the HEA. Her interest in plagiarism comes from attending a Netskills workshop, when the importance of deterring as opposed to detecting plagiarism was highlighted. This, together with her continued interest in learning and teaching, and role as a course coordinator, led to her being involved in the departmental Plagiarism Working Group and subsequently Bioethics Working Group.

Madhumita Bhattacharya is a senior lecturer at the College of Education, Massey University, New Zealand. She teaches both undergraduate and postgraduate courses in science, chemistry and technology education and in the Distance and Online Education Programme. Bhattacharya has more than 15 years of research and teaching experience in ICT in Education. She has published extensively. Some of her research interests are in the area of problem-based learning, e-portfolio, and e-learning in multicultural context. Recently she has received a British Council Research Exchange Programme Award. Currently Bhattacharya is working on a co-edited book titled *Managing digital diversity: Socio-technological perspectives.* Prior to coming to New Zealand, Dr. Bhattacharya had teaching and research experiences in Singapore, Australia, Japan, the UK, and India.

Dr. Mark Brown is an associate professor in the College of Education at Massey University, New Zealand. He is both an Apple Distinguished Educator and recipient of a National Sustained Teaching Excellence Award. Brown has published widely in the areas of e-learning and the use of information and communication technology in education. He currently edits the journal *Computers in New Zealand Schools* and serves on several other editorial boards. In his new role as director of distance education at Massey University, Brown is centrally involved in developing policy and strategies for learning and teaching.

Teresa Chen currently serves as associate professor in the Department of Educational Psychology, Administration, and Counselling at California State University, Long Beach (CSULB). She joined the CSULB faculty in the fall of 2000, after receiving her PhD in education in technology studies from the University of Illinois at Urbana-Champaign. At CSULB, she has taught classes in technology integration and instructional design. She also has published in the areas of computer-mediated communication (CMC) and computer-assisted language learning (CALL). She is particularly interested in examining computer technology as a medium that shapes students' learning and interaction in a global context.

Robert Clarke is a principal lecturer in computing at UCE Birmingham, UK. He completed an MSc in business information systems at Keele University, UK. His main research interests include contract cheating and online individualised assessment.

Barbara Cogdell, BSc(Hons), PhD, PGCHE, Registered Practitioner of the Higher Education Academy, has been employed as a teacher in the Institute of Biomedical and Life Sciences at the University of Glasgow for over 10 years. Her main teaching responsibilities are to Physiology and Sports Science students and her particular areas of expertise are ethics and numeracy. Her interest in plagiarism arose through her two opposing roles, first as a course coordinator which involves disciplining students and second as an adviser of studies which involves acting as an advocate for students.

Wilfried Decoo is professor of applied linguistics at Brigham Young University in Utah and at the University of Antwerp in Belgium. He is the author of *Crisis on Campus: Confronting Academic Misconduct* (Cambridge, MA: MIT Press, 2002) as well as of language learning textbooks with publishers in various countries. He has published articles on applied linguistics and language learning in journals such as *Bulletin de Psychologie Scolaire et D'orientation*, *Bulletin of the Canadian Association of Applied Linguistics*, *CALICO-Journal*, *Computer-Assisted Language Learning*, *Computers and Education*, *Educational Technology in Language Learning*, *Germanische Mitteilungen*, *Inostranie Jaziike v Shkole*, *International Review of Applied Linguistics*, *Language Teaching*, *Nova & Vetera*, *Speculations in Science and Technology*, and *System*.

Martin Dick is a senior lecturer in the School of Business Information Technology at RMIT University. He has been involved with teaching in the information technology area since 1996. Prior to that he worked for the Australian Customs Service in IT. He has published over 30 papers in international conferences and journals. His research areas of interest are cheating and plagiarism, assessment using oral interviews, the use of simulation games in education, and the adoption of new software development technologies. He is currently the deputy chair of the Asia-Pacific Forum on Educational Integrity.

Erik J Eriksson is a PhD student in cognitive science, Umeå University and will present his thesis in May 2007. Erik holds a master's degree in cognitive science from Umeå University. During his studies at Umeå University Eriksson has taught both in the Department of Computing Science and the Department of Philosophy and Linguistics. He has been a visiting student at the University of Sydney and North Carolina State University. His interest in plagiarism grew out of a doctoral level course taught by Kirk P. H. Sullivan and Ingmarie Mellenius in Forensic Linguistics.

Michael Hanrahan is the assistant director of academic technology and instructional technology and a lecturer in English at Bates College. He holds a PhD in medieval English literature from Indiana University and has held teaching and educational technology positions in the United States and in Great Britain. Recent projects include *Teaching, technology, textuality: Approaches to new media*, edited with Deborah Madsen (Palgrave, 2006).

Maurie Hasen comes from a background in social work and psychology practice, with particular interests in alcohol and drug rehabilitation and family therapy. He has developed and now teaches in a humanities based psychology discipline at Monash University. Behavioural studies coursework is often self reflective, so when issues around plagiarism became apparent, there were many questions raised and discussed about the pedagogy and psychology of addressing plagiarism and other inappropriate practices. This has now become a central interest for Hasen and his colleagues.

Niall Hayes (http://www.lums.lancs.ac.uk/owt/profiles/38/) is a lecturer in organization, work, and technology at Lancaster University. Niall's research interests centre on the social and organizational implications surrounding the development, management, and use of computer-based information systems in contemporary organizations. He is particularly interested in the areas of the social construction of boundaries, knowledge work, electronic government, and computer supported co-operative work (groupware and intra/extranets). His other research area explores issues pertaining to cultural values, technology, and higher education.

Lucas D. Introna (http://www.lums.lancs.ac.uk/owt/profiles/119/) is professor of technology, organization, and ethics at Lancaster University. His research interest is the social study of information technology and its consequences for society. In particular he is concerned with the ethics and politics of technology. He is co-editor *Ethics and Information Technology,* associate editor of *Management Information Systems Quarterly* and a founding member of the International Society for Ethics and Information Technology (INSEIT). More recently, he has been involved in a project studying the interrelationships between culture, academic writing practices, and plagiarism.

Kate Ippolito is the education development projects manager in Brunel's Learning and Teaching Development Unit. This role involves managing Brunel's Curriculum Innovation Fund, coordinating the annual Learning and Teaching Symposium, and teaching on the Postgraduate Certificate in Learning and Teaching in Higher Education and the Brunel Associate Practitioner Pathway programmes. She particularly enjoys supporting students' academic skills development through teaching on the Effective Learning Advice Programme and collaborating on curriculum development projects. Ippolito is also a learning area coordinator for the LearnHigher CETL project. Her research interests include exploring and evaluating approaches to making the HE curriculum more inclusive.

Lone Jorgensen is a senior at Massey University College of Education, New Zealand. She lectures in pedagogical studies and the teaching of science, biology, physics, and technology. Her current research interests are in comparative school system in Denmark and New Zealand and how these affect the retention of students in the science areas, as well as the philosophical implications of values education. After many years in secondary schools teaching the sciences, life-skills, and health to adolescents, she left to complete a PhD in environmental technology. She has a personal interest in philosophy and environmental issues.

Nai-Kuang Teresa Ku currently serves as adjunct instructor in the Department of Humanities and Social Sciences at University of the West (UWEST) and at California State University, Long Beach. After receiving her PhD in educational psychology and technology from the University of Southern California in 2002, she served as the director of student services at UWEST. At UWEST and CSULB, she has taught classes in child development and sociology. Her research interests are in the field of self-efficacy, self-regulated learning, motivation, academic achievement, and cross-cultural learning.

Thomas Lancaster is a lecturer in computing at UCE Birmingham, UK. He completed his PhD, titled "Efficient and Effective Plagiarism Detection" at London South Bank University, UK in 2003. His main research interests include plagiarism prevention and detection, electronic learning, and contract cheating.

Teri Thomson Maddox is professor of English and speech at Jackson State Community College in Jackson, Tennessee, USA. She has a BA in English from Lambuth College in Jackson, Tennessee, and an MA in teaching, an MA in English, and an EdD in higher education from the University of Memphis. She received a Developmental Education Specialist certification from Appalachian State University in Boone, North Carolina. She is active in community theater productions, sings in the choir and rings handbells at her church, and plays volleyball with a senior women's league. She and her husband enjoy traveling.

Ursula McGowan is deputy director and coordinator of the Academic Staff Development Program of the Centre for Learning and Professional Development at the University of Adelaide, South Australia. She provides academic induction courses for sessional, contract, and permanent staff and coordinates a broadly-based cultural awareness program for staff across the university. She is bilingual (German / English) with particular strengths and many years of experience in assisting staff and students with academic English development and the integration of English as a second or additional language learning into the academic curriculum.

Chris Park is director of the Graduate School at Lancaster University in the UK, and a senior associate of the Higher Education Academy. In a previous life, he was a geographer, with 10 books and many papers on the environment to his name, and in recent years he has published mainly on academic strategy and practice.

Jon R. Ramsey is currently a lecturer in the Writing Program at the University of California, Santa Barbara. He earned a doctoral degree in English from the University of California, Riverside. In his former position as the dean of studies and associate professor of English at Skidmore College in Saratoga

Springs, New York, he oversaw academic integrity cases for 23 years. His publications, including articles and two co-edited books, center on English literature and writing pedagogy; he also has presented papers on academic integrity, advising, and curriculum development at various conferences, especially those sponsored by NACADA (the National Academic Advising Association).

Janet Salmons, PhD, is an e-learning scholar-practitioner. Her consulting firm, Vision2Lead, Inc., provides curriculum, course, and faculty development services. She has served on the faculty of Capella University's School of Business and Technology MBA and PhD programs since 1999. Her research interests are focused on electronic collaboration in organizations and collaborative e-learning. She is editing *The handbook of research on electronic collaboration and organizational synergy*. Previous efforts include executive positions in nonprofit organizations and founding and directing a program at Cornell University that offered scenario-based management and diversity training across the U.S.

Judithe Sheard is a senior lecturer in the Faculty of Information Technology at Monash University. During the past 18 years, she has taught all levels of undergraduate and graduate level IT students. Judithe is co-director of the Computing Education Research Group at Monash and has published over 60 papers in international conferences and journals. Her main research interests are in student learning behaviour and in exploring the Web as a new educational medium. In 2000, Judithe was program chair for the 4th Australasian Computing Education conference. In 2001 she was awarded the Monash Vice Chancellor's award for team-based educational development.

Kirk P. H. Sullivan, is a reader in phonetics, Umeå University. Kirk holds a PhD from the University of Southampton, UK and took up his current position at Umeå University, Sweden after a post-doctoral fellowship at the University of Otago, NZ. His research interests focus on forensic linguistics and learning and range from first and second language acquisition to teaching, learning, and assessment in higher education. Together with Eva Lindgren, he recently has edited a book on computer keystroke logging and writing.

Frankie Wilson is a subject liaison librarian. The purpose of this role is to support the teaching, learning and research needs of all members of an academic school by purchasing (for the library) information resources and by providing training in how to effectively and efficiently use these resources. As a senior member of the library staff, she also has contributed to a number of university-wide projects and particularly enjoys working with colleagues from other departments to provide a seamless service for students. Her research interests include performance measurement, and quality issues in HE.

Craig Zimitat is senior lecturer and deputy director of the Griffith Institute for Higher Education, Griffith University, Australia. His interests lie in all aspects of teaching and learning. The current focus of his research explores all aspects of student experiences and engagement at university and the mediating role of learning technologies in those processes. Other interests include internationalisation of the curriculum, medical, and dental education.

Index

A

academic dishonesty 212
academic misconduct 11, 13, 20, 21
academic writing 12, 14, 17–18, 19, 20, 65, 69, 70, 72, 73, 75
algorithms 115–118
animal welfare and use of research funds 51
apprentice researcher 102, 106
assessment 11, 13, 14, 17, 19, 21, 39, 44, 47, 57, 195, 198, 211, 215, 218, 228, 229, 232, 234, 236, 239, 241
assessment design 199–204
assessment redesign 153–155
assessment rules 180
attitudes 28–29, 83–84
auction sites 146, 147, 148, 149
authorship 244, 245–246, 247, 250, 251, 252, 253, 254, 255

B

bid request 146, 148, 151, 156
biology 39, 45, 55
blogs 183–193. *See also* weblog
Bloom's Taxonomy 195, 208, 211, 214–215, 223, 224, 225
Boyer Commission 101, 102, 104, 105

C

case study 24–25, 60, 74
cheat 94, 100
citation 209, 210, 212, 213
citing 10, 12, 19
cognition 195, 196, 201, 202, 203, 204. *See also* knowledge
Colby, Bates, and Bowdoin (CBB) Plagiarism Project 183, 187, 190
collaboration 60, 71, 74

community college 124–143
community college student 125, 126, 128, 130, 132, 133, 135, 136
concept shifts 56
Confucius-heritage students 81
contract cheating 144–159
copyright permission 32
course evaluation 52
course information document (CID) 43
Creative Commons 184, 187, 190, 193
critical thinking 125, 129, 133, 134, 139
cross cultural factors 68–69
cultural commons 245, 251, 252
cultural factors 86–87
culture 196, 197, 198
culture of learning 81
curriculum 42, 44, 92, 94, 103, 104

D

definitions 25
definitions, institutional 29
detection 62, 68, 70, 74
detection sites 4–5
deterrence 62
deterring plagiarism 32, 33
discussion forums 144, 148, 149
domain 85
double publishing 51

E

educating students 60, 67, 72, 74
electronic detection tools 209
English-as-a-Foreign-Language (EFL) 77, 87, 91
English as an Additional Language (EAL) 93, 94, 99, 100, 103, 104, 107
essay mills 144, 147, 148, 149
ethics 39, 40, 41, 42, 44–45, 50–54, 55, 58, 208, 213, 222, 223

ethnocentrism 81
evaluation 48–50
examination 153, 154
extended post-use 236, 239, 240
extended pre-use 236, 237, 239

F

feed aggregators 144, 148
focus group 165, 166, 171
free culture 245, 249, 251, 252, 253

G

genre analysis 92, 103, 104, 105
group work 51

H

habitual cheaters 146
higher education 43, 61, 72, 74, 194, 199, 206
honor codes 6
honour codes 163, 175, 180
Howard, Rebecca Moore 250

I

idealists 6
imaginary plagiarism 248–250
inappropriate paraphrasing 212
individual assignment specification 179
individualisation 155
influences 161
information revolution 244, 246, 252, 259
informing students 27, 27–28
institutional approach 43–44
institutional policy 42, 56
intentional plagiarism 5, 126, 132, 139
International English Language Testing System
        (IELTS) 100
international students 92–107, 108–123
Internet 79, 83, 84, 85, 86, 87, 89, 90, 194, 195,
        196, 197, 198, 204
intertextuality 212

J

job market 256–257
Joint Information Systems Committee (JISC) 62
judicial 229, 230, 241

K

knowledge, definition of 198–204

L

learner 98
learning communities 189–190
learning environment 199–204
learning outcomes 199, 200, 202
lecturer attitudes 23–37
legal 229, 230, 231, 241
Lessig, Lawrence 252
lesson plan 64–65
library 245, 246, 247, 248

M

Mallon, Thomas 250
materials 61, 63, 64, 69, 71, 74
misleading 228, 230, 238
misuse of sources 212
monitored assessment 179
Moodle 54–56
motivations 164, 166, 168, 171
multimedia 190–191

N

non-native students 111, 114, 119
non-originality agencies 146, 148
note-taking 10, 12, 19, 20

O

offence 92, 94, 95, 99, 103
Office of Research Integrity (ORI) 230
online 70, 73, 74, 92, 93, 97, 100, 101, 102
online detection services 88
order of authorship 51
ORI 230, 231, 233, 234, 235, 237, 238
originality 234, 235, 236, 239
original work 212–213

P

paper mill sites 4
paraphrasing 14, 15, 17
patch-writing 110, 111, 114, 115, 117, 118, 119
patchwriting 20, 250–251, 255
pedagogy 55, 210, 223, 224
peer assessment 179
performance assessment 89
personal factors 84–85
phrase-mugging 231, 235, 237, 241
pilot study 61, 68, 73
plagiarism, definition of 24, 25–27, 29, 52, 114,
        125, 230

plagiarism, defintion 211–213
plagiarism detection 183, 184, 186, 197–198
plagiarism detection sites 4
plagiarism detection software 41, 57
plagiarism detection systems 108–123
plagiarism policies 96–98
policy 23, 25, 28, 29, 30, 33
pragmatists 7
prevention 160, 161, 162, 163, 177, 178–180, 182
principles 61, 63, 64, 65, 72, 73
project-based learning 205

R

realists 7
redundant publishing 51
referencing 10, 12, 18, 19, 20, 42, 45–50
relevant assessment 179–180
RentACoder 146, 147, 148, 149
reporting plagiarism 29
responsibility 24
roll out 69, 71, 72, 74

S

scholarly 92, 96, 97, 98, 99, 100, 101, 103, 104
scholarly work 97
self-efficacy 78, 80, 81, 82, 84, 85, 89
self-plagiarism 28, 31
seminar 63, 64–65, 66–68
sentence-lifting 231, 232, 241
situational factors 85–86
solutions 136–137, 179, 181
substantial 228, 230, 231, 233, 234, 235, 236, 238
substantial, verbatim, unattributed, misleading
        (SVUM) 238, 242

summarising 46, 47, 48, 49
SVUM-scale 238, 242

T

Taxonomy of Collaborative E-Learning 209, 216,
        216–219, 223, 224
teaching 245, 253, 255, 258, 259
terminology 94
text borrowing 77, 80, 82, 84, 86, 87
traceability 152–153
train the trainers 63, 73

U

unattributed 236–237
uncritical citing 212
understandings 164, 166, 168
unintentional plagiarism 5, 92–107, 124, 125, 126,
        130, 139, 233

V

values 94, 95, 96, 97, 98, 101, 102
verbatim plagiarism 234–236
verdict 240–241
virtual learning 39, 54

W

weblog 183, 184, 187, 189, 190, 191, 193
weblogs, controversies 187–189
workshops 38, 45, 55, 56

Z

zero tolerance 61, 62